# SOUTH CAROLINA 1775

## A Crucible Year

*Dedicated to the memory of my father-in-law, James L. Mayson, 1905-1993*

# South Carolina 1775

## A Crucible Year

Edmund Alexander Bator

Foreign Service Officer, retired

American History Imprints / American History Press
Franklin, Tennessee
www.Americanhistoryimprints.com
www.Americanhistorypress.com

Book Design by Stanford Alan Griffith

ISBN 10: 0-9753667-93
ISBN 13: 978-0-9753667-9-0

First Edition June 2009

Library of Congress Control Number: 2009922867

Printed in the United States of America on acid-free paper.
This book meets all ANSI standards for archival quality.

# Table of Contents

# SOUTH CAROLINA 1775

*A Crucible Year*

# *Foreword*
## *The Precarious Revolution*

THIS IS A BOOK THAT EVERY AMERICAN INTERESTED IN THE REAL story of the nation's history should read. With careful attention to seemingly minor details and the role that personality and self interest play in unfolding events, Edmund Bator has told us in this account of the first year of the American Revolution in South Carolina just how fragile and tentative the enterprise was, beyond the borders of New England. This is a reality that most Americans, mesmerized by the image of the supposedly heroic militiamen on Lexington Green, find very hard to digest.

Even in New England, until the British fired the first shots, the resistance to British economic imperialism was largely theoretical.

Too many 21st Century Americans still believe that as the British regulars swung into view, the captain of the Lexington company growled: "If they want a war, let it begin here." Instead, the entire company, with the captain's approval, had voted "not to make or meddle" with the King's men and had positioned themselves as far as possible from the road down which they presumed the regulars would march to Concord. They were totally flummoxed when the redcoated column came crunching toward them across the green.

South Carolina's resistance to the money-hungry British empire George III and his ministers were trying to create was complicated by two realities that Mr. Bator calmly and evenhandedly discusses. In a total population of 174,000, no less than 104,000 were slaves, who had already demonstrated a readiness to revolt. At least as daunting were the divisions between the low country, where the wealthy indigo and rice planters lived, and the more recently settled back country, where disgruntled Scots-Irish farmers were all too aware that they outnumbered the low country squires 2-1 and had virtually no power in the colony's legislature.

These little known facts turn South Carolina 1775 into a suspense story—and a superb introduction to the roller coaster revolutionary drama that unfolded over the next eight years. All the ingredients for a new under-standing of the struggle for independence are here, from defiant hotheads to agonized moderates to outraged conservatives —plus the presence of hostile Indians on the western frontier. Mr. Bator's unflinching realism will stir new admiration for the courage of our founding fathers – and for their political dexterity. Both were needed to prevent the infant republic from meeting an unpleasant demise in its cradle.

*Thomas Fleming*

# *Introduction*

On the 28th of August 1811, some 36 years after the beginning of the American Revolution, former Brigadier Andrew Pickens, a 72-year-old South Carolina back country war hero of the battles at Kettle Creek (1779) and Cowpens (1781), wrote a letter to his former comrade-in-arms, General Henry Lee, who lived in Virginia. Pickens was replying to Lee's request for first hand accounts of skirmishes during the southern campaign that 'Light Horse Harry' might include in his war memoirs.

My interest was piqued by the curmudgeon-like Pickens when he impulsively made the following comment: *"At the commencement of the war it was thought advisable by our council of Safety to have one or two Regiments raised & officered in the upper part of the Country—The candidates for Col of one of the Regiments were Robert Cunningham, James Mayson & Moses Kirkland—Mayson got the commission, which so exasperated the others that they immediately took the other side of the Question—They both being men of influence, but particularly Cunningham who lived on the east side of the Saluda River, & had considerable connections in that part of the country. If Cunningham had been appointed Colonel at that time, we would not have had so violent an opposition to our cause in this country."*[1]

Being engaged in research on Mayson, this struck me as an oddly biased opinion and a strangely prejudiced spin on the events of 1775—a year in which the foundations for South Carolina's brand of democracy were laid. For the sake of truth and accuracy, I decided to review that year in a detailed fashion, with a special focus on back country affairs, allowing the actual records to speak for themselves. The documented words and deeds of major characters, both low country and back country, provided unique insight into the hearts and minds of South Carolinians as the Revolutionary War struggle got underway.

To keep matters in perspective, it should be pointed out that the matter of establishing regiments and appointing commanders in 1775 fell to South Carolina's First Provisional Congress. It was established in January 1775, following a resolution of the First Continental Congress in Philadelphia which had urged the colonies *"to enter into a non-importation, non-consumption, and non-exportation agreement or association."*[2]

This resolution was shortly followed by a congressional document entitled *The Association*, also dated 20 October 1774, recommending *"that a committee be chosen in every county, city, and town, by those who are qualified to vote for representatives in the legislature, whose business it shall be attentively to observe the conduct of all persons touching this association."*[3]

The legislature formed in South Carolina after its delegates returned from Philadelphia took the designation of First Provincial Congress. James Mayson was elected a delegate to this Congress from the back country District of Ninety-Six. Neither Robert Cunningham, Moses Kirkland nor Andrew Pickens were members of this same Congress which, during its second session in June 1775, *"Resolved, That two regiments of foot, each to consist of seven hundred and fifty rank and file, be forthwith officered, raised, paid, and disciplined, and put under the direction of the congress."* It was further *"Resolved, That a regiment of rangers to consist of four hundred and fifty privates, be also forthwith officered, raised, paid, and disciplined, and put under the direction of the Congress."*[4]

Three days later a committee was appointed *"to receive the names of such gentlemen as shall offer themselves, or be recommended by any member of this Congress, to serve as Field-Officers, Captains, First Lieutenants, and Paymasters, in the horse and foot intended to be raised."* There is no indication whatsoever on record to show that the names of Cunningham or Kirkland were ever offered for consideration as a field officer. The record of 10 June simply reported the names of officers raised for the two low country regiments and further stated, with respect to the back country: *"Resolved, That William Thomson, Esq., be appointed Lieutenant-Colonel and James Mayson, Esq., Major, of the regiment of Rangers to be raised."*[5]

Andrew Pickens' interpretation of this process, to which he was not a witness, seems a bit incongruous. From his letter to Lee, one has the impression that Pickens had a burr in his saddle concerning Mayson. Yet both settled in the back country of South Carolina at approximately the same time, about 1759/60, emigrating from western regions of colonies where skirmishes during the French and Indian War were causing many Scots-Irish settlers to evacuate. The Maysons migrated from Virginia; the Pickens family from Pennsylvania.

By 1761 James Mayson had established himself as a planter, merchant, and justice of the peace in the back country of South Carolina. He became a leader in the Regulator Movement of 1768-69, as well as a militia officer, holding the rank of Lieutenant Colonel, second in command of the His Majesty's Militia of Ninety-Six District. By 1775, Mayson was a figure known and respected by settlers in and around the frontier regions of this district.

Mayson lived just across the Saluda River from Robert Cunningham, eight years his junior. Cunningham had arrived in South Carolina from Tidewater Virginia in 1769. Like Mayson, he also became a local leader, large landholder, justice of the peace and militia officer.

Moses Kirkland, three years older than Mayson, settled on the Wateree River of South Carolina in about 1752. He soon moved to the fork of the Broad and Saluda Rivers where he became an influential planter and mill owner. Like Mayson and Cunningham, Kirkland also became an officer in the King's Militia.

As hostilities between England and her American colonies escalated, so did the animosity among the American settlers, whether in support of independence or reconciliation with the mother country. Sharpness of opinions was particularly marked in the back country of South Carolina, as intimated by Pickens in his letter to Lee.

Pickens lived 22 miles west of Mayson in the frontier region of Long Canes. The dislike that seemingly arose between Mayson and the six-years-younger Pickens was most likely personal. Nevertheless, given historical facts, it is difficult to understand why Pickens remained so passionate in his charge, even 36 years later, that Mayson was inferior to Cunningham, and that his election as a field officer in the back country regiment of rangers in 1775 exacerbated hostility among settlers in the area. It is equally incongruous to believe that Mayson's election was the catalyst that turned Cunningham and Kirkland into Loyalist supporters of King George III.

Nonetheless, given the hostile pride, prejudice, and egotistical vanity evident among both low country and back country leaders on the eve of the Revolution, 1775 was indeed a crucible year in the advancement of South Carolina's independence. It was a year that pitted associators (Rebels) against non-associators (Loyalists) in a crucial struggle that would determine the nature of that colony's development after the Revolutionary War. This narrative, based primarily on original sources, is offered in an effort to set the record of 1775 straight, and to allow 'political junkies' to judge for themselves the nature of what Pickens oversimplified as "so violent an opposition to our cause in this country."

## *Notes to the reader*

With apologies to Carolinians who may prefer to see Lowcountry and Backcountry spelled as one word, the author has opted to use two-word spelling as found in many early histories of South Carolina.

All quotations used in this book taken from original sources retain their exact spelling and punctuation unless it was necessary to change the same for reasons of clarity.

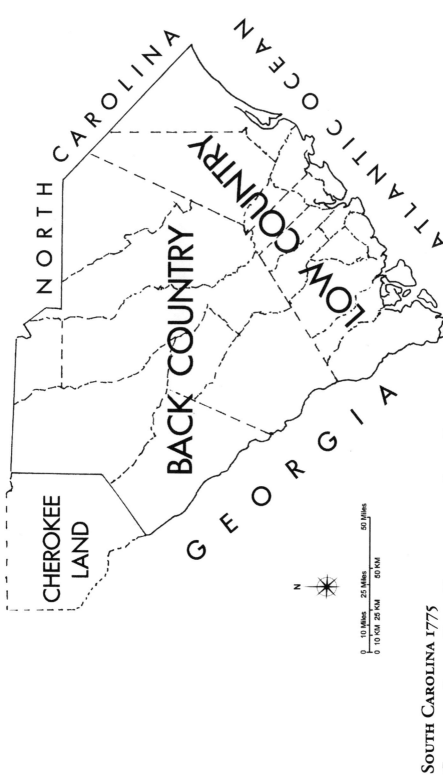

SOUTH CAROLINA 1775
CHEROKEE LAND, BACK COUNTRY AND LOW COUNTRY

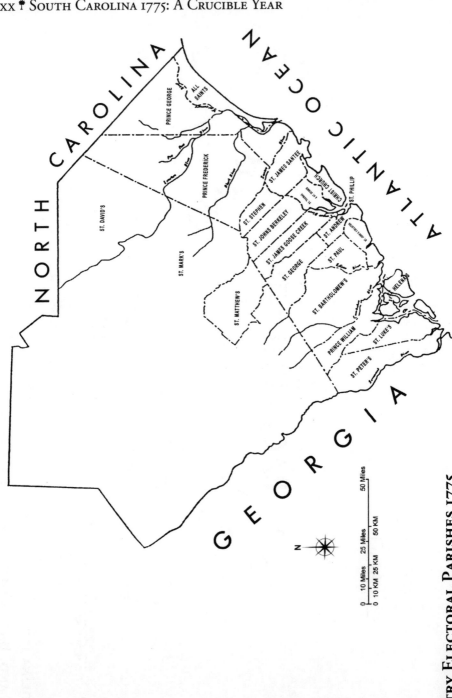

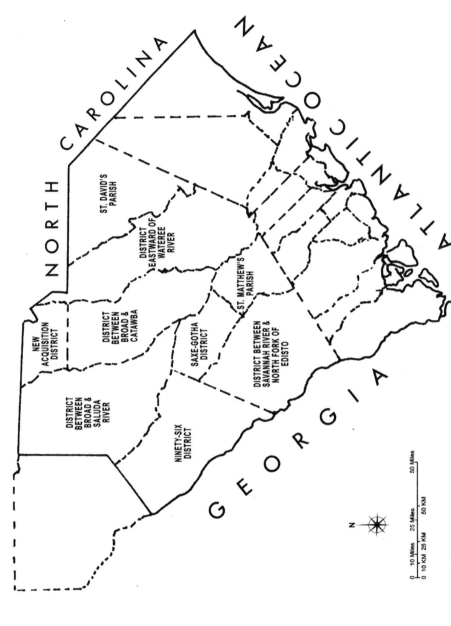

**BACK COUNTRY ELECTORAL DISTRICTS 1775**

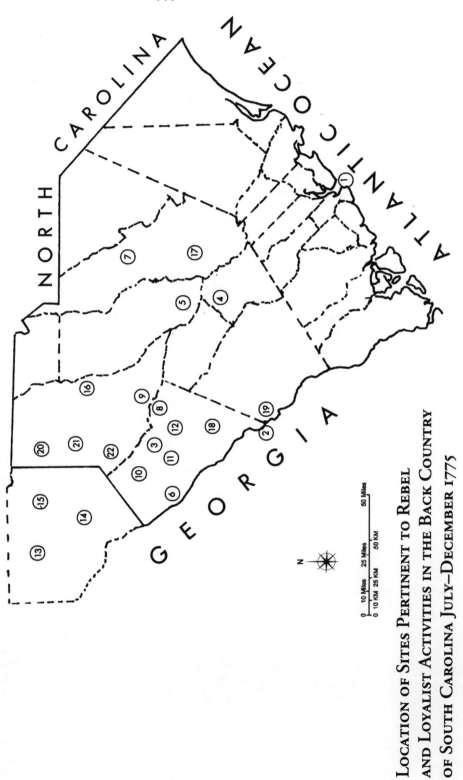

LOCATION OF SITES PERTINENT TO REBEL
AND LOYALIST ACTIVITIES IN THE BACK COUNTRY
OF SOUTH CAROLINA JULY–DECEMBER 1775

1. Charleston
2. Augusta
3. Ninety-Six Township and courthouse, site of confrontations between Rebels and Loyalists in July, September and November 1775
4. Amelia Township; home of Col. William Thomson; base camp area for Regiment of Rangers
5. Congarees Camp, gathering place for Col. Richardson's army in pursuit of Loyalists
6. Fort Charlotte, captured by Major Mayson on July 12, 1775
7. Camden
8. Glasgow Plantation, home of Major James Mayson, second in command of the Regiment of Rangers
9. Peach Hill Plantation, home of Loyalist Robert Cunningham
10. Whitehall, home of Major Andrew Williamson, militia leader
11. Cuffey Town - where Loyalist Moses Kirkland, after deserting the rangers, was sighted July/August 1775
12. Site where arms and ammunition en route to Cherokees was hijacked by Loyalist Patrick Cunningham on November 3, 1775; 18 miles south of Ninety-Six
13. Keowee, Cherokee Indian Town, site of meetings between Edward Wilkinson (Rebel government's Indian agent) and Alexander Cameron (King's Indian agent)
14. Camp of Loyalist Patrick Cunningham in Indian territory, after arms hijack
15. Home of turncoat Richard Pearis, Indian trader
16. Home of Loyalist Thomas Fletchall; nearby site of gathering of King's Militia, and other Loyalists, in back country, to sign a counter- association resolution in defiance of Rebel government, 13 July 1775
17. Home of Col. Richard Richardson, leader of joint Rebel army formed on 8 November 1775 to hunt down Cunningham and other Loyalists
18. Snowhill, home of LeRoy Hammond and gathering place for Drayton's Rebel militia in late August 1775
19. Home of George Galphin, Rebel government's appointee for liaison with Creek Indians
20. Col. Richardson's Camp Great Survey at Duncan's Creek; Fletchall and Pearis captured here December 1775
21. Col. Richardson's Camp at Liberty Hill, December 1775
22. Col. Richardson's Camp at Raborn's Creek near Reedy River; Cunningham's gang routed from here December 1775

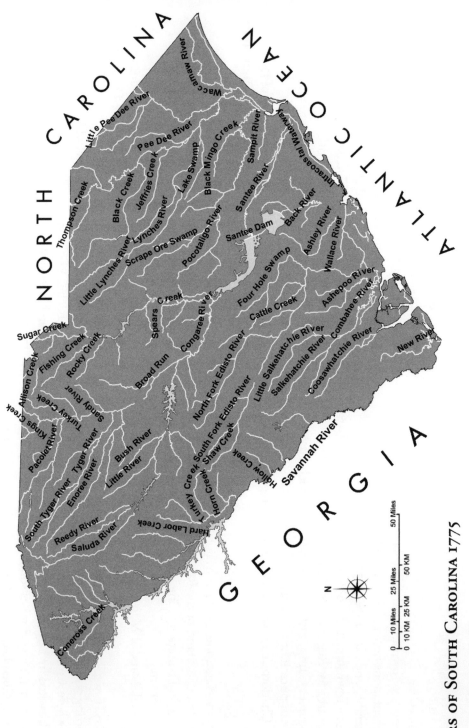

RIVERS OF SOUTH CAROLINA 1775

# SOUTH CAROLINA 1775

*A Crucible Year*

# CHAPTER I

## *The Politic and Right Thing to Do*

A
S OBSERVED BY EMINENT HISTORIAN THOMAS FLEMING: *"SINCE 1765, when the British passed the Stamp Act ... there had been a series of laws and regulations from London which seemed to point toward a comprehensive program aimed at the control and exploitation of Americans ... Although the Stamp Act was repealed, the British were back two years later with a wide-ranging set of taxes on paint, lead, tea, ... with these came a new customs organization, backed by vice admiralty courts ... the judges and the customs men were often little more than racketeers ... men such as John Hancock of Boston and Henry Laurens of South Carolina had their ships seized and their freedom threatened."*[6]

In this atmosphere of intimidation, spontaneous clandestine gatherings protesting the taxes broke out in Charleston. These meetings became more passionate after England passed the Coercive Acts in early 1774. Although aimed primarily at New England, these acts infuriated the merchants and planters of South Carolina, who recognized the handwriting on the wall. In Charleston, anti-British members of the Commons House of the General Assembly openly sought ways to rally Carolinians. But, having been prorogued by the Governor, the Commons House itself could not be convened as a rallying point.

Instead, instigated by restless members in July 1774, *"a purely revolutionary body had been assembled at the call of private individuals."* These low country men appointed an *ad hoc* governing body, in effect a revolutionary government. A *"General Committee assumed control of all public affairs."*[7]

They proceeded to select five delegates, all Charlestonians, to represent South Carolina at the upcoming First Continental Congress of all American colonies—a Congress promoted by the efforts of Virginia and the Massachusetts Bay Colony. This First Continental Congress was attended by members from all colonies except Georgia. It was in session in Philadelphia from 5 September through 26 October 1774. Representing South Carolina were low country aristocrats Henry Middleton, Thomas Lynch, Sr., Christopher Gadsden and the brothers John and Edward Rutledge.

In Charleston second thoughts and worrisome concerns began to set in. Because the July open meeting had *"few if any representatives of the upper part of the province, the General Committee, therefore, were of the opinion that the public union would be strengthened by having better representation from every part of the province."*[8]

Seeds for a more comprehensive future provincial Congress were thus planted. But low country Carolinians must have come to this decision with trepidation. After all, most of the low country aristocracy shared the view that the rough hewn, uneducated, back country settlers were of inferior social status. They were suitable for fighting Indians, as they did in the Cherokee Wars of 1759-61, but were they of a caliber to administer governmental affairs? How many uncouth back country frontiersmen could be relied upon to support the cause of liberty?

A glimpse into the suspicion with which the back country was generally regarded by Charlestonians is provided by Lt. Governor William Bull's dispatch to London on 3 August 1774. The revolutionary General Committee, ingenuously seeking to gain back country confidence, had requested that Bull arm frontiersmen. The Lt. Governor disdainfully declined, observing "they had prepared a Message to me ... to desire I would purchase a number of small Arms *to be given to many poor Irish and others in our western frontiers, with ammunition, upon the apprehension of an Indian war ... whenever that appears to me to be unavoidable, I shall take every step in my power to enable them to defend ..."* For the moment, however, Bull feared their guns might be turned against British authority, as he continues: *"It is not improbable but many of the poor Irish may have been White Boys, Hearts of Oak, who may have been accustomed to oppose Law and Authority in Ireland ... such men may not change their disposition with their climate."*[9]

In this way one learns that the reliability of back country settlers was suspect. Bull was reflecting the latent distrust that existed between low country and back country Carolinians. Only a few years earlier, during the Regulator Movement of 1768-69, frontiersmen had rebelled against the biased neglect shown by low country authorities toward back country grievances. To those lingering animosities were now added growing tensions with the mother country. Revolutionary minded Charlestonians had to find ways to ameliorate suspicions between themselves and their frontier neighbors in the event of war.

Settlement in the back country of South Carolina had begun in earnest only in the late 1750's. The majority of its settlers, as Bull intimated, had filtered down from the northern provinces of Pennsylvania, Virginia and Maryland. The French and Indian War, especially Braddock's Defeat near Fort Duquesne on 9 July 1755, induced thousands to migrate south. Indeed, during the period 1750-1780 the population of South Carolina tripled from approximately 64,000 to 180,000. Of these numbers, 39,000 in 1750 and 97,000 in 1780 were black slaves, who were brought predominantly to the low country. By far the greater number of white newcomers settled in the back country.[10]

It was with these new white settlers in mind that the revolutionary General Committee in Charleston *"parcelled out the whole of the upper country into four large districts ... one between the Savannah and Saluda rivers they called Ninety Six; the next was the district between the Saluda and the Broad; the next between the Broad and the Catawba; and the last, all east of the Catawba or the Wateree."* To each of these districts the committee allotted ten representatives because it was thought to be *"politic and right."* Accordingly, *"the general committee sent out writs for electing gentlemen in every parish and district throughout the province for the representation elected to meet in Charleston on the 11th of January 1775."* Still, as one local historian astutely observes, *"it was curious that the general committee, composed as it was of the leading men in the low country, seemed not to realize the great tide of population which had set in behind them ... the region which they were thus dividing into four election districts, with ten representatives each, giving them but 40 out of 184 representatives, then actually contained three-fourths of the people of the province."*[11]

In his own study, historian Edson L. Whitney mentions that the total population of South Carolina in 1775 numbered 174,000. Of these 70,000 were white and 104,000 were Negro slaves. Thus the provincial white population in 1775 included approximately 50,000 residents of the back country and 20,000 in the low country.[12]

Only 5500 whites resided in Charleston area in 1775, out of a population of 14,000. While whites were outnumbered by slaves in Charleston itself, the majority of slaves lived in the surrounding low country areas working on indigo and rice plantations, established over a period of 95 years by generations of English settlers from the Barbados. To preserve their heritage in a growing atmosphere of political change, with its concomitant fear of black insurrection, low country Rebel aristocrats would need the support of like-minded back country woodsmen.

To place South Carolina demographics of 1775 in perspective, one should keep in mind that the low country consisted roughly of that arc of land from the coastal border of North and South Carolina radiating southward in a 70 mile wide arc down to Hilton Head and the Dafuskie Island area. In 1775 the low country consisted of eighteen parishes. Until 1775, the colonial government was principally run by the indigo and rice planters surrounding Charleston, along with wealthy merchants and ship owners. They made up the membership of the Commons House of Assembly and the Governor's Council. As the taxes levied by the Coercive Acts became an issue, it would be the more revolutionary members of the Commons who voiced opposition. These same Rebels now sought to reinforce their ranks by bringing in delegates from the back country, once it was decided to form a provisional Rebel government. Even so, *"writs of election went only to certain influential gentlemen in every parish and district."* Consequently more than a few low country men appeared as representatives for back country districts; many of these men, while not actually residing there, owned land in the back country. *"The other representatives were almost exclusively the English Virginians who had recently come into the province."*[13]

Proud of this Virginia heritage, noted South Carolina historian A.S. Salley offers the reader insight with his footnote to *"A General Return to the honorable the Council of Safety of Colonel William Thomson's Regiment of Rangers from the time of inlisting to this 20th day of September 1775, inclusive ... it will be observed that very few of the men of this regiment were born in South Carolina. This is owing to the fact that this regiment was raised in the up-country of South Carolina which had not been settled twenty years before. It will also be observed that more of them were born in Virginia than elsewhere..."*[14]

James Mayson was one of these Virginians, although his origin is not stated on the muster roll to which Salley alludes. Mayson had been settled at Ninety-Six since 1761, having immigrated there with a wife and family a year or so earlier. He would become one of those newly elected delegates to the First Provincial Congress of South Carolina who would gather in Charleston on the 11th of January 1775 to elect Charles Pinckney as its President.

The deliberations of the First Provincial Congress, its delegation of authority to the Council of Safety when not in session, and the manner in which low country delegates wielded power over back country affairs, provides an incomparable insight into the workings of South Carolina's first Revolutionary government. Minutes of their meetings reveal the divergent anxieties that motivated the low country aristocrat and back country frontiersman while supposedly seeking common cause against British tyranny. These and other records reveal the volatile nature of a colonial Englishman's attitude toward the mother country in terms of allegiance—whether in quest for an amicable solution to perceived grievances, or in pursuit of independence.

The general restlessness in the air caused low country delegate Henry Laurens to cautiously reflect, one week before the Congress convened, "*I am persuaded from all the intelligence which I have received, that we are disposed to quietness & all the obedience that ought to be expected from us provided we are reinstated in the possession of those rights & privileges we had enjoyed antecedent to the year 1763— if this is denied us by the Mother country, there will follow infinite trouble and distress throughout the colonies of North America & I think it impossible but that Great Britain must participate largely in the general Calamity …every man here as far as I have discovered is agreed, opposition against the late acts of Parliament which are the subject of our dispute ought to be made, they differ only in sentiment on the mode—some are Red-hot & foolishly talk of arms & there is another extreme who say that implicit obedience is the Surest Road to a redress of Grievances— the majority of numbers lie between, & are Men of Wealth & consideration.*"[15]

Henry Laurens, an influential and wealthy Charleston merchant from an old, prominent Huguenot family, had only returned to South Carolina on 11 December 1774 from an extended stay in Europe. After his wife died in 1771, Laurens sailed for England to supervise the education of his sons and to travel on the continent. He was probably better attuned to British attitudes toward colonial grievances than most men in Charleston. While Laurens may have been swept up in the revolutionary movement upon his return, he approached it with apprehension as one of those "*in between.*" The conservative Laurens strongly favored negotiation to redress grievances in efforts toward a reconciliation with England, pleading "*Surely the dispute is now at a Crisis there will be Wisdom found in Great Britain to heal our divisions … Good God, what are we about to do, nothing less than destroy each other for Sport or Spoil to our enemies.*"[16]

A spoiler of the "Red-hot" variety in Laurens' eyes was William Henry Drayton, former King's Judge and member of the Governor's Council, a man recently turned revolutionary, now a leading radical and advocate of separation from England. Drayton had strongly defended British policy up to 1774. This docile attitude got him a seat on the Governor's Council and an assistant judgeship. In late 1774, however, he switched. His new strident, pro-revolutionary pamphlet "*A Letter from a Freeman in South Carolina, To the Deputies of North-America, Assembled in High Court of Congress at Philadelphia,*" produced in October 1774, represented a flip-flop in attitude—one that made Laurens suspect Drayton's motives.

Drayton, *"foolishly"* in Laurens' view, was urging a militant approach. Laurens gives us a taste of the times in his letter to Oswald: *"I cannot quit the subject without observing that the presentments by Grand Juries in three of the remote districts of this colony* [Georgetown, Camden and the Cheraws] *which seem to disclaim totally the authority of Great Britain, do not contain the Sense of the people, nay I am assured they are contrary to the Sentiments of even the Jurors themselves who were led into Subscribing a paper prepared for them without properly considering its importance—those presentments are the work of a person who was a while ago a violent Creature of the Administration, & one would be induced from Such conduct to believe him now, both violent & crafty in the Same interest in the guise of patriotism."*[17]

He was, of course, referring to Drayton who *"in the guise of patriotism"* had become a scoundrel and militant, a rabble-rousing propagandist and political opportunist promoting separation from, not reconciliation with, Great Britain. The extent to which Drayton rhetoric bordered on shameless spiritual demagoguery is reflected in a statement reportedly made in late 1774 in which he pontificates *"The almighty created America to be independent of Britain; let us beware of the impiety of being backward to act as instruments in the Almighty hand, now extended to accomplish his purpose."*[18]

Yet these two men, Henry Laurens and William Henry Drayton, despite their philosophic differences, would become key policy makers, working together to resolve the controversy that was about to erupt in the back country between Loyalists and Rebels. Their course toward the politic and right thing to do would rarely be smooth, but after South Carolina's delegates returned from Philadelphia on 6 November 1774, the curtain went up and the play began.

Three days later the General Committee called for elections to a Rebel Congress for South Carolina. Delegates from the back country were to be elected on 19 December 1774, while elections for low country delegates were scheduled for 9 January 1775. Even as this revolutionary spirit was incubating, the royal government carried on business as usual. On 9 January, the same day elections for low country delegates were scheduled, it was *"ordered by His Honour the Lieutenant Governor in council that the names of the Magistrates for the several Districts in the Provinces be printed."*[19] As a point of trivia these included a total of 301—almost half were from Charleston (141). Others on the list included Georgetown (40); Cheraws (12); Camden (51); Beaufort (27); Orangeburgh (30); and Ninety-Six (68). The vast majority of these magistrates were still King's men who preferred reconciliation to war.

# CHAPTER II

## *Rebels Gather in Charleston*

H ENRY LAURENS DESCRIBES THE SCENE OF THE FIRST MEETING: *"On the 11th all the deputies from the Several parishes & districts in this province except a very few who were unable to attend, met in General provincial congress at Pike's long room where C.Pinckney was called to the Chair & Elections adjusted—thence we adjourned to the Assembly's Room in the State House & there we have Sat every day, Sunday not excepted, from Morning to night ... during eight days we performed a multitude of Speechifying & Some business with all the solemnity & formality of a Constitutional parliament."*[20]

Chairman Col. Charles Pinckney, age 43, was from St. Philip's parish in Charleston. Other attendees—Thomas Lynch, Sr., age 55; Edward Rutledge, age 26; John Rutledge, age 36; Henry Middleton, age 58; and Christopher Gadsden, age 51—were chosen to represent South Carolina at the next Continental Congress. All were low country gentlemen.

The provincial legislators now gathered in Charleston reviewed resolutions adopted by the last Continental Congress in Philadelphia, approving of the Articles of Association passed by that body on 20 October 1774. It was essential that these articles now be propagated throughout the colony. The Provincial Congress decreed that Committees be established in all districts and parishes *"for effectually carrying into execution the Continental Association, and for receiving and determining upon applications relative to law processes aforesaid."* This act sought to curtail any legal actions initiated by the King's Court of Common Pleas *"without the consent of the committee of the parish or district in which the defendant resides."*[21]

Twenty-five parishes or districts in the province, with a total of 227 committeemen, stood ready to execute the resolution. James Mayson was one of 16 committee members named *"for the Ninety Six District;"* he and six others were members of Congress. Among the remaining nine, one was Moses Kirkland. Of Mayson's other supposed rival, Robert Cunningham, he was appointed one of a 17 member committee formed to promote the 'association' *"for the District in the Forks between the Broad and Saludy Rivers."*[22]

While neither Cunningham nor Kirkland was a member of the First Provincial Congress they, like all but two of the committeemen from back country districts, were either militia officers or justices of the peace. Committee members who held both positions included Mayson, Kirkland, John Savage, Thomas Fletchall, John Caldwell, Ezekiel Polk, Joseph Robinson, Champness Terry and Thomas Neel. All but Savage would play significant roles either as Loyalist or Rebel sympathizers in the upcoming struggle for the minds of men in the back country with respect to the "association."

By associating in common cause the Rebels hoped to force English compliance with American interests, namely greater autonomy over its own affairs and full rights as Englishmen. Whether defiance of British authority could be carried out peacefully remained the unresolved question. Therefore, the initial session of the First Provincial Congress, on 16 January, taking precautionary measures *"Resolved that a secret committee of five proper persons be appointed by the President of Congress to procure and distribute such articles as the present state of the interior parts of this colony renders necessary for the better defence and security of the good people of those parts and other necessary purposes."*[23]

The instrument was in place; but it would not become necessary to mobilize the Secret Committee until mid-April. During the interim, as one historian observes, *"the mass of citizens and men of prudence and moderation ardently longed for reconciliation with the mother country … awaiting manifestations of good will from the Throne … no one in south Carolina was bold enough to advocate independence."*[24]

The mood of Charleston was tense. Even the Provincial Congress, before adjourning its first inconclusive session on 17 January, reverently *"set apart the 17th day of February next as a day of fasting humiliation and prayer, before almighty God, to devoutly petition Him to inspire the King with true wisdom, to defend the people of North America in their just title to freedom, and to avert from the impending calamities of civil war."*[25]

In his memoirs published 27 years later in 1802, William Moultrie recalls, with rhetorical flourish, *"The Provincial Congress met at the State House of the 17th of February … went to St. Philips in a body … most of them in their military attire."* He offers a passionate description of attitudes prevailing on this day of prayer, making it clear that, although the people of Charleston *"were anxiously looking forward to reconciliation … a military spirit pervaded the whole country; and Charlestown had the appearance of a garrison town, every thing wore the face of war; though not one of us had the least idea of its approach*

*... the militia were forming themselves into volunteer companies, drums beating, fifes playing; squads of men exercising on the outskirts of town ... all joined in fervent prayer to the Lord to support, and defend us, in this our greatest struggle in the cause of liberty and our country. Among the women floods of tears rolled down their cheeks, from the sad reflection of their nearest and dearest friends and relatives entering into a dreadful civil war; the worst of wars! And what was most to be lamented, it could not be avoided."*[26]

These were moving words. Moultrie would himself emerge a hero of the revolution and later become Governor of South Carolina. In 1775, however, he was a delegate to the First Provincial Congress and still a colonel in the King's Militia—the commanding officer of a Regiment of Horse for the Charleston area. Another contemporary observer of the scene at this time was equally impressed. Henry Laurens, on 18 February, wrote to his son: *"there really appeared a more general Seriousness & Solemnity than I remember to have seen upon any other fast."*[27]

Bravado mingled with hope over the next few months. But hope was dashed when no response came from England. By April the mood in Charleston deteriorated to a point that *"without passing any formal resolution it was understood in the General Committee that public military stores should be immediately seized."* Members to the Secret Committee were now appointed by Charles Pinckney to do so. The five appointees, led by William Henry Drayton, immediately *"seized the public powder at Hobcaw magazine and the powder at Cochran's ... broke open the armory in the upper part of the State House and removed 800 arms, 200 cutlasses, besides cartouches, flints and matches."* These raids were carried out by *"many of the most respectable men ... including Col. Charles Pinckney, President of the Provincial Congress, Col. Henry Laurens, Chairman of the General Committee."*[28] In Moultrie's words, *"we were now fairly entered into the business, we could not step back ... at the shipyard, some 600 pounds, some little at Fort Charlotte in the back country ... the whole making about 3000 pounds of powder, all wehad to begin our great Revolution."*[29]

Fort Charlotte, hardly touched in April, would become a primary back country objective two months later, once intelligence reports began hinting that John Stuart, General Agent and Superintendent of His Majesty's Indian Affairs for the Southern District, might be stirring up the tribes along the Savannah River border of Georgia and South Carolina. It would then become imperative that the arms stored at Fort Charlotte on the Savannah, 40 miles north of Augusta, not fall into Indian hands. A mixture of defiance and foreboding was in the air.

During this same month, on 12 April, General Thomas Gage, Commander-in-Chief of British Forces in America, based in Boston, was drafting a letter to Governor Josiah Martin of North Carolina. This correspondence would further alarm South Carolinians when it fell into their hands two months later. In essence, Gage was promising to provide Martin with a supply of gunpowder, by way of New York, to bolster North Carolina Loyalists. This letter was intercepted and, on 6 June, forwarded to the New York Provincial Congress. The South Carolina Committee of Intelligence received word through a letter dated 1 July sent from its delegates in Philadelphia. When received, Charleston and its Provincial Congress would be furious, and would condemn North Carolina agents for *"attempting to arouse former Regulators in the South Carolina back country to oppose the patriot party in that province."*[30]

Meanwhile, only seven days after Gage wrote to Martin, matters came to a head in another quarter. On 19 April 1775 British troops fired upon farmers in Lexington, Massachusetts—the "shot heard round the world." The event occurred just three weeks before a second session of the Continental Congress was scheduled to meet in Philadelphia on 10 May. South Carolina's delegates who sailed for Philadelphia on 3 May were not yet aware of Lexington; nor were other South Carolinians. It was not until *"a few days later ... on the 8th ... that a vessel arrived from Salem, Massachusetts, bringing intelligence that civil war had begun ... the news of Lexington was immediately laid before the General Committee and a vote passed to summon the Provincial Congress to a second session on the 1st day of June.*[31]

Around this same time a letter from Arthur Lee, then practicing law in London, to Henry Laurens was forwarded under cover of a dispatch dated 8 May to South Carolina's delegates at the Continental Congress in Philadelphia. An insightful message, it sheds light on the rumor-filled thoughts permeating the revolutionary air of the times. Lee warns of a British 'black plan' to subvert slaves and Indians to revolt against anti-loyalist colonists. Thoughts of an Indian uprising were especially horrifying at this time. Reports were already rampant charging John Stuart, the Crown's Superintendent of Indian Affairs and a member of the Governor's Council, with nefarious attempts to stir up the Cherokees and Creeks to attack back country areas where British policy was being opposed. Lee's letter only reinforced such perceptions.

Arthur Lee of Virginia, age 35, was educated at the University of Edinburgh. He later studied law at the Temple in London, practicing there from 1768-1780. He was also a London agent for the Massachusetts Bay

Colony. Laurens, who himself had spent a few years abroad prior to returning to Charleston in late 1774, had known Lee in London. Through Lee, Laurens became acquainted with the British revolutionary John Wilkes, a man who had great influence upon Arthur Lee. In fact Lee *got deeply involved in Wilkes' brawl with Parliament and became a passionate no holds barred foe of the British establishment.* Wilkes' views no doubt rubbed off on Lee. Indeed, *"the Revolution was made to order for his temperament, which was a strange blend of acrimony and idealism."*[32] Lee's temperament regarding the mother country, expressed in his letter to Laurens, spreading tales of British deviousness, only indulged the rumor mills and added to suspicions about John Stuart.

Whether Stuart maliciously advocated Indian attacks still remains a subject of debate among historians, as does the question of whether British correspondence was deliberately misconstrued by Rebel leaders to encourage anti-British sentiments. By way of experiencing rumors of the times *"Stuart had, in fact, received a letter from Gage in January 1775, informing him that ill-affected people"* in the northern colonies were attempting to alienate the affections of the Indians from His Majesty. With this intelligence in mind, the Superintendent at once wrote to his deputies warning them *"against attempts of the like nature to debauch the Indians in their respective Districts."* In reporting to the King's Secretary of State, the Earl of Dartmouth, Stuart added the assurance that nothing in his power would *"be omitted to keep the Indians firm in their love & attachment to the King, & in a temper to be always ready to act in his Service."*[33]

Such remarks were widely interpreted by many Carolinians as inciting Indians toward aggressive action. Substantiated or not, suspicions about Stuart grew; the mere thought of Stuart rousing Indians to the attack infuriated colonists. To avoid the threat of mob action against him, the superintendent fled from Charleston and took refuge in Savannah. *"The story was spread that in consequence of his orders thirty four families on the frontier had been murdered by the Cherokees."* The accusation proved false but in Stuart's own words, *"by the most defamatory Reports and insinuations, they endeavored to make him obnoxious to the people ... to defend himself Stuart requested some of the opposition in Georgia to examine his correspondence with his superiors and his deputies ... they appear to have been inclined to to acquit him until a letter from his deputy in the Cherokee Nation, Alexander Cameron, was read."* In the letter, a reply to one Stuart had written in January 1775, Cameron assured his superior, with respect to Indians, he *"had the vanity to think that he could head any number thought proper whenever called upon in support of his Majesty and Government."*[34]

When they learned of these words, Charlestonians were incensed; they saw them in the worst possible light, interpreting them to mean offensive, aggressive actions to be taken at will by Cherokees against helpless frontier families. Stuart was impeached in absentia at the second session of the First Provincial Congress in Charleston, which then appointed its own agents, George Galphin and Edward Wilkinson, to handle Indian affairs.

While the Indian problem was festering during the month of May, it was really the events at Lexington that filled everyone's mind. News of the battle triggered a patriotic bonding among the zealous revolutionary-minded citizenry. A clue to the temper of the times is provided by Lt. Governor Bull, whose letter in late May to Lord Dartmouth reported that *"on the 10th instant Barnard Elliott ... resigned his seat as a member of his Majesty's Council."* Elliott would soon become second-in-command of the first regiment of foot to be raised by the revolutionary South Carolinians. In this same letter, Bull told the Foreign Office *"I have nothing new to add relative to the proceedings of the disenchanted in this province, they continue in the same temper ... the account of the skirmish or engagement between the King's Troops and the Provincials of Massachusetts near Lexington on the 19th of last month, seems to produce effects here very different from intimidation."*[35]

While Bull tried to play down the euphoria induced by Lexington, the people of Charleston seemed well aware that Lord Hugh Percy's British troops *"beat a disordered retreat to Boston. The Yankees followed them, singing Yankee Doodle; from that time the song has been considered an American patriotic air."*[36]

But the joy of victory was not shared by all in a province still sharply divided. Charles Webb, *"on that very day when the news was brought that hostilities had commenced ... declared he would go to England take a Commission & come Against the Americans."* Webb called the Lieutenant Governor *"a damn'd fool for not hoisting up the King's Standard."* He referred to the General Committee as a *"Sett of Mechanical, Ignorant Rascals, & all were Lousey Blackguards."* Webb's remarks would come to haunt him ten weeks later when the American cause was gaining favor. He would then be accused by his peers as *"an Enemy to this Province & America in General."*[37]

Webb was not alone in his opposition, but the Rebel factions were far more aggressive in displaying their feelings. News of hostilities in the north fired the imagination of Charleston's revolutionaries, who were now concerned over defending themselves, the city and the province of South Carolina. A special committee of the General Committee met to deliberate. Henry Laurens, its leading moderate, provides us with a peek into emerging events. Writing to son John in London on 9 May, having learned only one day earlier that "*the sword of Civil War was drawn in the environs of Boston on the 19th April … the committee here in which they have forced your father to be Chairman are exerting their utmost abilities I hope for wise & good—I recommend strongly to have always in view a happy reconciliation with the Mother Country & hopes of Saving her & our Selves from that destruction intended by wicked Ministers for both.*"[38]

While the conservative Laurens clung to hopes for reconciliation with England, radicals such as Drayton were simultaneously pushing for war. He, along with others in the General Committee, proposed military defense measures for Charleston harbor—far too belligerent and premature a posture for moderates to accept. Thus another proposition was suggested—an Association to be signed by the inhabitants generally, verbally protesting British oppression but taking no physical action.

An Association document, drawn up on 10 May, became an object of long debate during the following days. By a vote of 25 to 23 in the General Committee, action was delayed. Laurens commented to his son on 15 May, "*it will be recommended to the Provincial Congress at their first meeting on the first of June—I have no doubt of its favorable reception there. In the mean time the daily & nightly sound of Drums & Fifes discovers a spirit of the people … upwards of one hundred Men besides the common Town Watch mount guard every Night & Committees of observation, of intelligence & of safety find employment every Day.*"[39]

# CHAPTER III

## *Jingoism Prevails*

WHILE THE INITIAL JANUARY SESSION OF THE FIRST PROVINCIAL Congress in 1775 was filled with fanfare—pomp, circumstance and appeals to the Almighty—the armed skirmish between redcoats and farmers in Massachusetts on 19 April sobered Carolinians considerably once news filtered down to Charleston. When the second session of the Provincial Congress convened on 1 June 1775, its members were more seriously inclined to break from royal authority and place South Carolina on a war footing. For the first time backwoodsman would be assuming a serious role in the decision making process.

From the largest district in the back country, furthest from Charleston, James Mayson, militia officer and justice of the peace, would be joined in Congress by nine other elected comrades to represent Ninety-Six. Three of these men represented the top three officers of the King's Militia in that area— Col. John Savage, Lt. Col. James Mayson and Major Andrew Williamson. Their unit was one of 13 royal government militia regiments still existent in South Carolina, many of whose troopers would have a difficult time deciding whether to remain loyal or join the Rebels. The officers of Ninety-Six had no such difficulty; they were joined by additional delegates from Ninety-Six to the Provincial Congress—LeRoy Hammond, Esq.; Patrick Calhoun, Esq.; John Lewis Gervais, Esq.; Richard Rapley, Esq.; Edward Rutledge, Esq.; John Purves, Esq.; and Mr. Francis Salvador. However, when Congress met, some delegates still had their doubts *"Col. Charles Pinckney, then still President, for whom it is probable that matters were now going too fast, resigned … and Col. Henry Laurens, the late Chairman of the General Committee, was chosen in his place."*[40] On day two the first order of business *"Resolved unanimously, That a general ASSOCIATION is necessary …Ordered, that the Hon. Mr. Lowndes, Mr. Tennent, Col. Parsons, Mr. Harrington, Mr. Ferguson, Mr.*

*Thomas Heyward, Jun., and Mr. Thomas Lynch, Jun., be a committee to prepare the form of an association."*[41]

All these men represented parishes in the low country except for Harrington, a delegate from St. David's Parish on the northern fringe. Young Thomas Lynch was the son of a South Carolina delegate to the current Continental Congress sitting in Philadelphia; he would soon replace his father there and become a Signer of the Declaration of Independence in 1776. Regarding the Association in Charleston it was now *"Ordered, that the same be engrossed. And being engrossed accordingly, it was read:*
South Carolina

> *The actual commencement of hostilities against this continent, by the British troops, in the blood scene on the 19th of April last, near Boston—the increase of arbitrary impositions from a wicked and despotic ministry—and the dread of instigated insurrection in the colonies—are causes sufficient to drive an oppressed people to the use of arms; We therefore, the subscribers, inhabitants of South Carolina, holding ourselves bound, by that most sacred of all obligations, the duty of good citizens towards an injured country, and thoroughly convinced, that under our present distressed circumstances, we shall be justified before God and man, in resisting force by force; DO UNITE ourselves, under every tie of religion and of honour, and associate, as a band in her defence, against every foe: Hereby solemnly engaging that, whenever our Continental or Provincial Councils shall decree it necessary, we will go forth, and be ready to sacrifice our lives and fortunes to secure her freedom and safety. This obligation to continue in full force until a reconciliation shall take place between Great Britain and America, upon constitutional principles—an Event which we most ardently desire. And we will hold all those persons inimical to the liberty of the colonies, who shall refuse to subscribe this association."*[42]

This Association was a local NATO of its time—a document that left little doubt as to the mood of Congress regarding joint defense. Anyone not for liberty would be deemed suspect. Nevertheless, it was equally clear that liberty for many Carolinians did not mean complete independence from British rule, but rather equality as Englishmen. The resolutions left some wiggle room. Moderates, such as Laurens, were still hopeful that England would see fit to redress legitimate colonial grievances over trade and taxation without resort to arms.

But the wheels had been set in motion. By 3 June it was *"Ordered, That a sufficient number of copies of the said association be forthwith printed, on the largest paper that can be procured, and delivered in at the table to-morrow morning, in order to be signed by the members."* Congress then *"Resolved, That this colony ought to be forthwith put into a proper state of defence ... Ordered, That Col. Pinckney, Capt. Roberts, Capt. Lempriere, Mr. Tennent, Hon. Mr. Drayton, Col. Gaillard, Capt. Tucker, Capt. Joyner, Col. Gervais, Mr. Harrington, Doctor Farrar, Col. Bull, and Col Richardson, be a committee, to consider ways and means for putting the colony in a posture of defence; and to lay before the Congress a plan and estimate for that purpose."*[43]

No back country planters were included on the committee, unless one considers Col. Richard Richardson in this category. Richardson was a delegate from the District Eastward of the Wateree River. He was a well known and highly respected gentleman of 71 who, coming from Virginia, married into the Cantey family and served in the Commons House of five Royal Assemblies. Accepted as a low country aristocrat, Richardson was a recent convert to the Camden area.[44]

Following church services on Sunday, 4 June, the Provincial Congress continued deliberations and ordered *"that every member do now sign the association ... resolved that the representatives of the several country parishes and districts, do moreover subscribe their names to those copies which are to be signed by the inhabitants of the parts they respectively represent; and that the most effectual measures be taken to procure the subscription of the same generally as soon as possible."*[45]

Such a high handed order insisting upon a general signature by all amounted to intimidation. When representatives returned home, to sign or not to sign soon became a wedge driven between back country settlers. Many were uncertain of their feelings regarding loyalty to the King or premature rebellion. At this stage the degree of sympathy among the people at large for the cause of either Rebel or Loyalist was not well defined. And any nuances in back country attitudes were certainly not well understood by low country members of Congress; anti-associators still remained suspect. While copies of the Association were dispersed in handbills throughout Charleston, the deputies from the back country were told to *"retain the association papers ... and once every month certify and return lists of the names of subscribers thereto, and also of such shall refuse to subscribe, to the General Committee in Charles-Town."*[46]

Hardliners in Congress were in no mood to tolerate dissension or opposition, no matter how rational; they insisted upon compiling a blacklist of potential enemies—a reflex action typical of radical movements. In South Carolina of 1775 enforcement against enemies of the state would be carried out in the back country through economic sanctions, proselytization, intimidation and bodily harm over the next six months, pushing settlers to the brink of civil war. In the low country, enemies to association were tarred and feathered in political reprisal.

During congressional sessions legislators were getting down to other serious business. On 6 June, it was resolved *that two regiments of foot, each to consist of seven hundred and fifty rank and file, be forthwith officered, raised, paid and disciplined, and put under the direction of Congress ... resolved that a regiment of rangers, to consist of four hundred and fifty privates, be also forthwith officered, raised, paid, and disciplined, and put under the direction of Congress.*[47]

The Rebel Congress had now laid the foundation for a Rebel army to oppose the government of the mother country. Its two regiments of foot would be raised among low country men and would consist of ten companies each, 75 men in each company. The back country Regiment of Rangers would be composed of nine companies, 50 men in each company. Before Congress adjourned, however, after hot debate, these grandiose plans were tempered by fiscal restraints, and the numbers were cut to 50 men in each company of low country regiments and 30 to each company in the Regiment of Rangers. But the very accomplishment of organizing its own military inspired the Rebels—no easy feat considering that South Carolina still had 13 Regiments of King's Militia dispersed throughout the province, although these were troops of untested allegiance.

How many officers and men would remain loyal? How many would support the Rebels? One reading of the political barometer was clear—nineteen officers from the King's militia were already elected delegates to the Rebel Congress. Seventeen of them held field officer rank, including eight from the back country. But they made up less than half of the total officer corps of the King's Militia. Between officers and men there remained considerable indecision as to continued service to the King or support of a colonial association against the coercive actions of England.

In preparation for hard times Congress now turned its attention to the storage of rice and flour supplies. Food magazines, or storage facilities, were established at Jacksonburg, Pocotaligo, Beaufort, Dorchester, Watboo, Georgetown, Orangeburg, Ninety-Six, in the Fork Between the Broad and Saluda Rivers and at Smith's Ferry on the Broad River. Two persons in each of these areas were appointed to take responsibility for receiving stores. Col. James Mayson and Mr. William Moore were designated for Ninety-Six.

On 9 June the legislators returned to the task of military enlistments.

To wean men away from the King's established militia forces, Congress *"Resolved, That the sum of Fifteen Pounds, currency, bounty-money, be given to the soldiers who shall inlist in the service of the colony. That Ten Pounds thereof, be paid to them at the time of inlistment, and the other five Pounds, after one month's good behavior ... Resolved, That the sum of Three Pounds and five shillings, currency, be allowed to each officer for every man inlisted by him, brought to the headquarters, attested, and approved by the commanding officer."*[48]

Pay scales were agreed upon for officers and men in South Carolina's three regiments. Pay scales for rangers, however, differed from the foot soldiers in other regiments. Rangers were required *"to provide themselves with horses, guns, provisions, and such cloathing as shall be approved of by the commanding officer ... that the sum of Fifteen Pounds, currency, per man, be allowed to each Serjeant and private of the rangers, in aid of their monthly pay, for purchasing a pair of leather breeches, and such uniform cap and coat, as the Lieutenant Colonel shall think proper—which he is required to order ... the officers and men of the two regiments of foot be paid once a fortnight; and the rangers once a month, not otherwise."*[49]

Only in the late afternoon of the same day did the Provincial Congress get around to selection procedures for regimental officers. It was *"Ordered, That a committee be appointed to receive the names of such gentlemen as shall offer themselves, or be recommended by any member of this Congress, to serve as Field-Officers, Captains, First Lieutenants, and Paymasters, in the horse and foot ... to be raised ... Ordered, That Charles Cotesworth Pinckney, Esq; Col. Richard Richardson, Benjamin Waring, Thomas Heyward, Jun; and Isaac Harleston, Esqrs, be a committee for that purpose; and that they do sit immediately."* They did so, sitting through the night, receiving names of candidates. They reported the following day and laid the list on the table *"for the perusal of the members."* It was now *"Resolved, That the Colonels, Lieutenant Colonels, Majors, Captains, First Lieutenants and Paymasters to the three regiments, to be raised for the public service, be chosen by ballot."* Congress proceeded to vote accordingly, *"the following gentlemen being declared duly elected by a majority of votes. Resolved, That Christopher Gadsden, Esq., be appointed Colonel, Isaac Huger, Esq, Lieutenant Colonel, and Owen Roberts, Esq, Major of the first regiment of foot ... Resolved that William Moultrie, Esq., be appointed Colonel, Isaac Mottes, Esq., Lieutenant Colonel, and Alexander McIntosh, Esq., Major of the second regiment of foot ... Resolved, That William Thomson, Esq., be appointed Lieutenant Colonel, and James Mayson, Esq., Major of the regiment of rangers."*[50]

Each of these appointees was a member of Congress elected by his peers. There is no record of animosity regarding their selection. Contrary to Andrew Pickens' hindsight opinion 36 years later, there is no indication that Mayson's election was contested by either Robert Cunningham or Moses Kirkland, neither of whom sat in the Congress. However, someone did propose Kirkland's name for captain in the rangers. Accordingly, the record shows *"the following gentlemen be duly elected Captains ... to rank in the order they stand, viz. Samuel Wise, Ezekiel Polk, John Caldwell, Ely Kershaw, Robert Goodwyn, Moses Kirkland, Edward Richardson, Thomas Woodward, John Purves."*[51] All but Richardson and Kirkland were sitting members of the Provincial Congress.

Lieutenants were now duly elected for all three regiments. Of the nine 1st lieutenants elected to serve with the Regiment of Rangers only Samuel Watson was a delegate to Congress; the others were suggested by their friends and peers. Allen Cameron was a remarkable choice, submitted by Andrew Williamson, as he was the brother of Alexander Cameron, the King's Deputy Superintendent of Indian Affairs under John Stuart, who was currently considered to be an enemy of the province. Cameron would later decline the appointment.

While each of the two foot regiments were allotted three field officers, headed by a colonel as commanding officer, the rangers had but two, with a lieutenant colonel in command. All field officers of low country regiments, except for McIntosh, were second or third generation stock, born in or near Charleston. Major Alexander McIntosh was a recent immigrant from Scotland who settled in the Cheraws area in St. David's Parish. Both field officers of the rangers were also relatively new Carolinians with respect to pedigree. William Thomson, age 48 in 1775, came to Carolina with his parents from Pennsylvania sometime in the late 1750's. They settled in the Orangeburg area, St. Matthew's Parish. James Mayson, age 42 in 1775, received his first land grant in Ninety-Six District on 1 December 1761. As a Scots-Irish trader he filtered down into the back country of South Carolina, with a wife and three children, from western Virginia [Augusta County]. Like many others, Mayson was probably a refugee from the French and Indian War.

With appointments out of the way, legislators now *"Resolved, That Col. Moultrie, Col. Huger, Col. Motte, Col, Thomson, Major Roberts, Major McIntosh, Major Mayson, Capt. C.C. Pinckney and Mr. Bee be a committee to frame proper rules and regulations for better ordering the military forces of this colony."*[52]

Attention was then turned to the Council of Safety which had been established to serve as an executive arm of the Rebel government when

Congress was not in session. Its jurisdiction over military matters was laid out, The council *"shall have full power and authority to carry the acts of the Assembly for regulating the Militia of the Colony … Militia officers and men as shall be draughted and employed, shall be allowed a daily pay and rations, equal to the pay allowed in the new-raised regiments of foot: That if any just complaint shall be made against any officer in the militia … the council of safety may remove such officer … the Council of Safety in separate session elected Henry Laurens President and appointed Peter Timothy Secretary."* It ordered blank commissions for the army *"to be filled up"*, and then adjourned.[53]

As President of the First Provincial Congress and now President of the Council of Safety, Henry Laurens became the highest ranking official in the revolutionary government. Peter Timothy, although not a member of the Provincial Congress, was a politically powerful appointee. Born in Holland, he immigrated to Philadelphia in 1731 with his father, Lewis, who entered into partnership with Benjamin Franklin, whereby the Timothy family *"would establish a printing business in Charleston for Franklin."* The *South Carolina Gazette* was subsequently founded and managed by Peter from 1740-1772.[54]

The 13 members of the Council of Safety included Henry Laurens, age 51; Charles Pinckney, age 43; Rawlins Lowndes, age 53; Thomas Ferguson, age 45; Miles Brewton, age 44; Arthur Middleton, age 33; Thomas Heyward, Jr., age 29; Thomas Bee, age 35; John Huger, age 31; James Parsons, age 51; William Henry Drayton, age 33; Benjamin Elliott, age 50; William Williamson, age 45. Again, all were low country gentlemen and all were second or third generation Charlestonians except for Lowndes, a relative newcomer from the island of St. Kitts. They were the *de facto* government of revolutionary South Carolina, in opposition to the King's Governor.

The wheels had been set in motion. Inhabitants throughout the colony were now being asked to train diligently, at least once a fortnight. Congress had even authorized *"that the Council of Safety do, without delay, fix on some proper manual of exercise and cause the same to be printed and dispersed."*

Carolinians were also encouraged to form their own volunteer troops *"not exceeding 100 men in each troop or company or horse … subject to the orders of field officers of the district in which they shall associate and form."* All such field officers, however, *"would be subject to the rejection of the Council of Safety, by whom appointments shall be made out for all such officers as they may approve … Resolved, That the officers in the regiments of foot and horse now to be raised, shall in every case when acting in conjunction with officers of the militia of equal commission, take rank and precedence, without regard to prior dates of commission in the latter."*[55]

Given human nature and ego, as well as vanity and concern with rank and privilege once a uniform is donned, this last clause was an attempt to maintain honor and discipline where differences might arise. This was no small matter within a military buildup that included three regular regiments on one hand and, eventually, uncounted numbers of voluntary militia groups on the other. Psychological clashes over pride, honor and rank were bound to occur.

While in its final active days, planning for future gatherings, the Rebel legislators resolved on the 17th *that this congress shall expire on the sixth day of August next, that a new election be made on Monday the seventh and Tuesday the eighth days of August, except in Charles-Town; and that the members then elected, together with those elected in Charles-Town, do meet in General Congress, at Charles-Town, on the first day of December next, or sooner."*[56]

The Council of Safety held its own first business meeting on 17 June and signed commissions for all officers of the 1st and 2nd regiments to be established. On the 18th it signed commissions for officers of the 3rd regiment—the Regiment of Rangers.[57] The pieces were falling into place in readiness for potential conflict.

Auspiciously, on this same day, King George III's new *"Trusty and Beloved William Campbell, Esq., commonly called Lord William Campbell Our Captain General and Governor in Chief of Our Province of South Carolina in America,"* arrived in Charleston. South Carolina had been without a Royal Governor since Lord Charles Greville Montagu had departed in 1773, leaving his 63-year-old deputy William Bull in charge as the royal kingpin, to muddle through an increasingly volatile period in his colony's history.

Meanwhile, Campbell had been appointed in late 1773 or early 1774 to replace Montagu. On 2 April 1774 he was still in London dragging his feet over an unwanted assignment. On this day he wrote a grumbling letter to Lord Dartmouth *finding it impracticable to carry on his Majesty's service with any satisfaction while the affairs of the colony are in such a state disorder and confusion."*[58]

With great reluctance, on 20 June, the new appointee accepted his fate. Instructions prepared by the Earl of Dartmouth, his Majesty's Principal Secretary of State for America at Whitehall, were laid before the King, approved and handed to Campbell. This was nine months before he actually embarked for America. In the interim the First Continental Congress would take place and news of the "association" would become widespread. Indeed, only one week after the Continental Congress disbanded, on 2 November 1774, Brigadier Ruggles, a British officer posted in Boston, writing to his friend Israel Maudit, a Massachusetts agent in London, ominously observing, *"America is preparing for war and surprised at the apathy of great Britain … The desire for independence has spread over all the provinces, even parts of Nova Scotia are refractory. Only Canada is loyal and General Carleton has offered General Gage Canadians and Indians to assist if necessary."*[59]

The ominous tone of this information did not appear to concern Whitehall. It certainly did not stimulate Campbell's departure. But the comment about Carleton's potential recruitment of Indians eventually filtered south along the inevitable grapevine. It would arouse consternation among South Carolinians, reinforcing their suspicions about John Stuart's collaboration with the British. Major General Guy Carleton had only arrived in Canada in late 1774 and was appointed Governor of the Province of Quebec in January 1775, while still subordinate to General Gage regarding overall military affairs in the American colonies.

In England, the Ruggles letter, although disquieting, was given over to Lord North, Prime Minister of Great Britain, on 9 January 1775. There it languished. The seriousness of an American uprising had not yet registered among Whitehall's leaders. Nevertheless, North did send a reinforcement of British troops to Boston, along with General William Howe, who would later replace General Thomas Gage as Commander-in-Chief of British Forces in America. They landed in Boston in May 1775, in time to participate in the Battle of Bunker Hill.

Meanwhile, the appointed governor to South Carolina was still resisting his assignment, whining to Lord Dartmouth on 10 January about *"the decrease of the governor of South Carolina's salary owing to the proclamation prohibiting grants of lands owing to the late unhappy differences."*[60] Eventually, unable to procrastinate any longer, Lord William Campbell was forced to embark for America sometime in May; he and his family would arrive in Charleston harbor on 17 June, the same day the Battle of Bunker Hill was being fought in Boston.

Upon debarking Governor Campbell was greeted with all the pomp and circumstance of diplomatic protocol appropriate for a king's representative. But three days later the revolutionary Provincial Congress presented Lord William with a petition expressing its grievances. Excerpts from this polite document are instructive regarding the cautious mood prevailing among Carolina's Rebels: *"We his Majesty's loyal subjects, the Representatives of the People of this colony in Congress assembled, beg leave to disclose to your Excellency the true causes of our present proceedings … that we may stand justified to the world … When the ordinary modes of application for redress of grievances, and the usual means of defence against arbitrary impositions have failed, mankind generally have had recourse to those that are extraordinary. Hence the origin of the Continental Congress—and hence the representation of the people of this colony … We declare that no love of innovation, no desire of altering the constitution of government—no lust for independence has had the least influence upon our counsels, but alarmed and roused by a long succession of arbitrary proceedings … and deeply affected by the commencement of Hostilities … solely for the preservation and in defence of our Lives, Liberties and Properties —we have been impelled to associate and take up arms."*[61]

A more conciliatory petition is difficult to imagine given the growing gap between hawks and doves in Carolina. Guided by Laurens' tact and finesse, Carolinians still urged common sense in seeking equal rights under British law, not independence. The effort predictably failed when Campbell roundly condemned the actions of the petitioners as being illegal. They withdrew in anger to consult on their next move, hawks now holding the better hand.

Mobilization orders were issued by the Council of Safety to the province's three new regiments. Commissions for paymasters were signed—John Chesnut was assigned to the rangers. Commissions were issued for 2nd Lieutenants—blank ones to commanders where positions were not yet filled. On the same day, the 21st of June, the Committee of Intelligence received information from Savannah regarding the interrogation of John Stuart and the allegedly incriminating letter he received from his subordinate Alexander Cameron. Infuriated once again, Carolinians, led by William Henry Drayton, invaded Stuart's home in Charleston, harassed his wife and demanded all correspondence. John Stuart himself had, by this time, left Savannah and was presently residing in St. Augustine, Florida.[62]

At this point the Provincial Congress was itself disbanding; indeed many delegates had already left for their homes—some as far as 200 miles away. On the 23rd, in his usual lucid fashion, Henry Laurens wrote a letter to his son in London that reveals highlights of the Congress and offers insight into prevailing political attitudes as British-American relations deteriorated: *"last Night …1/2 past 3 o'clock I adjourned the Congress & got free from as hard a two & twenty Days labour as ever I went through in the course of my life … Mutiny Act or Rules & Regulations for the Army grounded upon the British Mutiny Bill was Read debated & agreed upon … Ordered upon a Motion & Question, that every man shall take with him his Fire Arms & Ammunition whenever he attends Church or other places of divine Worship in Charles Town—this foolish affair cost above two hours debate & carried by a Majority of one … Tuesday*

[20 June] *Mr. Lowndes moved that it be recommended by the Congress to the Council of Safety to restrain the number of foot soldiers ... to 1000 instead of 1500; & of horse to 270 instead of 450 ... this brought on very long debates—the parson* [William Tennent] *was exceedingly hot against the Motion at length we carried it ... Colonels are to inlist only 50 men in each Company of foot & 30 Men for each Company in the Regiment of Rangers & we save near 400,000 pounds ... It was moved on Wednesday that no Military Officer Should sit as a Member of the Council of Safety—& after long debate carried in the affirmative—another motion by an Officer , that no Commissioned Officer in the pay of this Colony Should be eligible to sit in the provincial congress, an hours debate ensued & then the Motion was withdrawn ... an impeachment of John Stuart, Esquire Superintendent of Indian Affairs, upon evidence from copies of his letters to his deputy Mr. Cameron, for endeavoring to incite the Creek & Cherokee Indians to act against this colony if his Majesty's Service should require it—this discovery was made to us by Jo. Habersham* [of Georgia] *to whom Mr. Stuart had produced Some of his letters in order to vindicate his conduct ... Resolved that the Committee of Intelligence do write to Mr. Stuart to answer the charge ... if he is guilty certainly he will feel public resentmen—His Estate will be held as guarantee for the quiet & good conduct of the Savages—Good God what horrible scenes are exhibited in Civil broils ... I am extremely sorry for the Man & most truly feel for the wretchedness of this family."* Although *"some things induce me to believe the charge not groundless,"* Laurens leaves the distinct impression that he is still not convinced of Stuart's guilt. [63]

In a lighter vein, Laurens continues, telling John that *"Our Young Officers have appeared in congress in their Regimentals, first Regimet Blue faced with buff Cap & feather—2nd blue Scarlet, Cap & feather with a crescent in front, motto Liberty. I think my memory has furnished you with a tolerable abstract ... & I have said enough to convince you that the people in this province mean to be in earnest in the defence of their Rights, you see they have taken in part into their hands both the Civil & military Government of the Colony—restrain the courts of law, Levy Troops, Coin Money—lay embargoes & command implicit obedience in all cases by Signifying what 'ought' and what 'ought not' to be done, terms well understood & more venerated by all Ranks, that ever I knew the laws of the province to be—at the same time every man in the Colony as far as I know ... are most sincerely desirous of returning to our ancient form of Government in subordination to the Mother Country upon constitutional terms. Surely the folly & madness of Administration must Soon be at an end—'tis impossible to go on long in their present course—the Glory of Britain is tarnished by their proceedings in New England."* [64]

Clearly Henry Laurens and many like him still wished to remain Englishmen, but with full rights. They felt that English authorities were being stupidly inflexible in refusing to admit the justice of their arguments regarding representation. In opposition stood Carolinian hawks who boldly proclaimed independence from Great Britain irrespective of any concessions offered by the British. Although obviously in anguish over the situation, Laurens had not lost his sense of humor, waggishly observing to son John, *"did I tell you that our Parson [Tennent] moved for a General Fast to be observed on the 27th July throughout the Colony, the Ministers to be desired to preach Sermons suitable to the occasion … in this Oliverian step he succeeded."*[65]

In the period from 23 June, when Laurens dissolved the First Provincial Congress of South Carolina, and beyond the 27th of July, designated as a Fast Day by the Rev. William Tennent, the Council of Safety would be in control as the executive branch of the revolutionary government. Most back country delegates to the Congress had already left Charleston by the 26th of June. Communication with their leaders would now be relegated to couriers on horseback, a relatively slow, tedious process given the lack of good roads between communities where rivers and streams were not always easy to cross. Military coordination would become all the more imperative once news of the Battle of Bunker Hill filtered down to Charleston. Meanwhile relations with the new Governor, William Campbell, had become increasingly more hostile since his rejection of the Rebels conciliatory petition of 20 June. And concern over the allegiances of Indians, always a major worry in the minds of colonial Carolinians, especially those living in the back country, remained in the forefront.

The Council of Safety obviously had much to contend with in organizing the colony for defense. A chronological, documentary diary of events, as they unfolded in South Carolina over the second half of 1775, offers the best description of struggles over policy, differences in attitude, and the fragility of pride and prejudice that continually faced men in Charleston and those in the back country. Views on "association" differed drastically, inciting confrontation more often than conciliation. The next six months would prove to be a crucible in which colonial Carolinians would mould their future as a state, coexistent with 12 other colonies, as they developed into the United States. But South Carolina's uniqueness as a state was founded on, and would ever remain based on, the relationship that evolved between men of the low country and those of the back country.

# CHAPTER IV

## *Organizing for Action*

W HEN MOBILIZATION ORDERS FOR THE REVOLUTIONARY regiments had been sent out by the Council of Safety on 21 June, many officers and members of Congress had already left Charleston. For the rangers, orders were sent by courier to *"William Thomson, Esq., Lieutenant Colonel Commandant of the Regiment of Rangers,"* who was already back in Orangeburg: *"Sir you are hereby directed forthwith to issue orders for levying in this and adjacent colonies, proper men, not exceeding thirty in each company, to serve for six months certain, and not longer than three years, in the Regiment of Rangers under your command; observing the articles agreed upon by the Provincial Congress for ordering and governing the forces in service in this colony."* This directive concluded with the hopeful thought, *"and it is recommended to all the good people of this and neighboring colonies to give you and the officers under your command all the necessary aid and assistance therein."*[66]

Although Thomson was given authority to recruit in Georgia and North Carolina as well, there is no evidence that frontiersmen from either colony actually joined the rangers. However, both Loyalists and Rebels from Georgia and North Carolina did serve in volunteer militia groups, formed in their own colonies as the war progressed. In 1775 the idea of recruiting rangers, even from the South Carolina back country, was a ticklish one. For many back country frontiersmen the word tyranny applied to Charleston's elite as much as it did to British authority. Many were reluctant to join an association in common cause with Rebels at this early stage, preferring simply to be left alone.

Stated another way, as South Carolina historian Edward McCrady observed, the back country had never been satisfactorily represented in the House of Commons. *"With what grace could the people on the coast appeal to them to join in a war against taxation without representation in the Parliament in England, when, though they had asked and petitioned for it, they were with-out representation in the Commons House of Assembly here in Carolina?"*[67]

According to Lt. Col. Thomson's order book, he received the courier's message on 24 June and on the same day, from his own camp established at Amelia, forwarded the information to his subordinate, Major James Mayson, with a cover letter, sent by courier to Mayson's home at Island Ford on the Saluda River 60 miles away, Thomson reports; *"Inclos'd is a copy of orders I rec'd from the Council of Safety ... observe the contents and give orders accord-ingly to the four upper companies Viz: Perwiss [sic], Kirkland, Caldwell, and Polk. ... you will also order an encampment in the most convenient place near Reedy River and that each Capt. as soon as he has enlisted ten men to send them to the camp in order to learn their Exercise and be in readiness with a good horse, and Rifle, and other necessaries."*[68]

Since the Regiment of Rangers was composed of nine companies, the gist of Thomson's letter seems to delegate command of the upper four com-panies to Mayson while Thomson retained control of the other five. Of Major Mayson's four captains, John Purves' and Moses Kirkland's came from areas closest to Mayson and were probably the most accessible. John Caldwell lived in the District Between the Broad and Saluda Rivers; Ezekiel Polk was settled in the District in the Upper Part of the New Acquisition, near the North Carolina border. With the exception of Purves, Major Mayson's other three captains, like Mayson himself, still retained commissions in the King's militia within their respective districts. All took a demotion in rank to serve in the Regiment of Rangers. Mayson contacted his captains and told them that an encampment on Reedy River, a few miles north of Ninety-Six village, would be established.

Undeveloped as the back country was with respect to roads, logistics necessarily would play an important role regarding communications and military strategy as hostilities between the convinced and unconvinced played out on the subject of "association." Horseback was the only means of transportation; a man could roughly cover but 30-45 miles per day depend-ing upon condition of roads, denseness of forest and number of streams or rivers to ford. Thomson's camp at Amelia was approximately 80 miles from Charleston, headquarters of the Council of Safety. Amelia was about 60 miles away from Mayson's camp north of Ninety-Six village. The distance from Ninety-Six village to the British Fort Charlotte on the Savannah River was 25 miles, and the fort was 45 miles north of Augusta. It was 140 miles to Charleston from Augusta and approximately the same distance between Charleston and Ninety-Six.

Enlisting men for the ranger companies proved more difficult than antici-pated. Many back country planters were only superficially aware of the dispute between England and America. Their sympathies were basically Loyalist, com-bined with distrust of the same Charleston elite who were now asking them to associate in common cause to take up arms against their mother country. The task required time, tact, compromise and patience. But the rangers would have little time for organization before they received their first marching order, which in itself created friction between Thomson and Mayson.

When the Council of Safety met in Charleston on 26 June, it *"Resolved, that a letter be written to Col. Thomson directing him to station the first troop of rangers that shall be raised from Fort Charlotte … to take care of the military stores … you will also cause the two brass field pieces and all the spare bayonets in the fort to be sent … to the Council of Safety in Charles-Town."* In this order, under Laurens' signature, Thomson was told, *"you will immediately send a copy of these instructions to Major Mayson, in order that he may not execute any thing relative to the directions he had concerning Fort Charlotte."*[69]

This last line must have puzzled, if not infuriated Col. Thomson as a breach of military discipline. What "directions" had Mayson been given "concerning Fort Charlotte?" Had he shared them with Thomson? If so, there is no record. Indeed, in later correspondence Thomson would irritably allude to this incident as a "secret" kept from him. Inadvertently or not, the Council had driven a wedge between a commanding officer and his second in com-mand. The results of this order will be taken up in context.

Meanwhile, on the 26th, the Council of Safety also discussed *"Proposals for supplying the Provincial troops received from Andrew Williamson, Peter Bounetheau and John Coram, esqrs."* Williamson got the contract which stated, *"Andrew Williamson for and in consideration of the said allowance of Three shil-lings for each man per Day to be paid monthly Doth hereby Covenant, Promise and agree to Provide and Furnish to each Man in the said two Regiments of Foot the following articles:*

> *One pound of good beef per Day or One Pound of Fresh Pork or Twelve Ounces of Salt Pork*
> *One Pound of wheat Flour per Day or One pound of Ship Bread or One Pint and a half of rice*
> *Half a pint of Vinegar per Week when in Barracks or Stated Camps.*
> *One Pint of Salt per week when they are served with fresh Provisions &*
> *One Pound of Black Pepper per Year if it can be procured."*[70]

A fascinating item of trivia was also raised on the 26th of June when the Council decided upon *"devices and mottos for the certificates to be engraved"* for South Carolina's currency. Mottos, as was customary, were written in Latin. In this case *"For the Five Pound note, the device was a bundle of rods and arrows tied together, representing the twelve United Colonies of America; motto Auspicum Salutis 1775."*[71]

Representation of twelve, rather than thirteen, original colonies was probably due to the fact that Georgia had not sent delegates to the First Continental Congress in Philadelphia; the second Congress, now in session, was attended only by an observer, Lyman Hall, from St John's Parish. It was not until 7 July that a full delegation was elected to represent Georgia. Meanwhile it remains questionable whether South Carolina actually printed her five pound note representing twelve colonies. If so, it would be a valuable collector's item.

*Tuesday, 27 June*

After signing his contract, Andrew Williamson remained in Charleston to receive special instructions from the Council regarding Alexander Cameron and the importance of maintaining friendly relations with the Cherokees. He left on the 27th and rode back home to Long Canes, approximately a three day journey. Williamson was asked to sound out the Deputy Indian Superintendent, Alexander Cameron, as to where he stood in the evolving struggle with England. Council members like Gervais, for example, feared that Cameron might be acting out of misguided duty if he was planning to stir up Indians at Stuart's bidding. That very thought was an abomination to Carolinians, especially those in the back country, so it was essential to be clear about Cameron's intentions.

In spite of current suspicions, Alexander Cameron was held in high respect by his Long Canes area neighbors, among them prominent families like Gervais, Hammond, Calhoun, Williamson and Whitefield. George Whitefield was currently in command of the British Fort Charlotte. John Lewis Gervais, who not only expressed his reservations in Council meetings, also penned a separate letter to Cameron on the 27th, for Williamson to deliver. In it he beseeches Cameron, *"My dear friend allow me to entreat you not to sully your hands Your heart & your honour under pretended duty—If your duty requires dishonourable acts you RESIGN and live admired, beloved, and make no doubt I may say rewarded among your friends … if the Indians break I should tremble for the Cameronian family ... no doubt people would exterminate them and all their possessions ... by Capt'n Stuart's exposing your letters he might have endangered your life ...I think it impardonable."*[72]

The Council's instructions to Williamson himself were more explicit. Because Cameron was still suspected of being part of a Stuart plot, Williamson was advised *"if Mr. Cameron's determination shall be in favor of the colony, Mr. Williamson shall assure him, the public not only will not permit him to be injured, in case Mr. Stuart should withdraw his salary, but will be mindful of his services. But, if Mr. Williamson shall have cause to conclude that Mr. Cameron's determination is inimical to this colony, the public will support Mr. Williamson in any steps he shall take to prevent Mr. Cameron's executing any plan that may be calculated to involve this colony in distresses."*[73]

Although the frightening prospect of using Indians as instruments of terror was a political weapon that should not be minimized, it was a threat exploited by both British and American agents. Within a few months it would be precisely this charge, leveled at the revolutionary government in Charleston by back country planters, which would bring South Carolina to the brink of civil war. At the moment feelings were running high. Williamson's mission to confront Cameron and report back was crucial; meanwhile the Council would again try to contact John Stuart.

*Thursday, 29 June*

When the Council of Safety's letter of 21 June to Stuart in Savannah had been returned, it was re-routed to him in St. Augustine on the 29th with a cover letter signed by William Henry Drayton and Roger Smith, admonishing the Indian Superintendent: *"We cannot but say that your precipitate departure from Georgia after you had an idea that you stood accus'd here has not vindicated you in the eyes of the public."* Drayton then wrote separately to rebut remarks Stuart had made to a friend in Charleston months earlier, accusing Drayton of launching a vendetta because he [Stuart] had been instrumental in having Drayton suspended from the Governor's Council. Drayton had originally viewed Stuart's action as a slur upon his honor and integrity. In his current mode, however, Drayton humbly boasted that *"the suspension placed me in a favorable point of view with the public, and brought an addition to my little reputation."*[74]

The Stuart affair would continue to percolate throughout the year. Nothing that Stuart or his deputies said seemed to convince revolutionary leaders in Charleston that the British were not bent on mobilizing Indians as mercenaries against any American uprising anywhere in the colonies. Revolutionary South Carolina's Indian policy would be based on that premise.

### Saturday, 1 July

The courier from Charleston reached Col. Thomson in his camp at Amelia, near the Congarees River, on 1 July carrying the Council's orders to occupy Fort Charlotte, drafted on 26 June—including Henry Laurens' cover letter. Thomson immediately relayed a copy to Mayson, 60 miles away, in Ninety-Six, tersely ordering Mayson *"to direct Capt. Perwis* [sic] *to take the Comand ... you may give Capt. Purvis orders to see that Mr. Whitfield* [sic] *is not molested if he will accept the offers made to him ... I expect to hear from you as soon as you have executed these orders, which I make no doubt will be on sight."*[75] Major Mayson received these orders on 4 July and immediately notified Capt. Purvis; but they were not executed "on sight."

### Sunday, 2 July

On this day, matters were progressing on another front. Lord William Campbell, the newly-arrived Governor of South Carolina, submitted his first report, Despatch #1, to Whitehall. He writes, it was *"with equal concern and great surprize, I was informed of the unhappy situation of the Province, people of the best sense and greatest prosperity as well as the rabble, have been gradually led ... unto the most violent measures, by a set of desperate and designing men ... I have not seen or heard from the Lt. Governor since my arrival ... he has remained at his country house about 12 miles from Town without favoring me with the slightest attention ... three days after my arrival the Provincial congress presented me with an address of a very extraordinary and criminal nature ... the violent faction ... ready to plunge ... into open and actual rebellion."* Now, eleven days after receiving the petition, Governor Campbell states in his dispatch, *"although the desperate views of some daring incendarys who had great influence with the lower rank of people on the congress are at present defeated, preparation for resistance continues ... I have wrote to both General Gage and the Admiral* [Graves] *... strongly recommending ... a few proper Cruisers with small craft to this coast. It would be a great check to a very brisk smuggling trade."*[76]

Campbell's letters to Gage and Graves had been written one day earlier, on 1 July, with the coordinating concurrence of Governor James Wright of Georgia and Governor Josiah Martin of North Carolina. General Thomas

Gage, age 54, was still Governor of the Massachusetts Bay Colony and Commander-in-Chief of British forces in America. He had his hands full with escalating hostilities in the northern colonies. Vice Admiral Samuel Graves, age 62, had taken up his post as Commander-in-Chief of British Naval Forces in America in July 1774. He, too, was based in Boston. Campbell's joint request was much delayed in reaching his superiors; no action was taken.

For the record, James Wright, age 61, was born in Charleston and had been a Lt. Governor of South Carolina from 1760-1764. In October 1764 he was appointed Governor of Georgia, where he served as a wealthy, worthy and respected defender of royal authority. Josiah Martin, age 38, was a former British army officer who sold his commission in 1769. He became Governor of North Carolina in 1771, replacing William Tryon.

In his dispatch of 2 July to Whitehall, Governor Campbell also primly confirmed that *"Mr. Stuart, the Supt. For the Southern District, having been suspected of tampering with Indians has thought it prudent to retire to St. Augustine. By what I can learn Mr. Stuart has incurred the displeasure of the people here by writing to Mr. Cameron his Deputy desiring he would be very vigilant and attentive to the Indians in his District that they might not be tempted to be drawn from their allegiance, and Mr. Cameron in his answer not only assures the Superintendent of their loyalty and affection, but goes a step further, and tells him there is a large body of them ready to take Arms if ever it should be thought necessary ... Mrs. Stuart was also forced by William Henry Drayton to turn over some dispatches her husband had received from a deputy in W. Florida."*[77]

The Governor concludes his message by reporting that on this very day, Drayton, along with colleagues John Neufville and Thomas Corbett, ransacked the Charleston post office, *"demanded the door be opened and in case of my refusal said they had plenty of assistance to open it by force and took away with them 26 packets"* of government mail meant for the governors of South Carolina, North Carolina and Florida.[78]

*Monday, 3 July*

As reported by Campbell, Carolinian *"preparation for resistance continues."* On this Monday, 3 July, the Council of Safety approved *"the manual of Exercise laid before them by the field Officers in the service of this Colony."* It was the result of a committee appointed by the Provincial Congress back on 14 June—a committee on which both Lt. Col. William Thomson and Major James Mayson had served. The Council ordered 500 copies printed for distribution and adopted forthwith by all militia regiments.

It was also on this day that the intercepted letter, dated 12 April, from General Gage to Governor Martin of North Carolina, forwarded on 6 June by Charleston's Committee on Intelligence to the Continental Congress sitting in Philadelphia, was read. The letter, concerning Presbyterian Loyalists in North Carolina, so upset legislators at the Continental Congress that they immediately alerted Presbyters of Pennsylvania to galvanize their preachers in both Carolinas to better organize efforts for countering Loyalist propaganda among former Regulators in the back country. This simply confirmed the growing anxiety among Rebel leaders regarding the allegiance of back country settlers.

## Tuesday, 4 July

The allegiance of frontiersmen and Indians were two major concerns of Rebel leaders in Charleston. Therefore, when Henry Laurens, President of the Council of Safety, laid before Council members a note received from Col. Moultrie, commander of the 2nd Regiment, alerting them to an upcoming visit to Charleston by two Catawba Indians, it was given priority consideration. The Indians were coming down from the border area of North and South Carolina along the Catawba River *"to receive news of the state of affairs between the colony and England."* The visit prompted the Council to *"immediately prepare a proper talk to be sent to the Catawba Indians."* The task was assigned to William Henry Drayton. [79]

It was on 4 July that former back country delegates to the recently concluded Provincial Congress—John Caldwell, John and James Williams, from the District Between the Broad and Saluda Rivers, members of the 17 man committee named for *"carrying into execution the continental association,"*—drafted a letter to Col. Thomas Fletchall, commanding officer of the King's Upper Saluda Regiment of Militia. Their purpose, of course, was to determine precisely where Fletchall stood. The text of this joint letter has not been found, but from Fletchall's later negative response we know that he was asked *"to call my regiment together in order to sign the Association paper."* [80]

## Wednesday, 5 July

The two Catawba Indians of whom Moultrie had written arrived in Charleston. Drayton spoke to them at length, extolling the need for friendship between the Catawbas and colonists. The Indians were given a copy of Drayton's talk to take back to their tribes. His letter ended with the words *"we desire that you will carefully remember this good talk. Send it, by a head man, to the Cherokees, and say you received it at Charles Town from the beloved men, as a good talk for you and them."* The Cherokees lived west of the Catawbas and north of Ninety-Six. A third group of Indians with whom Carolinians had contact were the Creeks, who lived along the Savannah River [mostly in Georgia] south and west of Cherokee lands.

At the same time that Carolinians were shoring up their defensive alliances with patronizing talk to Indians, the British were beginning to think in terms of offense, as learned from a dispatch being drafted on 5 July from Whitehall to South Carolina. Given the time lag in communications, the Foreign Office at Whitehall was actually responding to a letter from Lt. Governor William Bull written last May, after the Battle of Lexington but before Bunker Hill. Nevertheless, the Foreign Office observes *"the flame of rebellion seems to have extended itself to almost every colony."* To extinguish the fire the King was undertaking efforts *"to reduce His rebellious subjects to obedience by augmenting the army under General Gage."* Separate naval squadrons were being sent to New York, the Bay of Delaware, the Chesapeake, *"and upon the coast of Carolina."* Not having, as yet, received Campbell's Despatch #1, Lord Dartmouth disingenuously concludes, *"there is some hope that the Colonies to the southward may not proceed to the same lengths with those in New England."*[81]

The ignorance with which British leaders approached American events at this stage is striking. Much can be attributed to poor intelligence and delays in communications, but the facts of British obstinacy, over-confidence and a complete disregard for the basic rights of man remain—values upon which the British prided themselves. American colonists were simply regarded as second class citizens. As one American historian, John C. Miller, aptly observes: *"One of the convictions most firmly planted in the minds of eighteenth century Englishmen was the superiority of true born Britons to the American colonists. Too often Americans were regarded as degenerate Englishman or as the scum or off scouring of all nations … a hotchpotch medley of foreign, enthusiastic madmen … a mongrel breed of Irish, Scotch and Germans, leavened with convicts and outcasts."* Indeed, *"Americans in the eyes of many Englishmen were not heroes of liberty who had sought freedom in the wilderness rather than submit to tyranny in the old world. They were merely runaways who, had they possessed the least spark of courage, would have remained at home to assist their fellow subjects in the glorious struggle against arbitrary power in Church and State, instead of basely deserting them in distress, and running away like cowards to another world."*[82]

Backing up such thoughts with words culled from a contemporary newspaper, the *Public Advertiser* of London, dated 25 August 1775, Miller quotes *"the American struggle for liberty appeared to be of no greater consequence than the huzzaing of a few drunken yokels and mechanics at English hustings. It was not that the times were out of joint, it was merely that a few office-hungry politicians in Great Britain and America had taught the lower classes in the jollity of their drunkenness, to cry out that they were undone, and in this state signed papers that they have never read, and determined questions that they do not know; roared against oppression and tyranny ... and staggered home with impunity, swearing that they were in danger of slavery, while every one they met, who did not join in their cry, was in danger of a broken head."*[83]

Carolinians were not yet breaking heads, but intimidation against those who resisted the Association would increase over the next few months. Meanwhile it was still early July, and neither the British nor the Americans were completely sure of their positions or intentions, although both sides were making preparations for war.

It will be recalled that the Second Continental Congress had convened on 10 May, a few weeks after the Lexington battle. This skirmish was followed by the more brutal fight at Bunker Hill in mid-June. By July the atmosphere in Philadelphia was somber. Delegates were ambivalent, wrestling with their consciences. Few men desired a complete break from Britain, but subservience without due representation was unacceptable. Many remained in favor of reconciliation. Thus, coincidentally, on the same day that Lord Dartmouth was drafting his message of the 5th, one last effort was proposed by moderates in Philadelphia to draft a petition *"on the causes and necessity of taking up arms"* in hope that such end could be avoided. This so-called Olive Branch Petition, drafted by a committee of five, among them Edward Rutledge of South Carolina, was presented to the Congress three days later.

*Saturday, 8 July*

Few documents offer so clear an insight into the dilemmas confronting American colonial leaders at this point in history. While avoiding any tones of groveling, the Olive Branch Petition is a heart wrenching document clearly seeking reconciliation, but on rational terms of common sense:

*"Most Gracious Sovereign ... we your Majesty's faithful subjects of the colonies of New Hampshire, Massachusetts Bay, Rhode Island and Providence Plantation, Connecticut, New York, New Jersey, Pennsylvania, the counties of New Castle, Kent and Sussex on Delaware, Maryland, Virginia, North Carolina and South Carolina, in behalf of ourselves and the inhabitants of these colonies, who have*

*deputed us to represent them in general Congress, entrust your Majesty's gracious attention to this our humble petition … to redress grievances. We shall decline the ungrateful task of describing the irksome variety of artifices practised by many of your Majesty's Ministers, the elusive pretenses, fruitless terrors and unavailing severities, that have from time to time been dealt out by them, in their attempts to execute this impolitic plan, or of the unhappy differences between Great Britain and these colonies which have flowed from this fatal source."*

*"Your Majesty's ministers persevering in their measures and proceeding to open hostilities for enforcing them, have compelled us to arm in our own defence and have engaged us in a controversy so peculiarly abhorrent to the affections of your still faithful colonists, that when we consider whom we must oppose in this contest, and if it continues, what may be the consequences, our particular misfortunes are accounted by us, only as parts of our distress."*

*"Knowing what violent resentments and incurable animosities, civil discords are apt to exasperate and inflame the contending parties, we think ourselves required by indispensable obligations to almighty God, to your Majesty, to our fellow subjects, and to ourselves, immediately to rise all the means in our power not incompatible with our safety, for stopping further effusions of blood, and for averting the impending calamities that threaten the British Empire."*

*"We therefore beseech your Majesty, that your royal authority and influence may be graciously interposed to procure relief from our afflicting fears and jealousies occasioned by the system before mentioned, and to settle peace through every part of your dominion, with all humility submitting to your Majesty's wise consideration whether it may not be expedient for facilitating those important purposes, that your Majesty be pleased to direct some mode by which the united application of your faithful colonists to the throne, in pursuance of their common councils, may be improved into a happy and permanent reconciliation; and that in the meantime measures be taken for preventing the further destruction of lives of your Majesty's subjects; and that such statutes as more immediately distress any of you Majesty's colonies be repealed."*

*"For by such arrangements as your Majesty's wisdom can form for collecting the united sense of your American people, we are convinced, your Majesty would receive such satisfactory proofs of the disposition of the colonies toward their sovereign and parent state, that the wished for opportunity would soon be restored to them, of evincing the sincerity of their professions by every testimony of devotion becoming the most faithful subjects and the most affectionate colonists."*[84]

This noble gesture was a lost cause before it ever reached England. Given the great interval in communications, by sailing ship, between America and Europe, the petition did not reach King George until 1 September. One week earlier, on 23 August, the King had already signed a proclamation for *"suppressing rebellion and sedition."* This declaration of war would not reach America until 31 October. Meanwhile preparations for defense in all the colonies, including South Carolina, continued.

*Monday, 10 July*

Orders to take Fort Charlotte, received by Major James Mayson at Ninety-Six on 4 July had been immediately transmitted to Capt. John Purvis, whose company was told to execute the task. Now, on the afternoon of 10 July, Mayson learned by letter from Purvis that he had been unable to raise a company of rangers and therefore had not executed the Council's orders of 26 June. This placed Mayson in an unexpected predicament which only worsened when, on midnight that same evening, he witnessed a most melodramatic affidavit regarding *"mischief makers"* among the Cherokees: *"Ninety Six District … Before us James Mayson and John Caldwell Two of his Majesty's Justices assigned to keep the peace in Ninety Six District—Personally came and Appeared Mr. Robert Gouedy, who being duly sworn on the Holy Evangelist of Almighty God, Deposeth and Sayeth, That on this Day, a Certain Cherokee Indian, Named the Man Killer of Keowee Formerly now Seneca informed him this Deponent that Some Few Days ago, a certain John Vann told the Indians in the Cherokee Nation that they must fall upon the White people on this side Savannah River [South Carolina] and kill them … That the other side Savannah [Georgia] they must let alone, and Further says that Mr. Alexander Cameron Sent to the over hill warriors and That on their comeing he gave them Presents of Rum and That they returned home with it, and That this talk of Vann was delivered in Seneca Town House, That the Indians Told Vann they could not go to War, that they had no ammunition."* Robert Gouedy signed the affidavit, as did Mayson and Caldwell, stating, *"Sworn to us on this 10th Day of July at Midnight."*[85]

This report by Gouedy, although muddled and somewhat incoherent, must have sounded like an ominous confirmation of the circulating rumors condemning Stuart and Cameron. John Vann himself was a longtime Indian trader with a Cherokee wife; he and Cameron were undoubtedly acquainted. But was Alexander Cameron using him as an agitator? Whatever the case, Mayson and Caldwell quickly relayed the affidavit by courier to the Council of Safety in Charleston where, weeks later, it would raise yet more alarm.

But 10 July was auspicious for another reason. Allen Cameron, brother of Alexander, in a letter to Andrew Williamson bearing this date, writing from self imposed exile in Savannah, reports: *"I received your letter of the*

*15th ult."* [Williamson had written it while still attending the Provincial Congress] *And of course must thank you for the trouble it seems you have been at in procuring a commission for me."* But, he reminds the writer *"of the conversation that passed between you and I at Lokaber, in Long Cane … you could never infer from these words … that I would accept a commission in the Provincials …it really was not my sentiment … if I had been disposed for military service a lieutenancy would not suit me."* Allen Cameron, like other back country gentlemen, had a high opinion of himself. This kind of vanity would consistently plague recruitment for rangers over the next few months. On the other hand, the fact that he had exiled himself from Long Canes seems to show that this Cameron at least was not inclined to support the Rebel cause.

But Williamson would not receive Allen Cameron's response for weeks. Meanwhile, as directed, he had gone in search of brother Alexander who was presently among the Cherokees up at Seneca. The Council, in order to keep Williamson abreast of all matters concerning Cameron's superior, John Stuart, had sent a courier to him with copies of letters that had been forwarded to Stuart on 29 June. The courier, not finding Andrew Williamson at his home in Long Canes, followed him to the Cherokee Nation where he delivered his messages on or about the 8th of July. The courier then turned back to Charleston, again by way of Long Canes, passing by Fort Charlotte on 10 July. It was still a British arsenal not yet taken by the rangers, although it is doubtful that the courier was even aware of any plans to do so. When he returned to Charleston on the 12th of July the record simply shows that *"Bellard received from John Lewis Gervais Ten Pounds Currency in full for delivering letters to Major Williamson."*[86]

No mention is made of Fort Charlotte. But if the courier was questioned at all, he could only have confirmed that the Council's orders had not yet been carried out. Coincidentally, Lt. Col. William Thomson of the rangers had come to Charleston on 10 July. On that day, the record shows *"Col. Thomson attended the Council and represented the necessity of having an Adjutant to the Regiment under his Command."* The Council *"resolved to appoint one and ask the next congress for funds."*[87] Thomson was gone by the time the courier, Bellard, had returned.

## Tuesday, 11 July

On the active day of 10 July, as we know, Major James Mayson had been notified of Capt. Purvis' failure to act. As he would later explain, *"I thought it best to wait no longer but to go to Ninety Six where Capt Caldwell and Kirkland's companies were in Camp'd."* It is here that one finds the major on 11 July, where he found Caldwell *"having Twenty eight & Kirkland Twenty three men, and to take with me both these companies to Fort Charlotte; as I had been informed Capt. Whitefield had knowledge of what was intended by some imprudent expressions of Mr. Calhoun to the Serjant of the fort."*[88] The following morning Mayson and his two ranger companies set out for Fort Charlotte, 20 miles away.

*Wednesday, 12 July*

The manner in which Fort Charlotte was taken on 12 July is related in a document, signed under protest by Capt. George Whitefield, Fort Commander, and Lt. Louis D. St. Pierre, second in command. The deposition reads *"Be it remembered that on Wednesday the twelvth day of July in this present year of One Thousand Seven Hundred and Seventy five—between the hours Eleven & Twelve O'Clock P.M. appeared before this for—Major James Mason [sic]—having under his command Capts. Kirkland and Caldwell with a party of Rangers consisting of fifty men—Major Mason sent a message to Capt. Whitefield—that he then in the name of the council of Safety took possession of fort Charlotte. The Arms, Ammunition & Stores, and immediately demanded the Keys—of the Magazine & Stores, to which Capt. Whitefield as an officer without power—was under the absolute necessity of acquiescing—at the same tim—both Lieut. St. Pierre & himself protesting and do hereby protest against the said proceedings."*[89] This deposition was signed by both Whitefield and St. Pierre. When Mayson submitted his own report to the Council six days later, he commented: *"Capt. Whitefield did everything an officer could do without power & he submitted—he did it with a grace that will do him honor."*[90]

This gentleman's agreement offers an interesting example of military etiquette still in existence at the time—graceful submission by one officer when resistance was futile, and graceful acknowledgement by his opponent. In retrospect, the capture of Fort Charlotte is viewed by some historians as *"the first overt act of the Revolutionary War in South Carolina."*[91] To commemorate the event, a local American Legion Post erected a historical marker near the ruins of Fort Charlotte in 1941. Regrettably, the remains of the fort were inundated by waters of a holding lake for a new hydro-electric plant on the Savannah River in 1949.

While Mayson and his rangers were celebrating their achievements of the 12th, on this same day Major Andrew Williamson finally caught up with

Alexander Cameron in the Cherokee Nation. In his memorandum of conversation, also dated 12 July, Williamson reported to the Council that Cameron never interpreted *"Capt. Stuart's letter to him in February as an order to induce the Cherokee Indians to fall upon the Province of South Carolina, but only to keep the said Indians firmly attached to his Majesty's government … he never had any such thoughts as leading the Cherokees against the Province of south Carolina."* But Cameron could not be persuaded to resign; Williamson says that he looked upon the Council's offer of 26 June *"in whatever manner it might be given, in the utmost detestation."* Williamson then asserts *"I am willing to pledge myself for Mr. Cameron's performance of the above, as I have not the slightest doubt of its being his fixed determination."*[92]

The talk between Williamson and Cameron was held in the presence of Indian trader and Williamson confidante John Bowie. Cameron was given a copy of the memo that Williamson submitted to the Council. Although dated the 12th, this memo arrived in Charleston only on 21 July. In it Cameron comes across as an honest Scotsman, with integrity and a strong sense of duty, but a man who is not yet willing to join the revolutionary cause. But neither was he prepared to set the Indians against it, which may have been some consolation to Henry Laurens, if not to William Henry Drayton.

*Thursday, 13 July*

Back in his camp at Amelia near Orangeburg, Col. Thomson was still unaware that Fort Charlotte had been taken. The Council of Safety in Charleston, at this point, was becoming anxious over the state of its military organization in the back country. On this day, 13 July, it drafted a message to Thomson: *"Ordered, That Col. William Thomson do immediately make return to the council, of the several companies in the Regiment of Rangers … use his utmost diligence in order to complete them … on the 10th day of august next, 8 companies shall rendezvous at some proper place to be appointed by the colonel, and march by the following routes: Three companies to the southward, by Orangeburg to the Three Runs, down Savannah river to Purrysburg, thence to Pon Pon, then downward by the High Road. Three companies to the northward, by the King's Tree and the most populous part of Waccamaw and Pedee to Georgetown, thence by Wambaw to Huger's Bridge, and by the Strawberry Road going up to Childsbury Town to Biggin Bridge, Monck's corner, and thence downward by the High Road. Two companies through St. Stephen's Parish down to Monck's corner, thence to Edisto Saw Mills, and from thence to the Horse-Shoe and the Round O, to Parker's Ferry, Dorchester, and thence down the High road … Col. Thomson to march with the first detachment to the southward;*

*that Maj. Mayson to march with the second detachment to the northward; that the senior Captain on duty march with the third detachment of two companies ... the whole to meet and rendezvous at some convenient place within ten miles of Charles Town, on the first of September ... that orderly books be kept by the commanding Officer of each detachment, and the whole returned with a state of the regiment at the time of rendezous, on the first of sept, to the Council ... as there are attempts to alienate the affections of the inhabitants of this colony from the interests of America, Col. Thomson and all officers of the Regiment of Rangers, are ordered to take proper notice of such suspected persons ... confine such person or persons in the District gaol."*[93]

From the tone of this order, the Council of Safety desired to use the Regiment of Rangers as a display of force by marching them through various communities to show support for the Association. In addition it was asking Thomson and Mayson to implement the Council's own "patriot act," to intimidate anyone showing opposition. Before marching, Thomson was also *"to procure from Fort Charlotte, half a pound of gunpowder per man, and lead in proportion, for eight companies."*[94]

Other events would soon override these preparations, and the scheduled march would not be carried out. But the Council was right to be concerned about the alienation of affections among South Carolinians. Many still remained loyal to the crown, a situation that would shortly become all too obvious in the back country.

# CHAPTER V

## *The Loyalists Respond*

ON THE SAME DAY THE COUNCIL WAS ISSUING MARCHING ORDERS TO Thomson in Amelia, Col. Thomas Fletchall, commander of the Upper Saluda Regiment of the King's Militia, had mustered his regiment in the Fair Forest area [in present day lower Spartanburg County]. They were assembled in response to the Caldwell/Williams letter dated 4 July. In his own later commentary, dated 24 July, to the Council of Safety in Charleston, Fletchall would report on this gathering: *"Accordingly on the 13th … I did in obedience to those gentlemen … went to every Captain's company that was in my regiment, when drawn up, and requested Major Farry [sic] to read the paper to every company, which according was done."* [I believe the reader was actually Champness Terry of Col. Starke's Forks of the Saluda Militia Regiment]. But, Fletchall continued, *"I don't remember that one man offered to sign it, which was out of my power to compel them; but that it was agreed amongst the people in general to sign a paper of their own resolutions, and that application was made to Major Joseph Robinson* [of Col. Thomas Neel's New District Militia], *who was then present to draw a paper of some resolves, which the people in general did sign unto, from Savannah River to Broad River, which consisted of my regiment, Col. Stark's regiment and part of Col. Savage's regiment."*[95]

This news, when received in Charleston, would be a terrible blow to the Council's aspirations for unity against England. It also meant that efforts at recruitment to serve with the rangers were being greatly undermined. It was especially demoralizing to learn that half of Savage's regiment evidently sided with the Loyalists. This was the King's regiment in which James Mayson was a Lieutenant Colonel, and Andrew Williamson a Major. They, along with Col. John Savage, had been delegates to the late Provincial Congress and were fully behind the Association; it now appears that not all militiamen followed their lead. Given such attitudes it is easier to understand why Purvis had been unable to raise a force to capture Fort Charlotte.

The counter resolution drafted by Robinson on 13 July and passed around for endorsement states in part *"we resolve to Live in Peace & true friendship with the rest of Our Country men Notwithstanding Our Aforesaid Divercity of Opinions, and are Ready & willing at all times to assist in defending the Province in Order to Oppose and Suppress the Incurtions of Indians, insurrections of negroes, or any Other Enemy which may or Shalle invade this Province or unlawfully disturb the good People thereof, and that without any reward whatsoever when the Exegences of the case or Condition of our Province Require it—Or are called upon by a Lawfull Officer of Said Province. Moreover, that no laws bee executed amongst us but the Statutes of great Britain which are of force here, and the Acts of the general Assembly of this Province. In Testimony Whereof we Have subscribed Our names to this Memorial of Our Resolutions."* This memorial contained 95 signatures and *"62 names more not yet put down but in assent."*[96]

A full text of Robinson's Memorial was obtained by the Rev. James Cresswell; a copy was later sent to the Council of Safety by James Mayson, Cresswell's neighbor. The Council received it on 2 August. Meanwhile turmoil in the back country continued to change attitudes; and the delay in communications inevitably left the Council of Safety weeks behind. For the moment it was completely unaware of the events at Fort Charlotte or of the expanding Association opposition culminating in the Loyalist memorial of 13 July.

*Friday, 14 July*

Thus, when the Council of Safety met in Charleston on the 14th, it was taking care of small matters such as ordering the colony treasury to forward 1000 pounds to Col. Thomson for paying his Regiment of Rangers. It also *"signed a certificate for Dr. Alexander Rogers, appointed surgeon to the Regiment of Rangers ... upon application by Col. Thomson 10 July last."*[97]

Unaware of Fletchall's position, it was also ordered *"that the president do write a proper letter to Fletchall, to draw from him a declaration of his real disposition towards this country, in the present unhappy situation of public affairs."*[98] The draft was scheduled to be discussed on the following day.

It was also on the 14th that Major Mayson and Capt. Kirkland left Fort Charlotte in the hands of Capt. Caldwell and his company of rangers, returning to Ninety-Six where Kirkland and his company encamped *"about six miles southwest."* At this juncture, as we later learn from Mayson's letter to Thomson of the 18th, *"Lieutenant Middleton deserted the company & they all to a man deserted also, this you will see by Capt. Kirkland's letter to me and by a letter from Mr. Middleton & the Report from his serjiant to him, Copies of which I now send you.*"⁹⁹

Hugh Middleton had been commissioned a ranger 1st Lieutenant on 26 June, assigned to Kirkland's company. Neither copies of the Middleton nor Kirkland letter, nor the "serjiant's" report, have been found. Thomson's order book, as published by Salley, makes no mention of them, nor do the Council records. Notwithstanding, Mayson's report is additionally disturbing as he intimates that Kirkland, too, is wavering—although he would not resign until 28 July.

For the present, when Mayson and Kirkland left Fort Charlotte on the 14th they took with them *"two brass cannon, 250 pounds of gun powder, 500 lbs of lead, a crosscut saw and two old axes ... to make Camps for to keep the Rangers from bad weather,"* ¹⁰⁰ as Mayson explains. This was a portion of the gunpowder and lead so much desired by the revolutionary government.

On another front, on this same day, 14 July, Major Andrew Williamson, having returned to Long Canes from the Cherokee Nation, wrote a second report to the Council in Charleston regarding his confrontation with Alexander Cameron. This letter, along with the Williamson memo of 12 July, would be received in Charleston on 21 July. In his second note Williamson writes *"pursuant to your directions given me when in Charles-Town ... I found him* [Cameron] *gone to the Cherokee Nation."* In following him there, Williamson apologizes, *"this was exceeding your orders, but I thought there was an absolute necessity for seeing him as soon as possible ... I have inclosed you what passed between Mr. Cameron and me."* This second note also comments on local affairs in Long Canes, offering the reader a basis for comparison regarding unfolding events. Williamson observes: *"I was not a little surprized to find the most material transactions of the congress in the mouths of every person and to be told that there was an intention to seize Mr. Cameron, which occasioned his going to the Nation. At this time there is a good deal of confusion ... on account of the expected danger from the Cherokees."*¹⁰¹

Such apprehension among Long Canes settlers would alarm the Council. But, oddly enough, there was no mention of Fort Charlotte in this last message. Surely its capture by the rangers must have been known among the settlers who lived so close by. Nor does Williamson make any mention of the counter-association meeting held by Fletchall in Fair Forest on the previous day. Nor was the Major aware of storm clouds gathering in Ninety-Six, where part of Fort Charlotte's arms and ammunition had been taken. At this point, one is left with the impression that Williamson is unaware of any growing tensions between Rebels and Loyalists, at least not in the Long Canes vicinity. But Charleston was growing increasingly apprehensive.

*Saturday, 15 July*

Henry Laurens' draft of a letter to Thomas Fletchall came under discussion at the Council meeting. The letter is a passionate appeal to Fletchall's patriotism. It rhetorically outlines the cause of liberty in opposition to the *"arbitrary"* and *"despotic"* actions of the British government *"At a time when every colony from Georgia to New Hampshire are associated in arms, in order to oppose the torrent of unjust power and violence, and when this colony in particular is alarmed by the threats of invasions by the British soldiery—of instigated insurrection by our negroes—of inroads by the neighboring tribes of Indians— and of what is far more to be dreaded, the practices and insidious acts of false brethren, it cannot be wondered at that we are anxiously desirous of enrolling the number of our friends upon whom we may firmly rely for aid in the day of trial."* [102]

The comment regarding "insidious acts of false brethren" was motivated by a deposition forced four days earlier from Elizabeth Simpson of Camden. She reported on a conversation her husband had with the new governor on about 8 July. Simpson, paying a call upon Governor Campbell in Charleston, related news of the back country, expressing sympathy for the Loyalist cause that seemed to be gathering around Col. Thomas Fletchall. If true, this means that Fletchall was already active in opposing association long before the upcoming meeting of the 13th. Campbell, in turn, told Simpson of his letters to General Gates and Admiral Graves requesting military support. When the Council learned of this conversation from Elizabeth Simpson's deposition, they felt obligated to take action by writing to Fletchall.

In the Laurens letter, now dated the 15th, Fletchall is still approached with circumspection, but the Council was no longer averse to threatening him with intelligence reports, hinting that *"Fletchall is not a friend of liberty … there was room to apprehend that you have been covertly taking an active part against us."* To encourage a change in Fletchall's attitude, Laurens recites some recent battle statistics, *"further accounts received yesterday of the late battle on the 17th June"* [Bunker Hill in Boston]. Laurens reflects British losses *"killed, upwards of 900, among them two Majors, and about 60 other officers; and it is confidently asserted that General Howe is among the slain … the loss of the American troops, about 100 killed, and as many wounded or missing … when we seriously reflect that the number of the enemy was at least five to two of the*

*Americans, and when we consider that the united power of ships of war firing all kinds of deadly shot, at the same time with the mercenary soldiery, upon our friends, in that short, bloody, and to us glorious conflict, we may be allowed to express our belief, that God is truly on our side, because we fight for the cause of liberty and virtue, and because we plead for the sacred rights of mankind in future ages, who, as we humbly trust, will keep the fruits of our laudable strife against the cruel attacks of our fellow subjects."*[103]

It is hard to imagine anyone resisting the emotional sincerity of such spiritually noble sentiments, but Fletchall managed to do so. He was neither beguiled nor intimidated, and concluded only that he was being insulted and viewed as a traitor. The Laurens letter was received by Fletchall prior to his reply of 24 July, which would collate all his views. In the interim the council began to plan a strategy of defense.

On this same day, the 15th, having heard nothing regarding the occupation of Fort Charlotte, the Council began to show its frustration. It was suggested that a letter be drafted to Col. Thomson on the matter, for review on the following day. A communication, also dated 15 July, from Captain Samuel Wise of the rangers, writing from the Pee Dee area, to Col. Thomson in Amelia, offers a more optimistic perspective to the state of ranger recruitment. Wise reports: *"Sir, your favor dated, Amelia June 27th came safe to Hand on Sunday last 2nd instant."* In his response Wise notes that he left Charleston on the 24th and, *"upon arriving home I begun immediately to enlist Men, the number of which consisting this Day in 22 well chosen, young and well mounted Men ... I hope to set out at the Head of the whole company about the 1st of August, and join the Camp* [in Amelia] *with all possible diligence."* [104]

Thomson's letter of 27 June is not to be found in his Order Book but, following a letter to Major James Mayson dated 24 June, there is a notation saying *"same day gave orders to the remaining five Capts ... for levying thirty men with speed."* The fact that Wise's letter mentions nothing of back country disturbances seems to indicate that he was unaware of Fletchall's activities, or of the counter Association memorial drafted by Major Robinson that was being circulated.

## Sunday, 16 July

A frustrated Council of Safety met on this day. Some days earlier it had been *"alarmed by an intimation of Mr. St. Pierre's proceeding's with one Coffel ... as given by Capt. Whitefield in a letter to Mr. Gervais."* Whitefield, of course, was commandant at Fort Charlotte and St. Pierre his deputy. The letter to

Gervais was written before Mayson captured the fort but probably reached Charleston after the fact. The proceedings with Coffel are not explained but probably had something to do with foreknowledge that plans were afoot to take the fort. It will be recalled that when Mayson explained his reasons for moving quickly, once he learned that Purvis had been unable to act, he, too, referred to having been *"informed that Capt. Whitefield had knowledge of what was intended by some imprudent expressions of Mr. Calhoun."* Whether Coffel and Calhoun are the identical person is immaterial. The fort's officers had been forewarned and reported their misgivings to Charleston. Meanwhile the fort would be captured, but Charleston would still be in the dark.

Hence, on this day, 16 July, the Laurens letter to Thomson, under discussion, said it was *"anxious that you should carry out the order of the 26th June ... the gunpowder is most particularly recommended to your care ... I flatter myself with hopes that you will have anticipated the wishes of the council, and the fort is now in the hands of their officer ... if not, it is their order that you take possession of the fort without delay."*[105]

In closing, Laurens also makes clear that the council still *"entertains hopes that Capt. Whitefield will associate in the interest of America ... although he may not be content with a sub command—if he is a man of spirit he will not."* In that case Laurens suggests that Whitefield should come immediately to Charleston *"and apply to the Council for a commission to suit his stature."*[106]

John Whitefield, like Cameron, was a man of importance in the Long Canes area, a man worth flattering due to his potential influence among back country settlers. He was a nephew of the Rev. George Whitefield, a well-known fundamentalist and follower of the popular revivalist preacher, Jonathan Edwards. An Englishman and leader of "The Great Awakening", the Rev. Whitefield *"came to America in 1739 to add his voice to that of Edwards. Thousands of Americans thronged to hear both men on their tours."*[107]

Reverend Whitefield had an enormous impact among dissenters of the rigidity of the Anglican Church. Whitefield himself wrote, *"the established church is an excellent order as to externals; but many of its chief members were bigots."* More significantly, *"his controversial preaching left a great mark on the clergy who were active in the years just before the Revolution,"* encouraging *"the appearance of intinerant preachers"*[108] and critics of England.

To the more evangelical Baptist, Methodist, Presbyterian or Congregational preachers, with their less sophisticated followers in the back country, Rev. Whitefield was a hero. Given the ambivalence and suspicion developing among frontiersmen with respect to association with Charleston's elite in the Rebel cause, it would be a coup to bring the reverend's nephew,

Capt. Whitefield, over to the cause. Laurens was aware of human psychology and therefore willing to treat the Captain with deference in an effort to win his support.

### Monday, 17 July

According to Major James Mayson's report of the 18th, to Lt. Col. William Thomson, on 17 July *"about noon a Party of about 200 disaffected People from over the River* [east side of the Saluda] *headed by Robt & Patrick Cunningham, and Major Robinson of Col. Neill's Regiment came to Ninety Six armed with rifles & Capt. Cunningham order'd them to halt as soon as they got Round the court house, he demanded the Powder from us Rebells for the King & my orders for Robbing his fort—on my refusing he had me apprehended as also Capt. Kirkland who was present from the beginning—I was Committed to Gaol ... they took Every thing that came from Fort charlotte except the two field Pieces ... and about Nine O'Clock at Night they despersed ... Rangers present were Captain Kirkland, Lieutenant Warley & myself."*[109]

Felix Warley, age 26, born in South Carolina, had been commissioned a Second Lieutenant on 26 June to serve in Kirkland's Company. The company itself, along with 1st Lieutenant Middleton, had deserted three days earlier. Mayson and his two subordinates were left alone to face down 200 Loyalists under Robert Cunningham. Some historians have formed the impression that Mayson was set up by Kirkland, *"who changed sides and sent a message to Colonel Fletchall suggesting to him to take steps to recover the powder and lead which had been taken from the King's fort."*[110]

Nothing has ever been found to substantiate this allegation. Kirkland did not turn traitor to the Rebel cause until eleven days later, but he was leaning that way. In his letter of the 18th Mayson notes only that *"Captain Kirkland informed me that he intends to resign his commission ... I should bee very sorry for his resignation."* Such words show no animosity between the two men.

Of greater importance is Mayson's reference to the Cunningham brothers as leaders of the Loyalist raid at Ninety-Six. This is the first notice one has of anti-rebel feelings among the Cunninghams. Robert, 34 years old, and his younger brother Patrick, emigrants from Virginia, had been in the back country of South Carolina since 1769.[111] Robert is said to have sided with the "regulators" at the time but, unlike Mayson, he was not active. Nevertheless, it is quite likely that the Cunninghams attended Fletchall's counter-association muster in Fairfield Forest on 13 July, although neither would be mentioned in Fletchall's letter of the 24th to the Council of Safety. Living far closer to Ninety-Six village than Fletchall, it is not inconceivable that Cunningham became aware of the arms from Fort Charlotte after they were stashed there on the 14th. Whether he raided them at the instigation of Col. Fletchall, accompanied by the same Major Robinson who drafted the counter-association memorial, is another matter. It is possible; but I do not believe Kirkland was an accomplice. In any case, the arms were hijacked, thus dealing a major blow to the Council of Safety's defense preparations.

On the same day of the arms heist, Fort Charlotte's new commander, the ranger Capt. Caldwell, who was completely unaware of the hijacking, was responding to Mayson's earlier request for an inventory. His report, dated 17 July, captioned *"Return of Artillery Ammunition & Stores,"* also included the condition of buildings. It was sent to Mayson at his plantation, called Glasgow, near Ninety-Six, arriving the following day, in time to be included in Mayson's own report of activities since 10 July. Of interest, other than the inventory, Caldwell comments *"From the best information I can get Mr. Allen Cameron, has absolutely declined excepting the commission Conferred upon him by this Country, as I am told from good authority that he Received his Commission in a letter from Major Williamson that he did not think it worth his while to Return an answer I should be much Obliged to you to write to the Council of safety on this Occasion."* Mayson did so on the 18th, suggesting that Cameron was afraid of losing his estates in Scotland.[112]

Again, on this same day, 17 July, in his camp at Amelia, Col. William Thomson, commander of the Regiment of Rangers, was still completely unaware of any back country activities that had been playing themselves out since he wrote to Mayson on 1 July to convey the Council's original orders. Nor had he as yet received the Council's new orders of 16 July demanding that he take immediate possession of Fort Charlotte. On the 17th Thomson was only pre-occupied with carrying out the order dated 13 July, just received from the Council of Safety, to ready his regiment for a show of force, a flag-waving march to Charleston. Thomson therefore sent a copy of these orders to Mayson at Glasgow, stating *"You will please to give the three companies in Your District orders accordingly. I should be glad if you could have them all in Amelia by the sixth day of august as I could wish to have them together four days before the March. You'll observe the instructions about the Powder and Lead in Proportion and order down sufficient Quantity for the five Company's in this neighborhood, as prescribed in the General orders, that I may be able to make a return of the whole. You may supply those three Company's with their dividend of Powder and Lead before they come down in order to save Carriage. I make no doubt but you have comply'd with the orders concerning Fort Charlotte before this time I should be glad to hear from You immediately."*[113]

Amelia, Thomson's camp on the lower Congaree River, north of Orangeburg was only 60 miles from Ninety-Six. Yet on the 17th of July, it is obvious from Thomson's letter that he did not know that Charlotte had been taken five days before on the 12th. He was unaware that some of its arms and ammunition were stored at the Ninety-Six courthouse on the 14th, or that Lt. Middleton had deserted with most of Kirkland's ranger company on the same day. He was also uninformed about the counter-association meeting in Fair Forest on the 13th, and that a memorial then drafted was circulating throughout the upper back country. He didn't know that Loyalists had raided Ninety-Six on the 17th and stolen all the arms that rangers took from Fort Charlotte. Capt. Wise's letter of the 15th, the one positive aspect regarding ranger recruitment, was yet to reach him. Thus, on this 17th day of July, when Col. Thomson wrote to his officers—Major Mayson, Captains Wise, Woodward, Goodwyn, Kershaw and Richardson—it was merely to alert them to the marching orders dated 13 July from the Council of Safety, which he had just received.

Taking stock of the Regiment of Rangers at this point in mid-July, with each company requiring 30 men, recruitment stood as follows: Capt John Caldwell, with 28 men, was occupying Fort Charlotte; Capt. Moses Kirkland's company, except for Kirkland and Second Lt. Felix Warley, had deserted; Capt. Ezekiel Polk, from the New Acquisitions District, had not yet been heard from; Capt. John Purvis had five men, two sergeants and a 1st Lieutenant [William Martin]; Capt. Samuel Wise had 27 men; Capt Thomas Woodward had a full complement of 30 men; so did Capt. Robert Goodwyn; Capt. Ely Kershaw had 27 men; and Capt. Edward Richardson had recruited 24 men.[114]

Such statistics indicate that recruitment in the upper part of the back country was pretty much of a shambles, unlike recruitment in the midlands that had closer contact with the low country. The picture was becoming clearer to Mayson, as evidenced by his report to Thomson on the 18th. When his report eventually surfaced in Charleston and was evaluated along with other ongoing concerns, the Council of Safety worries would increase.

*Tuesday, 18 July*

Conversely, on 18 July, just as Mayson was drafting his report, Council of Safety members William Henry Drayton and Miles Brewton returned from a mission to Georgia, offering the reader a different perspective on revolutionary woes and triumphs. Drayton and Brewton proudly reported success in obtaining 5000 pounds of gunpowder from the Provincial Congress of Georgia and that *"upon the whole, the Congress had acceded to the Continental Associations and regulations."*[115]

This was welcome news; Georgia was safely in the fold and had finally sent delegates to Philadelphia, where members of the Second Continental Congress had developed an excessive, almost paranoid, concern over the shortage of arms and ammunition. Back on 1 July a frantic message had been sent, signed by the South Carolina delegation, to the *"Charleston Secret Committee ... By directions of the continental congress, we have sent the vessell by which this goes, to procure from you a Quantity of Gun-Powder for the use of the Armies actually in the Field of Service for America. The frequent & severe Skirmishing in the Neighbourhood of Boston have so exhausted their Magazines that an immediate Supply is absolutely necessary."* Charleston was asked to act *"with utmost Secrecy and Despatch."*[116]

It was on the basis of this message that Drayton and Brewton were sent to Georgia, where a British schooner with six tons of gunpowder had recently been captured. They succeeded in obtaining 5000 pounds of this booty—it would be shipped to Philadelphia on 21 July. Meanwhile the need for obtaining arms for local use had not abated. Charleston's frustrations would turn to anger when they eventually learned that some of Fort Charlotte's arms had been confiscated by Loyalist forces in the back country.

Major James Mayson's letter of the 18th, which reported this catastrophe, was addressed to Thomson, with a copy for the Council of Safety. It was a reply to Thomson's orders dated 1 July, explaining all that occurred since he received those orders on 4 July. The bulk of Mayson's message has been presented in context above, but his concluding emphasis is worth noting. When Cunningham's group *"despersed, they declared themselves intirely in favor Government & said they would ever oppose the measures of congress ...I fear this matter will spread on this side of the river if something is not spedily done in support of the resolves of congress & and it will be attended with very bad Consequence—Many people from the Savannah river have already come & subscribed to the Col. Fletchall & Capt. Cunningham association & many others are daily expicted for the same purpose."* Mayson warns that Ninety-Six could become *"a Santuary for all such who oppose the measures of the Continentall & Provincial Congress."*[117] Mayson's letter would catch up to Thomson at Granby on the Congaree on 22 July and later reach Charleston on 25 July.

Meanwhile, on this same day of 18 July, events unfolding elsewhere would have impact on the formulation of back country policy in Charleston. Having received letters of 21 and 29 June from the Committee of Intelligence, John Stuart, in St. Augustine, now replied. His letter of 18 July viewed the tone of Charleston's Rebel leaders as an insult to his integrity. He refused to relinquish his correspondence but assured the Council *"I have never received any Orders from my superiors which by the most tortured Construction, could be interpreted to spirit up or employ the Indians to fall upon the frontier Inhabitants or take part in the Disputes between Great Britain and her colonies, and I do not know that any part of my Conduct, thro all the various scenes of my Life, can fix upon me the Imputation of Cruelty or Inhumanity, or Induce a Belief that I would Wantonly use my Influence with the Indians to make them fall upon Innocent people. Yet such an Opinion has been most industriously propagated, altho it is absolutely impossible that it could or can be Supported by any Evidence of the least Credibility; and I will venture to say that every one and all of You do in your Conscience believe the charge to be false, I think I have a right to call upon You as Men of Honor to efface the Impression it has made upon the Minds of the People."*[118]

No matter how much Stuart protested, the Rebel leaders would continue to treat the Superintendent of Indians with suspicion. He was villified far and wide as a man who would unleash Indians as soon as the time was propitious to the British. Indeed, the bile of dissension among Carolinians was rising in many quarters between Rebel and Loyalist. Choosing sides was becoming inevitable, with concomitant mob action soon to follow.

It may be recalled that on 8 May, a citizen named Charles Webb made derogatory statements about the American cause. They were overlooked at the time. Now, ten weeks later, Webb was belatedly denounced by fellow citizens Allen Miles, Robert Miles and Melcher Garner—with references to witnesses John Jackson, William and James Ruggle, Jonathan Humphreys, Francis Bremars—regarding remarks Webb had made at *"Mr. Ramage's Tavern and Mr. Edward's Tavern on the Bay"* in Charleston. In those ten weeks a distinct sea change had taken place. The Council of Safety was now in charge as the *de facto* revolutionary government of South Carolina. Various committees of intelligence and vigilance had been organized throughout the province. Many pro-American vigilantes were on the lookout for anti-American malcontents. Webb's earlier remarks were now remembered by the committee in *"St Paul's Parish,"* where he was" *denounced an enemy to this Province & America in General & an Object of the Resentment of the Public."* The deposition of the Miles brothers and Garner was taken by *"one of his majesties Justices of the Peace for Charlestown District"* at the instigation of a

*"Committee for Vigilance in St. Paul's Parish."*[119] Although chastised, Webb was not imprisoned.

The emotional struggle for the hearts and minds of men was beginning to assume a position of major importance among revolutionary South Carolinians as the hot summer months unfolded.

# CHAPTER VI

## *Choosing up Sides*

ON 18 JULY, COL. WILLIAM THOMSON RECEIVED THE COUNCIL OF Safety's order [dated 16 July] to take Fort Charlotte. On this same day Mayson was writing to report that it had been taken on the 12th. Angry and puzzled by the new order, Thomson immediately sent a note to Capt. Robert Goodwyn to *"be in readiness to March at half a days Warnings … to take a tour of about ten days, owing to some intelligence I just now received."* But he urged that *"Lieutenant Hopkins still proceed on his journey to forward the Express to Major Mason [sic] with all possible speed."* This afterthought was a reference to the Council's marching orders of the 13th which Thomson had just sent out on the 17th.

Late on the 18th of July, Thomson cautiously responded to Council president Henry Laurens, stating *"I just now received your friendly letter of the 16th with the orders from the Council of Safety which shall be put into execution immediately. I do expect Major Mason [sic] has executed the orders of the 26th June long before this time, as I trusted that part of the service to him with particular orders to execute it, being in the neighborhood. I am very sorry the council of Safety had had to repeat their orders to me."*[120]

Thomson's letter would not reach the Council until the 21st. Meanwhile, still smarting from what he considered a rebuke, Thomson wrote to his other captains.

### Wednesday, 19 July

From Amelia, Thomson addressed letters to Captains Woodward, Richardson and Kershaw—Goodwyn had already been alerted. Captain Wise was not included. Thomson ordered his captains to *"meet me on Sunday next [23 July] at the Congarees in readiness for service to march to fort Charlotte."* At the same time he wrote separately to Major Mayson: *"Since the express I sent you yesterday* [by way of Hopkins] *I have rec'd a letter and orders of which I have sent you a copy. I desire you will immediately transmit to me a state of the whole affair as it now stands. I shall collect four of the lower companies immediately and be at the Congarees in five days* [at Granby] *in order to march up if the needful is not done already of which I hope to be acquainted from you before that Day. I desire that you will collect the four upper Companies to have them in readiness to join me when I come to Ninety six, that is if Capt. Purvis is not in the fort already according to the first orders. If so, the express of yesterday's will acquaint you what to do with the other three Company's. I shall be extremely sorry & surprized to find the orders of the 26th has not yet been put into execution by you, as I depended entirely on you, expecting to have them as absolutely executed as if I had been present.*"[121] Thomson does not mince words; his exasperation is evident, and he has not the slightest knowledge of what has transpired. Thomson was no doubt still fuming when Mayson's report caught up to him at Granby on 22 July, but at least he would now have some idea of the confusion and dissension that was percolating among settlers in the upper part of the back country regarding opinions of where to stand on the matter of loyalty versus rebellion. His own march to Fort Charlotte was canceled.

While back country Rebels were floundering, the low country was forging ahead with its war plans. In Charleston on this same 19th of July, Peter Timothy optimistically informed the Council *"that he had printed 200 copies of the Rules and Articles for regulating the Colony Forces"* for general distribution. In addition the Council *"ordered, that the resolution of the Congress relative to volunteer Companies be transmitted to the Colonels of the several regiments of Military throughout the Colony."*[122]

The local state of affairs, from the British point of view, also enters into the picture on the 19th as Lord Campbell prepared his second dispatch to Lord Dartmouth in London offering his own assessment of Rebel activities. The Governor now reports *"the people are ripe for any violence ... no subterfuge should be left them, things are come to such a pass my Lord that the whole world ought to know that the present measures proceed both from a Mob fired by oppression but that they are the result of a concerted plan and firm determination of a powerful party to establish independency by Acts as unprovoked as they are unjustifiable ... The intolerable Tyranny & oppression used by the committee in enforcing their mandates has already given offence to the Moderates of their own party, and has stirred up such a spirit in the back part of this Country which is very populous that I hope it will be attended with the best Effects. Several very respected people from Camden and Ninety six have been with me expressing their loyalty & Affection to His Majesty ... assuring me it is the sentiments of some thousands in those Districts. I have given them every encouragement to persevere ... earnestly requesting that they would cultivate this loyal disposition amongst their neighbors and promising them both protection and reward ... They proposed setting on foot an Address to me by way of a Counter association and I hope it will be signed by great Numbers. The boasted unanimity is notoriously false, very many who were obliged to sign the Association totally disapproved every measure.*"[123]

Campbell appears well informed about dissension in the back country and of Fletchall's efforts to counter association. But he haughtily ridicules the Rebels' efforts at mobilization, commenting, "*...the Continental Congress strongly disapproved of raising any Troops here and recommended they should drop the scheme but that is now impracticable.*" I find this statement a gratuitous improvisation on the Governor's part. No matter, he prattles on about the two low country regiments, telling his superiors that the Carolinian "*officers appointed are so pleased with their new garb and occupation that they dare not attempt disbanding them, and they are collecting such a set of vagrants from all quarters that I really shall not be surprized when they put them together and attempt establish discipline if they destroy their Officers and plunder the Country.*"[124]

Before concluding, the Governor again petulantly states that he has not yet heard from Lt. Governor Bull and then offers insight into his opinions about Georgia: "*By accounts received last night from Georgia, that Province has joined with the General Association and Appointed delegates to the Continental Congress. This apostasy will answer their purpose extremely well, as they are amply stocked with all kinds of European goods of which we already feel the want very much ... British schooner Phillipa ... bound from London ... recently boarded ... Georgians seized 15000 pounds of gunpowder ... to such a helpless state we are reduced here.*"[125]

Campbell and his Loyalist followers in Charleston were hurting. There were no British troops on hand for protection and he was relying upon sycophants for intelligence about the mood of Carolinians. It was precisely because rumors "*relative to certain recent transactions*" with the Governor had been circulating around town that Elizabeth Simpson had been taken in by William Henry Drayton and Arthur Middleton for questioning. Her testimony is psychologically revealing. Deposed before Peter Bounetheau in Charleston, "*the said Elizabeth Simpson, of Camden District ... being duly sworn, sayeth that on or about the eighth day of July instant ... together with her husband John Simpson, who is a relative of his Excellency, Lord William Campbell, went to see the said Lord William upon his arrival in this Colony, and being there, heard the conversation between the said Lord William and the said John ... Lord William asked the said John, how does the pulse of the people beat in the back country? The said John replied, that Col. Fletchall had 1000 men who would be for the King, and that there would be many friends for the King if they could hear from the Governor. To this the said Lord William replied that he did not know how he could procure a trusty hand to send on such an errand."*[126]

After a few more exchanges, the Governor suggested *"that as he, the said John, was dressed in a plain and poor way, he must go about the country and Town and hear all that was said ... and should always acquaint him, the said Lord William, with what he ... should hear from time to time. That he, the said Lord William, desired him, the said John, to go to sundry persons whom he named, who had been recommended to him, and to offer to enlist for the King, as he wanted to know whether he could trust them; that he intended, if those men were true, to order them to enlist privately for the kingdom, to keep them in readiness to come down when he sent for them; that he expected men of war to arrive soon, and that a man of war had carried away a negro pilot in order to bring them in."*[127]

Such intelligence alarmed the Council of Safety and had already prompted a letter to Col. Thomas Fletchall on the 17th. Meanwhile, as Campbell was drafting his dispatch of the 19th to London, Fletchall, on this same day, in Fair Forest, was composing his own letter to Governor Campbell, recounting the re-capture of arms from the Rebels at Ninety-Six two days earlier.[128] This letter would not reach Campbell until 1 August, at which time he would immediately reply. This is the only correspondence found between Fletchall and Campbell.

By mid-July 1775 rhetoric on both sides was escalating, along with tempers. It was on 19 July that Allen Cameron, still in Savannah, wrote a second letter to Andrew Williamson vehemently reiterating his rejection of a commission in the rangers, Once again he tells Williamson, *"I never gave you the least hint I would accept a commission ... I'm sure I did not say one word that you could infer from, that I would join the cause you all unluckily at present contend for. I always was and still is possessed of different sentiments ... I have returned the commission which you will find inclosed."*[129]

Cameron's uncompromising words were discouraging to the Rebel cause, but not everyone shared his opinion. A month had elapsed since the Rebels' Provincial Congress adjourned. News of its resolutions and follow-up actions had been circulating throughout the province. Sides were being chosen—even before directives for mobilizing volunteer militiamen were formally put into action.

*Friday 21 July*

Thomas Post wrote to the Council of Safety from Prince Frederick Parish on the Pee Dee River, 90 miles from Charleston, saying *"I live in a district on the south ws't side of the pee dee River, and on the north Es't side of Linches Crick … an area that has not bin Desciplined this fifteen years past."* Post reports that he has *"summoned the male inhabitants of sd District to Assemble together to Choose there officers to teach them the Military Discipline."* He has been chosen Captain, Hugh Giles was First Lieutenant, and Thomas Post, Jr. was Second Lieutenant. Post further suggests dividing the district in two, *"it being thirty miles in length."* He proposes taking control in the lower half, with a volunteer militia in the upper half *"above Willow Crick to black crick"* to be led by Capt. James Gregg and Lieutenants Robert Scott and John Gregg.[130] These men would be duly commissioned on 13 August.

The area where Thomas Post lived, the Cheraws, also contained numerous dissenters. Indeed, Capt. Wise and his Company of Rangers from the Cheraws, would be delayed in joining Thomson at Amelia precisely because interim orders requested him to round up malcontents before proceeding.

On the same day, in Charleston, the Council also received a letter "from Thomson dated Amelia 18th July 1775 … payment of forty pounds currency, to Thomas Singleton, for carrying an express to Col. Thomson at Amelia." Singleton returned on the 21st with Thomson's answer of the 18th. The gist of Thomson's letter has already been reviewed—essentially it apologized to the Council for having to repeat its orders of 26 June regarding Fort Charlotte. Thomson himself, by the 21st, was on the road to take the fort. By now he had reached Fort Granby at the confluence of the Broad and Saluda Rivers—the future site of Columbia—where he expected Mayson to meet him.

Meanwhile, Capt. John Purvis had joined Major Mayson at Ninety-Six with a company of only eleven men. This disheartening news was relayed to Thomson on 22 July. This letter has not been located but it is referenced in Thomson's Order Book.[131]

*Saturday, 22 July*

No sooner had Mayson sent off his message to Thomson on the morning of 22 July, as Mayson would later report, he *"received a Letter from Ezekiel Polk by express, informing me that he would be glad to see me immediately, as he was likely to be ambuscaded by some of Capt. Cunninhgam's party—accordingly I went and met him & his company about eight miles over Saludy river &*

*Conducted them hither"* to Ninety-Six.[132] All this and more would be reported in a letter dated 29 July.

This episode marks Polk's first appearance on the scene since recruitment orders went out last 26 June. Eight miles over the Saluda places him in Cunningham country, close to Peach Hill, the Cunningham homestead [today located in Laurens County]. Opposition to the Association was said to be most vehement in this part of the back country. As Mayson would later report, Cunningham's party on the 22nd *"consisted of about sixty men ... they stopped them on the road ... but Cunningham Ordered them to disperse."*[133]

It seems the Loyalists were not looking for a fight; they merely sought to intimidate Polk and his men. The incident occurred too late for Mayson to report in his earlier express of 22 July in which he noted Purvis's appearance; in this express he also enclosed a copy of a letter from Rev. James Cresswell with a copy of Fletchall's counter-association document of 13 July, *"which will farthur inform you of the confusion in the different parts of the Frontiers."*[134]

James Cresswell and James Mayson were neighbors who shared ferry responsibilities on the Saluda River. Cresswell, now 35, was an émigré from Virginia who had been *"licensed by the Hanover Presbytery in Virginia at Tinkling Spring in 1764 ... ordained at lower Lower Hico, North Carolina 1765 ... He settled at Island Ford on the Saluda,"* across from Mayson, around 1766. Like many itinerant preachers he was influenced by George Whitefield.[135]

On the same day that Mayson was rescuing Ezekiel Polk from Cunningham's clutches on the 22nd, Thomson had reached Granby, where his subordinate's letter of the 18th caught up to him. Thomson relayed its disturbing accounts to Charleston on this same date—22 July. Indeed, he now halted his march toward Fort Chartlotte and wrote three messages— two to the Council of Safety and one, a personal epistle, to Henry Laurens, his Commander-in-Chief. Such letters offer the reader psychological insights into the temper of the times, the difficulties of military organization, and the consequences of vanity in relations between men.

In the first letter, a short letter to the Council, Thomson was perplexed over disposition *"of about 50 Catawbas near Camden on a friendly visit. Mr. Kirshaw & I myself are both at a loss what to do with regard to taking some of them into pay for want of your instructions."*[136] By way of explanation, it seems that Capt. Ely Kershaw of the rangers, a resident of the Camden area, had been asked by his father, Joseph Kershaw, to bring this news to Thomson. The reader will recall that, when two Catawba Indians visited Charleston on 5 July last, they were given a pep talk by William Henry Drayton and a letter to share with the Cherokees reiterating the good intentions of the Rebels.

Drayton's letter, whose actual contents are worth recalling, cautions and cajoles the natives: *"The Great King, over the Great Water, has got some bad men about him, who every day give him bad talk about us ... Now we hope we have opened your eyes, and you see plainly that your case and our case is just the same; and therefore we expect that your warriors will join our warriors in this business, which concerns you as much as it does us ... and we acquaint you, that we are willing to pay some of your warriors in order to show that we look upon your nation as brother warriors. We are willing to hold you fast by the hand, and we think it is best to tell you, that we have a bad talk about you; and we tell you this because we hope you will let us see that you will hold us fast by the hand also."*[137]

What a delightful propagandist! Drayton, while obliquely referring to the rumors of Stuart's machinations, urges neutrality—but he nevertheless offers the prospect of compensation to the Indians who side with the Rebels. Fifty of these mercenary Catawbas had appeared in Camden asking Joseph Kershaw, an influential merchant in Camden, for help. Guidance was now being requested from Thomson, who threw the problem back at the Council.

In his second letter of 22 July, from Granby, addressed to *"the Honorable Council of Safety,"* Thomson writes *"Gentlemen—I arrived* [21July] *at this place with an intention to have march'd in the morning with Capts. Kirshaw, Richardson, Goodwyn's & Woodward's in order to carry into Execution your orders of the 16th instant. It was not in my power to collect the four Cympanys together sooner Capt. Wise being at the greatest distance and also near a Quarter where I was inform'd several disaffected Persons live say on Thomson's & Lynch's creeks, for which reasons I only sent him your orders of the 13th instant & intended leaving him there in order to watch the intentions of these persons. But on my way up hither, I met an express from Major Mason* [sic], *to the Council of Safety and also one for my self* [letters of the 18th], *a copy of which I herewith send you inclos'd ... I shall now camp a few miles above this place, with the four Company's above mentioned & dispatch an Express to Capt. Wise in the morning with orders for him to repair immediately with his company to this camp. I shall also send to Major Mason to have Fort Charlotte well guarded. If he finds it necessary with the whole of the other three Company's, or whatever part of them may be rais'd."*[138]

Having finally learned of the events concerning Fort Charlotte, Thomson perfunctorily tells the Council that he is calling off his expedition and is organizing forces for the still-intended three part march of the Regiment of Rangers through the province, for regrouping near Charleston. But, in a third letter of this same day, 22 July, addressed to Henry Laurens personally, Thomson lets his feelings vent, while protecting his self-interest: *I herewith send you Inclos'd Copy of orders I sent to Major Mason with the order of the 26th ult. from the Council of Safety. I am so sorry that Major Mason has so unfortunately lost the Gunpowder, & cannot tell why he brought it out of the Fort, perhaps the council of Safety ordr'd him to do so, as he told me when on his way up from Town, that he had orders relative to fort Charlotte, but did not inform me what they were, and kept it a secret from me, as I could wish he had done from all others."*[139]

Fitting the pieces together, Mayson left Charleston a few days later than Thomson, following the adjournment of the Provincial Congress. He evidently spoke with members of the Council of Safety prior to departure, and was given instructions pertaining to For Charlotte. Riding back to his home at Island Ford on the Saluda, Mayson passed through Orangeburg, where he consulted with his commanding officer. For reasons unknown, Mayson disclosed nothing about his instructions regarding Fort Charlotte. This unforgivable breach of military protocol is completely incomprehensible; it obviously annoyed Thomson and certainly affected their relationship from that point on. The loss of the gunpowder probably put Mayson further in Thomson's disfavor. Unfortunately, Mayson's original instructions, whatever they might have been, have never come to light.

On other matters, such as the escalating Loyalist danger, they were in agreement. In his letter to Laurens, Thomson concurred with the views expressed by Mayson, adding: *"I am doubtful that the officers in that quarter are not the persons esteemed among their neighbors & they have not told the men their duty at the time of their enlisting them, however you will be better able to judge when you Peruse the inclos'd papers, by which you will see how Fletchall, Cunningham & Robinson has deceived and deluded the poor people, in the Fork, Between Broad & Saluda Rivers ... I am clearly of the opinion that if some Gentlemen of the Council of Safety, or of the most noted Character together with Col. Richardson—as many of the people formerly belonged to his Regiment—could be prevailed to go up among them that could place these unhappy disputes between Great Britain & the Colony's in a proper Light that most of them might be brought over by fair means ... I do not mean Fletchall, Cunningham & Robinson, if they was Cherokees Chief or Leaders I would venture to loose my life or send their Scalps to the Council of Safety, But the poor people they have deluded, I am of the opinion might yet be convinced of the Error. I think Mr. Tennent would be a good hand to send up as a great many of these people are of his Religion."*[140]

William Tennent, a stoic Puritan who Laurens once likened to Oliver Cromwell, had been a politically active member of the First Provincial

Congress. A Congregationalist, Tennent was a graduate from the Presbyterian-tied College of New Jersey and a staunch opponent of Anglican leaders such as Loyalist Rev. Alexander Garden in Charleston. The back country was filling up with Presbyterians, Baptists and Methodists—all of whom suspected the English Church of papist tendencies.

In a postscript to Henry Laurens, Thomson adds a bit of gossip: *"I would just beg leave to mention that I am well informed of there being a private ... & great resentment between Mayson, Kirkland, & this Cunningham, the latter with some more of his neighbors think they have not been taken proper notice of—I only throw out those hints for you information."*[141]

Thomson offers no source for this gossip, but such innuendo sheds light on local allegiances and motivations as men struggled for recognition under times of stress. Having been himself censured by the Council, Thomson was in a querulous mood—angry because the Charlotte affair ended badly and disturbed because the Association was being challenged. But, if valid, his words can be interpreted to buttress the Andrew Pickens thesis offered 36 years later. History, like tabloid journalism, sometimes thrives on tenuous allegations, and one has to dig deeper for the truth.

All three letters from Thomson, dated the 22nd, reached Charleston on the evening of 25 July and were read before Council members on the 26th. The letter to Laurens in particular speaks volumes about Thomson's personality as an outspoken curmudgeon—he was fondly known among his men as "ol' danger." His observations about Cunningham—as "this Cunningham"—seem to suggest that he did not know the man personally. South Carolina historian A.S. Salley also makes this observation about Cunningham: *"So, after all, this chivalrous gentleman of the old school ... was nothing but a sorehead."*[142]

Personal misunderstandings aside, the two top rangers, Col. Thomson and Major Mayson, were on the same wavelength regarding confusion among back country settlers and their views of the mother country. Something had to be done.

*Sunday, 23 July*

Even as the news from Thomson and Mayson was enroute to Charleston, members attending a meeting of the Council of Safety were anticipating their fears and making arrangements. In the rhetoric of the times, they *"Resolved ... That the Hon. W.H. Drayton, and the Rev. William Tennent, be the two gentlemen to make a progress into the Back Country ... at public expense ... there to explain to the people at large, the nature of the unhappy disputes between Great Britain and the American Colonies; to endeavor to settle all political disputes between the people; to quiet their minds; and to force the necessity of a general union, in order to preserve themselves and their children from slavery."*[143]

How ironic and elitist such words must sound to libertarians today, not to mention black Americans. What must scholars of human rights think— might not the very idea of forced unity create a moral dilemma? It certainly did to the many Loyalists at the time, who persistently claimed to prefer neutrality. Yet here was Council of Safety saying that recalcitrant Carolinians would be forced to support the cause of liberty as viewed by revolutionaries—or else.

To understand how Loyalists viewed South Carolinians of 1775 we turn to Samuel Curwen, once a colonial Judge of the Admiralty in New York, later a *"loyalist-refugee in England."* Of this crucible year, he described South Carolinians as *"the settlers of the upper country, harmonious, and rapidly increasing in wealth and numbers. Devoted to the cultivation of their lands, they mixed little with the inhabitants of the lower country, and were disposed to consider the latter more as ambitious intriguers for place and power ... removed from the immediate sphere of British oppression the unjust taxation of the mother country was neither much felt or complained of by them ... and the commotions on their own seaboard, were attributed to the intrigues and ambitions of political demagogues ... it must be recollected too, that, in the early stages of the revolution, few thought or even dreamed of a separation from the mother country, and the only motives assigned for the extreme and warlike measures of enrolling troops ... were an express determination to resist the payment of unjust taxes, and the expectation that England would be induced to revoke her arbitrary acts by a violent and extended show of opposition on the part of the colonies. When, however, these demonstrations were followed up by acts of violence of the harshest and most vindictive character, against those those who wished to remain neutral, we cannot be surprised that the patriotism of the leaders of the movement party, whose deeds contrasted so unfavorably with their public declarations, should now be somewhat more than suspected by those who had always distrusted the purity of their motives ... Had it been declared at once that their objective was a separation, the violence of their conduct, , though quite unjustifiable, might have been susceptible of some palliation, in consideration of the magnitude of the stake for which they were contending ... But they asserted their movement to be strictly a defensive one, and to hold in abhorrence the idea of throwing off their allegiance ... It is difficult to reconcile the cruelties they perpetrated with honesty of purpose, and, after making every allowance for the enthusiasm, under the influence of which political, as well as religious bigots, in every age of the world, have endeavored by force to secure compliance, whenever their reasoning failed to produce conviction, the impartial historian will still have to record much to be accounted for only by the recklessness with which unprincipled men who assume, of their own authority, irresponsible power, are almost always found to allow their passions and the impulse of the moment to have uncontrolled sway over their minds."*[144]

This astute analysis of South Carolina's revolutionary leadership in 1775 is right on target. Passion, impulse, the use of force to assure compliance, aided by political and religious bigots—these are harsh condemnations. But here, in Curwen's imagery, we have William Henry Drayton [political bigot?] and the Rev. William Tennent [religious bigot?] about to set out on a patriotic crusade to either *"explain to the people"* or *"force the necessity of a general union."*

Thus, on the 23rd of July, fully aware of growing dissension in the back country, the Council of Safety: *"Resolved, That it is necessary to draught the Militia of the Colony ... ordering ... that the several Companies on their respective Regiments, to be divided into three Divisions, one third ... shall hold themselves in readiness ... to march on twelve hours notice, another third when called upon, and the other to remain for the protection of their respective Districts."*[145]

# CHAPTER VII

## *On the Eve of Crusade*

A S THE REBELS WERE ISSUING ORDERS FOR MILITIA MOBILIZATION on the 23rd of July, the Royal Governor of South Carolina was writing his third Despatch to Lord Dartmouth in London. It contained nothing relevant to back country matters, but his despondent attitude is apparent when he reports: *"It is hardly possible to conceive a situation more irksome than mine is at present scarce a shadow of authority left but I am resolved to keep my ground as long as possible."*[146]

*Monday, 24 July*

From his home in Fair Forest [present day Spartanburg County], Col. Thomas Fletchall replied to the Council of Safety's letter of the 15th. He took umbrage, writing: *"many reports have been maliciously asserted against me ... which I can make appear to be false."* Referring to his assembly of troops on the 13th, Fletchall reiterated, *"not one man offered to sign the Association ... it was agreed amongst the people in general to sign a paper of their own resolutions ... which the people in general did sign ... from the Savannah river to Broad River ... I must inform you, sir, there is some of our highland gentlemen who are very aspiring and fond of commission; thinking to get in favor with the gentlemen in town, will say anything but the truth ... I am heartily sorry that I am looked on as an enemy to my country ... but I am resolved and do utterly refuse to take up arms against my King, until I find it my duty to do otherwise and am fully convinced thereof."*[147]

These strongly held convictions seem to concur with Curwen's thoughts, and certainly intimate that personal feelings were running high. The comment referring to aspirations of sycophant "highland gentlemen" remains intriguing but speculative with respect to identities. Perhaps he referred to all who held commissions in the Regiment of Rangers. Fletchall's letter would not reach Charleston before Drayton and Tennent set off on their holy mission.

When the communiqués from Thomson reached Charleston late on 25 July, the contents would give the Council much to ponder over on the following day.

*Wednesday, 26 July*

From their minutes of 26 July, we find that *"The Council met. Present— Col. Henry Laurens, President; Hon. Mr. Lowndes; Mr. Brewton; Capt. Benjamin Elliott; Mr. Heyward; Mr. Ferguson; Mr. Williamson; Mr. Bee ... The President laid before, and read to the Council, sundry papers, contained in a dispatch from Col. William Thomson, received last night by Capt. Thomas Woodward, of the Rangers."*[148]

In response to the Catawba question, a letter was drafted *"by the president to Joseph Kershaw, esq., laid before the Council and approved of."* We learn at this point that a letter from Joseph Kershaw, dated 8 July, on this same question, had been received but overlooked. The Council now thanked Kershaw *"for his assiduity in treating with the old men and head warriors of the Catawba Indians ... hopes that forty or fifty of them will cheerfully enter into the service of the Colony ... the design of uniting them to the Regiment of Rangers is a measure which they altogether approve of, but to be under the particular direction of a white man."* The Council asks Kershaw to recommend *"a white man well qualified to lead them in scouts, and in action ... will give him a commission, and dispatch him with a letter to Col. Thomson, in whose camp he will meet with the Indians."*[149]

In this same letter, the Council optimistically tried to relieve Kershaw's concern over *"scanty store of gun-powder and lead for the whole colony ... quantities are at Fort Charlotte, and at Cheraw ... in proportion for the Western and Northern Districts needs."*[150]

The real problems of the day were dissension and hostility among settlers beyond the low country areas, difficulties they hoped to curtail with words and rational explanations. Therefore the Council now *"Resolved that the Rev. Oliver Hart be applied to, to join Mr. Drayton and Mr. Tennent."* Oliver Hart was a highly respected Baptist preacher and resident of Charleston. On this 26th day of July a letter was drafted suggesting *"your presence in the Western and Northern frontiers of the colony may be of great service, by explaining to the inhabitants, in a proper and true light, the nature of the present dispute ... your compliance will be esteemed by the Council of Safety as an instance of your zeal in the public service when the aid of every freeman and lover on constitutional liberty is loudly called for."*[151]

The mission to the back country was indeed becoming a crusade of bible and sword. The frontiersmen were a God-fearing people but, if they could not be swayed by the gospel of sweet reason from the mouths of Tennent and Hart, then Drayton would bring force to bear. Such was the sentiment emerging from the chambers where the Council of Safety was convened.

Nine months had elapsed since the First Continental Congress issued its resolution for "association." One month has passed since the First Provincial Congress of South Carolina adjourned. Since then the Council of Safety has been trying to implement congressional policies—to make preparations for possible armed defense and to encourage Carolina's native population to join them. Results thus far have been dismal. To counteract Loyalist hostility, the Drayton-Tennent-Hart mission was concocted, with Hart conducting his missionary efforts separately. But even before this expedition could be launched another crisis was brewing at Ninety-Six.

*Thursday, 27 July; Friday, 28 July; Saturday 30 July*

One later learns from a letter written by Major James Mayson on the 30th, wherein he says *"Inclos'd you will receive Mr. Kirkland's letter to me of the 28th by which you will see the reasons for resigning his Commission & that they correspond with the hints given you in a former letter."* Mayson reports that Kirkland came into camp on the 27th and *"immediately had a long private Talk with Capt. Polk, which I am a stranger to ... the next morning I gave Capt. Polk Orders to sett off with a Command of men to fort Charlotte for to conduct ammunition which you ordered me to send for in your Last Letter ... when I was told that he had discharged both the Grass & Quarter Guards from their duty—that he was their Officer & would not sacrifice their Healths for no Council of Safety's parading notions , that it was contrary to the rules of the Congress ... & a great deal of such like inflammatory Language ... I must confess that this sudden conduct of Capt. Polks surprized me very much ... His men were very impudent to me after his telling them that he would not order them below without their consent ... so that his jaunt to Fort Charlotte was not complied with—I am very certain it would be impossible for Capt. Polk ever to carry Command over his company, from what I have seen since his arrival here ... When I found Capt. Polk was determined to march his Company back again, I entreated him to reflect on what he was going to do, as his honor was at stake— He said he had already done it and would not take the Tour which was ordered by the council of Safety ... that he allways understood the Rangers were raised to protect the Frontiers & not their plantations ... directly after this conversation Capt. Polk Ordered his company to get ready for marching & left the camp about 10 O'Clock yesterday afternoon"*[152]

Polk and his company departed for their homes in the New Acquisition District on the 29th. With Kirkland also gone, Major Mayson was left stranded with Capt. Purvis and his eleven rangers. Meanwhile, 30 miles away, unaware that Polk had deserted, Col. Thomson, on 29 July, was composing a note to Henry Laurens assuring the president that *"I have at this moment been inform'd by a Traveling Man, that Capt. Polk Cross'd Saluda river with a compleat company of very Likely Men on Sunday Last, on his way to Ninety Six."*[153] How ironic! Sunday last was the day Polk had been rescued by Mayson from a Cunningham ambush. Now, a week later he was deserting Mayson's camp. At the same time Thomson was reassuring the Council that ranger matters were improving.

On this same day, from his camp *"near Congarees Creek,"* Thomson wrote a second letter, addressed to the Council of Safety. He reminded the Council *"My last to you was the 22nd instant by Capt. Woodward ... since which I have received the inclosed letter from Lieut. David Hopkins who I sent with the Association and a letter from the precedent* [sic] *to Col. Fletchall."*[154]

The reference is to President Laurens' letter to Fletchall of 15 July which was evidently transmitted through Thomson. The courier was Lt. David Hopkins of Capt. Goodwyn's Company. Hopkins was now returning with Fletchall's reply dated 24 July. There is a touch of mystery here for historical purists as one record indicates that Fletchall's letter, from *"Fairforest Munday July 24th 1775,"* was addressed to *"The Honourable Henry Lawrance, Esq."* Records state that this letter was *"docketed in Laurens' hand, Tho. Fletchall 27 July/1775. To Presid't of Coincil/ Read in council 11 Aug't."*[155]

If the letter was docketed on 27 July, why was it not read until 11 August—a full two weeks later? But the plot thickens or, perhaps, an explanation emerges, when one later reads that Drayton, in his message of 7 August from the back country, in a report to the Council, imperiously comments: *"We have taken the liberty to open a public letter to Col. Laurens from Fletchall."*[156] There can be no doubt that this is the letter of 24 July.

Because Drayton's own dispatch of 7 August was itself read at the Council meeting of 11 August, I suspect that Fletchall's letter, read at the same time, was included with Drayton's dispatch of 7 August—and not with Thomson's letter of 29 July. Why and how this happened, one can only speculate. However, knowing that Drayton, a Council member, was already on his way to the back country, it is likely that that Thomson held back Fletchall's letter, awaiting his arrival.

This question aside, in his letter to Laurens of the 29th, Thomson also acknowledges a second *"letter handed to me last night"* from Capt. Wise, dated 15 July. A third communiqué received was *"from Major Mason [sic] dated the 22nd inst: wherein he informs me of the arrival of Capt. Purvis the Day before & that he had only Enlisted eleven men—he farther informs me that he had expected Capt. Polk within Ten Days. From whom I have never yet received any account therefore cannot inform you with regard to the state of his Company, & neither Caldwell nor Kirkland have yet made a return of their Companys. Captains Kirshaw, Goodwyn, Woodward & Richardson are now in Camp with me & have all their Companys compleat except the Latter who wants four Men yet, which I hope to get in a few Days tho' I find some difficulty in raising Men, as the Enemies to the cause, take great pains to propagate differ- ent reports that the money they are to be paid with will not pass etc. ... I have order'd Major Mason, if he found that Cap. Caldwell's company was sufficient to guard Fort Charlotte to rendezvous the other three Company's near the Ridge, untl I rec'd farther orders ... from the moving of the gunpowder first of the Fort to ninety six, the different accounts of Capt Kirklands behavior on that occasion, Capt. Purvis having enlisted only eleven men, and not having intelligence from Polk, together with the minds of the back People being so much agitated at this time that I am really at a loss in what manner to act in regard to the Conduct & Behavior of the different officers in that Quarter ... shall be extremely glad of your direction."*[157]

Fast moving events in a world of sluggish communications would con- tinue to bewilder Col. Thomson. He was still unaware that Kirkland and Polk had deserted. As for directions from the Council, these would come directly from William Henry Drayton, who was then preparing with Rev. Tennent to leave Charleston in order to restore calm to the back country.

Meanwhile, in another letter of the 29th, Thomson continues confiding to Henry Laurens. It was in this letter that he enclosed a *"Copy of a letter from the Rev'd Mr. Cresswell to Major Mason which ... will farthur inform you of the confusion in the different parts of the Frontiers of the Colony,"* coinciding *"with different accounts that I daily have from the country."* All this confusion is affecting morale, as Thomson admits the troops *"seem rather dissatisfied at present."* He now requests favored treatment, observing *"I have four companys of my Regiment encamp'd near the Congarees, & I find it extremely difficult to keep them from suffering for want of provision, which causes much murmuring amongst my Men."* Thomson reminds Laurens that living off the country is not as easy now as it was *"in the late Indian War ... if you think any step could be taken to have the privates provided at the expence of the Colony, I am convinced it would serve a good purpose, and quiet the minds of the few I have with me. If a petition from all the officers would help,"* Thomson offers to supply one; but he believes the personal influence of Laurens *"would be of more service to the reg't than any petition."*[158]

When received, Thomson's request for special treatment would create consternation among high minded, public spirited members of the Council of Safety who viewed the request as unduly mercenary and unpatriotic. The rangers would shortly be told as much by Drayton. But, just as Thomson sent off his plea to Charleston, more bad news was on its way from Mayson.

*Sunday, 30 July*

Major Mayson's letter, sent from Ninety-Six, was addressed to Col. Thomson at Amelia, which indicates that the Major was not yet in synchronization with his commander's movements. Evidently Thomson's letter of the 19th, in which Mayson was told *"I shall be at the Congarees in five days"* had not yet been received. Consequently Mayson was responding to instructions *"to sett off with a command of men to fort Charlotte ... to conduct the ammunition which you ordered me to send for in your last letter per Mr. Forbes."* Since then much had transpired, including Kirkland's defection and Polk's desertion, now reported on the 30th. This news would continue to lower morale among Thomson's men. Despondency would grow when Mayson advised: *"I do not think it safe ... to send for any ammunition ... as there are so few rangers here to protect it ... the People seem to be in as great a ferment as ever, if not greater ... Several Gentlemen of Fortune have come from Savannah & Georgia & signed Fletchall's & Cunningham's Association & I am of the opinion many others will join them ... I shall be glad to know by the return of the Bearer whether you expect I will conduct Capt. Purves's Company down to Amelia as you ordered in your last ... but I have very little expectation of success."*[159]

One of the gentlemen from Georgia mentioned by Mayson was Thomas Brown of Augusta. He would soon play a key role as advisor to Thomas Fletchall. Leaving Mayson in a rather depressed mood at Ninety-Six, we turn to matters in Charleston. On this same date of 30 July, the Council, in a letter signed by Laurens, wrote to Thomson: *"Our orders to you of the 13th Instant respecting your march to Charles Town, are hereby Countermanded, as at this Juncture the Presence of the Rangers is necessary in the interior parts of the country."* Thomson is told to remain at his post and take all further orders from the *"Honble Wm. Hen. Drayton, & the Revd. Wm. Tennent, who are authorized to make a progress into the back Country, to examine into the present uneasiness & disturbances in those parts of the colony."*[160]

While the cauldron in the back country was heating up, and the Drayton/ Tennent duo were preparing to simmer it down, Lord William Campbell, in Charleston, was drafting another letter to Lord Dartmouth in England— Despatch #4. The Governor's mood was still pessimistic, but he tried to put on a good face: *"Some accounts from the Back country do not please them, the Association has been refused by numbers and I am told a strong party is formed against it by a Colonel Fletchall, a man who has great influence in that part of the province. They talk of sending some of their principal People to try what Art and Persuasion will, and if that fails mean to use force. They are indefatigable ... The late defection of Georgia—brought about entirely by the people here—was a matter of amazing triumph."*[161]

Campbell seems well informed of Council activities; but his back country information is still based on conjecture. Surprisingly, he has not yet received a letter from Fletchall that was supposedly sent out on 19 July.

To conclude this active day of 30 July, the historian is rewarded by a letter written by Henry Laurens to his son John, in London, which provides an overview of South Carolina affairs. With a tinge of exasperation Laurens writes: *"It is impossible but that you will hear of a defection to our cause in the Western & Northern frontier of this colony under the Banner of a Colonel Fletchall ... no less than 2500 fellows Some say more, Instigated by Fletchall, a Mr. Cunningham, Robinson & others have signed an Association to support his Majesty's Government & maintain good order according to law ... some of that party under Cunningham lately beset the Major [Mayson] & one of our Captains [Kirkland] of Rangers, Cunningham issued warrants against them for having 'stolen' as they charged, the Kings powder & stores out of Fort Charlotte, which was taken by order of the Congress—& was after a hearing, proceeding to Commit those Officers to the County Gaol but upon the Interposition of a lawyer who resides in the Neighborhood they were admitted to Bail at the same time, one of the Lieutenants [Middleton] of a Company of Rangers & his whole Company of privates disbanded & went to their habitations—every other company of that regiment have taken a step toward following then by loudly exclaiming against ... an order of March through the country towards Charles Town—& as loudly insisting upon terms which if granted would be derogatory to the honour of the Provincial Congress & Council of Safety & followed by other demands & acts of disobedience—this conduct is no more than I both expected & foretold."*[162]

Laurens' worst fears seem to be materializing. Meanwhile, continuing his letter, he tells his son: *"to cure this Evil ... I have written a letter to Coll. Fletchall & in addition to that preparatory step, W.H.Drayton, the Reverend Messr. Tennent & Oliver Hart are going into that part of the country in order to treat with those disaffected & to explain to them the nature of our unhappy differences with the Mother country ... I believe by proper applications all those people may be brought at least to promise absolute neutrality & many of them to join us ... no stone has been left unturned by Administration & their creature, to disunite us poor distressed Americans—Insurrections of our Negroes attended by the most horrible butcheries of innocent Women & Children—Inroads by the Indians always accompanied by inhuman Massacre—Civil disorder between fellow Citizen & Neighbor Farmer, productive of fraud perjury & assassination, are all comprehended within their plans, attempts have been made to carry them all into Execution—I do not desire you to take my word for proof of this assertion, I can prove the facts by producing letters from, A Secretary of State* [Dartmouth], *a Governor of one of the Colonies* [Martin of North Carolina] *& a Superintendent of Indian Affairs* [Stuart]." Rhetorically, the father asks his son, *"Are these dark hellish plots for Subjagating the Colonies, consistent with Lord Dartmouth's religious tenets?"*[163]

Adding to his litany of horrors, Laurens, in disgust, claims that South Carolina's own governor *"avows the expediency of exciting the Negroes to butcher their Masters ... he has in the most express terms excited an opposition to our measures by Fletchal ... pledged himself to be among them at a proper time ... when they had made up a respectable number & he could furnish them with Arms & Ammunition."*[164]

The despair reflected in Laurens' letter is obvious. His repugnance over potential Negro uprisings and Indian attacks is especially revealing of the fears that occupied people's minds both in the low country and back country. He was dismayed that Lord Dartmouth, a man of principle, would stoop so low. Indeed, as historian John C. Miller observes, it was common knowledge in Britain and America that *"Lord Dartmouth, who had become Secretary of State for the colonies upon the resignation of Lord Hillsborough in 1772, was a man of impregnable piety. Not a chink was to be found in his armor of righteousness; he was, indeed, a Methodist of such devoutness and evangelical fervor that the King's advisors feared to admit him to the royal closet lest he undermine the King's adherence to the High Church. As a humanitarian and philanthropist, he was one of the few members of the English Ministry during the reign of George III worthy of giving his name to an American college."*[165] Laurens could not believe that a man like Dartmouth would condone any *"hellish plots."*

In this letter to his son, Henry Laurens provides an excellent review of

South Carolina regarding the back country. The rumors of nefarious plots that he alludes to would continue to plague the populace.

*Monday, 31 July*

Three days after he deserted Major Mayson at Ninety-Six, Moses Kirkland appears to have turned into an active Loyalist. On 31 July, he sent a note to fellow backslider Hugh Middleton, proposing an attack upon Augusta. The message was intercepted by Rebels in Georgia and subsequently sent to Charleston, where it was received on 10 August, with repercussions to follow. Finally, on the 31st, intelligence from Fort Charlotte was received in Charleston, the nature of which is not revealed in records, except for a courier receipt stating *"Received 31st July 1775 of John Lewis Gervais Twenty five Pounds Currency for bringing down an express from Fort Charlotte ... James Banks."*[166]

As Capt. Caldwell and his rangers were in occupation of Charlotte at this time, one assumes the message originated from him. It, too, may have referred to rumors of attack. Meanwhile Drayton and Tennent were ready to set out on their holy crusade.

# CHAPTER VIII

## *Priming the Association Pump*

On the day before the Council of Safety's propagandists set out for the hinterlands, Governor Campbell must have received Col. Fletchall's letter written eleven days earlier. The record shows that Campbell replied on 1 August. The papers of Lord Dartmouth contain a paraphrased version of the Governor's answer: *"Lord William Campbell to Colonel Thomas Fletchall—1775, August 1. Charles Town.—Sends thanks to those who recaptured the stores and rebels at Fort Charlotte. Authorizes him to fortify that place by his own and Col. Neale's [sic] regiments. Regrets he cannot send further support. Desires Mr. Cameron Deputy Superintendent to assist him. Implores him to avoid giving offence and to do his utmost to preserve peace in the district."*[167]

The tone of this reply gave no comfort to Fletchall since it offered little more than moral support. But the reference to Neel's regiment is noteworthy. The King's New Acquisitions District Militia Regiment, commanded by Col. Thomas Neel, had as field officers Lt. Col. Ezekiel Polk and Major Joseph Robinson. Polk, a Rebel ranger captain, had recently deserted from Mayson's camp with his company. Would this testy, ambivalent officer now return to active duty with the King's militia? His intentions and attitude would become a source of future consternation for Rebel leaders in Charleston.

Robinson had drafted the memorial, anti-association paper that was being signed by so many in the back country. He had also accompanied Cunningham to Ninety-Six when Fort Charlotte's gunpowder had been recaptured. Not to be overlooked, however, both Ezekiel Polk and Thomas Neel would be elected as delegates to the Second Provincial Congress, even though their allegiance at this point was an enigma.

A second letter from Campbell, written on this same day, was addressed to back country Quakers. It, too, offers insight into the turmoil regarding allegiances. The Governor was *"pleased to receive reassurance of their loyalty which he will represent to the King and endeavor to preserve their privileges."*[168]

There were few Quakers living in South Carolina prior to the American Revolution. Their loyalty provides another means to evaluate the emerging quarrel. The assurances of loyalty probably originated from the "Bush River Meeting" located in present day Newberry County, then part of the district between the Broad and Saluda Rivers, where Loyalist sentiment was so strong. According to Quaker history, the Bush River Friends, formed in 1770, *"was the most important in South Carolina"* at the time.[169]

The Bush River Quakers were preceded in South Carolina by an earlier group. Among the ruins of old Camden there is a historical marker at the foot of Church and Meeting streets, approximately 200 yards from Joseph Kershaw's meadow burial site, stating *"Quaker Cemetery, circa 1759 was located here. Presbyterian Meeting House built on site of Quakers circa 1774."*

*Wednesday, 2 August*

According to a journal kept by the Rev. William Tennent, he and William Henry Drayton left Charleston at 6:00 a.m. on the morning of 2 August *"to endeavor to settle all political disputes between the people, to quiet their minds … by chaise from Charleston, arrived at Mr. Henry Middleton's plantation at Goose Creek … went on to Thomas Broughton's, a distance of some 30-40 miles due north … met about forty Catawba Indians on their way to town."*[170]

*Thursday, 3 August*

From Broughton's plantation the duo, on 3 August, *"reached Captain Flud's, thirty miles away."* Here, writes Tennent, they spent the night *"noways agreeably owing to the noise of a maniac."*[171]

Meanwhile, in Charleston, Henry Laurens was preparing a reply to Col. Thomson's letter of 29 July, *"rec'd by the hands of Gilbert Gibson,"* a private in Captain Robert Goodwyn's ranger company. The Council makes clear, *"Respecting the movement of you Reg't … You are to be govern'd by their late orders,"* meaning the orders of 30 July to cancel the march to Charleston. Having also received word of the defection of Moses Kirkland, the Council now urged Thomson *"to be diligent and circumspect in placing to the bottom the late conduct of Capt. Kirkland, as well with the respect to the disbanding of his Company, as in the affair of the Gun Powder said to have been taken from Major Mason by his contrivance. If he has been faulty take the surest evidence of facts and acquaint the council minutely ... as the Character & honor of an officer is at stake, secrecy will be necessary to save both from slander if he is innocent."*[172]

In this same letter of 3 August the Council applauded *"The Rev'd Mr. Cresswell's endeavors on the part of American Liberty,"* asking Thomson to *"signify to him their sense of his zeal & good service."* Character and honor were respected virtues among colonial Carolinians; references to honor and duty in the service of liberty, as envisioned in the eyes of its revolutionaries, are sprinkled throughout their correspondence. Indeed, a fascinating insight into the Council of Safety's thinking along these lines is offered in this same letter of 3 August to Col. William Thomson as it comments upon the Colonel's earlier request for special treatment regarding his rangers.

The letter berates the negative attitude of Thomson's malcontents as unworthy of soldiers, pointing out that *"each man must have been fully apprized of his obligations before he enlisted ... what other judgement can be formed but that they are disposed to distress the Council in order to force a compliance with exorbitant demands ... if, after the repeated assurances given in full Congress by the Coll. & Major* [Thomson and Mayson] *together with concurrent declarations of several of the Captains that upon such Pay & such conditions as were stipulated, there was no room to doubt of filling the Reg't with proper Men & ... If after the fair & eager Enlisting in the service upon terms previously declared & universally known murmurs are heard amongst the men, against those very terms, what rule can the Council of Safety adopt for their guide. Is it not likely that if the present attempt should be allowed to succeed new demands would thereby be created & somewhat else would be found wanting to pacify Men who have marked no limits to their desires."*[173]

Council members felt they were being blackmailed and didn't like it. Continuing its diatribe, the Council's letter testily observes *"If they are in earnest & mean to serve their country the pay to the Rangers is ample & when compared to the no pay of the Militia in Charles Town who perform daily & nightly service in the same cause, it is superabundant."* In condemning the attitude of Thomson's men, the letter emphasizes that *"like everyone else, the Rangers must be patriots and lovers of liberty ... if they are void of such sentiments, how shall we depend upon them to Act with us as Brethren & fellow sufferers in one united struggle, against the Power which now bears hard upon the general Liberty of All America."*[174]

These soul-stirring words, written by Laurens in the Council's name, conclude by advising Thomson to *"admonish the officers & Men of the Reg't of Rangers to reflect seriously upon the cause & nature of their establishment ...*

*And the Council have further ordered me to signify to you Sir, that they have no legal authority to allow a separate Pay for provision to your Reg't: a fact which you cannot be ignorant of ... & they are of the opinion that the Honour of the officers are much concerned in this case."*[175]

## Friday, 4 August

While Thomson was being upbraided by the Council, Drayton and Tennent, enroute to his camp, reached the Amelia Township area, St. Matthews Parish, on the 4th, *"arrived at Col. T at half past seven in the evening ... the col. not home ... his absence softened by an agreeable family"*—as recorded by Tennent in his journal.[176]

Col. Thomson was still encamped at the Congarees, where he was awaiting Drayton and Tennent. Meanwhile, in St. Matthews, the missionaries *"spent some hours at Gaillard's and we flatter ourselves the visit had good effect."*[177] Such self praise would be repeated ad nauseam over the next few months as the duo traveled throughout the back country lecturing on duty and honor.

Tacitus Gaillard, age 65, was born in South Carolina. His father was one of the original Huguenot settlers along the lower Santee River. Tacitus had been a representative to the First Provincial Congress from St. Matthews Parish along with William Thomson. Previously he had served in ten Royal Assemblies, and was still reluctant to break with the King. Gaillard was also John Savage's father-in-law; this was the same John Savage who commanded the King's Militia Regiment of Ninety-Six, many of whose men reportedly signed Fletchall's counter-association memorial. Savage, who played no active role on either side during the second half of 1775, was ill most of the time and died before 25 September 1776.

The ill health of John Savage goes a long way toward explaining why active leadership of the Ninety-Six Militia, or what was left of it, fell to Major Andrew Williamson, considering that the Major's immediate superior, Lt. Col. James Mayson, was now a Major in one of the revolutionary government's three "regular" regiments. Rank would create a major [no pun intended] controversy between Mayson and Williamson over assuming command of Rebel forces during the Battle of Ninety-Six three months later.

It was also on 4 August that Thomson received Mayson's letter dated 30 July containing confirmation of the Polk resignation; as Thomson would later put it, *"the first certain accounts I had of Capt. Polk's disobedience."* All this new data would be relayed to Drayton on the following day when they met.

*Saturday, 5 August*

Upon leaving the Orangeburg area on the 5th, *"a little after six,"* Drayton and Tennent *"passed sixteen miles over the worst road I ever saw … owing to the steepness of the hills and gullies made by yesterday's rain …arrived at Col. Chestnut's, paymaster, and there found Col. Thomson with sundry officers of the Regiment."*[178] The Chestnut family ran the Congarees store located close to Granby. The missionaries arrived there late on Saturday afternoon, where Major James Mayson was among the "sundry officers" gathered there. Capt. Wise was off on a mission to North Carolina. His company, led by 1st Lt. John Donaldson, had not yet arrived. Capt. Purves remained at Ninety-Six, while Caldwell was at Fort Charlotte, and Capt. Goodwyn was not yet in camp. Along with Thomson and Mayson, Capts. Kershaw, Richardson and Woodward were on hand when the Council's envoys arrived.

Also on hand was Lt. Thomas Charlton, age 29, from Capt. Kershaw's Company. According to Tennent, Charlton had originally come down from Philadelphia—other records state that he was born in Maryland. His presence, however, offers additional insight into motivations and aspirations of young Rebels. Charlton, who wished to be named a *"Surgeon's mate,"* had joined specifically with that goal in mind. In writing to the Council on the 7th, Drayton *"begged leave to recommend Lieutenant Thomas Charlton, a man of experience and reputation in physics."* However, the request was denied and Charlton continued serving as a line officer.[179]

Upon consulting with Thomson and his officers after their arrival, Drayton and Tennent confirmed to the rangers that their parade march to Charleston had been cancelled. At the same time the envoys were alerted to a pervasive reluctance among the German settlers from Saxe-Gotha to side with the Rebels in opposition to England. In particular, many Germans were afraid that the rangers had been organized specifically to coerce them to join the Association, and they resented such tactics. But it was not only the local farmers who were disaffected.

As Col. Thomson had mentioned in his letter of 29 July many of his rangers were also griping. The Council, as we know, had responded harshly to the soldiers' demands but, due to a delay in communications, Thomson had not yet received the Council's reprimand.

*Sunday, 6 August*

When Rev. Tennent preached a sermon in camp on Sunday morning, his diary tells us that he still *"found some disaffected among the soldiers."* Consequently, *"Mr. Drayton harangued them and was followed by myself ... all seemed well satisfied ... we returned to Mr. Chestnut's about two miles. At midnight were alarmed by an officer from the camp, who, informed us that they had mutinied and were determined to go off in the morning. We agreed to let matters rest until then."*[180]

Meanwhile, on the 6th a message had been sent off to Capt. John Caldwell, under Major Mayson's signature, ordering him to make repairs to Fort Charlotte.[181]

## Monday, 7 August

To pacify the potential mutineers among the rangers, as well as to mollify the local populace, it was agreed *"to disband the rangers for a few days to take off the fears of the people."* When Drayton later reported the mutiny, he also remarked *"We have engaged Col. Thomson to order a muster of two Dutch [volunteer] companies in this neighborhood on Wednesday next [9 August]."*[182]

The timing of the furlough can also be explained by the fact that it coincided with upcoming elections for delegates to a new Provincial Congress scheduled for 8 August. It was also on the 7th of August that Drayton and Tennent, from the Congarees, sent their first report, containing more that 1700 words, to the Council of Safety in Charleston. Although signed by both men, the letter has all the imperious earmarks of having been drafted by William Henry Drayton. It was replete with overbearing self-esteem, pompous, self-assured, and dictatorially decisive, yet erudite in that intellectually superior tone that Drayton cultivated. One should keep in mind that both men, unlike their frontier peers, were indeed highly educated—Drayton at St. Balliol College, Oxford, in England; Tennent at the College of New Jersey [later Princeton University]. Both men had a tendency to patronize their back country colleagues—if not to view them with the disdain of social superiority. Drayton's tone remained consistently haughty throughout his reporting. But his pronouncements would also provide marvelous insight into people and events in the back country of South Carolina in 1775, as viewed through the elitist eyes of a low country gentlemen and self-appointed taskmaster.

In his report of 7 August, Drayton says *"We have declared if the officers disobey they shall be broke [reduced in rank]. This threat was highly necessary as the Dutch Captains had some little time ago disobeyed such an order ... we hope this step will oblige a part of the Germans to give us a hearing; and we flatter ourselves that our discourses to them will not be entirely lost upon them. We expect these will induce others of their countrymen to be willing to hear what we have to say.*"[183] The Orangeburg area was composed almost entirely of German settlers; consequently their allegiance to the revolutionary government was crucial.

As for the ranger troopers, continues Drayton, *"their complaints respecting provisions were entered into, and they were assured the public could not so much dishonour them as to imagine that they had enlisted merely for pecuniary gain, but persuaded that they were being actuated with a nobler motive … that they could not in honor of conscience, desire more than absolute necessaries, and that, if they thought it a hardship to go abroad [to forage] to procure provisions, the Council were ready to save them that trouble by deducting a reasonable sum from their pay, and supplying them with provisions in the manner in which the foot were furnished … they had grumbled about tents, and were now informed that the British troops in America … not only generally used but preferred huts made of bushes … finally it was recommended to them … to pay the most perfect obedience to their officers … to defend those liberties and rights which they appeared so willing to protect … the consequences of mutinous conduct only expose them to the derision of their neighbors and enemies, and to cover them and the whole corps with shame, contempt, infamy and ruin … if they should prove unworthy … they would certainly be brought to condign punishment, and other … more worthy rangers be found to supply their places."* In this same letter, Drayton states that he made it clear *"that if any desert, they would be seized, for a reward would be put on their heads—no money would be thought too much to ferret them out … and dead or alive they would certainly be carried to Charles-Town."* Such an appeal to honor and duty may have hit home for, as its young, radical, aristocratic author, all of 33-years-old, boasts: *"This discourse we flatter ourselves had a full effect."*[184]

In any case, the rangers were sent home to vote. The First Provincial Congress had expired on 6 August; elections for a second Congress were set for 8 August. Drayton's letter tells us that orders were issued for the rangers to muster again at Amelia on 18 August. He also states: *"Major Mason [sic] is likewise under orders to appear at the same time with Capt. Purvis' Company. For the Major's presence in 96 is of disservice to the public affairs."* Just what provoked such a negative outburst from Drayton regarding Mayson at this time is never made clear, although it may have been precipitated by Robert Cunningham's taking of the gunpowder from Fort Charlotte, brought out by Mayson and deposited at Ninety-Six three weeks earlier. It is clear only that a mutual dislike seems to have developed between Drayton and Mayson.

Equally, Drayton's alleged "disservice" with respect to Major Mayson may have been derived from the defection of Capt. Moses Kirkland as, in his long letter to the Council of Safety of the 7th, Drayton also reports *"we find that Moses Kirkland is gone from town to the Governor ... to procure proper authorities from Lord William to counteract and oppose the provincial proceedings ... he has been very active in poisoning the minds of the people ... greatly interrupt our proceedings to calm them."* But Drayton was not yet aware of Kirkland's proposed attack on Augusta, for his report seems concerned only that Kirkland *"answer for his conduct in disbanding his men."* Curiously, however, he is reticent to condemn Ezekiel Polk's desertion, commenting rather enigmatically *"we are presently silent."* He suggests that the Council *"fill up the Captain's Commissions for those two vacancies by promoting the two eldest first lieutenants."* John Lewis Peyer Imhoff and Charles Heatley were shortly thus promoted. In conclusion, Drayton offers a condescending *"P.S.—The Rangers perform their exercise at least as well as the Regulars in Charles Town."* The man was truly incorrigible.[185]

With respect to the ever present unease over loyalty and allegiance to the cause that permeated the minds of the leadership in Charleston in these trying times, one other nugget in Drayton's letter to the Council is worthy of mention. Before departing Charleston, Drayton and his council colleagues had been mulling over the request for a militia commission for Thomas Sumter. Drayton now offers an ad hoc opinion from the field: *"Mr. Sumter's application to the Council ... the Colonel readily approved not only of the measure, but of the man, notwithstanding Kirkland recommended him as his successor in the company of Rangers, which he has so treacherously quitted ... The Colonel ... from this seeming connection with Kirkland purposes to keep a sharp eye upon Mr. Sumter's conduct."*[186]

Thomas Sumter, age 41, born in Virginia, is the "gamecock" who would later play so important a role in defeating the British in back country skirmishes after Charleston's fall in 1780. But in 1775 he was still under suspicion stemming from his association with Moses Kirkland. The colonel who was to keep Sumter under observation was Col. Richard Richardson, in the Camden area. Both Richardson and Sumter had served as delegates to the First Provincial Congress from the District Eastward of Wateree River.

From this lengthy communiqué one finally learns that *"Mr. Drayton shall quit the Dutch settlements on Sunday next* [13 August] *after having had on Saturday a meeting ... at one McLaurin's, a storekeeper, hitherto an enemy, but now, at least in appearance, a friend."* Drayton *"will then proceed up the fork to Col. Fletchall's."* Tennent, on the other hand, will leave on Tuesday, the 8th, and *"proceed through the Irish settlements on the north side of Broad*

*River up to Rocky Creek,*" before eventually joining Drayton at Fletchall's camp. Drayton confidently adds, *"these settlements are numerous and ready to sign the Association ... we flatter ourselves that we shall one way or another meet with success."*[187]

A brash optimist, Drayton was certain that his persuasive powers, and those of Tennent, would win over the hearts and minds of settlers, even those living in the hostile territories where many had already subscribed to Col. Fletchall's anti-association memorial. Perhaps his optimism originated with the Fletchall letter of 24 July, previously intercepted and held back for Drayton's arrival in the back country. On 7 August, he simply sends it on, stating *"we have taken the liberty to open a public letter to Col. Laurens from Fletchall."* This is the letter, along with Drayton's of the 7th, that would be read by the Council of Safety on 11 August.

Clearly, William Henry Drayton was taking charge; there is nothing indecisive about him. Since arriving at Chestnut's store in the Congarees on 5 August he has branded Moses Kirkland a traitor—anyone connected to him is suspect; he has harangued the men of the Regiment of Rangers over honor and duty—anyone who doesn't obey orders will be apprehended, dead or alive; he has arranged meetings with the local German populace to explain the case against England—any militia officer who doesn't bring his men to the meeting on 9 August "will be broke." Drayton exudes complete confidence in being able to convince any hostile elements as to the justness of associating themselves in the American cause of liberty and freedom from British oppression.

On the other hand, we know that thousands of settlers between the Broad and Savannah Rivers were said to have subscribed to Thomas Fletchall's counter-association—reports from the area continue to be pessimistic. We know that Loyalists led by Robert Cunningham have already raided Ninety-Six and confiscated the Rebels' gunpowder previously taken from Fort Charlotte. We know that Capt. Ezekiel Polk was subsequently ambushed by Cunningham, and we know that plots are being hatched to attack Augusta and that efforts are being made to contact Royal Governor Campbell for help.

A head count of the rangers was attempted on 7 August. Of nine ranger companies authorized by Congress, only two had been raised in the upper area. Capt. John Caldwell, just short of a full company, was occupying Fort Charlotte. Capt. John Purvis' company was growing in strength, but still lacked half its complement. The companies of Capt. Moses Kirkland and Capt. Ezekiel Polk had deserted. In the lower area, south of the Broad River, the rangers fared better. Captains Samuel Wise, Robert Goodwyn, Thomas Woodward, Ely Kershaw and Edward Richardson had either filled, or nearly filled, their quota of 30 men, two lieutenants, two sergeants and an optional drummer boy.

From a *"Camp at Mineral Springs, near the Congarees,"* we also know that Col. Thomson submitted his listing of *"all officers, non-commissioned Officers, & Privates"* to the Council of Safety on 7 August, noting *"Capts. Wise, Caldwell & Purves have not yet furnished me with a return of their Companys, and as to Kirkland and Polk, you'll see by their own letters of their having deserted the cause as has also their officers and Men except Lieut Mitchell of Kirkland's Comp'y who I have desired to recruit more Men, & have also desired the other officers now with me to list men in order to have the two Companys completed again."*[188]

Consequently, having achieved a coordination of efforts, it was on 7 August that Drayton told the ranger captains: *"You are hereby ordered to give your men leave to go to their respective homes, and you are to order them to get their horses recruited and themselves properly equiped, and on the 18th instant you are to rendezvous with your company in Amelia, place known by the name of Flechall's old field, where you are to camp till further orders."* In short, Drayton had now effectively assumed command of the Regiment of Rangers.[189]

In comparing the Drayton and Thomson messages, it is worthwhile to note that Thomson views both Polk and Kirkland as deserters, while Drayton reserves judgement regarding Polk. Thomson's reference to *"Lt. Mitchell of Kirkland's Comp'y"* is somewhat odd. Other sources indicate that the two lieutenants in Kirkland's company were Hugh Middleton [who instigated the desertion] and Felix Warley [who remained loyal]. Warley became a 1st Lieutenant when Peyer Imhoff replaced Kirkland—Moses Vance became a 2nd Lieutenant. William Mitchell was a 2nd Lieutenant in Capt. Goodwyn's company.

*Tuesday, 8 August*

With elections pending and a respite in the offing, Lt. Lewis Dutarque of Capt. Richardson's company was sent off at 11:00 a.m. to carry Drayton's dispatch to Charleston. Dutarque, like Capt. Woodward, had been the butt of Drayton's scorn two days earlier when both *"attempted to inveigh against the cruelty of keeping men encamped without tents."* Like their fellow troopers, both were being chastised into obedience.

On this same day, as Tennent's journal records, he was preparing for his tour of back country settlements. Today he *"rode five miles to an election for the Congress, where they refused to proceed unless we should enlighten them. We found persons had come a great way to oppose the election … I harangued the meeting in turns until every man was convinced, and the greatest opposer signed the Association and begged pardon for the words he had spoken to the people."* Preening with success, Tennent returned to the Congaree store and was there when *"Major James Mason* [sic] *came through from Ninety six and gave many melancholy accounts."*[190]

Presumably hostility toward the Association was still strong around Ninety-Six, although James Mayson was himself re-elected to serve in the Second Provisional Congress, along with Andrew Williamson, LeRoy Hammond, Patrick Calhoun, John-Lewis Gervais, Richard Rapley, Francis Salvador, Champness Terry, Rev. John Harris and William Moore. All had served in the First Congress, except for Moore, Harris and Terry, who replaced Savage, Rutledge and Purvis.

Champness Terry, in his mid-40's, came from Virginia, like so many others. Five weeks after his election he wrote out his will and declined to serve as a delegate to the provincial Congress. Terry died by June 1777. He appears to have been the same man, however, who took notes at Thomas Fletchall's anti-association gathering at Fair Forest on 13 July. He had also served in the Forks of the Saluda Royal Militia as a major under Col. Robert Starke and Lt. Col. Moses Kirkland.

John Harris, age 50, was born on the Eastern Shore of Maryland and, like Tennent, was a graduate of the College of New Jersey. He had been transferred to South Carolina around 1772, where he became a pastor to the Fort Boone, Bull Town and Long Canes congregations.[191]

Little is known of William Moore's background. He did not take part in the "Regulator" movement of 1768/69. He was a member of the Committee to promote the Association in the Ninety-Six District; and also served with Mayson as a commissioner to oversee the storing of rice and flour for Rebel use in the Ninety-Six District. It is said that he died around 1791.[192]

On this election day, but irrelevant to it directly, a unique document with the dateline *"Chote 8 August 1775,"* was being drafted as a message to Alexander Cameron from the Cherokee Indians. For history enthusiasts it offers rare insight into Indian attitudes toward the escalating quarrel between England and America. The Cherokee letter was intercepted by *"liberty caps,"* and forwarded on to Charleston. How, when and where intercepted does not seem to be recorded. But the communication, in English, is reasonably literate, and may have been written by an Indian trader [probably John Bench].

It begins *"a talk from Indians to Alexander Cameron ... we are not a little alarmed to see our brothers the traders return without ammunition and it is not customary for them especially at this season of the year & we will be glad if you will inform us why a stop is put to our having that article which we have it not in our power to purchase clothing. What makes this circumstance more alarming is ammunition is likewise stopped from our younger brothers the Creeks. This we are informed by one of our chiefs who arrived here a few days ago from that country & are both of the opinion that we are equally imposed on. We have found in some measures that the Carolinians are the cause of this stopage ... in this case we see but through a small light but almost conclude that the people of Carolina have something bad at heart against us & as our Father the Governor has left us to follow the dictates of our own minds & what to us shall appear almost proper & knowing that the white people are our Elder brothers we are apprehensive that did we say anything disagreeable to ... them that is their intention to endeavour to trample us under their feet—they must think that it will be very disagreeable to us to hear that they have drove our Father Capt. Stuart from his house in Charles Town & you from your house at Long Cane, as you always gave us talks that were very agreeable to us & as we have no other friends to apply to in our necessities. Our great Father over the water was ever kind to us & gave us agreeable talks & we can't see what was in the people on this side of the water can have for quarreling with him & trying to drive his people away. As we thought good of him & all his talks. We will abide by him. The actions of the Carolinians are so contrary to our way of thinking that when we look towards Savannah we see a small light & believe the governor has some good thoughts of us, as he lets the ammunition come as usual which will further bind our friendship to him ... that the Bearer hereof is our friend John Bench we beg you will ... tell the Governour of Savannah that we wait impatiently to hear his Answer that we may know whether the Carolina People intend treading under foot as they have already ... & to serve our Great Father over the Water."*[193]

The original of this letter is mutilated along the edges and some words are difficult to read, but the substance is apparent. The Cherokees are alarmed; they believe that the differences between America and England are harming trade and negatively affecting their lives, and they desire that trade be re-established. If not, the letter implies that the Indians will blame the Americans [Carolinians], not the British, for this breakdown. This message, unwelcome news for the Council of Safety, would create considerable consternation when it became known. From its tone, moreover, the Cherokees were evidently unaware of the talk Drayton had given to the Catawbas one month prior, asking them to distribute it among other tribes.

# CHAPTER IX

## *Exploring the High Ground*

HAVING BEEN IN THE CONGAREES AREA FOR FOUR DAYS, DRAYTON and Tennent would now separate to cover different ground during their proselytization tour to recruit back country settlers to sign the Association in support of the American cause. To bolster their credentials, Drayton would be accompanied by the trusted Rebel, Joseph Kershaw, and Tennent would have the company of Col. Richard Richardson, both men from the Camden area.

*Wednesday, 9 August*

William Tennent's diary of this day tells us that he *"rode four miles to Mr. Beard's on the banks of the Saluda, a romantic situation—Col. Richardson accompanies me."*[194]

On the 9th, as scheduled, Drayton went on to meet with the Orangeburg Militia and people in Saxe-Gotha. He would write, later this day, to the Council of Safety, stating that *"During our dicourses, the falling tears from the audience showed that their hearts were penetrated, that we might hope for success ... in conclusion all who were present signed the Association, except for fifteen persons ... All persons joined in the election, which we judged it necessary to postpone yesterday and the day before, as no person appeared; and we judged we had authority so to do ... to compose the people by giving them an opportunity of electing Representatives after they understood the nature of the dispute."*[195]

The fact that no one showed up on the designated days of election, 7 and 8 August, is a good indication of the distrust in the area. Yet Drayton believes he has overcome local wariness with his speech on the 9th. By this time it also appears that the activities of Moses Kirkland have become better known through rumors circulating in the back country. Accordingly, in his report of the 9th, Drayton would enclose an affidavit as further evidence of

Kirkland's perfidy. No copy of this sworn statement has been found; we have only Drayton's word for its existence. But, in his report, Drayton elaborates: *"I shall not forget him in my return to Town, but this you will be pleased to keep secret; for if he shall be allowed to remain in the country after our return, our progress will have been in vain."*[196]

In this same report, Drayton now proposes economic sanctions against all those from the back country who send goods to Charleston without first having signed the Association. To coerce compliance, he recommends a *"constant guard of regulars be placed at the Town gates, to inspect and enquire of all wagoners from the Congarees, the fork between Broad and Saluda Rivers and Fair Forest, for certificates of their having associated."*[197]

While Drayton was laying down the law, Col. Thomson was pre-occupied by his own relations with the leaders in Charleston. Separately on the 9th, Thomson wrote to the Council of Safety: *"rec'd a letter from the President written by your orders."* This is the letter of 3 August which berates Thomson over the complaints of his men. Thomson also acknowledges awareness of orders canceling the march to Charleston and the authority of Drayton and Tennent over his Regiment of Rangers. Groveling a bit, Thomson concedes that the complaints of the rangers have been satisfied by Drayton's speech which *"has been of great service."*[198] Col. Thomson was not a man to make waves.

At this same point in time, 9 August, a letter was being drafted by George Galphin, the Provincial Congress' newly appointed agent to the Creek Indians. When received by the Council of Safety, and reviewed in conjunction with the correspondence to Cameron from the Cherokees, it would increase apprehensions regarding relations with Indians. Galphin's letter was actually addressed to Georgia's Council of Safety in Savannah. In the division of responsibilities among the revolutionaries, Georgia had jurisdiction over Creek affairs. A copy of the letter was later forwarded to Charleston by the Savannah Council.

Born in Ireland, Galphin had settled on the Carolina side of the Savannah River at Augusta. He begins his letter to Savannah acknowledging having been *"appointed by the Gent' of the committee in Charlestown to be a Committee of correspondence for the Creeks ... they had settled that point with you, and you were to take the Creeks under your care & they were to take the Cherokees & Catawbas under theirs."* It now appears that a shipment of goods and ammunition to the Creeks from Savannah has been stopped, greatly alarming Galphin, as he had promised this shipment to them. He warns the Council *"I always take care to avoid telling the Indians a Lie & that is the reason they put so much Confidence in me, for Once they find a person tells them lies*

*they never put more confidence in him Afterwards. Any person that advised the
Stoping the goods from the Indians knows nothing of Indians and are not your
friends for once they find the trade Stoped from them it will not be in the power
of any Man to keep them Peaceable Longer ... if any person has a design of setting
the Indians upon us it will be a fair opportunity for them to gain their point."*[199]

This sage psychological insight into Indian mentality would come back
to haunt the Rebels. But Galphin had additional intelligence to offer. He had
been consulting with his neighbors *"Mr. Hammond & Mr. Zubly"* who were
aware of rumors concerning an impending attack upon Augusta. Galphin
assumes that Savannah is also *"aware of the danger ... from one Fletcher ...
against them with Seven or Eight hundred men."*[200]

This ominous information from Galphin would later be relayed from
Savannah to Charleston, along with Kirkland's letter of 31 July. But from
Galphin's intelligence it was Fletchall [Fletcher] and not Kirkland who would
be leading the attack. News of a similar nature may have been contained in
the affidavit that Drayton had sent to Charleston on the 9th. All of these
rumors would generate alarm among Council members.

Meanwhile, on the British front at the same time, one is offered a glimpse
into their northern problems, which will have an effect upon southern strategy, or lack thereof. On 9 August we find General Gage finally penning a
reply to Governor Campbell's plea for help sent on 1 July. Gage, responding
in curt fashion, called the governor's attention to extensive casualties suffered by the British at Bunker Hill, concluding: *"I fear a long and bloody war
between Great Britain and the Colonies."* He offers no hint of help whatsoever
to Campbell. In fact, General Gage has been pre-occupied with the American
invasion of Canada which began on 27 June; he had no troops to spare for
South Carolina. Surprisingly, the Royal Governor of South Carolina would
not receive this message until three months later, when he refers to it in a
communiqué to London dated 1 January 1776.[201] In the meantime, Carolina
Loyalists and Rebels were left to battle it out between themselves, without
official British interference. Their struggles for allegiance would take place
primarily in the back country, where the majority of Carolinians now lived.
Civil war now seemed imminent.

*Thursday, 10 August*

In the back country on this day we find William Tennent crossing the
*"Saluda River in the early morning ... traversing the Fork."* He met with a
guide *"at Fur's ford, on Broad River,"* as well as with *"some disaffected men,*

who became converts by proper arguments." The reverend is ever the optimist. These particular converts were skeptical about the value of the new bills being issued by the revolutionary government. Tennent soothed their fears—"we gave them gold for them … then reached Capt. Woodward's of the rangers after sundown." He refers to Woodward as "an honest man who informed me that his Company had universally signed."[202]

## Friday, 11 August

Having spent the night at Woodward's, Tennent left in the morning to journey northward along the eastern bank of Broad River, where he continued to meet with "refractory people … obstinately fixed against the proceedings of the Colony", but " … after much pains brought over some chiefs" and local militia "to cheerfully subscribe to the Association."[203]

With messages and rumors now flying between the low country and back country, coordination of Rebel strategy and tactics at the Charleston end became rather complicated. On 11 August the Council of Safety drafted a letter to Col. Thomson, but withheld transmittal until the 13th when a second message was prepared. The letter of the 11th criticizes Thomson for not revealing "that Capt. Polk & his Company of Rangers had renounced the cause of liberty & abandoned their duty … affairs of such moment should be Communicated by Special messenger & without delay."[204]

The tone of this letter, signed by Henry Laurens, President of the Council, is one of anger and frustration. But is Thomson at fault? Polk's defection was reported by Mayson on 30 July, received by Thomson on 4 August, passed on to Drayton by Thomson on 5 August, and alluded to by Drayton in his letter of 7 August to the Council. Evidently the Council had not yet read Drayton's message prior to drafting its rebuke to Thomson. The fly in the ointment seems to be, as Laurens states in his letter, "the Council have been informed [of Polk's desertion] by a private Letter … by one of your officers to Mr. Gervais." Such personal correspondence, out-of-channels, is precisely what tended to throw bureaucratic discipline to the wind. In this case it created an atmosphere of suspicion and distrust. Ever sensitive to slights, such laxity annoyed Laurens, who now scolds: "to this disagreeable tiding," was added the irritating matter of the Kirkland letter of 31 July "relative to … dangerous attack threaten'd upon Augusta."[205]

The Council had just received word of Moses Kirkland's plot from its counterpart in Savannah. Laurens enclosed a copy of Kirkland's intercepted letter for Thomson's perusal. In the name of the Council of Safety he requested the colonel to take action—to contact the commanding officers of all volunteer militia groups in his area and be prepared to *"raise as many Volunteer as may be necessary. In a word the council rely upon your Zeal & good conduct in this dangerous conjuncture, when it is impossible for them to give explicit orders, and they will expect to hear from you by return of this messenger ... & as frequently afterward as there shall be occasion."* The Council was close to being in a state of panic. Thomson could not have been pleased to be dumped on in this manner. As an afterthought, Laurens snaps: *"You know what will be proper to be done with Capt. Kirkland when practicable & safe."*[206] Laurens was no longer concerned with "character and honor" as he was one week earlier. But Col. Thomson would not receive this message until 18 August.

Meanwhile, on the 11th, William Henry Drayton, as he reported in a letter dated the same day, *"left the Congaree store and proceeded to a Dutch Church about ten miles higher up Saluda"* where he gave his discourse *"to the congregation consisting entirely of Germans."* Before them he employed *"many texts of Scripture"* and gave reasons why sanctions on *"trade and communications with non-subscribers ... was not any force put upon them. To my great surprise only one of the congregation subscribed to the association."* According to Drayton they had been *"perverted"* by the non-subscribers who had attended his meeting at Saxe-Gotha two days earlier. He now discarded the velvet glove of scripture and began waving the sword, declaring *"that no miller who was a subscriber, should grind wheat or corn for any person who was a non-subscriber. This gave an immediate shock, and has given a general alarm among the Dutch, from which with some other operations I expect a desirable result."*[207]

Drayton's anger over German refusal to associate in common cause was compounded by the fact that some officers of the Orangeburg Militia had ignored orders to muster on the 9th, but agreed to meet with Drayton at the Dutch church on the 11th. They reneged. Frustrated, Drayton was provoked into writing a nasty complaint to Godfrey Drehers of the *"committee for carrying into execution the Continenal Association in the Saxe-Gotha District."* His note, dated 11 August, gives one a flavor of his fury and displeasure with back country Carolinians' misunderstanding of, or lack of concern with, the crisis that faced America's founding fathers: *"Dear Sir—Captain Shrams has not attended ... neither has any of his company come to us, altho this place was of the Captain's own choosing. This disobedience to Military orders ought not to go unnoticed for fear others seeing so criminal a conduct pass with impunity, they should be encouraged to imitate a behavior that may lead to ruinous consequences. I therefore think it would be proper immediately to let Captain Shrams know that you recall his commission & discharge him from his command & take measure to call the company together & influence them to elect a Captain, who will receive a Commission from the council, Your presence will greatly facilitate this work, & their choosing a Captain will naturally I hope lead them to sign the association. But do not mention this affair to them till after they have chosen their Captain. We have had very bad success here today & I declared that no Mills shall grind flour & no dealings shall be had with any non-subscriber.*"[208]

While Drayton was running into resistance among the Germans, his good friend and Council colleague Arthur Middleton took up pen to brief Drayton on events in Charleston. The tone of Middleton's letter, dated 11 August, beautifully depicts an elitist view of class distinction and admirably captures prejudices of the period. Case in point, Middleton writes: "*your letters from the Congaree Store were opened ... I am sorry to hear you have been under a necessity of exercising your abilities upon the soldiery by sermons and harangues—I wish you may not have thrown your jewels among swine ... Fletchall's letter promises nothing favorable ... I confess I have not the slightest hope of your succeeding in that quarter; my opinion is, that we shall at least be obliged to have recourse to your device and motto 'Et Deus Omnipotens.'*" [Here Middleton adds a sketch of an arm with drawn sword].[209]

Fletchall's letter had been read at the Council meeting on 11 August. Middleton's pithy reaction to it would be sent to Drayton along with the Council's more formal message, also dated 11 August. An archetypical intellectual and low country aristocrat who epitomizes the sophistication of privilege, Middleton's words provide readers with a precious glimpse into Charlestonian thinking—and the place to which back country planters have been relegated in the low country scale of social strata.

The Council's letter, less picturesque, states: "*inclosed you will find Copies of three letters the Contents of which are very alarming—ne dated the 6th inst. From the Committee at Augusta to the Council of Safety at Savanna—one from that Council dated the 8th to the council of Safety in Charles Town & the third from Capt. Moses Kirkland to his late Lieuten't Middleton [Hugh] which are recommended by the Council of Safety to your particular attention.*"[210]

The letters from Savannah had reached Charleston only on 11 August. One week later, as Laurens again wrote to his son in London, we learn that one of these enclosures to which Laurens referred contained "*an account ... imputing that a certain somebody whose name I don't recollect was marching at the head of 200 Men of Fletchal's band in order to lay Augusta to ashes.*"[211] This tallies with Galphin's earlier comment. But the person whose name Laurens can't remember is probably Thomas Brown, a Loyalist Georgian from the

Augusta area—one of the "gentlemen of fortune" to whom Mayson referred in his letter of 30 July to Thomson.

Meanwhile, in the Council's letter of 11 August addressed to Drayton, President Laurens tells his emissary: *"I have by order of the council & by the bearer of this written to Coll. Thomson & inclosed to him copies of the above mentioned letters ... Coll. Thomson is enjoined to exert his utmost endeavours for the Interest of the general Cause in this dangerous conjuncture & to avail himself if possible of your advice—if you are in the Neighborhood of his Camp he will lay before you his instructions, which from necessity are general, & the council of Safety being perfectly satisfied that you will leave nothing undone that shall appear to be necessary have not charged me with any particular direction to trouble you with ... I flatter myself with hopes that your success in the main business of your journey will be found to have anticipated our wishes & and that the intelligence from Augusta will prove unbottomed ... P.S. you know what ought to be done when practicable with Safety in the case of Kirkland."*[212]

The instructions to "leave nothing undone" will be interpreted by Drayton as *carte blanche* authority to act unilaterally, as he pleases, with respect to military action. This interpretation will lead to subsequent conflict between Drayton, Thomson and the Council of Safety in Charleston.

*Saturday, 12 August*

As events unfold before Charleston's eyes, Drayton, disappointed by the German rejection yesterday, was ready to make an effort again on the 12th. He *"proceeded into the Fork Between the Broad and Saluda river to McLaurin's where I had a pretty large meeting of Germans ... here I did not procure one subscriber. McLaurin threw a damp upon the people, as did some other leaders whose names I have taken down."*[213] Once more Drayton met with opposition, motivating him to start a blacklist—a record of recalcitrants for future retribution. In truth, the Germans were not so much inclined to oppose the Rebels; they simply wished to remain neutral in this internecine fight between Americans over their allegiance.

While William Henry Drayton was left swallowing his bitter disappointment at McLaurin's place, the Rev. William Tennent was to be found further north around Sandy River, a tributary of the Broad River 45 miles from the Congarees. Here he came across *"a part of Col. Neal's [sic] Regiment laid contiguous to Mr. Tim's Tavern."* Tennent arranged a rally, for the following day, of local settlers at Rocky Creek, and invited the companies of Col.

Neel's militia regiment to attend. Messages were sent to *"Captains Martin and Richard Sadler ... and to Mr. Fisher, all on Fishing Creek."*[214]

## Sunday, 13 August

Tennent's rally took place at the Rocky Creek Meeting House with *"some hundreds of the inhabitants,"* as he would record in his diary. He *"harangued them at large ... supported by Richardson. The heat almost melted me ... but I had the pleasure to see all the people eagerly sign the Association fully convinced of the necessity of it."* The good reverend also provides the reader with an amusing picture of prevailing conditions in the back country with respect to sleeping quarters, as he mentions *"the fury of the little inhabitants of the bed. After a sleepless and wet night, I was shocked by the blood and slaughter of my callicoed shirt and sheets in the morning."*[215]

Leaving Tennent to his bedbugs, we find people in other quarters catching up with rumors and hearsay. On this same 13th of August it seems that *"Jonathan Clark, resident upon the banks of Saluda river in the Cherokee country ... conversed with John Garwick, an intimate friend and countryman of Alexander Cameron, Deputy Superintendent among the Cherokee Indians ... touching the danger of the Cherokees commencing hostilities."* The conversation, later reported to Drayton, is mentioned in Clark's sworn affidavit taken on 21 August. In sum, Garwick told Clark on 13 August of a meeting Cameron had with 400 Indians in *"the last week of July ... and did all he could to influence the said Indians to join the King's forces against the people of Carolina."*[216]

At the same time that Garwick was telling his story to Clark deep in the back country, Arthur Middleton, in Charleston, was again keeping his friend William Henry Drayton informed about Council debates. Under the name of Andrew Marvell, a pen name he often used when offering commentary to local gazettes, Middleton, on 13 August, wrote to his coy mistress in the countryside. Marvell agrees that: *"The affidavit* [which Drayton had enclosed with his letter of 9 August] *proves Capt. K* [Kirkland] *a seditious, rebellious son of a b*[itch]*, and the letter declares Capt. P* [Polk] *not to be one of the best of folk ... for God's sake as you come down sweep the chimney of the State, or we may shortly have a bonfire."*[217]

Such erudite punning, pompous but delightful, shows that Middleton is also highly perceptive of the dangers of increasing hostility in the back country. In general, he agrees with Drayton's actions and writes that *"the proposal of having wagoners examined ... will be taken up the first time we have leisure for considering it ... I have mentioned your request respecting the vacancies in the Regulars ... blank commissions are all forwarded to Thomson by this conveyance ... I also ... urged the necessity of entrusting you with blank commissions for Volunteer Companies on the back of Fletchall, and with some difficulty carried my point; so that the President will inclose you six setts; it is expected, however, that you will have the resolution of congress strictly complied with before delivery of the Commissions, I mean as to the associating of fifty men and the election of officers, and that you will bring down with you copies of such associations and lists. The Continental congress strongly recommend the dividing the militia of each colony into regiments or battalions. If we should carry that point in Council, it will be a means of diminishing the influence of Fletchall and every scoundrel like him in the colony."* Vituperation in Middleton's attitude toward Fletchall is palpable. After reading his letter, he says the Council condemned Fletchall for *"abusing authority vested in him as a Justice of the Peace ... a weighty argument ... in your discourses among the poorer sort."*[218]

Regarding the question of volunteer militias, activists such as Arthur Middleton had to argue diligently for them against more conservative men like Henry Laurens, who felt that Rebels were moving too far too fast. Revolutionary Carolinians were far from unanimous about the extent to which the mother country should be opposed by military force when peaceful reconciliation was still a possibility. Five years later, after Charleston had fallen, the war against the British would be waged and won in the back country almost exclusively by volunteer militia groups led by such men as Andrew Pickens, Francis Marion and Thomas Sumter—men who played minor roles during the growing pains of military buildup in 1775.

Another of Drayton's pen pals in Charleston was Peter Timothy who, along with Arthur Middleton, provided out-of-channels intelligence on the contemporary scene. In his letter of 13 August, Timothy offers news of clandestine Loyalist activities. He suspects *"Robinson is coming to town, and I think it will not be amiss to have a look out for him, as well as the man you have mentioned,"* namely Kirkland, who was thought to be on his way to see Governor Campbell.[219]

Joseph Robinson, by this time, had become the suspected link between Col. Fletchall and Governor Campbell. Indeed, it was probably Robinson who brought Fletchall's message of 19 July to Charleston and he may well have been the courier who returned with the Governor's reply of 1 August. Speculation about enemy activities was becoming rampant in Charleston; meanwhile the Council's missionaries in the back country continued in their dogged pursuit of converts.

Having been twice disappointed at previous meetings, Drayton now reported, on 13 August: *"On Sunday I intended to have been at another place of Divine worship, but when I got near, I found Summer … a leading man in the neighborhood"* deliberately planned to be absent and *"by his absence manifested a dislike to what I came about … I thought I might save myself the mortification of preaching to a people who were obstinate and would not hear."* Both Kershaw and Drayton agreed it best to move on. *"We made the best of our way from that stiff necked generation to this place* [King's Creek] *… I may pronounce the Dutch are not with us."*[220]

Back in Charleston, the Council members continued issuing their instructions. The record shows that a letter dated 13 August was addressed to Col. Thomson, with enclosures for Drayton and LeRoy Hammond. Thus both Thomson and Drayton were to receive packets of instructions dated 11 and 13 August respectively. In its letter of the 13th to Thomson, the impatient Council of Safety waspishly nags: *"from the total silence of yourself and Mr. Drayton upon the expected attack upon Augusta we are willing to hope, that our friends have been cautiously alarmed."* Council members had no way of judging how this danger was perceived by Drayton and Thomson in the back country—or even if they were aware of it. Hence the enclosure, a *"Letter for Capt. Hammond which we request you dispatch by special Messenger."*[221]

Hammond lived in an area on the Savannah River just above Augusta. The Council was anxious that he and his neighbors be apprised of any danger but, as we know from Galphin's letter of 9 August, Hammond was already aware of an "imminent attack." The unavoidable time lag in communications made it inevitable that a constant gap in intelligence sharing would exist among Carolina's revolutionary leaders, which made the formulation and implementation of policy to advance the "cause" haphazard at best.

# CHAPTER X

## *The Crusade for Association Continues*

ETWEEN 13-22 AUGUST, BACK COUNTRY MOBILIZATION EFFORTS WERE beginning to fall into place. Lieutenants John Lewis Peyer Imhoff and Charles Heatly were promoted to the rank of captain, each with his own company, in the Regiment of Rangers. Moses Vance was made a 2nd lieutenant retroactive to 1 July. Six additional blank commissions, as per Middleton's suggestion, would be received by Col. Thomson with the usual caveats offered by a sarcastic Henry Laurens who, in his letter of 13 August, cautions: *"this is an extraordinary measure which we have consented to in the present unsettled state of your Regiment, hoping that by a discreet distribution of these Commissions the Company's will be filled up by good Men & that the Public may reap some advantage from the vast charge which has already been incurred by that establishment, but it must not be drawn into Precedent."* The prudent Laurens was still annoyed, not only over the escalating cost of maintaining Rangers with dubious return, but also over the miscarriage of the Council's order of 30 July, the letter Thomson claimed not to have received. A substitute copy was now enclosed with the admonishment, *"the original we believe went by the Hands of Capt. Woodward & ought to be inquired for."*[222]

Woodward, it will be recalled, carried Thomson's letters of 22 July to Charleston, where he remained for a week before being given messages to tote back to Thomson. One of these was the 30 July order to cancel the march to Charleston. One also learns that, on his return trip, *"by the Hands of Capt. Woodward we have sent the sum of five thousand Pounds for the Payment of the Rangers."* Woodward may have lost the letter, but the money was safely delivered—as would be reflected in the regimental return of 29 September 1775.

Additionally, in his letter of the 13th, Laurens tells Thomson, tongue-in-cheek, *"It affords us some satisfaction to learn by Your Letter of the 9th that the remaining Rangers were Content & Perfectly disposed to do their duty, we hope that disposition will be lasting, the effect of a true sense of their duty & not the transient product of an harangue."*[223]

In taking stock of the two months that have elapsed since the First Provincial Congress adjourned and the Council of Safety assumed its role as the *de facto* revolutionary government of South Carolina, a "true sense of duty" meant one thing to the Council, and quite another to those colonists who still felt that legitimate government was represented by the King's Governor, Lord William Campbell. There were thousands of honorable people, in both the back country and the low country, who couldn't decide which way duty lay or on whose bandwagon they should jump. Ironically, political opportunism was often the deciding factor in doing the "right thing." In the process of choosing sides, back country settlers were nearing a showdown. The Council of Safety sensed this, as is evident from the tone of their advice to William Henry Drayton.

Having digested its first communiqués from Drayton and Tennent [messages of 7 and 9 August], the Council, in its letter of the 13th, bravely replied to Drayton *"sensible of your Zeal & Diligence … rejoice to hear that your endeavours have been so far crowned with success."* Still concerned over personal allegiances, however, the Council suggests: *"it may be best to postpone the consideration of a Military appointment for Mr. Sumpter until your return or till we more clearly understand what Duty he proposes to take upon himself."* The Council was still cagey about Thomas Sumter's past connections with Moses Kirkland, who was currently their public enemy #1. The letter to Drayton now advises; *"You were probably misinformed of Capt. Kirkland's intention of coming to Charles Town—the copy of an intercepted letter which you will receive [Kirkland's letter of 31 July to Lt. Middleton] shews that he was to have attended an Election at Cuffee Town on the very date of your Letter [of 7 August]—such a Watch is set as will not suffer him to pass unnoticed … We desire you will spare no expense to secure & have him brought hither if that can be done."*[224]

The anxiety exhibited by these words would have a disturbing effect on Drayton, who would be in the area of King's Creek when he received the Council's message. It would be equally disturbing to Tennent, in the area between the Broad and Saluda. Most of all it would affect Col. William Thomson who, closest to Cuffey Town, would be asked to investigate. Cuffey Town was located between the Savannah and Saluda rivers approximately ten miles north of the present county seat of Edgefield. For Kirkland to be active in this area, so close to Augusta and Fort Charlotte, was a frightening prospect.

*Monday, 14 August*

Enjoying better success than Drayton, we find the Rev. Tennent *"laying the foundation for a company of volunteer rangers"* in the District Between the Broad and Catawba Rivers adjoining the New Acquisition District. With pride he notes in his journal that *"Robert Allison, Esq., undertook to enlist and swear a hundred men to be ready at a moment's warning, and to be at the command of the council of Safety ... enlisted three more volunteer companies at which the Ministerial heroes were much chagrined ... had desultory talk with a collection of the most staunch of Fletchall's friends."*[225] These friends included Robert Cunningham and Thomas Brown.

It was at this stage that the reverend once again met up with Drayton at the Enoree River. The character and personality of Drayton begins to emerge more clearly now, as he is forced to come to terms with rising belligerency among Loyalists—although neither Drayton nor Tennent are fully aware, as yet, of Kirkland's machinations. The Council's letters of 11 and 13 August won't catch up with them until 20 August.

*Tuesday, 15 August*

Drayton's spirits must have risen slightly at this point, as is evident from his report to the Council dated 16 August, when he speaks of reaching *"Hendrixs' mill, upon Enoree ... yesterday I had a pretty large gathering ... and I gave a discourse which was generally satisfactory ... the people expressing their pleasure and readiness to sign ... Cunningham was at hand, and he hoped that the people would stay and hear what he had to say ... I was to be made a public disputer in spite of my teeth. Cunningham arrived and I asked him and his company to a dinner ... after dinner I took Cunningham aside and spoke to him seriously and politely; all was in vain."* Clearly local residents were undecided. While the crowd was still collected, Thomas Brown, *"a Scotchman* [sic]*, took out Dalrymple's address from the people of England to the people of America; which he may have received from Lord William Campbell."*[226]

This 12,000 word pamphlet had only lately made its way to America. It had been written by Sir John Dalrymple at the request of the British government. Dalrymple is the same propagandist who, *"at the request of the best of Princes, some time ago wrote and published his Memoirs of Great Britain and Ireland,"* in which he denounced Irish patriotism, as he now denounced American patriotism.[227]

Brown's reading evoked mixed feelings from the Council's crusaders in the back country. In his diary Tennent commented that *"The pamphlet sent over by the Governor has done much damage here, it is at present their Gospel ... it seems nothing can be done here ... people have been industriously taught ... that no man from Charles Town can speak the truth, and that all the papers are full of lies. Some angry discourses between Brown and Drayton sent us to bed."*[228] In his version of the gathering, Drayton proudly observes: *"I so answered the whole, that the company rejoiced, and Cunningham had not one word to say in reply. The people are perfectly satisfied, and I am heartily glad this pamphlet was produced for people have heard both sides of the question and the general conclusion is—that Cunningham is beat out of the field."*[229]

The true effect that Dalrymple's words were having upon the people at large undoubtedly lies somewhere between the Tennent and Drayton versions. Local settlers were still suspicious of the Charleston elite. However, after his experience with the German settlers, this encounter in Cunningham territory on the 15th seems to have renewed Drayton's self confidence. It showed in his letter of 16 August to Charleston in which he tried to balance the scales.

*Wednesday, 16 August*

All his activities since 11 August were reviewed by Drayton in a letter sent to the Council of Safety on 16 August. His comments provide insight into the residual misgivings that remained among back country farmers. For example, he divulges that on 7 August, *"at the day of election the people of this part of the fork assembled at Ford's, on Enoree, to choose representatives ... a letter from Cunningham, Kirkland, and others arriving, the election was quashed ... I have given notice there will yet be an election in the lower part of the Fork, and that I have appointed one to be holden on the 24th."* In a postscript, Drayton suggests that his answer to the Dalrymple pamphlet be printed *"and copies sent into the country, it would have a good effect."*[230]

Like Tennent, Drayton was worried over the effect of Dalrymple's words on the undecided settlers—in spite of his claimed debating success over Cunningham and Brown. But his suggestion for publication would die on the vine when the men in Charleston, led by Laurens, thought it supercilious. Meanwhile, Drayton now informed his peers that he was about to set off to Colonel Fletchall's headquarters for the crucial encounter.

Other back country events were also taking place this day. Alexander Cameron, on 16 August, wrote to Andrew McLean, an Indian trader in the Augusta area. Intercepted by Rebel forces in Augusta before reaching its destination, the letter was forwarded to Drayton approximately one week later. He in turn would forward it to Charleston on 24 August with a cover letter. Cameron's letter, dateline Keowee in the Cherokee Nation, discusses a visit from Occonostatah Indians who are *"cross about the usage their father [John Stuart] met with in Charles Town … they see plainly that the white people mean a war with them, and they will be glad to know, if they intend it this winter or next spring … they are to a man resolved to stand for the great King and his warriors."* A second item in the Cameron/McLean message would be equally disturbing to the revolutionaries in Charleston, as Cameron observes: *"About Long Cane the people begin to change sides. The people see their error and are determined to stand in support of law and government."*[231] This assessment is contrary to Williamson's report of 14 July.

These words, when they reached Rebel leaders in Charleston and the back country, would raise the stakes in the game of "association." Meanwhile the time was approaching for the Regiment of Rangers to muster in Amelia on 18 August, as previously agreed.

*Thursday, 17 August*

The Council of Safety's packet of information, drafted on the 11th and 13th, reached Col. William Thomson in Amelia on the 17th of August. Its contents would galvanize him into action. A joint message from Col. Thomson and Major Mayson was immediately sent to Major Andrew Williamson, along with the Council's letter for LeRoy Hammond. Under cover of his own letter dated 21 August, Williamson then sent the Hammond letter to Capt. John Caldwell at Fort Charlotte in order to be forwarded. In his response dated 22 August, addressed to Thomson and Mayson, Williamson writes: *"Dear Gentlemen—I received your favor of the 10th instant the express to Mr. Hammond from the council of Safety, I immediately sent to him, also at the same time wrote to Captain Caldwell advising him to be on his guard."*[232]

The packet received by Thomson on the 17th also contained messages for William Henry Drayton. These, too, were immediately forwarded to Drayton who was now in Col. Fletchall's territory. They would be received by him on the 21st at Lawson's Fork.

Writing to John Lewis Peyer Imhoff, Thomson tells him: *"This day I rec'd from the Council of Safety a Captains Commission for you. On recep't hereof you will wait on me in Amelia in order to receive the same. In the interim & on your way, you may enlist Men for yourself."* Meanwhile, writing from Amelia, Col. Thomson left *"general orders … to the sev'l Capts of the Regt. Of*

*Rangers ... Charles Heatly will shew you your place of Encampm't near Fuguetts old Field & the form you are to camp in ... you will order out of each Company every Day sufficient Grass Guards & Fitague Men. I am order'd on a Tour to the Beaver Dam near little Saluda."*[233]

Beaver Dam was 45 miles distant from Amelia, located in the vicinity of Cuffee Town, where Kirkland had last been sighted. Thomson had been ordered to investigate, and was gone until 21 August. Meanwhile Major James Mayson would be touring the countryside on a recruiting trip with Capt. John Purvis. Other ranger companies, except for Caldwell at Fort Charlotte, were ordered to muster in Amelia. Momentous events were beginning to take shape, actions which would shortly affect the rangers.

For the moment, on this same 17th day of August, William Henry Drayton *"reached Col. Fletchall's ... Thursday morning before breakfast, and there I found Brown, Cunningham and Robinson, who had arrived the evening before, as had Mr. Tennent and Col. Richardson."* After breakfast, as he later reported, *"we engaged Col. Fletchall in a private conversation during near three hours,"* before being joined by Fletchall's counselors. Dayton and Tennent spent two days with Fletchall at Fair Forest, after which Drayton would make a full report on 21 August from nearby Lawson's Fork, saying: *"We endeavored to show him that we had confidence in him. We humored him. We laughed with him. Then we recurred to argument, remonstrance and entreaties to join his countrymen and all America."* But Fletchall *"insisted he could never take up arms against the King, or his countrymen, and that the proceedings of the Congress at Philadelphia were impolitic, disrespectful and irritating to the King."* Fletchall also admitted to have been in correspondence with Governor Campbell—that Robinson *"brought up a letter."* Robinson admitted that he had a commission from the Governor *"to raise men for the King."* This comment vexed Drayton, who declared in exasperation that *"this man's looks are utterly against him."* Appraising the other men, he comments: *"Much venom appears in Cunningham's countenance and conversation ... but Brown is the spokesman and his bitterness and violence are intolerable."*[234]

Thomas Brown's bitterness had a legitimate foundation. A few months earlier, according to local historians, *"he had indulged himself in indiscreet censure of the Revolutionary party. He had done worse—he ridiculed them. Apprised of the resentment his conduct had excited, he attempted to escape, but, closely pursued, he was brought back to Augusta ... sentenced to be tarred, feathered and carted unless he recanted and took the oath of allegiance to the new government. Browne [sic] was a firm man and resisted with a courage which should have commanded the respect of his persecutors. But the spirit of the mob was aroused, and after undergoing the painful and mortifying penance prescribed … he was doomed to have his naked feet exposed to a large fire … at length turned loose by his tormentors, who were surprised when this simple Indian trader reappeared an armed, vindictive, and implacable enemy."*[235]

Thomas Brown, however, was not a "simple Indian trader." The son of a wealthy English merchant, Thomas has come to Georgia in 1774, where he was awarded an extensive land grant in the Augusta area and made a magistrate by Governor Wright. Brown and his servants established Brownsborough in St. Paul Parish above Augusta. He was 23 years old when he tangled with Drayton who complained that, in their meetings of the 17th, Brown tried to provoke him with insults. But, ever the incorrigible authoritarian, *"in a firm tone I severely checked him,"* reports Drayton. Before their meeting broke up, however, it appears that Fletchall agreed *"to call out his regiment on the 23rd inst … at the same time and place of election at Ford's."*[236]

Fletchall's attitude sounds rather conciliatory, but Tennent, in his own letter to the Council, dated 20 August from Bullock's Creek, disparagingly comments *"we have at length visited the great and mighty nabob Fletchall. We found him surrounded by his Court, viz: Cunningham, Brown and Robinson, who watch all his motions and have him under great command. We soon found the unchangeable malignity of their minds and the inexpressible pains they were at to blind the people and fill them with bitterness … But we surprised him into a promise to assemble the regiment next Wednesday."* After the encounter with Fletchall, Rev. Tennent traveled back to the upper part of the fork between the Broad and Saluda rivers, whereas *"Drayton is gone up to his iron works, and to the people about Lawson's Fork."*[237]

## Friday, 18 August

Ezekiel Polk, who defected from Major James Mayson's camp at Ninety-Six on 28 July, reappears in the chain of events once more. As Justice of the Peace in the New Acquisitions District, he took an affidavit from a man named Zacariah Bell. This same Bell *"swore that, walking near the house of Col. Fletchall, he heard one of six or seven men in a group say that a person, whose name he did not hear, was to go within ten days to seize upon powder— the deponent could not hear the name of the place"* at which the robbery was to take place. But the statement was taken *"near Fair forest"* and given to the Rev. Tennent, who enclosed it with a cover note to Drayton. It was forwarded to the Council by Drayton on 21 August, wherein he says: *"I inclose a letter from Mr. Tennent to me the day we parted at the Colonel's."*[238]

*Saturday, 19 August*

The parting of Drayton and Tennent did take place, but not before they had spoken with Ezekiel Polk. In Tennent's journal, he states; *"Capt. Polk came now."* In Drayton's words *"Polk came to us, appeared much concerned for his past conduct, attributing it to a mistake touching upon the station of the rangers, which he had thought had been by the Congress fixed to the back country and frontiers. He has since been active in our favor as a person of influence in his part of the country on the back of Fletchall; his brother is a man of great influence in Mecklenburgh* [North Carolina]*, and ready to march to our assistance when called upon."* Because Drayton now viewed Polk as someone needed *"to quash Fletchall's expectations ... it is absolutely necessary"* to give Polk permission *"to raise an additional troop of rangers to immediately lie on the back of Fletchall ... we have given Captain Polk such a lesson, which he has received with all due submission, as I believe will render him more obedient to orders, than he has been."*[239]

Ezekiel Polk was now restored to the good graces of the revolutionary forces. When their talk with him ended, Tennent rode back to Tims' Tavern and Drayton left for Lawson's Fork—but not before *"dispatching an express to the commanding officer at Fort Charlotte, and directions to Major Williamson, to throw into the fort a reinforcement of thirty militia ... the garrison here will now consist of seventy-odd men."* He also advises the Council of his orders, adding *"I have also given Major Williamson directions to hold the militia in readiness to march in case of any commotion."*[240]

This flurry of activity was generated by the affidavit taken by Polk and Robinson's cryptic remarks about raising forces under the Governor's commission. Tennent was *"no longer doubting of the infernal design to take Fort Charlotte by the Governor's order."*[241]

And where does the Governor stand? Coincidentally, on 19 August, Lord Campbell was writing his own discouraging report to London: *"I am still in hopes of hearing from General Gage and the Admiral soon,"* a reference to his letters of 1 July to which he has not received replies. *"Since my arrival here I have seen Georgia a Province at present of the last consequence ... warped from its duty by a very insignificant internal faction aided by the people in this Province. The friends of government here have been so sunk, so abandoned to despair for sometime that it is hardly possible to make them believe the British Nation is determined to assert their just rights over the colonies ... Sorry am I to find myself unable to protect or assist the King's loyal subjects here, it is a cruel mortification."* In the Governor's opinion, the Rebels have been *"amassing great quantities of warlike stores, ammunition particularly, which they can easily do as there is not Force by Sea or land to prevent them."* He encloses a letter *"received from Colonel Fletchall with my answer ... Regiment of Horse to be raised in the back country ... I am told the levies there have been much checked by Fletchall, Robinson and one Cunningham mentioned by Colonel Fletchall in his letter who is a very active man and remarkably spirited."*[242]

Conspicuously absent from Campbell's dispatch, as he was from the meeting in Fair Forest, is Moses Kirkland. He does not seem to have had contact with Fletchall. Nevertheless, fears persist among Rebels that Kirkland might still attack Fort Charlotte or Augusta. The Rev. William Tennent, in particular, was quite apprehensive.

### Sunday, 20 August

*In reporting to Henry Laurens on the 20th, Tennent wrote: "I discovered on my way, a scheme to surprise Fort Charlotte and take all the powder and arms away. Took an affidavit [Bell's statement] and sent it express to Mr. Drayton, so hope it will be prevented. The Governor has undoubtedly given orders for it, and they are privately enlisting volunteers to the service ... I shall this morning privately obtain affidavits to prove that Major Robinson has attempted to enlist many in the King's name ... they think that they are nearly ripe to show themselves, and make no scruple to threaten the whole province with devastation in a short time. They say that Cameron is among the over hill Cherokees and will soon join them with 3000 gun men. I have just heard that the lower towns will not join them, but confess that the over hill Indians are preparing to fight for the King ... In short your friends in town are preparing a great dish of blood for you, and expect soon by their army not only to have an asylum to fly to but to bear down all before them. This both you and I have prophesied many times, but a lethiferous slumber seems to have sealed the eyes of some of our brethren ... Robinson assures the people here that a great multitude in town of those who have signed the association are in the scheme and will join them upon notice. I am now convinced that a certain affidavit which some have despised, is with a small exception true, in every particular. There is here all the appearance of a hellish plot." In a postscript, Tennent cautions Laurens: "if you do not keep a look out, these people and savages will receive ammunition by wagons from town."*[243]

The "despised" affidavit to which the cleric refers is that obtained from Elizabeth Simpson in Charleston on 11 July. Not stated in his letter but mentioned in his journal, dated 20 August, Tennent divulges a meeting with 100 people assembled at King's Creek on this day, where his speech in support of America was undercut by *"two gainsaying Baptist preachers ... who disssuaded all but ten of the gathering from signing the Association."* Consequently, when these same non-associators asked Tennent for help in obtaining *"powder to defend themselves from the Indians,"* he self righteously refused to *"try to do something for them"* until they signed the Association. *"This I hope will have its influence."*[244]

Tennent has a flair for the melodramatic and tends to panic easily, but his reports give the reader a taste of the rumor mill continually grinding in the back country. Truth was a slippery thing to grasp, and this would create even more consternation among the Charleston leadership with respect to its Indian policy. There, on the same day that Tennent was filing his report, Henry Laurens was writing to his son John in London—Laurens' letters are indispensable as rational judgements of the mood in South Carolina.

Despondent over military organization, he tells John: *'I am frequently told that there is no prospect of our receiving greater advantages from the 1st & 2nd Regiment of Regulars, as they are Stiled, than from the Rangers ... these people cost us now upwards of 150 Pounds Sterling Per Day ... I informed you some time ago that one Company of our Regiment of Rangers had disbanded themselves, that was Capt. M. Kirkland's who was himself at the bottom of the plot & we have made Such discoveries as will probably bring him to Death if he can be Seized—Since then another whole Company with their Capt. E. Polk at the head, have followed the example & the remaining Seven Companies are true Carolina Rangers ready to receive the Public Money & determined to follow their own Orders ... the Council of Safety have had much trouble with them, forced to coax & at last Suffer them to make their own way—this is no more than I foresaw & against which I forewarned my Country Men."*[245]

On the Indian question, not being inclined to the Tennent view, Laurens writes: *"Our Cherokee Indians according to advices we have just received ... are well disposed towards us—they blame King George ... for quarreling with his children about 'the leaves of a tree'—they say 'he is foolish ... why does he not see that the people in America don't love it ... if they did, would they have thrown a whole shipload of it unto the sea,' and they moreover 'think it very hard that the King will not give us powder & bullets & blankets because we won't drink his tea.' They wonder too at the attempt to make Men 'slaves by pieces of paper'—meaning Acts of Parliament, they can form no idea of the possibility of making the Americans drink 'the Leaves of a tree'— 'give their money for Nothing'— by means of writing upon Paper over the Great Water—their Brothers they say 'would be foolish as old Women to mind paper'."* With greater concern, however, Laurens points out that the Indians *"lament the Scarcity of Gunn Powder &*

*Bullets.*" But pragmatically he concedes "*it would not be consistent with sound policy if we were just now to supply them with those articles.*"[246]

Laurens does not divulge the source of his information about the Cherokees, although he seems to be quoting from a letter—perhaps one received from Edward Wilkinson, the Rebels' agent to the Cherokee Nation. Unfortunately, nothing to verify such speculation has come to light. In any case, Laurens was by this time privy to the "talk" sent to Cameron by the Cherokees at Chote, dated 8 August, and intercepted by the Rebels. Such thoughts aside, it is fascinating to hear the Indians metaphorically allude to the Boston Tea Party. More meaningful, however, is Laurens' comment that it would not be "sound policy" to arm the Cherokees. This attitude would change within six weeks; the seeds of change would be planted by Drayton's communiqué of 21 August.

### Monday, 21 August

Having parted with Tennent on 19 August, Drayton went to visit his ironworks some miles north up the Tyger River at Lawson's Fork. This was close to Indian country in what is now part of Spartanburg County. From Lawson's Fork, Drayton reported to the Council, covering events from 11 August. Commenting upon the Clark affidavit [see 13 August], Drayton writes: "*you will see that there is no dependence upon Cameron. I have sent up a short talk to the Cherokees inviting them to come down to me within twelve days to Amelia.*" This "talk" was to be transmitted to the Indians through Richard Pearis, an Indian trader living in the area. Drayton tells the Council that Pearis has been directed to "*conduct six of their head men to me ... and I should be glad within the time mentioned to receive from you 70 Pounds or 80 Pounds worth of shirts, watch coats, blankets, linen, strouds and paints,*" with which Drayton hopes to win their allegiance.[247]

Presenting gifts to Indians was normal procedure but, if one is to believe Richard Pearis, it was more than the Indians' allegiance that Drayton hoped to influence. Pearis would subsequently accuse Drayton of an attempt to swindle the Cherokees out of land at Seneca for his personal use through the use of these same government gifts. This accusation, later made in a deposition of 11 November, when Pearis turned Tory, would set in motion an acrimonious rebuttal from Drayton. For the moment, however, the Pearis deposition serves another purpose. It confirms that, on 21 August, Pearis, "*at the plantation of Capt. William Wofford ... did meet with the Honourable William Henry Drayton,*" and that Drayton "*did tell the Deponent that he*" *wanted very much to see some of the Indian Warriors and asked the Deponent if he would Bring Them to see him at Col. Thomson's—saith that Mr. Drayton Did give the Deponent a letter of Talk for the Indians, which he was to Explain to them that the purport of that letter was to desire the Indians to meet him at Col. Thomson's & to inform them that Cammeron [sic] Deceived them."*[248]

Indians aside, in his current letter of 21 August, Drayton tells of plans to attend the election and to review Fletchall's regiment *"at Ford's, at the mouth of Cedar Creek on the Enoree,"* on the 23rd. Pensively, he admits, *"I do not expect any success; I apprehend some insults … within twelve days I purpose to be at Colonel Thomson's camp, where I think it advisable that I should remain till I shall see every spark of insurrection extinguished … I shall regulate myself by your orders on the subject."* Much depends on the state of affairs with regard to Moses Kirkland. Therefore Drayton, who has apparently become obsessed with the man, warns: *"if Kirkland shall be seized, without doubt a commotion will follow, and if he goes off with impunity … it will be fatal to the discipline of the army—especially the rangers."*[249]

This assessment of the situation in the back country clearly conveys a mood of pessimism and apprehension. Drayton recommends a hard line stance against anyone who opposes association: *"Vigorous measures are absolutely necessary. If a dozen persons are allowed to be at large, our progress has been in vain, and we shall be involved in a civil war in spite of our teeth. In giving you this information, I tell a Melancholy truth; but I do my duty … if certain persons should be secured, some commotion, in all probability will follow, but I am so well acquainted with the situation of the disaffected parts of the country and with such parts that may be brought against them, that I am under no apprehension for the consequences, provided prompt and vigorous measures attend every appearance of insurrection. I would beg leave to observe, that as this business is of the highest importance, so your orders on the subject, must be clear and general, to vest proper authority, to take such measures as may tend to suppress this threatening insurrection, that will assuredly break out by delay and come upon us unexpectedly … Perhaps my being arrived at the camp [Amelia] in my return home, may be construed as an expiration of the powers vested in Mr. Tennent and myself, and his return to Charles Town may work an annihilation of powers, to be exercised by us together. For, as our continuance in the country will be of little benefit in the Dutch settlements and the disaffected quarters while inder the influence of Fletchall's people, so I make no doubt but that Mr. Tennent will choose to return to town, sensible that his presence in the country will not be of any advantage in the way of expounding our political texts to the people. I have the honor to lay all these things fully before you, that you may regulate yourselves thereupon, and send orders to me at Amelia by which I shall either remain with the camp or return to Charles Town. But I pray you to be expeditious, for a delay on your part will allow the enemy to recover many of our converts; and I know they are active, malicious, and bent upon mischief."*[250]

Drayton's fears are explicit; the propaganda mission is failing. Vigorous measures must be taken immediately to apprehend Loyalist ringleaders—people such as Fletchall, Kirkland, Robinson, Brown, Cunningham—who must be dealt with forcibly. To do so, Drayton needs a clear mandate of authority, especially if Tennent returns to Charleston. The time for palaver, Drayton intimates, is over. Joseph Kershaw and Col. Richard Richardson have already returned to their homes. As Drayton admits, *"they could not, in these parts, be of any assistance."*

Political differences among back country residents over breaking away from England were becoming more acrimonious. Families such as that of William Wofford, at whose home Pearis and Drayton met, were becoming divided. Wofford, originally from Maryland, settled in the back country of South Carolina in the 1760's, establishing an iron works in the vicinity of the Tyger and Pacolet rivers. William had only recently been elected to serve in the 2nd Provincial Congress; his son, Benjamin, remained a leader in the anti-association movement and would later be jailed along with many other followers of Fletchall.

Others, such as long time friends Ezekiel Polk and Joseph Robinson, fellow officers under Col. Thomas Neel in the New Acquisitions District Militia, were also feeling the moral and ethical pressures of separation from the mother country. Because it remains one of the very few letters of its kind from a Carolina Loyalist in 1775, and because it bares his soul, Robinson's letter to Polk is herein offered almost in its entirety. Written four days after Drayton had met with Fletchall, and on the same day that Drayton was drafting his own report to the Council of Safety—the 21st of August—it reads:

*"Dear Sir ... my sincere compliments to you and Madame Polk—Great are the Convulsions Of this Country & particularly of this Province, which I am Infinitely sorry for! ... that Verbal Communication between us should cease is dissatisfactory. It is of Great unhappiness to me that I cannot persuade my Conscience to approve of the Present Measures ... Ever since a short time after I enjoyed that interview with Col. Polk at your Dwelling House."*

*"Especially since a conference with Col. Moses Kirkland Esq I have had no occasion to borrow a Pair of Political spectacles to Detect a Division in the Prime Intentions & Machinations of some of the Principal Leaders of your Party—how*

*the Dose works in some of the Southward Colonies Distant I have not Learned Sufficiently. But if they have Cut as deep in their Pockets in the same Ratio, like symtoms will be produced … but all are smothered by the picture of General Unanimity—The Chapter began with lies and so continueth."*

*"The first thing that offended me was that I must be fed with second hand lies touching the unanimity of the Colonies & their Miraculous Success at Boston … & that I must be amused with the Pacific idea of an Accomodation, a thing much dreaded by some of those Gentlemen if they would Plainly tell their deluded Countrymen … that they do in fact, fight against the King, Desire an Ultimate Separation, & are to be Lords in these New States, to lay off the Country into Manors, have the Taxes paid to themselves & to be Lords, Knights … at the expense of their poor countrymen's blood … that there were above forty hundred of the Bostonians Slain in all at the time of the Battle of Bunker Hill & that they … i.e. the Americans, left six cannon of their Battery & Entrenchment charged."[251]*

One cannot help but pause over so harsh [and mistaken] an indictment, accusing revolutionary Carolinians of wanting to create a land of lords and manors at the expense of their poor countrymen's blood. Was such disdain held in common by back country farmers? Not likely—yet Robinson's accusation was a reminder of the Fundamental Constitution of Carolina dated March 1669, wherein the charter actually authorized the establishment of nobility, the creation of hereditary ranks, manors and manor lords. The eminent American historian, Wesley Frank Craven, once observed: *"The elaborate political and social structure outlined by the proprietors, however absolute may have been the terminology of the document itself, clearly intended to serve as ultimate rather than an immediate objective … the effort to transplant into America the feudal usages of England's rural society may seem foolish in the light of previous and subsequent experience … let it be noted that the effort did not prove a complete failure; though landgraves and caciques in Carolina showed an early disposition to drop the title … many of the conventions of aristocracy took root."* Craven suggests that the *"aristocracy of later Carolina"* may have been *"distinctively American … it must also be admitted that the aristocracy envisioned in the proprietors plan … to award large acreages with contingent responsibilities and prerogatives to selected individuals was a very practical promotional device."[252]*

The year 1775 was "later Carolina" and, for Robinson, these criteria— "conventions of aristocracy" and "prerogatives to selected individuals"—still seemed to apply to the low country elite in Robinson's mind. For the past 20 years, as another historian reminds us, *"the low country elite had been consolidating their privileged positions."[253]*

To be fair, Joseph Robinson believed that such elitist authoritarians existed not only in South Carolina but in the north as well, where misguided revolutionaries were attempting to force independence and "association" upon others under false pretenses. Thus, continuing his letter to Ezekiel Polk, Robinson writes: *"the Nothward Gentlemen do feed the southward ones on lies and after they have showed it awhile it is delivered to their tools as Proper Political food for our poor deluded People ... Dear Sir, be not offended & in the deepest Cordiality I Declare myself not only Ready to serve you in honor, person & Family, But also my Country. I understand those people [Council of Safety] have sworn Extravagantly against me, oath upon oath, that I intended to enlist all kinds of Enemies against the Congress ... I cannot help what Prejudiced People say or swore against me. I do averr that I never did, nor intend to Tamper with Indians, Negroes or the Devil against my Rebellious Countrymen ... I should be infinitely glad to see you on this important occasion, but am sensible of my Danger; the Consequence is known to me. Every step of it if I am taken it will cost some Person a pretty Dear price if Circumstances will permit of it. I make free to Invite you to at least a solemn Consideration of the Natural circumstances of this Province Before you—you will be engaged with Enemies shortly & I dareth not & greatly fear Viz. Christian & Savage, External, Internal & Fraternal. Good God! For what? Nothing at all."*[254]

Robinson closes on a somber note: *"I think I understand the subjects of Difference in the great Debate ... it will be much to the honour of Col. Kirkland that when he Detected the Poison he Departed—you are a Gentleman of Sense, & I am sorry to part with you. I know not the minute when I shall set out on the Path of spirits to unknown climes—you will do me perhaps this last favour, if you blot out my name from the book of Death. I confess the Epistle may appear Contemptuous. But please Sir, Not to attribute the least thought of it to yourself, it never was imagined. I am with great Esteem and Particular Regard yours ... Joseph Robinson ... Broad River ... August 21, 1775."* In a postscript, he adds: *"I cannot think that you will ever lift arms on this occasion ... I would wish you knew as much on the other side of the Question as I do ... my enquiry is not who is the Wronged Party, but who is in the Right?"*[255]

This is a troubled man. Saddened though he may be to lose a friend such as Polk, Robinson seems ready to stand by his convictions. He attributes treachery not to the King but to misguided Rebels who would assume authority at the expense of the people. The ingenuous nature of Robinson's distrust over motives of low country Rebels is striking—as is the degree to which he admires Kirkland. The extent of contact between Robinson and Kirkland from the time Kirkland left the rangers on 28 July is nowhere made clear. Polk, too, was supposedly influenced by Moses Kirkland, which is why he deserted the rangers, according to Major James Mayson. But three weeks later, Ezekiel was as easily influenced by William Henry Drayton to return to the Rebel fold. Whether the Robinson letter made him waver once again is not known.

These were trying times for many in the back country whose politics were not yet defined. Robinson's soul searching, Drayton's pronouncements, and Polk's indecision all reflected the dark clouds mounting over the back country. Insurrection seemed imminent, Indian intentions were unknown, and rumors of attack against Augusta or Fort Charlotte persisted. Contact between the governor and his back country supporters, although marginal, bolstered Loyalist confidence and made Rebels uneasy. These accumulating fears began to imbue revolutionary leaders in South Carolina with a sense of urgency—a need to nip in the bud any cohesive counter-revolutionary movements. To force compliance with Rebel policy, a strict imposition of trade sanctions would have to be adopted.

Trade with Charleston was a bread and butter issue for the back country planter. Word of the revolutionary government's intention to restrain trade had spread since Drayton initiated the idea in his earlier letter to the Council. Now, on 21 August, he again encouraged more of the same to force the malcontents into line. In addition, he also warns the Council of double dealing: *"In particular, I must earnestly recommend that no more goods be allowed to be sent up to McLaurin's store. His partner in town is one McCurry, or Curry ... This man has signed the Association, and under this sanction, he means to supply McLaurin, by which means the Dutch will be encouraged to persevere in their obstinacy. And I beg leave to caution you even against McLaurin's signing the Association, if he should think proper to do so to procure goods; for the Dutch agree, if there should be a necessity, that he should be allowed to subscribe, and then they would be supplied as usual without acceding to the Association."*[256]

On the same day that Drayton wrote his lengthy report to the Council of Safety, on the same day Robinson addressed Polk, Andrew Williamson was taking action. Writing from his plantation home, Whitehall, located 10 miles west of Ninety-Six village and approximately 20 miles from Fort Charlotte, he penned a response to the first of the communiqués he had received regarding rumors of an attack upon Augusta. On 21 August Williamson wrote to *"Captain John Caldwell, Commandant at Fort Charlotte ... I just received a letter from Col. Thomson and Major Mayson, dated the 10th inst [sic]. At the Congarees, informing me ... of a body of men ... headed by some of the disaffected about Stephen's Creek, to attack Augusta ...They desire me to give you every intelligence for the defence of Fort Charlotte, that you may be on your guard. I have heard nothing as yet of the above report, but you may depend upon it that if ever they make such an attempt they will have Fort Charlotte in their view."*[257]

As a precaution, Williamson offered Capt. Taylor and his company, from Williamson's militia regiment, as reinforcements for Fort Charlotte. Williamson also suggests that Caldwell send a scout to Stephen's Creek to assess the situation. Stephen's Creek lies 10 miles south of the fort, in the region between present day Edgefield and McCormick—an area in which Kirkland was thought to be operating. In making this suggestion Williamson provides a glimpse into the emerging military attitudes toward protocol and authority as he adds, *"Excuse me taking the liberty of dictating to you."*

Williamson, as a militia man, had no authority over a regular officer. Such concern indicates that he was quite sensitive to status in these early days of military buildup. In another situation a few months later, under different circumstances, Williamson would be less accommodating when differences of opinion arose between himself and Major Mayson.

While Andrew Williamson was writing to Caldwell, Col. Thomson returned from his own scouting tour of Beaver Dam. The record shows that on 21 August he was back in camp at Amelia penning a note to his new Captain, John Lewis Peyer Imhoff, requesting that the Captain *"as soon as possible … inlist 30 private Men—2 Sarjeants, and a Drummer. As soon as you have listed ten Men, you will send them to camp."*[258] Evidently, in the four days that had elapsed while Thomson was on tour, none of Imhoff's company had yet appeared.

*Tuesday, 22 August*

Williamson, still at Whitehall, wrote a second letter, replying now to the Thomson/Mayson communiqué of the 17th. As previously stated, he confirms: *"Gentlemen … I received your favour of the 10th instant. The express to Mr. Hammond from the council of Safety, I immediately sent to him, also at the same time wrote to Captain Caldwell … I have heard nothing of any Body of Men going to attack Augusta …"* In addition he reports, *"I this day heard from Mr. Drayton directing me to reinforce Fort Charlotte with Militia, which I am now giving orders to do."* In this same letter, Williamson passes the news to Thomson and Mayson that Drayton is to address Fletchall's regiment on the 23rd, observing that Drayton *"has some opinion that they may use violence to his person … if that should be the case, I shall endeavor to have the Militia under my Command, to march whenever he may be carried a prisoner. I have sent this day a Young Man whom I can well depend upon to be at the Meeting tomorrow.*"[259]

This intelligence from Williamson may be the first that Thomson and Mayson received regarding developments in the back country since Tennent and Drayton left the Congarees two weeks earlier. In closing his report, Williamson compassionately adds that he *"shall acquaint Mrs. Mayson that you are well."* Within a week Mrs. Mayson would be dead.

Meanwhile, having mined a rich lode of information from the back country during the past ten days, Charlestonians were in a good position to re-evaluate recent developments from a townsman's perch of privilege.

# CHAPTER XI

## A View From the Top

ON THE 22ND OF AUGUST, PETER TIMOTHY—FRIEND, COLLEAGUE and advocate of Draytonian adamancy in support of forced unity— sent Drayton a brief news report from Charleston, confirming that the governor's dispatches of 19 August were carried off by *"the Eagle packet which sailed yesterday."* Their contents were unknown, but Campbell's attitude of late must have been stirring uneasiness among Rebels. Timothy, who had doubts about the Council's indecision, comments: *"What to say about sound policy. I am at a loss; it does not seem to have been well defined. This week will be spent in matters relative to our election. The merchants ... at a meeting today, either have, or will, nominate ten of their body to represent them in the ensuing Congress. At a previous meeting they proposed fifteen for their quota, then twelve, and at last condescended to be content with ten. The Germans have taken an alarm, and had a meeting—and the mechanics are not thoroughly pleased; they also will have a meeting this week in regard to war and peace—but the Noblesse are perfectly pacific."*[260]

Echoing Timothy, Arthur Middleton, on this same day, provides additional insight into the aristocratic mindset. He writes to Drayton, saying *"I have received the Orders of the Council to acknowledge the receipt of yours of the 16th ins't by Elias Lindsey; they are greatly obliged to you for your unwearied Diligence in the Publick Service, lament that your Success has not been more general, & sincerely wish you may be more fortunate at your future Gatherings ... The mode you have pursued relative to Elections is entirely approved of—The letters from the Council to you & particularly one of the 11th ins't are so full upon most points, that they do not recollect anything just now necessary to recommend to you for your Government upon progress, & they confide wholly in the good understanding & Discretion of yourself & Colleagues. Your messenger has been paid, according to your Desire, tho' the Treasury leaks so fast that 50 Pounds is looked upon as a great deal of money."*[261]

The rate of seven pounds currency to a pound sterling was in effect at this period. The courier, Elias Lindsey, was a Rebel sympathizer who resided in the upper reaches of the Broad and Saluda Rivers, near King's Creek. This is where Drayton had written, on the 16th, regarding his failure to convert the German populace, before going on to see Fletchall. John Lindsey, his brother, had been a representative to the First Provincial Congress from this area. Another Lindsey, James, would side with the Loyalists in the next few months.

Continuing his letter, Middleton consoles Drayton for his lack of success with the Germans, but cannot long refrain from intellectual sarcasm. The rest of his letter is quoted at length because it so well characterizes elitist low country feelings of superiority over frontiersman and offers the reader much to reflect upon: *"So much for the Council ... & now a slice entre-nous ... As I expected you have not hitherto made many Proselytes, & I am sorry to prophecy that you will not meet with much more success, at the same time I wish I may be set down in your memorandum Book, as a false prophet ... I am certain both you & the Dr. [Tennent] would do much more good by your Harangues in the Senate House, than by Field-preaching, notwithstanding the watry Eyes of the Mynheers & their Frows ... but to be serious, lasting Effects are not to be expected from any Operations on the passions; Emotions quickly rous'd are as soon allay'd—arguments to the purse strings will have much weightier impressions, especially among the Hounhununs; in short pray come down soon, for you are much wanted, both of you, I really believe your absence is very agreeable to the cool, dispassionate, timid, lukewarm, disinterested, disaffected, &c. &c. &c in short all who are will'g to make a retrograde progress."*[262]

With respect to Hounhununs, I am indebted to Frederic G. Cassidy of The American Dialect Society, for pointing out that *"Arthur Middleton had in mind the Houyhnhnms of Gulliver's Travels but confused them with the Yahoos, which he seems to have meant. The Houyhnhnms ... were the horses with reason, whereas the Yahoos were human-like in form but brutish beasts in their conduct."* This is indeed what Middleton had in mind in his description of German settlers in the back country. As a literary snob, Middleton was undoubtedly familiar with Jonathan Swift's novel, first published in 1726.

On the subject of "non-associators," the scholarly Middleton turns to allegory in siding wholly with Peter Timothy in his disdain toward those who oppose the revolution. If necessary they should be intimidated into compliance. But, *"all is mum as yet respecting our mighty doings with Non-Associators ... however, W.W. will have full leisure to get a compleat insight into the Nature of vegetation, & the Art of Agriculture—The Tory fishing Club is broke up, it is thought dangerous for them, as the hurricane season is approaching."*[263]

Such double meaning and innuendo is typical Middleton—literally, hurricane weather was approaching, a potentially destructive force; figuratively, a hurricane of revolution against British authority was also en route. Tories, like W.W. [William Wragg] should know this and take care. Wragg, a venerable old Charleston Tory, was a man of integrity in the eyes of moderate men such as Henry Laurens. He found it contemptible that a man of Wragg's stature should be treated in so shabby a manner by men like Middleton, who suggests that Wragg be exiled to his farm and garden in the country.

In this same letter, Middleton scathingly observes: *"Milligen has taken himself off; his flight was precipitate; he skulks between the fort* [Johnson] *& the Tamar* [British gunboat anchored in the harbor]; *I don't know that he had any pressing necessity for such a Manoevre, but undoubtedly he longs to be a great man, & by this step has begun his Career of Glory; probably he has an unconquerable Dislike to the mode of Cloathing lately adopted in these scarce times, & by no means wish'd to be exalted in this damn'd pot of a Country, but would rather a high place in Scotland."*[264]

Dr. George Milligen, Chief Surgeon to his Majesty's forces in South Carolina, was one of the 21 Charleston royal officials refusing to sign the Association. All would be condemned, on 23 August, by order of the South Carolina General Committee, as inimical to the liberties of America.

Continuing in his facetious style, Arthur Middleton derisively writes: *"Our Great, noble, & most Excellent Governor, has found out a mode of talking over some of our Statesmen: he wheedles, & assures, & reasons, & cries like anything, & how is it possible to withstand such reasoning; Mr. J.S., the Lt. Gov'r according to the old woman is a very good friend to this Country, & has nothing at all to do with politicks. Mr. I is a very good man, he loves the Governor, & the Governor loves the Country, ergo—you may draw the Conclusion—there is however one unanswerable argument in favour of this Connexion of the Noble Lord, that his Lordship cannot possibly do without him."*[265]

One needs hip boots and a Middleton thesaurus to wade through his meanings, but the "old woman", "Mr. I," is most likely Alexander Innes, Secretary to the Governor. J.S. is James Simpson, Attorney General for South Carolina, a relative and confidante to Campbell.

Mention of Governor Campbell's wheedles refers to a recent incident still fresh in the memory of Charlestonians. On 11 August a slave, Jemmy, was condemned to death by the Rebels for alleged implication in a plot of insurrection. Campbell opposed the sentence and self-righteously appealed to the Council of Safety for justice. The Governor still considered himself to be the *de jure* head of government in the province; thus, decisions regarding capital punishment fell within his prerogative. A spate of communications was traded between Campbell, Innes and Laurens on 17 and 18 August concerning Jemmy, before he was pardoned on the 18th. Moderate revolutionaries, such as Laurens, still had respect for the Governor's authority. Nevertheless, Laurens, in his letter of 17 August, had been careful to point out: *"I understand the unhappy Man in Question was found Guilty after a fair Legal trial, that the Justices and freeholders were unanimous in their opinion of his Guilt—In the Calamitous Situation of this Colony under the threats of Insurrections, strong proofs of which the people are possessed of, no wonder they are alarmed at the Sound of Pardon to a Man circumstanced in all respects."* [266]

The fear of black insurrection in Charleston is more clearly understood when one reflects that the city's white population numbered only 5000, compared to 9000 slaves. The threat of insurrection from the inside, along with potential Indian attacks on the outside, made many Carolinians uneasy in 1775.

Arthur Middleton, in his long epistle of 22 August, now waggishly concludes, *"I could write you more but our friend P.T.* [Peter Timothy] *writes by my side, & I am sure his accuracy will leave nothing untold—he tells me he has wrote you nonsense but as you are in the back woods, anything will do for you."* In this same humorous vein, Middleton offers, *"My best complim'ts attend the Lord-High-Admiral* [Tennent] *… pray ask him when he intends to turn his Coat, & cry out with patriotick fervour 'Divinity lie there.' He is generally known in Town by the name of the Firebrand parson."*[267]

Although Drayton's message of the 21st had not yet reached Charleston, Timothy independently echoed his own observations over deception regarding trade sanctions. His letter of the 22nd to Drayton shows awareness of the McLaurin/Currie connection. Timothy records that *"Yesterday the Committee of Observation stopped McLaurin's wagon; it seems he is in partnership with one Currie, now in town. Currie is much blamed, and begs to leave the goods unsold … till he goes up and brings down McLaurin's name subscribed to the Association … offers to give security … and if he does not succeed, to send the wagons' loads back."*[268] Evidently the policy of trade sanctions was working.

Meanwhile, on this busy day of 22 August, there was movement elsewhere. In Boston, Admiral Graves finally replied to Governor Campbell's plea of 1 July for help. His message, like that of General Gage, would not reach Campbell until sometime in November. But it was not encouraging: *"So far as being able to encrease the number of King's ships at South Carolina, I am under the necessity of ordering the Tamer hither. Your Lordship may have been informed of her very bad condition from Capt Thornborough and the almost impossibility of her remaining any longer on service without the greatest risque."*[269]

This would be demoralizing news for a man who had led his Loyalist followers in South Carolina to expect reinforcements from the north. Meanwhile both Rebels and Loyalists would continue to recruit supporters, neither yet confident in their stance.

*Wednesday, 23 August*

Although unknown in America as yet, actions were being initiated on the other side of the Atlantic which would dash the hopes of moderate Rebels who still felt reconciliation was possible, and strengthen radical Carolinians who preferred a showdown. On 23 August, King George III issued a proclamation for *"suppressing rebellion and sedition"* in America. The King proclaimed: *"Whereas many of our subjects in divers parts of our Colonies and Plantations in North America, misled by dangerous and ill designing men ... have at length proceeded to open and avowed rebellion, by arraying themselves in a hostile manner, to withstand the execution of ... law, and traitorously preparing, ordering and levying war against us ... we have thought fit, by and with the advice of our Privy Council, to issue our Royal Proclamation, hereby declaring, that ... all our Officers, civil and military, are obliged to exert their utmost endeavours to suppress such rebellion, and to bring the traitors to justice."*[270]

This proclamation of war was issued seven days before the British government received the Olive Branch Petition from the Continental Congress seeking a redress of grievances. The olive branch withered when superceded by the King's uncompromising proclamation. But Americans would not get word of the sovereign's order until 31 October. By then much of the momentum for reconciliation had dissipated. Three months later, when Thomas Paine published his pamphlet *Common Sense,* many more fence sitters would have second thoughts, and become convinced to join the Rebel cause.

In South Carolina, after the King's proclamation became known, even moderates such as Henry Laurens would become more willing to jump into bed with radicals such as William Henry Drayton. But before this happened, Carolinians still had to weather the threat of provincial storm gathering in the back country. And, so far as many Carolina revolutionaries were concerned, the clouds looked blackest in the closing days of August. Hopes for peace were further discouraged when the meeting at Ford's took place. The assembly was far smaller than expected, and was another major disappointment for Drayton, as evident from his report of the following day.

*Thursday, 24 August*

In a joint message from Drayton and Tennent to the Council, dated 24 August, dateline *"Ford's upon the Enoree,"* the duo reported that Fletchall, Robert and Patrick Cunningham, Kirkland and Brown were all present. However, they had contrived to keep most area residents away. Thus, they angrily comment: *"One thousand men meet here in general … when Fletchall's paper was signed there were about 1500 … we had but 250 hearers, and a great many of these were friends from other parts … not one man of Cunningham's Company was present … Kirkland treated the congress, the committee, the Council, and ourselves with the highest insolence … on the point of assaulting Mr. Drayton."*[271]

This was the first, and very likely the only occasion at which Drayton and Kirkland met face to face. Kirkland had not attended the meeting at Fletchall's home on 17 August. The Enoree gathering was a failure; the elections were again postponed for a fortnight. As the Drayton/Tennent communiqué stated, *"the very small audience clearly manifests that the sentiments of the party who oppose association are clearly inimical."* It ended weakly, noting: *"we inclose two affidavits & an intercepted letter. Fort Charlotte is in good condition."*[272]

The affidavits refer to those deposed by Zacariah Bell [on the 18th] and Jonathan Clark [on the 21st]. The intercepted letter was that of Alexander Cameron to Andrew McLean [16 August]. Reference to Fort Charlotte was made on the basis of news brought by the young man who had been sent by Andrew Williamson to attend the meeting. Meanwhile, Drayton and Tennent would now head for the Ninety-Six, a town consisting of 12 homes and a courthouse.

The disastrous results of the 23 August meeting, news of potential Indian hostility and the fact that the back country Loyalists seemed to be in contact with Campbell, who still expected reinforcements, conjured up a grim picture for Rebel leaders. The ranger muster at Amelia began to take on greater importance. The status of these preparations was now reported to the Council by Col. Thomson.

*Friday, 25 August*

Surprisingly, Col. Thomson, in Amelia, had not caught up with events at this stage. Writing to Henry Laurens on the 25th, he remarks that the courier sent to Drayton on the 17th has not yet returned. This is odd, as

Drayton claims to have replied on the 20th; but the letter appears not to have reached Thomson as yet. Consequently, the colonel was not aware of Drayton's meeting with Fletchall, of Polk's return to the fold, of the "hellish plots" alluded to by Tennent. Nor, it appears, had he received Williamson's reply of 22 August which acknowledged receipt of the Thomson/Mayson order to alert Fort Charlotte and to pass on a letter to LeRoy Hammond—on which Williamson had duly followed through. It was Williamson's letter that also mentioned Drayton's upcoming meeting at Ford's on the Enoree and the fact that Drayton might be threatened. Being unaware of these happenings, Thomson's letter to Laurens was a bland report on the status of the regiment. We learn that he is encamped at Amelia *"with five Companys—Capts. Wise, Kirshaw, Goodwyn, Richardson & Woodward; Capts. Imhoff & Heatly are out recruiting, as is Capt. Kirshaw … Major Mason* [sic] *who has some time been at the Congarees waiting for them I expect at the same time to join the Camp."*[273]

All will soon rendezvous at Amelia to await Drayton's arrival and further orders. Strangely, Thomson doesn't mention Capts. Purves or Caldwell; the former is still recruiting; the latter is occupying Fort Charlotte. But he does submit a list of Capt. Wise's company, recently arrived, although Wise himself is still in North Carolina. Thomson merely reports that *"his men came in with Lieut. Donaldson … Capt. Wise I presume will be in Camp in a few days."*[274]

With respect to the Polk matter, Thomson was still chafing from the Council's criticism over his failure to expeditiously report Polk's defection from Major Mayson's camp. In his letter, Thomson carefully explains: *"the first certain accounts I had of Capt. Polk's disobedience, I rec'd by a letter from Major Mason* [sic] *the day before Mr. Drayton came to the Congarees, & on his arrival I deliver'd it to him. I did not chuse to write from report, where the reputation of a Gent. was at stake, my officer, who wrote to Mr. Gervais/ yet unknown to me/ had he acquainted me, I should have had it in my power to have wrote the facts. Whatever certainties might have come to my Hands of consequence, either for or against the cause of Liberty, You may depend upon I shall / both as a point of my Duty & my strictest regard for the welfare of the Country / make immediate report of."*[275]

At the same time that Col. Thomson was mending fences, we find the Rev. William Tennent approaching Cunningham country. Following the encounter at Ford's on the Enoree, Tennent and Drayton parted company. On 24 August Tennent *"forded Enoree river, & rode twenty miles … arriving in the evening at Mr. James William's, one of the committee, an honest and liberal man, who lives in the midst of Cunningham's company … met with Rev.*

*James Cresswell, minister at Ninety Six and this place … met with the greater part of Robert Cunningham's Company, & two of his officers in a large congregation at the meeting house … preached to a large & concerned audience … the most fixed people that I have ever yet seen. This is the center of the opposition … I conjured them by all that was sacred, that they should not give themselves to the dupes of ministerial artifice, or the instruments of the opposition & slavery, & by God's help, so touched their minds, that the greater part of them clustered around me afterwards & wanted to hear more; many seemed much shocked; some declared themselves convinced; others went away silent; a few were very angry.*" He concludes his journal note optimistically, writing *"the force of violence is broken here."*[276]

*Saturday, 26 August*

On this day we find Rev. Tennent visiting with *"Rev. James Cresswell only six miles away,"* preparing to cross the Saluda River on the following day, where he again would meet with Drayton.

*Sunday, 27 August*

According to his journal, Tennent *"crossed the Saluda at Mr. Cresswell's ferry"* and went on to Wilson's Creek, where *"the fresh was so high, as we were obliged to put the chaise onto a flat and cross the mill pond … went the eight miles to Ninety Six … put up at Wm. Mores* [sic].*"* At Ninety-Six Tennent was joined by Drayton before *"a considerable meeting … Drayton harangued them, and was followed by me. The audience appeared fully convinced, and as I learned, there remained not one who had not subscribed before that did not subscribe now."*[277]

Among the congregation on this day was Anne Elizabeth, wife of Major James Mayson. Tennent, who had by then moved on to Long Canes, reports in his diary that on the evening of the 27th, we *"were alarmed in the night by a messenger to inform us, that the wife of Major James Mason was drowned in crossing Wilson's creek, on her return from the sermon."*[278]

The major, at this time, was in the Congarees area where ranger regiments were still mustering. It is not certain when he was notified but it was undoubtedly at some time during the following day. Presumably he returned to his plantation, Glasgow, near Wilson's Creek, to bury his wife. Anne Elizabeth left him with six children: Maria, the eldest, was 21, three years married to David Anderson, a magistrate who would soon be serving with the volunteer militia; Luke was 19—he would join his father's regiment in 1776; James Robert, age 15, would serve with the militia in 1781; two daughters, Christina and Elizabeth, were about ages 9 and 12; and a young son, William, was approximately 4 years old. Major Mayson returned to his regiment at Amelia sometime during the first week of September, leaving the farm in the hands of his sons and eight slaves.

*Monday, 28 August*

The record shows that Dr. Alexander Rogers, now with the rangers at Amelia, wrote to the Council on the 28th, asking: *"Please send Medicines by the first opportunity ... for use of Col. Thomson's Regement of Rangers ... pray don't Disapoint us."*[279] It was also on the 28th that Drayton and Tennent met with Andrew Williamson in Ninety-Six for a brief discussion before departing the area. None of the participants reported on the conversation; Tennent simply wrote in his diary, we *"parted; Mr. Drayton for Augusta, Mr. Tennent to cross Saluda."*[280]

*Wednesday, 30 August*

Having recrossed the Saluda and spent the previous night at Rev. Cresswell's home, William Tennent tells us that, on the 30th, *"I rode to dinner with Major Terry ... conversed plainly with the Major, and have reason to think he is firm in the cause of America; he is now become a Captain of a volunteer Company."*[281] This is Champness Terry, whose majority refers to a rank in the Forks of Saluda Regiment of Militia commanded by Col. Robert Starke, in which Moses Kirkland had been a Lt. Colonel. It is likely that Terry is also the man to whom Col. Fletchall referred to as "Farry" when he attended the counter-association meeting in Fair Forest on 13 July. Terry now seems wholly converted to the Rebel cause. Three weeks ago he had been elected a delegate from Ninety-Six to the 2nd Provincial Congress. However, he would decline to serve.

While the back country was sorting itself out, Loyalist activities would soon surface once more, affecting South Carolina's Indian policy. On 30 August, John Stuart, now exiled in Florida, sent two messages: one a letter to David Tait, an Indian trader who operated under Stuart in Georgia and Florida; the other a "talk" to Cherokee Indians, directed to *"the Great Warrior and Prince of Chote, and to all the Warriors and Ruling Chiefs of the Upper and Lower Cherokee Nations."* These messages were intercepted by Georgia Rebels and turned over to the Council of Safety in Savannah, through whom Charleston would be informed.

In his talk to Indians, Stuart refers to his forced exile of which *"Mr. Cameron will undoubtedly have informed you."* Stuart apologizes to the Cherokees for the *"gunpowder ... seized and taken out of the ship by some bad people at Savannah, which prevented your being supplied by your traders with the necessary quantity for hunting & defence."* Stuart planned to replace the loss with *"ammunition from this place, which I shall send to Augusta, as soon as I can be provided with pack horses to carry it, and now I write to Mr. McLean to send some for it."*[282]

McLean is Alexander McLean of Augusta, a commissioner of roads and an Indian trader—the same man to whom Cameron had written on 16 August, only to have his letter intercepted. McLean, like many other traders, had not yet made up his mind as to which side he would support; Stuart was, after all, paying him and he had to make a living. However, within a year, McLean would renounce his allegiance to Stuart, recanting before the Council of Safety in Savannah, vowing that he had broken off communications with Cameron and Stuart *"or any other professed enemy to America."*[283]

In his talk to the Indians, Stuart also admonishes them: *"the murder of two white brethren in your Nation was not like friends ... this is not what I expected from you—it is not fulfilling your engagements."* He also berates them for assisting Shawnees *"to kill white people in Virginia ... I hope you will stop all such proceedings ... the difference between the people in England and the white people in America is a matter that does not concern you; they will decide it between themselves ... I shall do all in my power to procure for you a supply of necessaries but I expect you will put confidence in the great King's protection, and not listen to any talks against him, or his officers and governors ... I have sent Mr. Cameron amongst you to take care of your interest."*[284]

Stuart's rather innocuous words do not sound menacing. Indeed, the Loyalists, as much as the Rebels, wished to keep the Indians neutral. While both sides decried Indian involvement in the dispute, each seemed willing to use the Indian menace as a scare factor. It placed the Natives in an excellent bargaining position, patronizing the side that kept them supplied with goods, guns and powder. Tennent and Drayton had no knowledge of Stuart's activities but, from previous rumors, they were still under the impression that Loyalists planned an offensive, perhaps with Indian support. In the Long Canes region, where we now find Drayton, such frightening stories had to be taken seriously.

Having parted with Tennent at Ninety-Six, Drayton journeyed toward Augusta. On 30 August we find him at the plantation of LeRoy Hammond, a transplant from Virginia, now a prosperous landowner outside Augusta. Hammond had been a delegate to the First Provincial Congress from Ninety-Six District; he was re-elected to serve in the Second Congress. The Council of Safety relied on Hammond to help mobilize settlers in his area to defend against any attack on Fort Charlotte or Augusta.

# CHAPTER XII

## *To Fight or Not To Fight*

ROM HAMMOND'S PLANTATION, SNOW HILL, DRAYTON WROTE A report to his peers in Charleston on 30 August saying: *"I came here to see the people of Augusta and the settlements in these parts on my way to Amelia. By various accounts that I received on the road yesterday afternoon, last night, and this morning, it appears to be a fact that Kirkland is actually in arms to attack Augusta and Fort Charlotte."* Just nine days ago, Drayton had dismissed such rumors, telling the Council "the alarm respecting Augusta was without any foundation." After making this remark on 21 August, Drayton ran into Kirkland at Enoree on the 23rd. Since then, on the road to Hammond's place, he has traveled through Cuffey Town, where Kirkland had been active. The picture had changed. Drayton now reports: *"the King's men as they are now called were summoned to meet yesterday at a place about 20 miles from here."* Drayton believes they plan to meet again and *"have been very diligent in obtaining arms. Cunningham and Brown are of the party."*[285] Therefore, says Drayton, he has taken it upon himself to order out three companies of Carolina militia.

They will be joined by Georgians from Augusta. Additionally, *"I have ordered Major Williamson to march with three hundred men to Harden's ford on the Savannah about thirty miles above this place. I have also ordered Col. Thomson to march his Rangers, and as near three hundred militia as he can, and take post at the Ridge; and Col. Richardson with three hundred men, to take post at the mouth of the Enoree, to be a check on Fletchall's people, in case they show any intention of assisting Kirkland."* In the process of mobilizing 1000 men, Drayton was in his element—a foreshadowing of the Napoleonic style he would assume in the absence of direction from Charleston. In essence, he became the government. After all, as Drayton himself points out in this letter of 30 August, *"I have not been honored with any letters from you, but those of the 11th and 13th instant."*[286]

These last mentioned letters were in the batch of correspondence Thomson had forwarded to Drayton on the 17th. Both Drayton and Thomson received similar directives at the time. That of 11 August to Thomson categorically states: *"You will immediately consult the Hon'ble Mr. Drayton if he is in your neighborhood & pursue such measures, relative to the dangerous attack threaten'd upon Augusta as shall appear most likely to suppress the insurgents … should Mr. Drayton be at any coinsiderable distance you will act in this important & alarming circumstance as shall seem best in your own opinion without delay."*[287]

To Drayton on the 11th, the Council wrote: *"Coll. Thomson is enjoined to exert utmost endeavours for the interest of the general Cause in this dangerous conjuncture & to avail himself if possible of your advice—If you are in the Neighbourhood of his Camp he will lay before you his Instructions, which from necessity are general, & the Council of Safety being perfectly Satisfied that you will leave nothing undone that Shall appear to be necessary have not charged me with any particular direction to trouble you with."*[288]

These orders seemed to give Col. William Thomson, the highest ranking regular officer in the field, command over military matters, in conjunction with William Henry Drayton, a civilian agent of the government, as an advisor. Drayton, however, took matters peremptorily into his own hands by unilaterally issuing orders for mobilization, undercutting Thomson's military authority. Moreover, on 30 August, from the Hammond home, Drayton drafted a circular, for general distribution in the District of Ninety-Six, which left no doubt about his political authority as a representative of the revolutionary government. It stressed his mandate from the Council and is a fine example of how one willful, determined, decisive Rebel leader could impose direction to a cause. It deserves to be quoted in full: *"Snow Hill, August 30, 1775. By the Honorable William Henry Drayton, Esquire: Whereas by Commission from the Honorable the Council of Safety for this Colony, dated 23rd day of July last, I am upon a progress through the country, to explain to the people at large the nature of the unhappy disputes between Great Britain & the American Colonies; to endeavor to settle all political disputes with the people; to quiet their minds; & to enforce the necessity of a general union, in order to preserve themselves & their children from slavery: And, whereas, the progress having been continued almost through the Colony with success to the State, satisfaction to the people, &, upon the most perfect principles, tending to promote peace & good order, for the purposes of progress aforesaid, I did appoint that a meeting of the people should be held on Friday next, the first day of September, at the Ridge in the district aforesaid: But whereas one Moses Kirkland having, without lawful authority, assembled men in arms, in the district aforesaid, it is but too evident, that, to his treachery against this Colony, he means to add crimes of a deeper dye, &, by the force of arms, to violate the public peace: Wherefore it becomes inexpedient that the intended meeting of the people should be held as aforesaid, lest the meeting should furnish occasion for civil bloodshed, which it is our purpose to avoid as long as may be possible: And, whereas, by the arts, frauds, & misrepresentations, of the said Moses Kirkland, some weak & ignorant people have been led into measures of so criminal a nature, as, if persisted in, must inevitably involve then in destruction, from motives of humanity, I, therefore, do hereby recommend to all such persons, that they forthwith desist from following the counsels of the said Moses Kirkland in points tending to sedition & hostility; and I hereby notify, that all such persons as, without lawful authority, shall assemble in arms, in company with, or by instigation of the said Moses Kirkland, will be deemed public enemies to be suppressed by the sword ... Given under my hand, at Snow Hill, in the district aforesaid, this 30th of August, 1775."*[289]

Having made a military and political command decision in the field without consulting either the Council of Safety or Col. Thomson, Drayton would open himself up to criticism from Charleston as being unnecessarily provocative. He had unilaterally mobilized troops and thrown down the gauntlet before Kirkland. The decision between war and peace was now up to the Loyalists. If they followed Kirkland, he and his followers would "be deemed public enemies to be suppressed by the sword." Were other Loyalist leaders ready for war? Or did they [Fletchall, Cunningham, Robinson, Brown], believe that the hearts of minds of the people could still be changed without violence? For that matter, was Kirkland actually in a position to attack Augusta, or was his alleged aggression being interpreted by Rebel leaders based on rumor alone? No matter; by mobilizing, Drayton sought a preemptive strike designed to nip any potential aggression by Loyalists in the bud. Of course, none of his moves were known to the Council of Safety, which was still playing catch-up, replying to earlier correspondence in the pipeline.

*Thursday, 31 August*

Henry Laurens, in a reply to Thomson's letter of the 25th, approved the dismissal of *"several disaffected Captains from service in your Regiment of Militia,"* a reference to Shram and the others drummed out of the Orangeburg Militia. Thomson was requested to fill the vacancies and *"to encourage volunteer Companies."* Laurens also approved of commissioning Moses Vance a Lieutenant in Capt. Imhoff's Company. In a show of petulance, he acknowledges receipt of Capt. Wise's *"Return,"* but complains that it is *"neither dated nor signed, an Omission which you will guard against hereafter by issuing proper Orders for that purpose."* This comment strikes one as rather finicky, but it is indicative of the mood in a Council of Safety that doesn't think it is getting much value for its money. In this same letter Thomson was informed of the Polk matter, confirming his militia appointment *"to a command by Mr. Drayton & Mr. Tennent, but not to be incorporated with your Regiment."* Laurens also consented to *"your coming to Charles Town about the 10th September according to your request, but we desire you will in such case leave the Regiment under the Command of the Major* [Mayson].*"*[290] Given the rapidity with which the situation in the back country was changing, Thomson would not make this trip.

Of more significance, in this same letter, was Laurens' statement *"we have found it necessarty to grant the Honble. Mr. Drayton enlarged powers hoping thereby to promote peace & good order in those parts where you are at present threatened with distraction; we therefore enjoin you to Cooperate with that Gentleman … in order to avoid repetitions we recommend a careful review of all our former Instructions & especially to keep the important Post of Fort Charlotte & the Safety of our Associated Friends at Augusta objects always in sight."*[291]

Laurens was unaware, of course, that these "enlarged powers" had already been pre-empted by Drayton, not to "promote peace," but to instigate war. At the time Laurens' letter went out to Thomson, similar instructions were being sent separately to Drayton, who would interpret them as a stamp of approval, giving him supreme command. This interpretation would later make the Council furious. Curiously, a copy of this letter to Drayton, dated 31 August, is not found among the Laurens papers. References to it do, however, appear in the book *Memoirs of the American Revolution*, published in 1821 by John Drayton. In defense of his father, John observes at length: *"Upon an alarm from Georgia, that Kirkland was going against Augusta, the Council of Safety wrote Mr. Drayton, on the 11th of August, that on such an occasion, they were perfectly satisfied he would leave nothing undone … it was by virtue of this letter that he collected an army against Kirkland. After Mr. Drayton had taken this decided and vigorous measure, partly on the above implied authority, and partly on his own responsibility, he received a letter from the Council of Safety, dated the 31st day of August, stating that they viewed with horror the spectacle of a civil war, and were not ashamed to own, that they could not hastily determine, upon measures which at first sight may promise to avert the calamity; but which for aught they knew, might rush them upon the very danger, which they would wish to avoid If the removal of twelve mischievous men, will really quash the growing opposition, that work may be easily accomplished; but, may not our enemy prove a hydra, and start twice as many heads to bring on their four thousand adherents, with fury, to rescue their first leaders, or to revenge their cause?"*[292]

The fact remains, when the Council wrote to Drayton on 31 August, they had no idea of the action already taken by him to mobilize troops; they were yet unaware of his ultimatum being distributed among the populace. The Council, with mixed emotions, was responding to Drayton's notion, expounded in his letter of the 21st, to take "vigorous measures" to capture Loyalist leaders, if possible, but to avoid provoking a war. Indeed, as Drayton would later learn from his friend, Arthur Middleton, the powers granted to him on 31 August *"had been much debated in the council; and had been carried only four to three."* Those in opposition called Drayton *"hot ... rash ... a young man perhaps unaware of the Danger of creating a Civil war ... he may raise the people, and set them to cutting one another's throats."*[293] Too late, the fat was in the fire.

Meanwhile, on 31 August, in his sixth Despatch to Lord Dartmouth, Governor Campbell is blissfully unaware of the crisis in the back country. He, at the moment, agitatedly refers to a letter from Arthur Lee in London to Henry Laurens in Charleston. In this letter, which Laurens received last May, Lee was alerting Carolinians to British plans for subverting both slaves and Indians in America to revolt against colonists who opposed British rule. This is the same letter that the General Committee in Charleston forwarded to its delegates at the Continental Congress. The contents have now become common knowledge. The Governor bitterly labels Lee's opinions as *"fictitious,"* an *"instigation of rumours."* But these rumors are now being widely spread; moreover it is *"universally believed, that to effect this plan 14,000 Stand of Arms were actually on board the Scorpion."* Such rumors *"inflamed the populace ... was the conversation of all companies. ... no one dares contradict them."*[294]

The *Scorpion* was the ship that brought Campbell to Charleston last June. No evidence has come to light to confirm that it also carried "14,000 stand of arms." At the moment the *Scorpion* was in North Carolina waters. The only two ships in Charleston harbor were the *Tamar* and the *Cherokee*—both had limited firepower. True or not, such rumors undermined Campbell's authority in Charleston and strengthened that of the Council of Safety.

### Friday, 1 September

Following debate in the Council over Drayton's competence to assume extensive powers, Henry Laurens sent Drayton a copy of Stuart's "talk to the lower Cherokees" which had been intercepted by "liberty boys" in Augusta and forwarded to Charleston by George Galphin. Knowing that Drayton had invited Cherokees to meet with him in Amelia, Laurens felt that the Stuart letter *"may be of some use to you in your intended interview with the Six Head Men ... Mr. Loocock's Account for certain Indian presents now delivered to Thomas Dean & Thomas Pierce who have promised to convey the whole safely to you—which when done you will Certify in order to entitle them to Five Pounds Curr't money for the safe carriage."*[295]

Dean and Pierce were privates from Captain Samuel Wise's company of rangers. They had brought in a muster report, and had remained in town long enough to take messages back to the interior. The thread of back country intrigue is now taken up by the firebrand preacher, William Tennent. By 31 August he had recrossed the Saluda into Long Canes territory. On 1 September we find him holding forth at *"one of Mr. Harris' preaching sheds on Long cane Creek in Boonsborough ... the congregation was small and affected."*[296]

On this same day, in a letter to the Council, Tennent showed deep concern about the forthcoming elections in the Enoree River area, now scheduled for 7 September. He was equally filled with foreboding over the presumed *"intrigues"* of Governor Campbell among Loyalists in the back country. Tennent found *"the inhabitants here in great terror ... because they have no ammunition"* to defend themselves against Indians. If Indians do join the Loyalists, he warns, then *"the rest of the inhabitants will be forced to join them, to save their families from massacre ... I am taking proper measures in this district to prevent the horrible conspiracy. Three volunteer companies are formed. One under Major Terry ... another under Capt. Pickens; a third under Capt. James McCall,"* of Georgia. But, *"the great difficulty is want of ammunition."* Tennent also reports of a *"design upon fort Charlotte."* Consequently, he has promised settlers that the Council would supply ammunition for its defense; then he departed to visit the fort in person.[297]

At this point it appears that Tennent was not yet aware of any conspiratorial meetings held by Kirkland, or of Drayton's mobilization plans.

*Saturday, 2 September*

Tennent's journal for this day reveals that he preached at a meeting house *"about fifteen miles from the Indian line. The assembly was the most crowded I have ever seen ... the people, through mostly opposers, appeared very affectionate ... the people seemed satisfied, and many of those who had signed Fletchall's Assocation now subscribed ours."*[298] So goes the struggle for hearts and minds.

On the following day Tennent received a message from Drayton which forced him to cancel subsequent meetings, spend the night at Patrick Calhoun's and leave for Fort Charlotte on the 3rd. Tennent does not elaborate on the contents of Drayton's message but one assumes it alerted the reverend to Kirkland's plans and Drayton's mobilization efforts. Similar messages were sent to Col. Thomson, Major Williamson and Col. Richardson, ordering them to mobilize their respective troops.

Thomson's Regiment of Rangers, it will be recalled, had disbanded temporarily on 7 August to permit men to return to their homes, vote in congressional elections, restock their provisions, and then regroup at Amelia on 18 August. Still under complement, Major Mayson continued recruiting for the regiment throughout August, returning home only to bury his wife in the final days of that month. Whether he had returned to camp at Amelia when Drayton's message arrived there on 1 September is not known; but he was most certainly on hand four days later.

Meanwhile, replying to Drayton on 2 September, Col. Thomson reports, *"Your orders I rec'd late last night, shall putt them in execution immediately. I shall march from this camp tomorrow, I shall do my best endeavours to take as many of the Militia with me as possible, tho I am I afraid shall not be able to procure the Compli't you mentioned … I have disp'd your orders to Col. Richardson & your letter to the Council of Safety."*[299] The latter referred to Drayton's letters of 30 August.

Thomson now sent word to *"Lieut. Coll. Rowe & Major Golson"* of the Orangeburg militia, ordering them to *"meet me on Saturday the 9th Inst. At the Ridge, with two hundred Men well armed, out of our Regim't of Foot, if you can't raise them as Volunteers, You must draft them."*[300] The Ridge is an area between Augusta and Ninety-Six.

Upon receiving Drayton's news of mobilization, the excitable Rev. Tennent himself turned into a military commander. By the 3rd, he was on his way to Fort Charlotte, pausing long enough to send ahead a message containing orders *"to Capt. John Caldwell … to employ six workmen to build to build platforms for fighting … carry out orders from Major Mason, bearing the date August 6th, 1775 … mount two of the best four-pounders on high wheels, that they be fit for either field or fort service … Take great care that no man enter the Fort on any pretense, that you do not know … Be much upon your guard against surprise, especially at night … In case of an alarm, and when the approach of an enemy is no longer dubious, you are to fire three cannon toward the thickest settlements as a signal … And whereas there is a great scarcity of ammunition among the militia, and an attack from Indians is to be apprehended, you are directed to give out 150 lbs Weight of the powder, and lead in proportion, under your care to the captains of the volunteer and other militia companies in the upper part of your district ... taking a receipt from them ... you are also ordered to dismiss your horses for the present, and not hazard your men by grass guard; but the horses are not to be sent to such a distance as that they cannot be commanded within the space of a day and a half."*[301]

We learn from his journal that the reverend reached Fort Charlotte late the same evening, *"surveyed the fortifications ... reviewed the soldiers and the militia, discoursed with them on the goodness of their cause ... prayed with them ... and then took my leave accompanied by Lieutenant Cawan to his house, eight miles on the same side of the the river."*[302]

We leave the militant preacher momentarily to catch up on activities elsewhere, where another bit of skullduggery was being planned on this day, which wouldn't come to light until a deposition was taken six days later at Fair Forest in Fletchall's area. The settler deposed was Edward Morrow, who *"on his way to Broad River ... fell in company with Philip Wells"* on 3 September, about three miles from Wells' home. *"They there met with about 33 men, who were all well armed ... went aside with Capt. Benj. Wofford and Capt. John Ford ... Wells came back,"* asked Morrow if he would *"would go along with them to take some powder from Cpt. Ralph Smith* [a Rebel militia officer] *and four others who had gone to Fort Charlotte to obtain powder and was expected ... to be brought along the Indian Line and to cross Enoree."* Morrow accompanied the raiders to the Indian line where they lay in ambush until noon the next day. While waiting, Morrow says *"there were several schemes proposed among them to take Fort Charlotte ... it was also much talked of, among the Company, that Cameron had a body of Indians that was ready to fall on the country when Cameron got orders from the Governor."* The Morrow affidavit was taken before *"J. Thomas Jun., Clerk of the Committee,"* at Fair Forest on 11 September."[303] The deposition had no effect on Drayton's plans; it was merely another of the many rumors circulating in the back country at this time. The raid would never materialize.

## Monday, 4 September

Thomson's courier, with Drayton's orders, reached Col. Richardson on 4 September. The courier returned to Amelia without a response from Richardson. Six days have now elapsed since Drayton took command, six days during which the process of mobilization continued. However, nothing more has been heard about Moses Kirkland and his intrigues. On this same day we find the Rev. Tennent taking a tour on the Georgia side of the Savannah, on the lookout for conspiracies, which he duly found. As reported in his journal, he *"arose with early dawn, took a guide and crossed Savannah river at Cawan's ferry; the river swelling much by the rains; was on the Georgia side before sunrise ... had to avoid a place where an ambuscade was suspected ... met with one of the King's men, as they are so absurdly called, from whom I learned, that they expected a meeting on Wednesday [6 September] of all their comrades on the banks of the Savannah, about twenty miles above Augusta."*[304]

Tennent's journal intimates that these men were meeting to plan some sort of attack, but it is not clear whether they were coordinated in any way with plans that Kirkland might have had. On the same 4th, Tennent rode on to Augusta *"forty-seven miles, some say fifty-five ... crossed the river to Capt. Hammond's; found his house forted in, and a large body of militia there, ready to move with Mr. Drayton."* Once again in Drayton's presence, Tennent informed the commander of his intelligence regarding a planned meeting of King's men on the 6th. The preacher and the general discussed strategy while at Hammond's, wherein it was determined that Drayton would march with the troops, while Tennent, *"consented to make the best of my way to Charles Town, to lay a state of the whole matter before the Council of Safety."*[305]

There is no evidence that Drayton reported separately to the Council at this stage, probably relying on Tennent to fill them in. Actually, Drayton has not filed a report since his letter of 30 August; his next message to Charleston would be on 11 September. General Drayton now girded his loins for battle, preparing to march off with local forces to meet up with his gathering troops near Ninety-Six village. According to Tennent's journal, the forces at Hammond's consisted of *"the two hundred men here ...the quota that Georgia sends."* In his last letter, of 30 August, Drayton had reported only *"one hundred men from Augusta ... and three companies from this place* [Carolinians]." They would march out on Wednesday, the 6th.

*Tuesday, 5 September*

The record shows that the Council wrote to Drayton on 5 September, having received his letter of 30 August. It refers to its communiqué of the 31st and now, somewhat nervously, confirms *"the confidence which we have responded in you & we assure our selves that you will make such use of your authority & of the means which are in your hands as will be productive of great advantage to the colony & give general satisaction ... we are not under the doubt of your ability to defeat any plots which Kirkland may have concerted against Fort Charlotte or Augusta & since you are seriously entered upon a contest with him, it will be absolutely necessary to subdue him, or drive him out of the country.*"[306]

No matter how ambivalent Council members may have been, they were making the best of Drayton's rash action; it was a *fait accompli*, and they sat back and hoped for the best. To aid and assist his efforts, the Council told Drayton that, "*in addition to the supplies of gunpowder previously sent to Col. Neel's Regiment of Militia, we shall now send two barrels of Powder & about 400 lbs lead to Mr. Kershaw's Store at the disposal of that Gentleman & Coll. Richardson.*"[307]

The reference to Neel's regiment is interesting; this is the same "Neale" to whom Governor Campbell referred to in his letter of 1 August to Fletchall, suggesting that Col. Neel be assigned to occupy Fort Charlotte, once it was recaptured from the Rebels. Evidently, Col. Neel was no longer a fence sitter.

More significant, however, is the fact that the Council had "*come to a resolution to distribute Powder throughout the colony among our friends,*" a shift from previous policy. The Council, on the 5th, also acknowledged receipt of the Drayton/Tennent letter of 24 August, delivered by Mr. Downs. But, ever the penny pincher, Laurens cannot refrain from chastising Drayton for not warning him earlier of the agreement to pay Downs 35 pounds for delivery. After all, he complains, it did not "*appear to us that he came expressly for that purpose.*"[308]

Meanwhile, from Hammond's home, on 5 September, Drayton wrote to Col. Thomson to inform him that he was moving out with his army on 6 September and hoped to rendezvous with the rangers on the Ridge—an area halfway between Augusta and Ninety-Six. Col. Thomson, already on the move, would receive this message at 2:00 p.m. on 6 September.

### Wednesday, 6 September

This day brought forth a series of messages that serve to illustrate how muddled, and difficult, communications could be in these times. On the morning of the 6th, moving out of Amelia, Thomson dispatched a rider to Hammond's plantation with a letter for Drayton, not realizing Drayton was also on the move. The reader may recall that, before leaving Lawson's Fork, Drayton reported to the Council on 21 August that he had sent "*a small talk to the Cherokees*" and asked Richard Pearis, an Indian trader, "*to conduct six of their head men to me*" at Amelia.

Thomson's letter was now meant to inform Drayton that "*yesterday*

*...came an express from Capt'n Paris* [sic] *informing us that himself and five Cherokee Indians were stopt from coming down by Captn. Hendrick & some others belonging to Fletchall's regt. of about 10 miles distant from the Congarees."* Some of Thomson's rangers *"marched to rescue them, which they did & took Hendrick prisoner, who is now confined to camp ... Captn Paris* [sic] *is now here with the Indians."* In this same letter, Thomson tells Drayton that he plans to march for the Ridge *"early tomorrow morning ... where I expect to be ... on Friday evening & where I shall stay until I receive your further orders."* He adds that his men from the Orangeburg militia have been *"order'd to meet me at the Ridge by Saturday."* In closing, Thomson comments that Drayton's orders to Col. Richardson had been duly relayed. The courier returned without a written message, but reported that Richardson *"is much hurt from a fall from his Indico Vatts ... the express from the Council of Safety arrived here last night with the inclosed Letter for your honor, also two bundles which I expect are for the Indians."*[309]

Separately on the 6th, having received Drayton's orders, Col. Richardson responded directly to the Council of Safety. He confirms *"having broke two or three of my ribs ... I have sent the necessary orders to Major Cantey* [Samuel] *to assemble the regiment ... new Irish settlers are distitute and many unable to provide themselves"* with weapons. Moreover, the regiment lacks a second in command; Lt. Col. James McGirth *"has left this province ... there are several Volunteer Companys assembling ... some nearly Compleat."*[310]

In a second letter written on 6 September, Col. William Thomson also reported to Henry Laurens in Charleston, confirming receipt of *"your favor of the 31st Ult. Which gives me great satisfaction. You may depend that I will as soon as possible exert myself for raising Volunteer Comp'ys & inform you of my progress therein."* The Council's letter of 31 August had been received by Thomson on the evening of 5 September, along with letters for Drayton and gifts for distribution to the Indians. Thomson forwarded these letters to Hammond's home. As for himself, in response to the Council's queries, Thomson wearily observes: *"I find it impossible at present ... to make a proper return of my whole regim't but will endeavour to do it as soon as I meet with the Hon'ble Mr. Drayton."* He states that he has issued orders to all ranger captains to turn in muster reports. Indeed, those for Kershaw, Richardson, Goodwyn and Woodward have been submitted *"but the omission of Capt. Wise was owing to his not being present ... nor did he join the Reg't before yester-day ... his reason for not joining before was owing to orders he received from the Hon'ble Council of Safety."*[311]

This is the second time that the Council seemingly issued orders to one of Thomson's officers without informing him. It will be recalled that Major Mayson was supposedly given secret orders regarding Fort Charlotte before he left Charleston, following the adjournment of the Provincial Congress last June. Now Wise has been on a mission to North Carolina, presumably on the Council's order, but without Thomson's knowledge.

In this same reply of 6 September, with respect to a possible attack on Augusta or Fort Charlotte, Thomson again assures Laurens *"I, to the best of my ability follow your own and Mr. Drayton's instructions & will give him all the Military aid in my power ... I shall carefully review all your former instructions give such orders with regard to ... Fort Charlotte & for the safety of our associated Friends at Augusta, as prudent."* Regarding the Polk affair, Col. Thomson wryly expresses hope that Polk *"will gain credit by his future behavior."* He also informs the Council that the Indians have arrived at the Congarees.[312]

Col. Thomson was on the move. He had written his first letter dated 6 September from a Camp at the Congarees. Later in the day he had progressed to Fairchild's Branch, where he received Drayton's *"of the 5th inst: at Mr. Williams about 2 o'clock this afternoon on our march hither."* The colonel replied immediately, telling Drayton that he had sent an earlier dispatch by William Weatherford *"to Augusta."* Thomson now tells Drayton that Pearis and his Indians were left behind at the Congarees camp with some of his Orangeburg Militia because they were too tired to march further. Before he dispatched this letter, a note arrived from Capt. Arthur of the Orangeburg Militia stating that Pearis and the Cherokees have changed their minds; the Orangeburg militia would escort them to the Ridge. Therefore, Thomson now tells Drayton that he will stay at the Ridge to meet with Pearis and his group while the rest of the rangers will travel on to join Drayton's army. He closes: *"for further particulars I refer you to Major Mayson with whom I have consulted & who will deliver this with his own hands."*[313] Mayson had taken leave to bury his wife, who died on 27 August; Thomson's reference confirms his return to the rangers.

By the 6th, the Council of Safety was aware of Drayton's mobilization. In its letter to Thomson of this date, Laurens reluctantly informs the Colonel: *"Mr. Drayton may from necessity have anticipated he has not exceeded the powers vested in him by calling forth the Rangers & Militia in order to prevent or defeat the Plots of our Enemies—We have great doubts of Kirkland's boldness in the face of danger & consequently no sanguine hopes of your taking hold of his Body—this is a serious matter & of the utmost moment therefore we shall wait in great anxiety for your further accounts."*[314]

In effect the men in Charleston have become resigned to Drayton's initiative, but they don't think Kirkland will fight. Thomson is being politely told to defer to Drayton's command while the Council awaits the outcome of the current crisis, with fingers crossed.

# CHAPTER XIII

## *Standoff at Ninety-Six*

L EFT BEHIND AT HAMMOND'S PLANTATION, WAITING FOR HIS CHAISE to be brought from Long Canes, the Rev. William Tennent spent his spare time visiting Augusta, talking to whomever settlers he could find along the Savannah, bolstering their spirits and gathering intelligence.

*Thursday, 7 September*

A notation in his journal shows Tennent *"was alarmed by intelligence that two of Drayton's men had been killed ... sent to inquire ... could not find the certainty ... another report ... that Kirkland, with a large party, was about twenty five miles up the river ... and intended to take advantage of the absence of the men to attack this place."* With valiant determination, Tennent leaped into the breach. Intent on defense, he *"went with speed to Wilson's fort,"* where settlers *"were greatly alarmed at our coming."* The rumor of attack proved baseless but, while at the Wilson home, Tennent's chaise was delivered to him *"by Mr. Taylor from Saluda."* The reverend now learned that Taylor had conversed with Robert Cunningham sometime during the past few days, thus providing Tennent with another rationale for warning against Loyalist plots. In the preacher's words, *"The discourse he* [Taylor] *had with Cunningham confirms me in the belief of the extent of Lord William's conspiracy."* Such an interpretation was vintage Tennent who, since he left Fair Forest 20 days ago, had been shouting "hellish plot" at each and every opportunity. Consequently, at his urging, *"Mrs. Barnet's fort had loaded thirteen muskets for service, and were preparing to repel an attack ... every valuable house in Augusta is surrounded by a strong wooden fortification, formed of three inch plank."*[315]

In its inimitable way Tennent's journal provides excellent insight into the mood of the times. Its writer reflects the fears of back country settlers, with the addition of a patina of drama as he reports each rumor. But he now had his chaise and was ready to depart for Charleston. His journal would continue through to 15 September, at which point, having arrived home, all Tennent's difficulties would be *"compensated by the joy of my dear family and friends on my safe arrival."*[316] Tennent's final report from the back country is dated 10 September and will be taken up in chronological order.

### Friday, 8 September

William Henry Drayton and his army had marched from Hammond's near Augusta last Wednesday [6th], and arrived at Ninety-Six on Friday evening the 8th of September. Major Mayson and the rangers now rendezvoused with Drayton, and the Major passed on Col. Thomson's message of the 6th.

### Saturday, 9 September

It was on this day that David Anderson, son-in-law of Major Mayson, and a justice of the peace for Ninety-Six District, took an affidavit from Edward Morrow, mentioned in context above [see 3 September]. It pertained to a planned attack on Fort Charlotte by Loyalists from the Spartanburg area, and was conveyed to Drayton at Ninety-Six for his evaluation. Meanwhile, on the 9th, Drayton sent a message back to Thomson at the Ridge to notify him of the army's arrival at the Ninety-Six courthouse.

### Sunday, 10 September

Col. Thomson's order book shows that he replied to Drayton's message. In his response, Thomson says *"I shall strictly observe the contents thereof ... I shall march for Ninety Six early tomorrow morning."* In addition, Thomson reports the arrival of *"Captn. Arthur and Captn. Geiger with twenty volunteers ... from the Congarees with whom I expected Captn. Paris & the Indians ... they chose to stay at the Congarees until your return."* Finally, he expects the arrival of *"Major Golson ... with a draft of Men & Volunteers this day."*[317]

On this same 10th of September, Rev. Tennent was some 78 miles away from Augusta, en route to Charleston. It was Sunday, he wrote in his diary, and *"having no opportunity for the worship of God in a country destitute of the least form of religion, and no time to warn a meeting, and, indeed, not being happy where I was, I concluded it best to spend the day on the road ... pushed hard to get to a Mr. Hudson's about forty-two miles ... found his house on a high bluff of Savannah river … here wrote letters to the Council of Safety in Savannah, giving them the most interesting intelligence."*[318]

The letter was datelined *"St. Mathews Parish,"* in Georgia, not to be confused with a similarly named parish in South Carolina. At this point the reverend was approximately 45 miles northwest of Savannah city, and about to ferry across the Savannah River into South Carolina. The letter reads: *"Gentlemen … I think it my duty to acquaint you that there exists … a most dangerous conspiracy against the lives and liberties of these colonies. Encouraged by Government and the tories in your town and in Charlestown … they do not hesitate to boast that they are furnished with ammunition and even artillery … This I have by a trusty friend from Cunningham's mouth."* In Tennent's mind Cunningham, not Kirkland, was now emerging as the back country Loyalist ringleader. Moreover, the Loyalists *"depend upon the Cherokee nation to join their camp … I am in possession of an affidavit by which it appears that the malcontents on the frontiers expect to gather into forts, and suffer the savages to pass on and massacre the associated inhabitants."* He urges the Council to mobilize *"at least one thousand five hundred, if not two thousand men … the King's men are already assembling … above Augusta … the tour which Mr. Drayton and I have made through the back parts has greatly weakened but not discouraged them … supplies of ammunition go up by single horses and in covered wagons from both Savannah and Charleston. And Cunningham openly confesses that he has fifteen thousand pounds weight of good powder lately received."*[319]

The "trusty friend" who informed on Cunningham's activities was Taylor, the young man who had delivered the reverend's chaise from Long Canes. This is probably Francis Taylor, age 25, originally from Virginia, who Tennent first met on 26 August at Rev. Cresswell's home on the Saluda. On that day, Tennent had written in his journal that Taylor *"seems so much engaged in the cause that he got the promise of a commission, if nothing prevents."*[320] The record shows that Francis Taylor was indeed commissioned a 2nd Lt. in Capt. Charles Heatly's Company of Rangers on 15 September.[321]

These were ominous tidings; but there was no basis on which to make such charges, except rumor. The supplies looted by Cunningham from Major Mayson on 17 July didn't come close to 15,000 lbs. of good powder. And there are no records of a continuous line of munitions trains from Charleston or Savannah destined for Loyalist hands. William Tennent, however, had a vivid imagination and was prone to take every rumor seriously. The times were troubling and hard intelligence was difficult to obtain. With the benefit of retrospect, we do know that Loyalists outnumbered Rebels in South Carolina in 1775, especially in the back country where 75% of the population lived. Here, the American/British dispute was not yet considered a cause for open rebellion against the mother country. These settlers wished to be left alone. But they were being forced by Rebel and Loyalist leaders to take sides. Each side accused the other of the most scurrilous charges, such as employing Indians as mercenaries. Tennent's cry of "wolf" to rally the Rebels was the natural reaction of a frightened man.

*Monday, 11 September*

Again, from the vicinity of modern day Spartanburg, another affidavit was taken on the 11th under the heading *"South Carolina—Ninety Six District."* Sworn to before justices of the peace John Thomas, Jr. and David Anderson, Joseph Wofford confirmed the earlier deposition given by Edward Morrow. He, too, vowed that his brother, Capt. Benjamin Wofford, was sent with Capt. John Ford to ambush a wagonload of arms that the Rebels were bringing out of Fort Charlotte. The order to seize these arms was given by Col. Fletchall.[322]

On this same day, John Thomas, father of John Thomas, Jr., acknowledged receipt of a letter, dated 10 September, from Drayton, requesting Thomas to raise troops. In his reply, Col. Thomas adds to the rumor pot, commenting that *"from good information ... the malignants are forming the most hellish schemes to frustrate the measures of the Continental congress."* Otherwise, the elder Thomas says he will comply with Drayton's order to raise troops, but *"your Honor must suppose it is impossible to raise the whole Regiment, as several have families, and no man would be left about the house if they should be called away."* Nevertheless, he promises to *"make as large a draft as possible from every company"* of the Spartan Regiment.[323] John Thomas reflects the concern of all settlers who live near Indian Territory. Under threat of Indian attack, few men would be willing to leave their family and farms to fight for liberty in an uncertain quarrel with Great Britain. Thomas enclosed the affidavits taken from Morrow and Wofford in this letter to Drayton.

Incidentally, John Thomas, Sr., age 55, was born in Wales, from where he immigrated to Pennsylvania. He fought with General Braddock in the French and Indian War before settling in South Carolina, and was an active militia man during the Cherokee Indian Wars of 1759/61. Now that Fletchall had opted to side with the Loyalists, Drayton was asking Col. Thomas to recruit a volunteer regiment to replace Fletchall's troops. Before the month was out, John Thomas would also be elected a delegate to the Second Provincial Congress.

By 11 September, as supreme commander of Rebel forces in the back country, William Henry Drayton, at Ninety-Six, was basking in the glory of power as he drafted a report to the Council of Safety. In this message he confirmed receipt of the Council's letters of 31 August and 1 September. He thanked the Council *"for the confidence you have placed in me by your letter of the thirty-first. I hope I shall prove myself worthy of it, and I make no doubt but that I shall fully answer your expectations in restoring the country to a state of quietude by eradicating the opposition."* He proceeded to give *"an account of my conduct since my letter from Hammond's,"* observing that his declaration of 30 August *"was published ... as generally as I could. It had the desired effect ... Kirkland is now invisible—is never two hours in a place, and never sleeps in a house. He has sent to me to make terms, offers to quit the province ... I neither could or would make any terms with him but on unconditional surrender ... he means to flee the country ... but I mean, if possible, to seize him ... the King's men were terrified by the march and the cannon. We picked up a few prisoners ... the people now daily come in to make their peace ... immediatley upon my arrival here I sent a party to surprise Cunningham. He was absent ... but our men took his letters ... I refer you to two letters from Fletchall."*[324]

These two letters were sent to the Council. Although the texts have not been preserved, they probably helped prove the conspiracy theory so far as Drayton was concerned. In his own letter, he continues: *"Yesterday I received notice that a party of men were forming twenty miles off, and over the Saluda ... immediately detached one hundred horsemen to observe their motions ... received what appeared to be well authenticated information, that Fletchall ... will attack us about 2 in the morning ... consulted with Major Mason [sic], Major Williamson and Capt. Hammond."*[325]

Major Mayson was acting commandant of the Regiment of Rangers in Thomson's absence—the colonel was still at the Ridge. Williamson had originally been ordered "to march 100 men to Harden's Ford on the Savannah," but was now at Ninety-Six. Hammond was in charge of a volunteer militia company from the August area on the Carolina side.

A decision was taken to ambush the enemy. As Drayton explains: *"The enemy coming to surprise us, would never expect to be surprised by us ... and in the night, would be fatal to them ... sent Major Mason to post"* a hundred man cavalry *"in ambuscade at a ford on the Saluda, about six miles off."* This was Island Ford where the major's own plantation, Glasgow, was located. Then, *"after dark I marched 110 infantry about a mile and a half from Ninety Six and posted them in ambush on this side ... with Major Williamson, mounted and proceeded to the river. I took the liberty, in as polite a manner as I could, to alter the Major's* [Mayson's] *disposition, with perfect approbation of Major Williamson."*[326]

Such delicate posturing from an overbearing egotist tickles the fancy, but has the aroma of an ongoing personality clash. Drayton's tinkering was not likely to amuse Mayson. The gratuitous mention of this action in his letter to the Council is but another example of Draytonian arrogance peppered with a firm belief in low country intellectual superiority—vintage Drayton. He continues, saying *"I have the pleasure to assure you the men behaved with the most perfect obedience, and demonstrated the firmest resolution ... I trust myself, gentlemen, that your confidence in my prudence is not misplaced. I readily advise with those about me, who, I think, are prudent men, and then I form my own judgement."*[327]

The man is precociously arrogant but, one must admit, decisive and thorough, even though the *"alarm was false."* Drayton's letter closes with the words *"I have been particular in my account of the steps taken ... not out of ostentation, but, because as this is a new business in my hands, you may full judge whether I have conducted it with propriety."* He goes on to offer his assessment of the military situation. Fletchall, Brown and Cunningham *"have no force embodied ... their influence is declining ... their people are terrified. And this last, I assure you, is a fact. They never dreamed we would take the field ... I have well grounded information,"* that, if Loyalist leaders are assembling, it is *"with a view to make terms of accomodation ... they have no determination ... in all human probability this cruel opposition will be crushed without blood spilt in battle."* but if necessary I will *"march into the heart of Fletchall's quarters with about 800 men and 6 pieces of cannon."*[328] Drayton sat back to await war—or peace.

On the subject of Kirkland, he was not far off the mark. Moses indeed "is now invisible." On the very day that Drayton was penning his letter to the Council, Kirkland came to Charleston in disguise to meet with Governor Campbell. This bit of news would be relayed to Drayton on the 15th.

### Tuesday, 12 September

Documents from this date offer further insight into the effects of rumor and reality in the back country. An unsigned letter, from the upper part of the area between the Broad and Saluda, dated 12 September, addressed to Drayton, tells us that the election at James Ford's on the Enoree, set for 7 September, had not gone as well as expected. *"There was but a small gathering—the chief of the whole were liberty boys. They put fourteen members up but did not close the poll."* A new election was rescheduled for *"the 26th of the month ... at Hammond's Old Store on Bush river."*[329]

Loyalist support in these parts was evidently not entirely lacking in determination, as Drayton believed. The writer of this unsigned letter also refers to *"a dedamus come up from the Governor, authorizing Col. Fletchall, Lt. Col. Kirkland, Capt. Cunningham, Champ Terry and John Ford to administer the oath of allegiance to all officers, both civil and military, on which they are advertised to meet the 19th of this month at James Ford's."* In this way one learns that contacts between back country Loyalists and the governor supposedly continue. On the other hand, the writer encouragingly reports *"the people seem very favorable to Liberty, and a great many have signed the association paper."*[330] What is one to believe?

The anonymous letter writer also mentions *"the taking of Majors Robinson and Hendricks,"* both Loyalists. A Capt. Hendricks, as we know, was taken into custody by the Orangeburg militia for hindering Pearis and his Cherokees, but Major Robinson was not involved. Indeed, he was part of the contingent of Loyalists now gathering to face Drayton at Ninety-Six. The anonymous writer was reporting hearsay. Another rumor stated: *"Lord Moses ... it is said, intends to get aboard a man-of-war."* This would prove to be credible; but the writer couldn't possibly have known that Kirkland was already in Charleston by 11 September and would board the *Tamar* on the 12th. Moreover, *"it was being said that loyalists were very much disgusted"* by Kirkland. On the other hand, *"Col. Fletchall is very much displeased with Mr. Terry; lays all the fault to him of taking the powder and ammunition from Ninety Six ... speaks disrespectfully ... Mr. Terry came to his muster* [13 July] *and joined with them, and then informed where the powder was, and insisted on their taking it; and said if they would not, he would go with a small party and take it himself."*[331]

This curious bit of information refers to the incident of 17 July when Cunningham confiscated the powder brought out from Fort Charlotte by Major Mayson and Capt. Kirkland. Kirkland's role in this affair, if any, is not recorded. According to this new intelligence [or rumor], it was Terry who inspired the raid. In any case, with respect to Terry and Kirkland, our anonymous writer states that Fletchall and other Loyalists *"are almost ready to shake the two in a box."* Completing this potpourri of intelligence, the author alludes to the same Loyalist plot of 3 September [previously mentioned]—to ambush an ammunition train from Fort Charlotte where *"five liberty boys"* were sent ten days earlier for powder. Loyalists, led by Benjamin Wofford, *"with about 40 men resolved to take the powder from them. About 100 liberty boys set out immediately, resolving they should not. However, the two companies did not meet in the woods."* The five men, *"instead of following their directions, returned through the settlements with the powder."* Our writer concludes *"To serve some particular reason, I subscribe myself BLANK … you cannot fail to know who the paper comes from."*[332]

The writer was probably Col. William Wofford, who had been Drayton's host at Lawson's Fork three weeks earlier. If so, as father of a Loyalist son, Benjamin, and a Rebel son, Joseph, he was faced with a dilemma of conscience. One can understand why he preferred public anonymity.

Mid September was a time of escalating tensions and growing apprehensions in the back country. From Augusta, also on the 12th, Alexander McLean sent a note to Drayton at Ninety-Six. Having just returned from a trip to Fort Prince George in the Cherokee Nation, where he had seen Cameron, McLean wanted to convince Drayton that Rebels were wrong to think that Cameron was stirring up Indians: *"Let me assure you sir, so diabolic, so very infernal a thought never once entered his head, and if any person could be devilish enough to give him such orders … he will not comply … the people on the frontier of your province were much alarmed as I came through Long Canes last Sunday* [10th]; *they heard that Messrs. Brown, Cunningham … were bringing down Indians upon them. I eased their minds, by assuring them that neither one or the other were true."* McNeal volunteered to visit Drayton at Ninety-Six to further clarify matters—the offer would be spurned.

A third document submitted to Drayton on the 12th was a petition, signed by 56 residents of Long Canes, subscribers to the Association. They offered to form a Volunteer Militia, *"ready to march at 24 hours notice, under the command of our proper officers, commissioned by the Honorable Council of Safety … to defend our country in her liberties from any invasion whatsoever."* But they expected to be reimbursed *"according to the pay of the other troops commissioned and paid by the Government."*[333] Among these volunteers was James Birmingham, who would later become back country South Carolina's first Rebel fatality of the America Revolution, killed at the Battle of Ninety-Six two months later.

Meanwhile, another episode took place on the 12th that would soon raise hackles on many a neck among settlers in the Long Canes region. On the Georgia side of the Savannah, 10 miles west of Fort Charlotte, four Indians were attacked by white settlers near Buffalo Lick, a Creek Indian area bordering Cherokee lands. One Indian was killed, two were wounded and the fourth escaped *"to set up the war whoop."*[334]

This was precisely the kind of incident that could ignite indiscriminate retaliation from Indians if the white culprits were not swiftly brought to justice. As word of the murders spread, frontiersmen in both Carolina and Georgia began to fear for their lives. Tremors of anxiety would soon be felt in Charleston. Meanwhile, Carolinians still remained ambivalent in choosing sides with respect to England or liberty.

*Wednesday, 13 September*

Denunciations, neighbor against neighbor, were now becoming commonplace throughout the province. On the 13th, the Committee of Intelligence at Little River, composed of Samuel Dwight, Josias Allston, William Pierce, Alexander Dunn, John Allston, Jr., and Samuel Price, wrote to the Council of Safety, denouncing Daniel Robins for *"trading with persons who had not signed the Association ... We desire that the said Daniel Robins for his despicable Behaviour ... should be publickly advertised."*[335]

It was on the 13th as well, although the news had not yet reached the back country, that Moses Kirkland's companion, Bailey Cheney, a bodyguard who accompanied Moses to Charleston, was picked up and interrogated by the General Committee. As Laurens would write to Drayton two days later: *"amidst heaps of Shuffling & prevarication they collected enough to confirm not only their belief of Kirkland's being actually on board the Man of War [the Tamar] but also that His Excellency Held a correspondence with our Enemies of a very different nature from that which he had endeavoured to represent to us as the true motive of his writing to Fletchal & others of that party; in order however to obtain more Satisfactory proofs Some of the gentlemen of the Army by a Stratagem which succeeded to their wish procured Such from his own Mouth as were indubitable, the particulars of which we Shall inclose & refer you to ... henceforth we can depend upon this Gentleman [Governor Campbell] only as upon one who under the guise of Neutrality & even pretended friendship is devoted to work our destruction."*[336]

Such words have a strange ring of naiveté coming from a politician as astute as Laurens, but they emphasize the high level of moral and ethical behavior that he prized in personal relations between individuals. Laurens had not yet abandoned all hope of reconciliation with England; he had looked upon Lord William Campbell as an honest broker. Now that Campbell admitted to deviousness in corresponding with Loyalists in the back country, Laurens' eyes were opened. But just what did the Governor say?

After interrogation, Cheney was released, and went immediately to Campbell. The "strategem" used by "the Army" was to send a spy along with him, Capt. Adam McDonald of the First Regiment, who took the pseudonym, Dick Williams. He reported their conversation, which was later repeated by William Moultrie in his memoirs:

"Lord William: *Were you not before the committee today?*

Cheney: *Yes.*

Lord William: *What did they say to you? What did they take you up for?*

Cheney: *Because I came down as a life-guard to Mr. Kirkland.*

Lord William: *They could hurt you for coming in company with Mr. Kirkland.*

Cheney: *I denied it, at first, that I came in company with him.*

Lord William: *I am sorry for that, you should always tell the truth; you need not fear the committee; they can do you no harm; is that one of your acquaintances* [pointing to McDonald].

McDonald and Cheney: *Yes.*

Cheney: *This is Dick Williams.*

McDonald: *I am a serjeant to Kirkland; I am as much concerned as any of them; I want to get out of town early to-morrow, and I am afraid I shall be taken up by the committee; I will carry any message or letter safe to Fletchall, Brown or Cunningham.*

Lord William: *I have nothing to send them, but tell them to keep all the men in good order, to make a circuit and ride constantly round to one another.*

McDonald: *I suppose you correspond with one another.*

Lord William: *Yes. Yes.*

McDonald: *I suppose they must not take up arms now.*

Lord William: *No, not without they have ammunition plenty, and think they are strong enough.*

McDonald: *They are not strong enough, and they have not ammunition enough; for Drayton is there, and getting them over fast.*

Lord William: *If they are not strong enough, tell them by no means to take up arms yet; and that they will be released in a little time.*"[337]

Campbell's advice to Loyalists to bide their time, help was on the way, did not sit well with the Council of Safety. Active measures were immediately initiated to defend Charleston harbor. Men such as Laurens, who favored reconciliation, now felt deceived. He would reluctantly draw closer to the more radical views of Drayton.

While the Council was digesting McDonald's report, William Henry Drayton, self-appointed supreme commander of forces in the back country, was savoring his position at Ninety-Six. Since issuing his ultimatum of 30 August Drayton had encountered no opposition. But, to preclude any thought of hostility on the part of the King's men, he now issued a second ultimatum which, in Caesar-like rhetoric, outlines the nature of the struggle: *"Whereas the liberties of America being treacherously and cruelly violated ... the thirteen colonies ... virtuously, gloriously, thanks to the Lord of hosts! Successfully are confederated ... to wrest from the hands of traitors their liberty ... And whereas ... certain inhabitants of this colony ... oppose and counteract the virtuous efforts of america ... knowingly deceiving their neighbors, and wickedly selling their country, have practised every art, fraud and misrepresentation to raise in this Province an opposition to the voice of America."* To oppose their hellish plots, *"the Honorable the Council of Safety for this Colony, commissioned the Reverend William Tennent, and myself, to make a progress through the disturbed parts of this Colony"* to explore the dispute. But the leaders of opposition *"resolved, by the din of arms, to drown the voice of reason. For such an infernal purpose, by the instigation of Moses Kirkland, on or about the 29th of August last men did actually assemble in arms, and with hostile intentions. My immediately assembling, and marching, with a part of the militia, caused these men to disperse; but now other leaders, of the same malignant party ... have assembled in arms on the north side of Saluda river ... these men threaten to attack the troops under my orders ... Wherefore, to prevent the effusion of civil bloodshed, I think it my duty to issue this declaration ... that I may leave no moderate step untried, to recover ... our unhappy countrymen from these delusions."* Embellishing upon this rhetoric, Drayton called attention to *"the dangerous and disgraceful situation,"* having filled settlers' minds *"with fears and apprehensions that that their lives and properties are in danger from the designs of Congress."* Not true, says Drayton. *"I solemnly declare, that all such apprehensions are ... groundless ... in the name of the council of Safety."* He assures the people of *"perfect safety of their lives, persons and property ... so long as they shall choose to behave peaceably ... we abhor the idea of compelling any person to associate with us,"* but *"any person who will not associate with us ... in this arduous struggle for our liberties, cannot, by us, be considered as friendly ... and, therefore ... we cannot aid and comfort such person, by holding that intercourse and communicating with such person as is usually held between friends ... It is my duty to declare, that I shall march and attack, as public enemies, all and every person in arms ... in opposition to the measures of Congress."*[338]

This declaration was meant for distribution to hostile areas in order to induce Loyalists to negotiate a truce. He sent a copy to Col. Richard Richardson, but deviously sent it so that it would be intercepted—*"a device ... to persuade the enemy that I would persevere in this plan."*[339]

It was also on the 13th that the rest of Major Williamson's forces from

Hardin's Ford on the Savannah showed up at Ninety-Six. Col. Thomson, from the Ridge, had appeared in camp the previous afternoon.

*Thursday, 14 September*

We learn from a later Drayton report that his "declaration was publicly read" in camps of the opposition on the 14th, and that it induced a climate for mutual discussion. The stage was now set for truce talks. Meanwhile, back in Charleston, Rebel leaders were reacting with apprehension to what they perceived as the Governor's own deviousness.

*Friday, 15 September*

A portion of the Council's letter, written on this day, pertained to the whereabouts of Moses Kirkland, who was about to be whisked off to Boston by the British—but the Council did not know this, and they still feared him. Thus, in responding to Drayton's message of 11 September which had *"this moment … by the hands of Fields Pardue been delivered to us,"* Henry Laurens writes, *"we approve of the measures you have taken & you may clearly perceive that even in instances where you have not been altogether clear & explicit in your advices we have imputed the deficiency to the right Cause & put the most favourable construction on all your Acts. Kirkland has eluded all your schemes, but we will not yet think him out of our Reach, tis possible we may Still bring him to answer for his misdeeds—his Companions Robinson, Brown & Cunningham we hope will be taken or driven out of the Colony by you."*[340]

While started on the 15th, Laurens now continues this letter, in obvious annoyance, on the following day: *"16th September—last night a packet arrived from Capt. Pearis who was at Congaree with four Cherokees who were waiting for you—Mr. Pearis laments your delay, represents the anxiety of the Indians … fears bad consequences will follow if they Should return without seeing you or Some person to Talk to them in your stead—this appears to be a matter of great moment & will require your immediate attention—we need not inform you of the contempt in which Indians hold the Man who deceives them & they Scarcely know a difference & never will make the distinction, when their friendship is Courted, between disappointment & deceipt—Cameron too will exult & repeat his Slanders, we therefore recommend this business to your most Serious attention."* From his tone it is obvious that Laurens has taken to heart the admonitions of Indian agent George Galphin, submitted in an earlier letter. The need for a wise Indian policy was beginning to loom large in Charleston's thinking. But the Pearis crisis would linger.

With this letter, Laurens also enclosed a separate message from Drayton's brother, Charles.

*Saturday, 16 September*

Having heard from the Council of William Henry Drayton's success in the back country, his brother Charles, in Charleston, congratulated him. He reports *"Kirkland is aboard the man-of-war ... Chayney with him as friend and guard ... has been before the committee."* Charles mentions that Chayney has also spoken with the Governor, who *"advises the back people not to take up arms, unless they think they are full strong enough—if they think they are, they may—and that they will soon be relieved by troops expected to be here soon."* The governor's expectations were based on his letters of 1 July to Gen. Gage and Adm. Graves in Boston—the letters were ignored. But, so far as Carolinians were concerned, the threat of reinforcements was always imminent.

Meanwhile, on the 16th in the back country, Drayton was about to enter into negotiations for a truce with the Loyalist opposition. As Drayton would report on the 17th, his *"declaration was read in their camp ... together with a series of negociations, procured a deputation ... to me ... I drew up, and, with them, signed the enclosed instrument."* This was the *"Peace Treaty of Ninety Six,"* signed on 16 September. Paraphrasing, it reads in part: *"Wherefore, for the clearing up of the said misunderstandings ... Colonel Thomas Fletchall, Captain John Ford, Captain Thomas Greer, Capt. Evan McLaurin, the Reverend Philip Mulkey, Mr. Robert Merrick and Captain Benjamin Wofford ... have repaired to the camp of the Honorable William Henry Drayton, Esquire, acting under the authority of the Council of Safety for the colony as aforesaid on the one part, and the deputies aforesaid, in pursuance of powers vested in them by the said part of the people on the other part,"* agreed to the following stipulations:

That the Loyalists did not act out of *"unfriendly principle or design"* in declining to associate, *"but proceeded only from a desire to abide in their usual peace and tranquillity."*

That the Loyalists *"never did mean to aid, assist or join the British troops ... if any British troops shall arrive ... the said deputies ... on the part of the people ... shall not, and will not give, yield, or afford, directly or indirectly ... advantage or comfort of the said British troops.*

In these two clauses Drayton's tactful, diplomatic, face-saving language allowed Loyalist leaders to withdraw with pride intact. But the carrot was followed by a stick.

Any person who criticizes *"the proceedings of the Congress of this Colony, or authorities derived from them ... shall be delivered up to the authority of the Congress ... to be questioned and tried and proceeded against."* If any such accused critic does not turn himself in within 14 days of a request, *"the Congress or Council of Safety, or General Committee, may and shall be at liberty to use every means to apprehend every such person."*

But, if any subscriber to the Association should molest a non-signer *"without authority of Congress,"* that person will be punished. In short, all Loyalists *"not offending in or against any of the premises aforesaid, shall, and may continue to dwell and remain at home as usual, safe in their lives, persons, and property ... All persons who shall not consider themselves as bound by this treaty must abide by the consequences ... Done at the camp, near Ninety Six, this 16th day of September, 1775."* Drayton signed for the revolutionary side; Fletchall, Ford, Greer, McLaurin and Wofford for the Loyalist side.[341]

One has to admire Drayton's astuteness in drafting so reasonable a document of common sense. He was no longer asking the Loyalists to take up arms against the King—which is precisely what Fletchall refused to do in his letter of 24 July. Drayton merely asks that Loyalists refrain from aiding and abetting British forces in the struggle—exactly what many Loyalists wanted in the first place, without having to sign the Association document.

The compromise appeared to be something both sides could live with. Unfortunately, other Loyalist leaders such as Robert Cunningham and Thomas Brown would see things differently, thereby prolonging the struggle in the back country, bringing it closer to the brink of serious bloodshed.

Although William Henry Drayton was the only one to sign the Treaty of Ninety-Six for the Rebel side, it was witnessed by three others—Col. William Thomson, Commandant of the Regiment of Rangers, Ely Kershaw, a ranger captain, and Francis Salvador, a young man of 28, born in Middlesex, England.

Salvador had inherited a fortune from his father, married a cousin, and settled in America in 1773, where his father-in-law held 100,000 acres in the Ninety-Six District. Francis was already a well-educated, widely-traveled man before settling in the back country. He served in the First Provincial Congress of South Carolina and had been re-elected to serve in the second. With his aristocratic and heraldic background, he and Drayton found common ground in social equality. It is not surprising that Drayton selected him as a witness. Had he not died the following year, it is likely that Francis

Salvador would have played a prominent role in the political life of South Carolina following the revolution. Unfortunately, on 1 August 1776, he was shot and scalped by Indians in the area of Keowee in the Cherokee Nation. According to a biographer, *"Francis Salvador has the distinction of being the first man of Jewish faith to be elected to the South Carolina legislature and the first to die in the American Revolution."*[342]

### Sunday, 17 September

Having unilaterally concluded an agreement with Loyalists, Drayton reported to Charleston. His letter of the 17th was also a response to the Council's message dated 5 September, in which some Council members were beginning to find Drayton's activities *"somewhat irregular."* Such concern did not bother Drayton in the least. Riding a wave of euphoria, he explains: *"My assuming and exercising the powers contained in your letter of the 11th was only in consequence of the event mentioned in the letter from the Committee at Augusta, on the 6th of August, viz: 'Fletchall's men ... marching to Augusta.' When I received that letter, there were no such men, or any men in arms against us, or Augusta, therefore those powers could not be exercised, and I could not possibly, from them, deem myself authorized at every risk, to seize such men as I thought were enemies to the public. But when, on the 29th of August, I found Fletchall's men, that is, those who had signed his association were, under Kirkland, actually in arms, and, by general account, upon a design of marching to Augusta or Fort Charlotte, then I though the letter of the 11th, was applicable to the time and the event."*[343]

The sophistry with which he defends himself is a wondrous example of political dexterity. Drayton seized unilateral control for the good of the cause—as anyone with confidence in his superior intelligence might do. Thus he can observe with complete equanimity *"I flatter myself, gentlemen, this conduct will shew, that I mean to execute your orders punctually; and that I am clearly sensible that I have the honor to be invested by you."* The treaty, which Drayton now forwarded to the Council, would speak for itself. To make certain it was properly understood, Drayton rationalized the steps leading up to it. To summarize, in Drayton's hopeful words, the Loyalists *"are bound, neither by word or action, to censure, or oppose proceedings of Congress ... with this treaty the spirit of discord is gone forever among them, and there is now a great quarrel between Fletchall and Cunningham."* But, he claims, *"the people approve of Fletchall's conduct ... Cunningham is now left with only about 60 men who, I suppose, will soon disperse ... I have employed people to watch Cunningham, and if he offends, he will be delivered up ... Fletchall and his people will be true ... the affair is now crushed,"* except for Kirkland. *"I continue to pursue him."*[344]

Drayton, of course, does not know that Kirkland has left the back country. But now that a treaty has been signed, he suggests *"that the trade with the back country be opened,"* and that the treaty *"be printed generally in the Gazettes, and in sheets to be immediately circulated throughout the colony ... that they be published in England."* Finally, tackling the Indian question, Drayton reports: *"I have not yet seen Pearis and his Indians, but I expect to see them in a few days, after which I shall return to Charles Town."*[345]

The Indians, who were specifically requested by Drayton to come down to Col. Thomson's camp in Amelia to meet with him, have been cooling their heels at the Congarees since 5 September. But Drayton is no hurry to see them. He blithely says that he plans *"to stay to stay here* [at Ninety-Six] *with the rangers for a few days ... I shall send off a company of rangers to quiet the fears of the people above ... with orders not to advance any thing near the Indian line ... I shall discharge the militia. To-day I returned the army public thanks—they are really a fine body of men."* Drayton, at this point, was confidently wrapping up his mission. On one final item, referring to the Council's letter of 5 September, he cautions: *"In respect to your intended distribution of powder, I beg leave to advise that no powder be distributed into the Fork, or Ninety six District."*[346]

Such caution was necessary because, in spite of his optimism, Drayton was well aware that his treaty was not acceptable to all Loyalists. If opposition spread, the treaty wouldn't be worth the paper on which it was written.

# CHAPTER XIV

## *Taking Toll as the Plot Thickens*

BOTH ROBERT CUNNINGHAM AND THOMAS BROWN WERE ADAMANTLY opposed to the Treaty of Ninety-Six. An enlightening letter from Thomas Brown addressed to Governor William Campbell on 18 October reviews events between 11-16 September. It offers insight into Loyalist feelings during the period of treaty negotiations that disagree with Drayton's interpretation, and views the Loyalist/Rebel quarrel from a different perspective, as the battle for the hearts and minds of back country settlers continues.

After Drayton and his army arrived at Ninety-Six, Brown states: *"Captain Cunningham & I immediately began to embody Men for the security of our Friends & having in the course of 5 days* [between 11-16 September] *collected 2200 men and encamped about 10 miles above Saluda & near 16 from Ninety Six … Colonel Fletchall joined us with about 250 men & as Colonel of the District we resigned our Command to him—his presence foreboded no good—his Timidity which he could not conceal from the People gave such general Offense that Captain Cunningham's men & mine insisted upon having him drummed out of camp. As our Camp consisted chiefly of men of property … near 1000 of which had been in his Majesty's Service the last war* [Cherokee Indian War], *'twas with extreme Difficulty we moderated their Resentment against Fletchall."*[347]

Fletchall wasn't actually drummed out, but resentment against him was building. Brown recalls events in his letter, as follows: *"When Drayton received intelligence of the Strength of our party he dispatched two messengers, Messrs. Anderson & Moore with overtures of peace."* In the Loyalist camp *"a Council of Officers was called & a Person dispatched to know their Conditions. Colonel Fletchall fixed upon a man almost as timid as himself tho' of somewhat better understanding."* When this emissary [name unknown] arrived at the Rebels camp on 12 September, it seems that *"Drayton ordered his men to form the 'hollow square' by which politic Manovre the poor Dastard* [the emissary] *unacquainted with military Evolutions concluded their body which consisted of 1250 men was innumerable ... struck with terror, he went so far as to acquaint Drayton that it was his Opinion we would submit to any terms. Drayton judging of the Disposition of our Troops by our Messengers issued the Declaration [13 September] with an answer by Letter, the purport of which was after promising the peaceable Intentions of himself and Congress with some Observations on the Number of their friends in the Province, that if Cunningam, Fletchall & I would surrender ourselves the non-subscribers would meet with no molestation or disturbance in the future ... In this Stage of our Negociation we apprehended an Express from Drayton with a Letter to a Colonel Richardson, the Substance of which was as follows that he should raise a Body of men with all Expedition and entrench near the river Inoree until he [Drayton] had sufficiently strengthened his party, for which purpose he had dispatched Expresses to every part of the Province, that he had sent orders to Colonel Thomas to burn the houses & destroy the Plantations of all the non-subscribing Absentees."*[348]

The Loyalists, of course, were meant to intercept the letter to Richardson—as part of the game of intimidation played by Drayton. But rather than cow the opposition, Brown tells us: *"This letter of Drayton's I read to the People, which having commented upon, the People were raised to such a Pitch of Fury that it was with the utmost Difficulty we restrained them from attempting an Attack in the Indian mode upon their Camp that very night which was at that time impracticable from the River Saluda's not being fordable ... Captain Cunningham & I had mediated an Attack in the night with a party of 800 men. As soon as we could command the Pass of the River, which I'm convinced from Drayton's ignorance in the Disposition of his Swivels & men & the little Confidence he placed in People drafted contrary to their inclinations, would have been attended with all the success we could wish."*[349]

This empty boast from Brown at least offers better understanding of his agitated state of mind. In his letter to the governor, he continues: *"In answer to the letter from Drayton [to initiate peace talks], at the Request of our military Council I dictated a Reply which to the best of my Recollection was as follows. We acknowledge the Receipt of yours. Your public Declarations little correspond with the private communication of your Sentiments in your Letters to Colonels Richardson & Thomas ... We profess ourselves as averse to the Effusion of human blood as Mr. Drayton & Congress & to have as sincere Desire for Peace on such a proper solid footing as may restore tranquility to this distracted Province ... We must further observe we have as true & real Regard for Liberty established on constitutional Principles as any Men on the Continent by whatever name distinguished & shall take very proper legal Steps in our Power for its Preservation &*

*Support … As to the boasted Numbers of Mr. Drayton, it will never intimidate Men actuated by the true spirit of Freedom & as to the ignominious Surrender he speaks of we are sorry he entertains so contemptible & Dishonorable an Opinion of us as to think it will ever be complied with."*[350]

Words to this effect were evidently transmitted to Drayton by letter from the Loyalists for, as Brown continues, *"on Drayton's receipt of the above he dispatched a Major Williamson with Captain Cohoun [sic] & Hammond requesting a Conference with Fletchall, Cunningham and myself, these officers to be left as Hostages for our Security … this proposal was rejected with indignation by our men for the following reasons … that as Drayton had solicited Peace it was his Duty to attend at our Camp & that the Officers proposed to be left as hostage were not of that Consequence to them as we were to our own People but that if it was the inclination of Fletchall to attend with some Officers of inconsiderable Consequence as Messengers they had no Objection but would not on any Account consent that Cunningham or I should attend."*[351]

From such words, Brown clearly thought that the majority of Loyalists supported him and Cunningham, not Fletchall, and they were not about to allow themselves to be entrapped by Drayton. Consequently, it was on his own, says the unapproving Brown, that *"Fletchall … selected 6 as ignorant and illiterate as himself"* to negotiate for the Loyalists. But, *"with the Approbation of Captain Cunningham, I proposed the following instructions to be delivered by our Messengers … which were unanimously agreed to with this further clause that if complied with fully by Drayton in such case they* [Fletchall's team] *were at liberty to act as Plenipotentiaries."*[352]

The nature of Brown's instructions is not revealed. Nonetheless, *"Fletchall and the rest of the Messengers having received their instructions set off for Ninety Six … on his arrival distressed with apprehensions in order to revive his spirits had such frequent Recourses to the Bottle as to soon render himself non compos—whilst in this Condition Drayton without consulting anyone drew up the Articles. Fletchall having heard the Articles read which I'm convinced neither he or the rest understood, Meyrick & Mulkey excepted, & without mentioning a Syllable of the Instructions, signed the Articles prescribed by Drayton & prevailed upon the rest to follow his example."*[353]

If we are to believe Brown, Col. Fletchall was completely drunk when he signed the treaty, along with four of his followers; part of Fletchall's delegation, the two Baptist preachers, Philip Mulkey and Robert Meyrick, declined to sign. When Fletchall returned to the Loyalist camp and read the articles to those assembled, Brown reports: *"The People no sooner heard the shameful disgraceful conditions … seized with Rage & Indignation they swore* to a man nay even the *Officers who had signed, upon explaining the Nature of these Articles, that they never would abide by them but execrated Fletchall who had betrayed them.*"[354]

If indeed this was the true sentiment in a Loyalist camp of 2500 men, then Fletchall was a traitor to their cause, and the treaty was worthless. However, Brown has a propensity for bluster. Although there undoubtedly were divisions among the Loyalists, it is hard to believe that Fletchall was overwhelmingly condemned. If that were true then Brown and Cunningham should have had no difficulty in leading an attack upon Drayton. After all, the Loyalists had more men and, as Brown himself maintained, *"the Camp of Drayton lay at our mercy & … we could have commanded 5 thousand men."* He further claims that, after the terms of the treaty were read in camp, *"men made a Tender of their services to Captain Cunningham & myself that they were ready & willing then to sacrifice their fortune & Lives in our Behalf."* Yet no action was taken. In his later letter to the governor, Brown simply explains that *"Captain Cunningham & I having retired for about an hour and considered what steps we could most prudently take in such circumstances, concluded upon dismissing our troops until we had received your Lordships instructions … which Captain Cunningham & I hope will meet with your Lordships approbation."*[355] So, for the moment, Loyalist opposition fizzled out with barely a whimper.

When the Loyalists dispersed, Thomas Brown headed off for Charleston *"in Expectation of the Honor of a conference with your Lordship & to receive such instructions as might appear necessary for the regulations of our Conduct."* The curtain was falling on Brown as a back country agitator. He did not obtain his requested audience with the governor. Brown faded from the stage of 1775, but would reappear at a later date. The treaty would receive mixed reactions among Loyalists and Rebels when made public. Meanwhile, during this period of 11-16 September, other corollary and significant events had been taking place. Fort Johnson in Charleston Harbor was occupied by Rebel forces on the morning of the 15th. On the same day, Governor Campbell took refuge aboard the HMS *Tamar,* a British gunboat. These events triggered some soul searching in South Carolina's conservative Chief Executive Officer, Henry Laurens. A perennial letter writer, he had a knack for summarizing his feelings while describing unfolding events.

*Monday, 18 September*

Writing to son John in London, after a bizarre weekend, Laurens laments: *"Our poor people here are proceeding by hasty Steps, attempts too mighty for their abilities, & every day convinces me that I was not wrong when I endeavoured to dissuade them from taking the Reins of Government into their hands ... for my part I remain tranquil, patience is my happiness, I oppose every wrong measure although it is necessary to give motion to many by my signature.*"[356]

As a reluctant revolutionary, Laurens has reached a point of struggle with his conscience. He prefers reconciliation, but compromise seems to be slipping away. He deplores violent means to justify a revolutionary end, but is willing to sanctify them with his imprimatur. Unable to oppose the radicals, Laurens tells his son: "*I lament the fate of a people who Seem forced & impelled to do very improper acts on Support of a good Cause.*" Recounting recent events, Laurens observes "*the King's Officer's have been disarmed—Capt. Innes banished—Mr. Roupel [Deputy Postmaster] confined to his own house—Wm. Wragg to his plantation near Dorchester—Lord William is gone aboard the Tamar Man of War—the House of the Assembly dissolved—the Judges have shut up the Courts of law—the custom house will probably Soon follow the example— Fort Johnson is taken into the hands of the people Garrisoned by 400 of the new raised Troops commanded by Col. Motte—New Batteries they say are to be raised & Vessels equipped for defence of the Harbour— W.H. Drayton is at the head of 1200 Men reasoning with some of the disaffected in the back country—You think people in England are acting madly. I am sure we may Safely compare Notes with them in this country—I am ready to cry out, a pox on both their Houses; we are all Mad; all wrong; but if I am to die it Shall be on the right side, I honestly mean on this Side—I detest & abhor the measures of Administration.*"[357]

Henry Laurens has also come to the conclusion that Campbell is indeed "*privately spiriting up the People on our Frontiers to oppose our Association & to hold themselves in readiness to act against the colony ... to this untoward circumstance add the unfavorable accounts which we have received from the Indians, the danger which we are always exposed to & more especially at this time from domestic Insurrection & the expectation of British Troops & Ships of War.*"[358]

Laurens was discouraged over the situation in South Carolina; but so was Governor William Campbell during his self-imposed exile aboard the HMS *Tamar*, where he was now drafting his Despatch #7 to Whitehall.

## Tuesday, 19 September

Justifying his hasty departure from Charleston, Lord William comments: "*The King's Dignity and the Honor of His Government would not permit me to remain any longer in Charles Town ... fresh violences have every day been committed.*" He acknowledges receiving Whitehall's message #18 drafted on

5 July, which arrived in Charleston only on 13 September. It gave the Governor *"most sincere pleasure, as I hope to see a respectable force in this province."*[359] This was the letter the Council had demanded to see, the one Campbell alluded to in conversation with Cheney and McDonald. Its contents, as reported by McDonald, upset Rebel leaders, motivating them to take defensive measures. Thus, on the 14th, the Council of Safety requested the governor and his entourage to relinquish their arms. Not being able to comply with honor, the governor chose to exile himself aboard the *Tamar*, anchored off Fort Johnson. Before leaving town, however, the governor dutifully dissolved the Assembly—a meaningless but necessary symbolic gesture, in order to maintain his dignity of office.

Of particular interest in Campbell's letter of the 19th is confirmation of the fact that *"a few days before I left Charles Town Mr. Kirkland, a Lieut. Colonel on the Back Country Militia, who has great influence amongst the People here, came to see me requesting to be sent to Boston. He assures me they want nothing but Arms, Amunition and a few experienced Officers and he will engage to raise 4000 men for the service … winter is best for action in this Country, and I am well convinced part of General Gage's Army deployed to the Southward during that season would effectually reduce the three Provinces of Georgia, South and North Carolina."*[360]

Early military action in the soft underbelly of the colonies might well have worked. Fortunately for the Rebels, no America-based British troops could be spared. And the reinforcements now being mobilized in England would not reach South Carolina for eight months. However, Campbell's spirits must have been buoyed by Kirkland's appearance. He writes of *"the loyalty of those poor, honest, industrious people in the back country … the rebels here very justly dread so formidable a body at their backs and have drawn together 1500 men amongst which are 60 Catawba Indians … to crush and oppress them … I have ever since my arrival made it my anxious study to encourage and keep the spirit amongst those loyal people, and have succeeded so well that I have incurred … the detestation and hatred of the whole faction. I shall send Mr. Kirkland to Boston the first opportunity … Mr. Kirkland acquaints me Fort Charlotte is also in the hands of the rebels."*[361]

Although Campbell seeks to put a favorable spin to his actions vis-à-vis the back country, he is blowing smoke at this point. His contacts with the back country have been tenuous at best; Loyalist settlers saw the handwriting on the wall. Their dwindling expectations induced jumbled reactions—from Thomas Brown's blustering to Moses Kirkland's loose cannon extremism—all talk and little action. This was in marked contrast to William Henry Drayton's decisiveness in propagating the Association and negotiating a truce. His treaty of Ninety-Six might well have marked an end to Loyalist resistance in the back country had not the misfortune of a bungled Indian policy intervened.

*Wednesday, 20 September*

Aboard the *Tamar*, Lord William Campbell composed a letter for Kirkland to carry to General Thomas Gage in Boston. He comments, not without sarcasm, "*I ... was in hopes his Majesty's service to the Northward would have permitted some little to have been paid to his Southern Provinces. I have now only to acquaint your Excellency that this Province has some time been in a state of open Rebellion, and after undergoing many mortifications and insults I was at last obliged a few days ago to take refuge on board the Tamar, and leave the Officers of the Crown disarmed & confined to Charlestown ... the bearer of this, Mr. Kirkland, was a Lieut. Colonel of Militia in the back part of this country, I know him to be a man who has great influence there and by his attachment to Government has I fear sacrificed all. He has acquainted me with all the particulars of what he means to communicate to your Excellency, and I am convinced, if the execution is not delayed too long, he may be made very useful in this and neighboring Provinces of Georgia and North Carolina.*"[362]

Unknown to the Governor, Loyalist fortunes in the back country have taken a turn for the worse. Those who do not adhere to Drayton's treaty will be hunted down.

*Thursday, 21 September*

Drayton wrote to Robert Cunningham, again explaining his mission "*to promote peace.*" He expressed his pleasure that "*Fletchall and other gentlemen*" signed his treaty, "*but it was with concern, that I have heard that you will not be bound by it.*" In his velvet glove mode, Drayton asks Cunningham to write to him, "*assuring me that that you hold yourself included.*"[363] This letter was datelined the Congarees; Drayton by now had removed himself from Ninety-Six and, one assumes, will finally get around to meeting with Pearis and his Indians, who have been waiting for him since 5 September. Drayton, however, delayed the encounter another four days, while basking in the glory of his achievements.

Meanwhile, the Council in Charleston was becoming increasingly anxious. As of 21 September, the last bit of news received from Drayton had been a letter dated 11 September, to which the Council replied on the 15th expressing concern over relations with Indians. Now, on the 21st, in another rebuke to Drayton, the Council hopes that he was on his *"way to meet with those Indians, who, led by Capt. Pearis, came from the Cherokees at your command, and who have, in the utmost anxiety and impatience, been many days waiting for you."* In addition, Drayton is told *"We have several copies of intercepted letters from the superintendent* [John Stuart] *at St. Augustine to his agents in the Nation. They look so much like design to amuse us."*363 Nevertheless, Drayton is cautioned to be on his guard.

The intercepted letters referred to Stuart's of 30 August to David Tait and to his "talk" to the Cherokees. The Council views these as counterfeit, meant to be intercepted. For Rebels in Charleston, Stuart's desire to keep the peace was a ploy. They remained anxious about real feelings among the Indians. Consequently, it was feared that Drayton's indifference might antagonize the chiefs waiting for him at the Congarees with Pearis. The Council also informs Drayton, in their letter of the 21st, that *"Capt. Pearis applies for commission … if one is granted it must be especial … you will be the best to judge."* It notes, as well, that Col. Wofford has applied for *"commissions to organize a regiment against Fletchall."*

When he applied for commissions, Wofford was ignorant of the peace treaty signed by Fletchall and Drayton. As of the 21st, neither was the Council of Safety yet aware of it. But the treaty would soon be known throughout the province; reactions began to trickle in.

## Monday, 25 September

In the Tyger River region, which remained strongly pro-Fletchall, a different interpretation of the Drayton treaty was taking place. On the 25th, John Prince, a newly elected representative to the Second Provincial Congress from the lower part of the Broad and Saluda, took time to pen a cautious letter to Drayton. Prince informs his *"honor … some of Fletchall's party"* are gloating over treaty *"concessions … you were forced to make in their favor."* If so, Prince believes these were made *"purely from the dictates of humanity."* Nevertheless, Prince seeks reassurance from Drayton that he did not give away too much to Loyalists, *"considering the ignorance and malignancy of their natures."* Such a reaction is strikingly opposite to Thomas Brown's analysis. The Loyalists in Prince's area believed that Drayton had been conned. In either case, the extent to which they might still resist the inducement to violence was still in question.

Meanwhile, Moses Kirkland, on the 25th, surfaced in St. Augustine,

Florida, from where he planned to sail for Boston. This information would be conveyed in a letter dated the 29th from Frederick Mulcaster in St. Augustine to Governor Grant of West Florida. It was intercepted by Rebel forces and eventually found its way to Charleston.

On the 25th of September, as well, Indian affairs were about to assume center stage in South Carolina. It was on this day that Drayton finally turned his attention to Pearis and his Cherokees. Drayton presented his usual "talk" to them, a patented, flowery discourse, redundant with imagery to suit Indian mentality as perceived by the white man. It was entitled *"A Talk from the Honorable William Henry Drayton Esq., one of the Beloved Men of South Carolina to the Beloved Men, Head Men, and Warriors of the Cherokee Nation at the Congarees, September 25, 1775."*[365]

Such speeches offer the student of American history an incomparable insight into White/Indian relations and attitudes. They are historical gems, of which only a sliver is herein quoted: *"Before our forefathers left England … they made an agreement with the Great king … that they should contnue to have and to enjoy the same rights and privileges … the king broke the agreement … has made laws which … have a right to take our money away without our consent … Friends and Brother warriors … is it not now as plain as the sight at the end of your rifles that these laws and proceedings are like so many hatchets chopping our agreement to pieces."* The talk continues to discuss the tax on tea and other injustices before Drayton observes: *"Friends I have now told you the causes of our unhappy quarrel. I hope that your eyes are opened, that you see plainly that your interest is as much concerned in the quarrel as our interest … we have put on our shot pouches and have taken up our rifles, only to defend our rights and privileges … and to defend your deer skins against those who wish to rob you … let us act together … I am informed that you have been told that your brothers the white people in Charlestown used you ill when they seized some ammunition which your traders intended to have sent you. It is true, my friends, that we did seize the ammunition … knew it would distress you … but blame the king … we had to defend ourselves … were compelled to seize it … our behavior was natural and just … we knew you would understand … to show you that we regard you as brothers, we intend to make you a present of some of these arms … we will share."*[366] This last offer would later come to haunt the revolutionaries.

In meeting with Pearis and his Indians, Drayton would also mention the recent murders of Indians by whites on 12 September. The incident greatly enhanced tensions along the frontier, a matter to which the Council was privy, having heard from its agent to the Cherokees, Edward Wilkinson. Only a week earlier Wilkinson had met with Drayton and Col. Thomson in Ninety-Six, bringing news of the murders. It was this news that prompted Drayton to send the rangers on a tour of the Indian border to calm settlers. Drayton now expressed sorrow to the Cherokees at the Congarees. He knows that *"the Indians want satisfaction … and wait to see what the white man will do."*[367]

Another version of this encounter between Drayton, Pearis and the Indians on 25 September would later be given by Richard Pearis himself in a sworn affidavit signed on 11 November. The pertinent part reads *"he the Deponent went to the Congrees with five Indians—to meet Mr. Drayton—saith that he the Deponent & the Indians did stay 20 days—waiting for Mr. Drayton and that on his, Mr. Draytons conversation with the Indians he Delivered them a Talk—Telling—that the white man here were Oppresed by Britain—that if they did not soon prevent and resist … the price of goods for skins would increase threefold … and that the Indians would also be oppressed & asked them to be their friends in the Dispute against Britain—that the Indians Did tell Mr. Drayton they took him by the hand—Desired him & the White men his friends be strong—and if they were not able to fight the Battle Themselves that they the Indians would Assist them—that he Mr. Drayton said to the Indians—he was sorry to tell them that he & his friends were obliged to detain the powder which was sent by their Great Father to them as usual for their own defence—but still of the little ammunition which they had—they would spare the Indians a Part."*[368]

The affidavit then lapses into topics of a more personal nature: *"saith he the Deponent Did tell Mr. Drayton that he understood that the council of Safety were to appoint a superintendent of Indian affairs—Desired that if they thought him worthy—he might be appointed to the office—& that Mr. Drayton did promise that he the Deponent should be appointed—and that the commission should be sent up along with the Ammunition & presents for the Indians & that he did then ask Mr. Drayton if he had considered of the purchase—about which they had talked at Capt'n Woffords upon which Mr. Drayton replied he thought the price mentioned at the time was Very high but that he Mr. Drayton was still very desirous of making a purchase conjointly with the Deponent & saith that he Mr. Drayton Did tell the Deponent—that he thought that when the Indians were assembled to Receive the Ammunition he the Deponent might very well get them to sign a Deed for the land to the Deponent & Mr. Drayton without any further presents—upon which the Deponent seeing that Mr. Drayton— Intended to make the Ammunition the payment of this land—told him that were the Deponent to Endeavor to such a thing— Both whites and Indians would consider him as Cheating the Indians out of their land … Upon this reply of the*

*Deponent Mr. Drayton seemed Dissatisfyed—uttr'd a swear and walked off—saith the Deponent he did immediately go to Ralph Humphreys a Tavern Keeper at the Congarees—& told him what Mr. Drayton had said to him—saying he wanted to cheat the Indians."*[369]

With respect to the appointment as Indian agent sought by Pearis, Edward Wilkinson would first have to be dismissed. This may be why Pearis, in his sworn statement would also say that *"he did go to Mr. Drayton & told him that Mr. Wilkinson was a Roague—and Desired that he be taken out of the Nation—that Mr. Drayton told him that they should first get Cameron, then think about Wilkinson."*[370]

With all this conniving going on, the truth is difficult to ascertain. However, the statement made by Pearis, *"saith he the Deponent is assured that from what Mr. Drayton did say to the Indians—that he intended to Employ the Indians to fight against the white men for the committee,"* probably did the most damage to Drayton's reputation. It will be taken up in context. In making his statement on 11 November, Pearis had also switched to the side of the Loyalists. But on 25 September, all one knows is that Drayton was trying to calm the fears of Indians over trade, attempting to rectify matters by offering them a part of the Rebels supply of available gunpowder.

*Monday, 26 September*

Before leaving the back country, Drayton once more assumed the mantle of supreme authority as he writes to Alexander Cameron in a letter of the 26th: *"In consequence of the powers vested in me by the Council of Safety … in this time of public calamity, when the King's troops have unnaturally commenced … to prosecute a cruel war upon the people of America … when we have just cause to shortly expect the arrival of the King's troops in this colony to spread slaughter and devastation, we feel strongly actuated by the prevailing principles in human nature … to remove at a distance every object that has any ability … to impede our means of defence, or to assist the enemy."* Drayton's objective was to get Cameron to leave the Cherokee Nation, so he very bluntly tells him: *"we look upon you as an object dangerous to our welfare … we do most ardently wish to procure your removal by the mildest measures, and politest mode of application.* But, should Cameron resist, Drayton reminds him that his word *"carries all the force of a command, and that you cannot disobey, with safety to your person."*[371] But disobey he would. Twenty days later Cameron would reject Drayton's ultimatum.

Drayton was now wrapping up his mission to the back country, preparing to return to Charleston. The Regiment of Rangers, back in camp, was concerned with updating their muster rolls. Captain Caldwell, who has been occupying Fort Charlotte since 12 July, finally submitted his first roll call and pay bill showing a full complement of men except for one lieutenant and a drummer boy. Surprisingly, it was *"sworn to Before me this 26th September 1775, George Whitefield,"* former commanding officer of the fort. *"John Caldwell being duly sworn upon the Holy Evangelist of almighty God, maketh Oath that the above is a just and true Pay Bill."*[372]

The muster list shows William Cunningham, age 19, as a private in Caldwell's Company. Born in Virginia, young William, a cousin to Robert and Patrick Cunningham, would soon become famous in his own right. According to Loyalist historian Samuel Curwen, William's *political opinions leaned to the Whig side, and, being a great favorite with the young men of the district of his own age, he exercised considerable influence over them. On this account, he was applied to by John Caldwell, to assist in raising a company.* William Cunningham served with Caldwell until the following year, when he fought under Andrew Williamson during the Indian campaign in the autumn of 1776. After this, *"he declared that, having seen reason to change his opinions, he was determined to continue no longer in the service of the Whigs."* According to Curwen, it was because *"a party of lawless Whigs took William's crippled brother out of his house at night, whipped him to death."* This act set in motion a vendetta of atrocities against the Whigs [Rebels] by William, who spent the rest of the war on the Loyalist side, holding the rank of major. His *"life was passed in a series of wild adventures, so often ending in such fearful tragedies, as to earn him … the significant cognomen of Bloody Bill."* John Caldwell would turn out to be one of Bloody Bill's victims in 1781.[373]

The 26th of September was a busy day for correspondence. From Charleston, once again, the incomparable Henry Laurens offers a glimpse into his thoughts as he writes to son John in London. Quoting only from those parts which affect back country matters, we learn that Tennent *"returned from his Embassy some days ago—Mr. Drayton still remains & will remain some time longer. He has just transmitted to the council of safety a Treaty which he had concluded with the heads of those Malcontents on the 16th inst. Together with a Declaration which he had previously put forth & which had the desired effect of bringing them in … if we have received any pleasure from the knowledge of this flattering Treaty which between you & me I look upon as a very bad & imperfect Cure, our joy is a little damped by a Shocking Account of a Cherokee Man killed & two others wounded in an attempt to kill, in cold blood by four White Men unknown which we have just receiv'd from Mr. Wilkinson at Keowee there is therefore no doubt of the fact, & the Act is looked upon as a contrivance by our Enemies to set those barbarians upon us—Many attempts have been made to exonerate the superintendant under the first charge against him but I say it with concern that I am more & more convinced his design was to keep the Indians always disposed to Act for His Majesty's service."*[374]

To the chagrin of Laurens and other Council members, his convictions would soon be challenged by events, and Loyalists would accuse the Council of a similar nefarious alliance with Indians.

# CHAPTER XV

## *The Limitations of Patriotism*

AS THE MONTH OF SEPTEMBER DREW TO A CLOSE, IT APPEARED THAT back country Loyalists were in headless disarray. Kirkland was gone, Fletchall was cowed, Cunningham and Brown were sulking and Robinson was nowhere to be found. Drayton's army had been disbanded and he had returned to the Congarees. The treaty had been received with skepticism in Charleston on 25 September. Laurens labeled it "a bad and imperfect cure."

### *Wednesday, 27 September*

Replying to Drayton on this day, the Council, nevertheless, stated *"we will send the declaration and the treaty to be printed in London, but shall defer a publication here until we have an opportunity of discussing the propriety of such a measure in your presence, which, we suppose, will happen in the course of a few days ... we hope that you have sent away the Good Warrior and his fellow-travelers in good humour, and that they will influence their countrymen to remain quiet and give us time to discover the perpertrators of the murder intimated by Mr. Wilkinson; in the meantime we trust you have taken the proper measures for that purpose."*[375]

Wilkinson had already conferred with Drayton and Col. Thomson in Ninety-Six—they were aware of the murders before the news reached Charleston. Rangers had been sent on a reconnaissance tour of the frontier to "ease the minds of the people." But the good warrior [Pearis] and his fellow travelers were not in good humor. Thomson's own report to the Council of his activities after the treaty gives one a clearer picture of events as they unfolded.

*Friday, 29 September*

Col. Thomson, back in Amelia, now writes that he *"has just returned from Ninety Six."* Recounting events after the treaty was signed, *"I took a ride to Fort Charlotte, & examined the whole; I think it is in very good order for defence & that there is a very good Company in it."* Returning to Ninety-Six, *"I met with Mr. Wilkinson from the Cherokee Nation who informed me that one of the Indians was killed & two wounded by some of the Georgia people. I immediately gave orders to Lieut. Taylor of Fort Charlotte to take a party of Men with him & go in search of the Persons ... whose names Mr. Wilkinson mentioned to me ... Mr. Drayton's opinion in this case concurs with my own ... that the Rangers were raised in defence of the country, the back Setlers would think hard if they were not with them in case of danger ... We have order'd them to march for some time amongst them but not to proceed within fifteen Miles of the Indian Line, for fear of alarming the Indians, & in order to appease the minds of the inhabitants in those parts."*[376]

While the rangers were away, Drayton returned to the Congarees. Thomson and his men remained on their reconnaissance tour for a week before returning to Ninety-Six around 26 September. The regiment then gathered at camp in Amelia by the 28th. It was from here that Thomson wrote to the Council. This same letter enclosed *"A General Return of my regiment of Rangers from the time of enlisting to the 20th instant."* The rangers were now given leave once more *"in order to recruit themselves & horses ... they are to meet at the camp in Amelia on 24th October."* In this same letter Thomson says that *"Capt. Wise ... resigned his commission to Mr. Drayton ... as he will inform you."*[377]

Drayton had left Amelia, accompanied by Samuel Wise. They would be in Charleston by the 30th, where Samuel Wise would write a letter to the Council of Safety to explain his resignation. This offers the reader another glimpse into the sensitivity of men in revolutionary South Carolina to the values of honor and integrity.

Meanwhile, on the 29th, Thomson wrote a second, private letter to Henry Laurens, as was his custom in this special relationship. He assures Laurens *"you may depend that I shall always make a proper Distinction in my Private & Public Letters to You ... Your present situation of President & Chairman I am convinc'd must be very fatigueing, & tho I cannot but think it is high time that you ought to be relieved of your burthen Yet I am afraid they will not find a Person to supercede You, who will act in both capacities & be of as much Service to the Country as you have been."* Having completed his ablutions, Thomson agrees that *"Kirkland ... be severely punished for his*

*Villainy.*" Commenting on the treaty, Thomson observes "*I was informed that Cunningham & Brown were not well pleased with Fletchall for what he had done.*" On the subject of Pearis and his Indians, "*they are very well pleased but wishes to have the ammunitin that was promised as soon as possible.*" Finally, Thomson hints that he intends "*going to Town sometime next week, when I will do myself the pleasure of waiting on You & converse more fully on the news of the country.*"[378]

### Saturday, 30 September

From "*Charles Town*" in a letter addressed "*To the Honorable—the Council of Safety,*" Captain Samuel Wise apologizes for resigning: "I *having entered into the service with a heart full of zeal & for the legal freedom of myself & fellow subjects of this Province in particular, & the constitutional rights of America in general; so, nothing less than being dishonored by a suspicion of a want of integrity to the great cause of constitutional liberty, would have induced me to have taken this step; & I hope your honors will be pleased to consider the bitterness of my feelings, when Mr. Drayton refused to tell me the name of the man who had thus disgraced me.*"[379]

Who complained about Wise, or why, is not revealed. Commenting upon the affair, one local historian would later write: "*Captain Wise was a man of the nicest sense of honor, and doubtless betrayed a morbid sensibility under the wound which must have been unjustly inflicted on his reputation. He was induced to withdraw his resignation.*"[380] One year later Wise would become a major in the rangers when Mayson was promoted to Lt. Colonel and Thomson to full Colonel.

The perception of honor played a significant role in the minds of revolutionary Carolinians. For example, Major Mayson complimented Capt. Whitefield on his honorable surrender of Fort Charlotte. He asked Capt. Ezekiel Polk to consider honor before deserting the rangers on 28 July. Expressing remorse, Polk was later forgiven by Drayton, who suggested he be given a commission with the volunteer militia instead. In this capacity, Ezekiel Polk is once again heard from.

### Monday, 2 October

Writing to Henry Laurens from the New Acquisitions District, "*with zeal & Esteem Your most Obed't Humble Servant Ezek'l Polk*" pays due homage and then complains "*I am partly in a State of inactivity. I took my company & five Companies of the Militia & Volunteers, in order to join Coll. Thompson*

[sic], *but had not Marched far till we Received Certain Intelligence that Coll. Fletchall had Decamped; I have made a Tour among tories on Kings Creek some of whom Seem Determined not to subscribe the association; I have Thought that forcing them to Subscribe would not sufficiently Secure them, therefore I have taken a middle course ... as you will find by the Inclosed Deposition; I thought it prudent at this Dangerous Crisis to proceed in this manner as Some have already Declared, that although the Want of Necessaries has Obliged them to Subscribe yet they would join the other party if they must fight."*[381]

Such intelligence implies that Drayton's trade sanctions are working, that back country farmers are signing the Association, but only as an expedient. If it comes to an actual conflict, they will side with the Loyalists. This news could not have amused leaders in Charleston when Polk's letter reached them.

Meanwhile, on 2 October, the Council of Safety was drafting a letter to George Galphin to corroborate his designation as Commissioner for Indian Affairs. This letter spells out Galphin's authority *"to treat with the said Indians in the name & on behalf of the united colonies in order to preseve peace & friendship with the said Indians and to prevent their taking part in the present commotions."*[382] The administrative organs of the revolutionary government were taking shape, and the Indian question continued to remain a priority.

## Tuesday, 3 October

Keeping in mind the recent murder of Indians by white men on the upper Savannah, Laurens solicitously writes to his counterparts on the Georgia Council of Safety: *"we find that the Cherokees ... were killed & wounded in your colony, we think it very necessary to Advertise & offer a reward for discovery of the perpetrators."*[383] Twenty days had elapsed since the crime was committed; Laurens had not yet received Thomson's letter of 29 September in which he says that he was given the names of the killers by Wilkinson and has sent Lt. Taylor with a party of men from Fort Charlotte to apprehend them. They were eventually captured, but whether by Taylor is not confirmed.

## Wednesday, 4 October

After George Galphin was sent his commission on the 2nd, Laurens followed up with a personal letter on the 4th, saying: *"I think I should be deficient in point of justice to a Gentleman in the service of my country & and an old acquaintance if I did not inform you of an attack upon your character as a friend to the American cause."* Again, honor and patriotism are at stake, trivial though the charges may seem. It appears that the Rev. William Tennent, upon return from his back country mission, was spreading tales about Galphin's disloyalty. Tennent had been Galphin's guest at Silver Bluff when he passed through the Augusta region on his return home, at the same time that a Dr. Gould had been there. Laurens now tells Galphin that *"the Reverend Mr. Tenant who had twice before intimated doubts of your attachment, expressed strong desires that a certain Dr. Gould should relate a conversation which passed between you & him on Public Affairs ... this seemed very alarming to some People."* Consequently, Gould was brought in for questioning. It seems that he had requested the loan of a horse from Galphin *"for the country's service. You said Damn the country I have lost enough by it already."* Tennent was ready to condemn Galphin for blasphemy. Laurens found it amusing; as Gould confirmed *"the liberties of America"* were in no way involved. Laurens face-tiously closes his letter saying *"I have taken a resolution that whenever I learn or hear of a very Rascally attempt to traduce a Man's character, I will call it Parson Tenents Golden Evidence."*[384]

In its separate express to Galphin on this same day, the Council of Safety informs him that a decision has been taken, on the basis of Drayton's promise of 25 September, *"to send to Keowee in order to be properly distributed among the Cherokees One Thousand weight of Gun Powder & 2000 lead, of which you will be pleased to inform Mr. Wilkinson immediately & that he may expect it on the 20th inst. Or a day or two sooner."*[385] This attempt to arm the Cherokees would rekindle Loyalist hostility. During the interim, mutual sniping continued.

### Thursday, 5 October

On this day, Robert Cunningham replied to the Drayton letter of 21 September, although a few days would elapse before it reached Charleston. Datelined *"Page's Creek,"* Cunningham replies that he *"only this day"* received Drayton's letter, commenting: *"I think sir, at this time the question is rather unfair; however ... I must confess I do not hold with that peace* [Treaty of Ninety-Six]—*at the same time as fond of peace as any man— but upon honorable terms ... according to my principles, that peace is false and disgraceful from beginning to ending. It appears to me, sir, you had all the bargain making to yourself ... I expected you would have acted with more honor than taken advantage of men half scared out of their senses at the sight of liberty caps and the sound of cannon."*[386]

Drayton must have been furious upon receiving a response that impugned his honor. Cunningham's view of treaty negotiations paralleled those of Thomas Brown. Nineteen days after the signing Cunningham was still angry; his attitude would make the Rebels uneasy. Indeed, the degree of sympathy for Loyalists throughout South Carolina continued to bedevil the revolutionary leadership.

For example, on the 5th of October Thomas Ferguson, a member of the Council of Safety, wrote to Christopher Gadsden, a delegate to the Continental Congress in Philadelphia: *"I have just to acquaint you with the fact that after … the council agreed"* to fortify the harbor *"one of the council, Thos. Bee, did privately withdraw and get up a petition from the people of Charlestown"* against fortification. *"I am sorry to say many of our people seem more inclined to lay down their arms than defend their country."*[387] It was still touch and go between Rebels and Loyalists—and preparations for possible armed conflict continued.

### Saturday, 7 October

In a letter bearing this date, Col. Richard Richardson submitted a muster roll to the Council for Captain Matthew Singleton's volunteer militia company—30 men—*"of Sait Mark's Parish, on the High hills of Santee."*[388]

### Monday, 9 October

A return was submitted from Capt. Robert Lide's Company, *"sixty of the inhabitants on the North East Side of Pee Dee River, from Brown's Creek to the Three Creeks, in St. David's Parish."*[389]

On this same day, curiously enough, a return was submitted for "Ezekiel Polk's Co. of Rangers … Commanded by Col. William Thompson [sic], Esq. From 18th day of June to 7th day of October … sworn before Tho. Charlton." This return was delivered to Charleston by Capt. Eli Kershaw. It would later be corrected; Polk now commanded a volunteer militia unit.

### Friday, 13 October

The Council belatedly apologized for the mix up. It seems that Polk had written to the Council on 12 September, long after his encounter with Drayton, inquiring about his new status. He received no reply. Hence he had sent his letter of 2 October, wondering about his state of "inactivity."

Meanwhile, a return of his men was submitted as though he were still with the rangers. In its apology of 13 October, the Council admits *"two occurences occasioned our not answering your former letter … Mr. Henry who was to have called … neglected to do so."* Second, because the Council thought that Drayton had given Polk instructions, *"concerning your new raised company it appeared unnecessary to repeat them."* The rest of the Council's letter to Polk is herein quoted because it succinctly portrays the Council's attitude toward the role of Ezekiel Polk in the revolutionary government's overall plans: *"After you had retired from the Regiment of Rangers we filled the vacancy, & then it was impracticable to rejoin your Troop to that Corp—but in order to give due encouragement to your recollected zeal in the public Service, we Resolved to confine the order of Mr. Drayton & Mr. Tenent [sic] & authorized the former to assure you that your new company should be kept in pay equal to that which is allowed to the Rangers, & we had reason to conclude that Mr. Drayton had given you the proper information on this head until his late return to Charles Town when we learned from him that he had omitted it … Your letter of the 2nd inst informs us that you have been active in the public cause as a Magistrate & as a friend to liberty & we approve of the measures which you have pursued for retaining the Enemies of their own & of American freedom in a state of Neutrality, we hope that such Steps will lead them on after further consideration, to be our friends—& in order to to keep your Troops in proper exercise we desire you will immediately upon receipt hereof March to Dorchester & there offer your Service to the Commissioners for fortifying that Town who will probably assign to you the guarding of the public Store of Gunn Powder—inform us of your arrival there & we will transmit such farther orders as shall appear to be necessary. If you should not arrive at Dorchester before the 1st November, you will then leave your Company under the Command of your eldest Lieutenant & give your attendance in provincial congress … we shall make an early representation of your peculiar circumstances & submit to the Representatives of the people whether it will be proper to add yours as a tenth Company to the Regiment of Rangers or continue it under your sole Command independent."*[390]

### Saturday, 14 October

Up to this point, Loyalist activity in the back country has been muted. On this day a letter was sent to William Henry Drayton, drafted by Edward Musgrove from Fletchall's area. At the request of *"the people,"* Musgrove has been asked to report on the situation following the Treaty of Ninety-Six. Edward Musgrove, age 59, a justice of the peace and a tax collector, came directly from England and settled north of Broad River around 1755. He took part in the Cherokee wars as a militia captain. At this time, his son, Beaks, and his brother, John, sided with the Loyalists. Edward himself seemed but a lukewarm Rebel. In any case he now reports that Fletchall's company returned from Ninety-Six *"very much displeased with the conduct of their Colonel."* Musgrove hints at various plans for hostile retaliation *"by particular persons."* But *"the scales seem turned very much now, and you are much applauded for acting at Ninety-six ... I am sure they never will go with the colonel again."* Nevertheless, *"there is a contentious spirit yet reigning in the hearts of some ... a wheel within a wheel ...it will be precarious."*[391] Such personal speculation only added to the rumor mill—indicating that the Rebels have not yet consolidated attachment to their cause.

*Sunday, 15 October*

Alexander Innes, secretary to the self-exiled Governor Campbell, wrote from Charleston to Patrick Tonyn, Governor of East Florida, on this day. He refers to his last letter sent via Moses Kirkland, who landed in St. Augustine around 25 September, enroute to arrange transportation to Boston. Kirkland would subsequently be intercepted on his voyage north, captured off the coast of Massachusetts, and eventually jailed in Philadelphia. Meanwhile, Innes, having received mail from London, was now forwarding it to Tonyn, with an apology for having read his newspapers *"as by some neglect Lord Williams were not sent ... and in our present forelorn situation you may judge how anxious we must be to read any thing from England."* Since the Governor left Charleston to board the *Tamar*, complains Innes, he *"has left me with very little interesting to say of affairs here ... there are great divisions amongst the* [Rebel] *leaders, & I firmly believe the majority of the people of Charles Town are against all their measures."* With respect *"to the state of the back Country ... Mr. Kirkland could fully inform you of, & the event of Draytons expedition plainly shows what might have been done there; by what infatuation or neglect these unhappy provinces to the southward have been so totally abandoned I cannot imagine, but the reflection of what I have seen drives me almost distracted."*[392]

The Innes letter clearly reveals the demoralized state of mind among Loyalist officials in Charleston, their pleas for help having been totally ignored. Moreover, in Innes' eyes, the British government seems to be living in a dream world. Inconceivably, in this period of stress, they have sent a man out to survey the country. William deBrahm, Surveyor General of his Majesty's American Dominion in the Southern District, had arrived in Charleston on

7 September aboard the HMS *Cherokee*, captained by Lt. John Ferguson. In his letter to Tonyn, Innes now caustically comments, *"A fine time to talk of his survey of a country that we are in a doubt to whom it may belong."*[393]

As Innes was sharpening his sarcastic wit in Charleston, a remarkable letter was being written on this same day by George Galphin in Augusta. It offers the historian a unique glimpse into the mind of an Indian trader turned administrator. Galphin reports to the Council of Safety that half of the upper town of Creek Indians is now under British jurisdiction of *"west floarada."* He claims the British *"has youse'd all there interest to bringe the rest of the nattion to there way of thinking but they Could not perswade them to it nor it will be in there power to do it in Case they are sepleyed from hear as usuall."* Galphin notes that all the Indians *"are at home & very unEasy for want of amnison to go out a hunting as this is the month they go out for there winter's hunt … they Disiere that this talk may be sent to the beloved men of Ch:Town & Georgia & for me to send up there ancer Emedeatly."* He bluntly admits *"wee have Lost half the uper Town allredy & if they had been suppleyd as usall wee should not have Lost of them but they have sent trade to pensacollo and they* [British agents] *have broght up plenty of Amnison for them."* Galphin warns that if the Indians don't get any ammunition from the American side until *"the Commissionor meetg at Salisbury* [scheduled for mid-November] *has finished there bissness there, the season for hunting will be over & there will be no passeyfying them & they will say all the talk we have sent them is nothing but Lyg* [lying] *for they ware told there wood be nothing but Lying talk sent them from these two provences."*[394]

This was a pragmatic argument; Galphin, in effect, was recommending some quick-fix diplomacy to counteract the "bad talk" being spread by British agents. For Galphin, credibility regarding Indian relations is essential; without it a commissioner is powerless to carry out policy. At the moment the credibility of Carolinians is suspect. If it comes to a crunch, Galphin intimates the Indians will follow British commands. The fact that an arms shipment was on its way to the Cherokees must have pleased him, although he makes no reference to it in this communication. Elsewhere pieces are falling into place.

### Monday, 16 October

After the Treaty of Ninety-Six was signed, Major Andrew Williamson made a tour of the Savannah River area from Augusta through Long Cane. On 16 October he reported by letter to the Council of Safety: *"From the best intelligence I can learn since Mr. Drayton went from hence, I have the pleasure to acquaint your Honors, that everything seems in perfect tranquillity, both here and on the other side of the river. Volunteers are there and here forming."* Their greatest complaint remains *"their want of arms and ammunition ... hopes your Honors will order a sufficient supply to Fort Charlotte where they can be safe."* In conclusion, Williamson reports *"I am sorry to be under the necessity of returning the commission for Mr. Allen Cameron ... his letters which I received a few days ago."*[395] These letters were written last July.

As for Allen's brother, Alexander Cameron, his position still remains of urgent concern to the Rebels. On this same 16th of October, Alexander responded, from Keowee, to Drayton's letter of 26 September, after having *"maturely considered"* the situation. Cameron comments *"the contest and confusion in America at present gives me real concern, but who the aggressors are I am not competent to judge ... nor will I pretend to blame men who have already advanced so far as the Americans have done, in support of a cause which their conscience dictates to them is just ... the concern you express for requesting me to remove to some distance from my present residence among the Cherokees ... I cannot find myself at liberty to comply ... At the same time I think that the chiefs of your province can be under no apprehension of danger from me or my connection with the Indians, if we are at liberty to enjoy peace and tranquiity where we are ... while I have the honor to serve in my present office, I must implicitly observe the directions and orders of my superiors, and cannot recede from my part without first obtaining their leave ... From the day I commenced as Mr, Stuart's Deputy, I received no instructions injurious to the frontier inhabitants, but on the contrary and agreeably to my duty I have assiduously endeavored to cultivate peace and friendship between the Indians and them."* Finally, in obvious anger, Cameron refers to Drayton's "talk" to the Indians of 21 August, in which Drayton accused Cameron of speaking "with two tongues." Writes Cameron, *"I think sir, you might well have omitted such uncourtly expressions ... I defy you or any man breathing to make good these assertions, and if it was to a view to prejudice the Indians against me, all the rhetoric Mr. Pearis is a master of, could not affect it; although he is well known to be a person who will not stick to the truth to accomplish his designs."*[396]

Refusing to be intimidated by the imperious William Henry Drayton, Alexander Cameron's defense of his honor tells us a good deal about the man, whose integrity has previously been upheld by his Long Canes neighbors, Andrew Williamson and John Lewis Gervais, both revolutionaries. Cameron also provides a different insight into the motivations of Richard Pearis, an unabashed opportunist in Cameron's eyes. Most significant, however, is his forceful assertion that he has never sought to stir up the Indians against frontier settlers—nor has this ever been British policy. The honorable stance taken by Cameron must have had an impact upon some of the Council members in Charleston who appreciated honor and integrity; but it didn't alter any opinions.

On another Indian front, namely the Catawbas, it will be remembered that 50 warriors came to Camden last July to enlist in the American cause. They were turned over to Joseph Kershaw, who placed them under the jurisdiction of Lt. Samuel Boykin of the Camden militia. Boykin was told to integrate them into Col. William Thomson's Regiment of Rangers. We now learn, from a Boykin letter of 16 October from *"Granbey,"* that he has been unable to fully comply, since *"so many were taken very sick … I was taken extremely ill with the feaver, or should have wrote you before this … as the Sickly season of the year is now Over,"* the Indians are *"willing to come down at any time you may think proper. I have paid twenty five Indians Under my Command two hundred & fifty pounds which is ten pounds Each man."*[397]

All told, the situation in the back country, as of mid-October, seemed to be relatively calm. The Rebels were becoming better organized while Loyalists were in a state of disorder. A letter from Loyalist leader Thomas Brown to Governor Campbell at this point provides additional perspective. Brown went to Charleston soon after the Treaty of Ninety-Six was signed; he was immediately picked up for questioning and confined for a period of time before being released.

### Wednesday, 18 October

Released by this date, Brown now drafted a letter to the exiled governor, requesting a hearing. He tells Campbell *"The Council of Safety upon information of my arrival in town, with their customary Politeness took me into custody & proceeded to interrogate me concerning the Contents of the Letters your Lordship had sent."* He shrewdly observes *"any interrogation was an infraction of the Articles of Peace & that Gentlemen who had a proper regard for their integrity & Public Faith would never be guilty of a violation of what by the most barbarous Nations was held sacred."* Brown was posturing, but such game playing was standard with respect to honor; here we have Brown putting a fine line to Article 4 of the Treaty of Ninety-Six, a treaty he has denounced, accusing Rebel leaders of violating their own stipulation against molesting non-signers of the association without cause. Yet, self righteously, Brown threatens *"I was determined never to claim Security under a most scandalous disgraceful treaty. I insinuated that should any violence be offered to me it would be attended with the most fatal Consequence in the back country."* On this basis, *"I presume I was released."*[398]

The fact that Brown, a known opponent to the Rebel cause, was not denounced for sedition seems to indicate that opinions within the Rebel leadership were mixed with respect to Drayton's treaty. Therefore, Brown was able to place his interrogators on their honor, based on words contained in the treaty. But attitudes were changing; five days later Robert Cunningham would be denounced for sedition and a warrant issued for his arrest. For the moment Brown was free and in his letter to the governor he seeks guidance: *"Whatever Directions or instructions your Lordship may think proper to send us will be strictly adhered to ... I have this moment received intelligence from the back parts of the Province that the People ... had burnt Colonel Fletchall in effigy."*[399]

Brown's letter was delivered to the Governor by Richard Lambton, the King's Deputy Auditor General in South Carolina. Campbell received it on the 21st and enclosed it with his letter to Lord Dartmouth, Despatch #8, written on 19 October but not sent until the 22nd. Thomas Brown himself never got to see the governor, nor did he return to the back country. He went south to Florida where he raised his own regiment of volunteers to ride against the Rebel frontiersmen of Georgia. In 1776 Governor Patrick Tonyn commissioned him a Lt. Colonel in British service.

### Thursday, 19 October

Writing on this day, before receiving Brown's report, Governor Campbell's attitude is still one of despondency: *"I have the honor to inclose a Georgia paper containing the only Account I have as yet been able to procure of the Rebels transactions in the back Country for they are as secret, as they are wicked, and by it your Lordship will see my best endeavours were not wanting to promote the King's interests had I been but supported."* Sixteen weeks have passed since he pled with Boston for help; no answer had been received. *"I am now informed that they [Rebels] are tampering with the militia ... have formed volunteer companies to obey orders of the Council of Safety ... when I look towards the back country, my distress and vexation is increased."* Nevertheless, he bravely implies that the proselytizing mission of Drayton and Tennent *"could not draw settlers from their allegiance to His Majesty,"* even though *"they embodied troops and marched against them with the Catawba Indians in their Train, by way of striking terror."*[400]

Again, each side was prone to vilify the opposition by exploiting the threat of Indians as mercenaries. But Campbell didn't have a corner on pessimism. From another quarter, the increasingly disturbed political mood of the colony is reflected in Henry Laurens' letter written to his brother James in London.

*Friday, 20 October*

Laurens' letter of the 20th demonstrates fear and indecision regarding the questionable manner in which his own government operated. He was not at all comfortable with the extremism of men such as Drayton. Laurens' conscience bothered him, but: *"I am resolved to hazard all … rather than to submit to the tyranny of those brethren who are on your side of the water."* Even so, *"we might have acted with more wisdom than we have discovered in South Carolina. I have been uniformly of that one opinion from the hour in which I dared to plead against taking the Reins of Government into our hands & every hour since has verified & confirmed my declaration of what would naturally follow that injudicious determination—at length we have driven ourselves into a labyrinth—rash Men have devised means for affronting the King's Government in many instances too grossly to be borne—ingorant & timid men have been persuaded to join them & to make up a Majority; they have gone too far to retreat, & know not how to get out, & are at their wits to find out Men & means for defending against the Powers which we are told are on the way to destroy us … hundreds of familiies have already sent their household goods & valuables into the Country & stand ready to take the same course upon the first account of Men of War & Troops upon our coast."*[401]

The reader will recall that Laurens expressed similar sentiments to his son one month ago. He remains apprehensive. Coming from the chief executive of Rebels in South Carolina, these are distressingly pessimistic words. They reflect the split in opinion, according to historian John Drayton, between radicals like William Henry Drayton, Arthur Middleton, Col. Charles Pinckney and Thomas Ferguson, men who would coerce the colonists, fight tyranny with tyranny to oppose Great Britain, and conservatives like Rawlins Lowndes, Thomas Bee, Col. James Parsons and Thomas Heyward, Jr., who still sought compromise. Swing votes on the Council of Safety were in the hands of moderates like John Huger, Benjamin Elliott and William Williamson. Henry Laurens himself was highly conservative but, as president, did not vote. The last member of the Council, Miles Brewton, had simply *"quitted the colony"* in discouragement.[402]

Laurens was of the opinion that denunciation and mob action was getting out of hand, and that guilt by association was too often being used as a tool for intimidation. If a person was not for the Association, extremists considered him against it. Such was the common mob attitude. Laurens deplored it; he viewed such behavior as dangerous to the very liberties America sought. While he agonized over tyrannical methods, Drayton was not averse to employing them. While Laurens sought to avoid conflict, Drayton prepared for it—advocating stronger defense measures to his colleagues on the Council of Safety. Laurens felt they were going too far; it was too expensive. Thus, in his letter to brother James, Laurens hoped that the upcoming session of the provincial Congress *"may think that burthening the whole people with immense Taxes for vain attempts to secure Charles Town may not be best calculated for Promoting the Welfare of the colony & the real interest of America."*[403]

On the other hand, one senses that Laurens may be wavering, as he exhibits uncertainty over initiatives like the Treaty of Ninety-Six. *"General Drayton,"* he quips, *"has established a Treaty of Neutrality with Col. Fletchal at a great expense to the Treasury ... amounting to the Colonel's declaration made to me in answer to a letter which I wrote him a Month before the General began his March ... if Mr. Drayton is right in his treaty of Neutrality with those People, how very wrong have we been who have refused to grant the same terms to some of our most worthy & valuable citizens ... on the subject of the Association when I was ordered to sign—I saw what would be the consequence of forcing Men's consciences & what I thought I then foresaw is come to pass ... the Clergy & others"* share his sentiments.[404]

Forcing conformity and employing excessive zeal to induce symbolic patriotism was no substitute for honorable relations in the eyes of Henry Laurens. He and William Henry Drayton saw honor and duty in dissimilar ways.

# CHAPTER XVI

## *Defining Parameters of Common Cause*

CONSIDERING THE ANTI-BRITISH PASSIONS BEING AROUSED AT THE time, it is not surprising that anyone who sought rational compromise was often labeled an enemy of the people by men such as Drayton and, scruples aside, so treated. Robert Cunningham would soon fall into this category. But, for the moment, the Council of Safety had a more pressing problem—the formulation of an Indian policy.

### Sunday, 22 October

Replying to George Galphin's letter of the 15th, Laurens wrote to him on the 22nd: *"It appears from your opinion … that we have no other means for keeping our Indian Allies in peace & friendship with us but that of supplying them with Ammunition Clothing etc as usual, we therefore cannot withhold our Assent that such Goods should be sent among them, & we shall impart our sentiments on this head by Tuesday's Post to the Council of Safety at Savanna."* Coordination of policy with Georgia was precisely what Galphin had recommended; Laurens and the Council concurred. In fact, Georgia had been notified that the Carolinians had already sent a shipment of arms to the Cherokees, which was supposed to arrive at the Nation around this time, fulfilling Drayton's promise of 25 September. Edward Wilkinson, in Keowee, the Council's agent to the Cherokees, had been alerted to expect it. Galphin, meanwhile, was urged to stay on in Augusta: *"we think it of great moment that you should have a personal interview with those Indians expected at the latter end of this month at your House & therefore recommend, to delay your intended journey to Salisbury even to the 5th or 6th November."* [405]

A conference of all American Commissioners for Indian Affairs from all the colonies was scheduled to take place in Salisbury, North Carolina, in mid-November, for the purpose of coordinating policy to prevent Indians from succumbing to British blandishments. Before Galphin left Augusta, Laurens and the Council were anxious that *"Indians be well informed of the appointments of Commissioners for the purpose of conducting the Trade with them, & of the several departments of Commisioners, as well as by what authority appointed—the novelty and dignity of this grand plan will excite their curiousity, strike them with awe & tend to confirm their resolutions to remain neuter."*[406]

Revolutionary Americans had become serious contenders to replace British authority. For the Council, it was important that Charleston be viewed by Indians as a reliable, steadfast partner. With this in mind, one can understand why the Council would soon become furious when it learned that its arms shipment to the Cherokees had been arbitrarily halted by parish leaders in Saxe-Gotha. This unilateral action, taken together with the arrest of Cunningham, would precipitate a crisis.

Meanwhile other pieces were falling into place. William Campbell, now aboard the HMS *Cherokee* in Charleston Harbor [he had transferred from the *Tamar*], wrote a short postscript to his message of the 19th to Lord Dartmouth, commenting upon the letter from Thomas Brown, stating that it corroborated *"the account I have already given your Lordship."*

The Governor's knowledge of back country events remains limited, as is the Rebels' knowledge of Campbell's intentions. His supposed conspiracy with back country Loyalists continues to be simply a "hellish plot." Part of this plot, for Rebels, involves belligerents such as Robert Cunningham, who seems to be emerging as a chief enemy of the people in the eyes of men such as Drayton. In the spirit of denunciation, so prevalent in Carolina at this time, Cunningham was next to be pilloried.

*Monday, 23 October*

Cunningham's opposition to the Treaty of Ninety-Six was made clear in his reply of 5 October to Drayton. But was this language seditious enough to arrest him? Some members of the Council thought it was. According to Loyalist writers, Cunningham's *"bold expression of the opinion that Drayton had taken dishonorable advantage of the fears of loyalists,"* caused his arrest. *"On the 23rd day of October he was arrested at night, in his own house, by a party sent by Major Williamson, for that purpose, under the pretence of 'seditious words' on the affidavit of John Caldwell."*[407]

The affidavit, *"taken before Richard Rapley, Esq., at Ninety six, October 23, 1775,"* justified apprehending Cunningham and bringing him before the bar of justice at the Second Provincial Congress then convening in Charleston. He appeared on 1 November, and was speedily tried, convicted and jailed. At the same time we learn that it was Capt. Benjamin Tutt from Williamson's militia who actually captured Cunningham and brought him before Congress, where Tutt *"related the cause and manner of his having taken and brought Robert Cunningham to Charles Town."*[408]

The record is not more explicit. Details of the capture remain unknown except for hearsay, such as that of an unknown person in Savannah writing later to *"a Gentleman in London"*—on 19 November. This individual tells us: *"The Province of South Carolina is involved an all the horrours of a civil war, Colonel [sic] Robert Cunningham, a very considerable planter in the back settlements, being suspected of attachment to the king's cause was seized by a party sent in disguise of Indian traders from Charlestown, by the Committee of Safety."*[409] Such allegations add a fanciful touch to Cunningham's capture, but remain of doubtful accuracy.

According to local historians, *"the arrest of Cunningham was deeply resented by the people of the Upper Country."*[410] This resentment would be further fueled by a train of events that would lead to a major predicament.

## Tuesday, 24 October

The record shows that the Council of Safety in Charleston angrily wrote to the Committee for Saxe-Gotha on the 24th, chastising it for over-reaching its authority by unilaterally stopping a wagonload of gunpowder destined for the Cherokee Nation. Irritably, the Council wrote: *"Gentlemen—the affairs of this Colony must be reduced to a very precarious situation when one can supercede the orders of those who are authorized & required to do every thing which shall to them seem needful & expedient for the defence security & protection of this Colony—how do you think public business can be conducted if the orders of men properly authorized & who devote their whole time to public service without fee or reward, are to be thus interrupted & impeded."*[411]

Saxe-Gotha Rebels had acted without authority, and the fact that a courier from that area, who had been in Charleston recently, neglected to mention this action infuriated the Council of Safety. Their letter indignantly observes: *"Mr. Lewis Dutarque was in the Council of Safety a very few days ago after he had come from the Congree—he gave us no such information … he has therefore either too hastily informed you or has been extremely deficient in his duty as an Officer & Associate, by failing to lay before us, intelligence of such vast importance—We should have hoped that he would have forwarded the execution of the Council of Safety's Orders & we hope you will do so upon receipt hereof—be assured we act upon good grounds & have nothing else in view but the public welfare."*[412]

Lt. Dutarque of the rangers had arrived in Charleston in early October to deliver the regiment's muster roll. He was told of the Council's intent to ship arms to the Cherokees, and the reasoning behind this action. Evidently Dutarque, on his return through Saxe-Gotha, did not make clear the Council's newly adopted Indian policy. As frontiersmen, the Committeemen of Saxe-Gotha area did not take kindly to arming Indians who might then attack them. Being unaware of policy, stopping the arms shipment appeared to be in their best interests.

Coincidentally, during this same time, John Stuart in West Florida was initiating actions of his own to cultivate Indians. But he, too, had political problems. A letter, dated 15 September, from British General Gage in Boston, had just been received by Stuart, urging that southern Indians be encouraged *"to take arms against his Majesty's enemies."* Stuart was faced with a dilemma; Gage's aggressive instructions seemingly contradicted the defensive posture Stuart had adopted in his "talk" of 30 August to the Cherokees. Gage's order, however, stemmed from the belief that Americans *"brought all the savages they could"* against the British. Consequently, back in June, he *"proposed to Lord Dartmouth that Indians be used against Americans who were marching against Quebec."* Dartmouth responded on 24 July, agreeing that Indians should be induced *"to take up the hatchet against his Majesty's rebellious subjects in America."* Gage interpreted this response as *carte blanche* permission to recruit Indians as mercenaries. Based on Dartmouth's response, Gage wrote to Stuart on 15 September urging him to actively recruit southern Indians for use against the Rebels, reminding him that the *"Rebels had open'd the door."* When Stuart received this message in October he *"ordered supplies of guns and ammunition and Indian goods to be sent to Pensacola,"* as a distribution point. At the same time he ordered precautions implemented to prevent Rebels in Georgia and South Carolina from supplying the Indians with goods, *"for the Indians would be inclined to give their aid to those who could and would supply them with these necessities."*[413]

Indians, apparently, were up for grabs. Both American and British authorities were now playing the same game, trying to woo Indians to their respective sides, although, at this point the Carolinians were as yet unaware of the Gage letter to Stuart. On the 24th of October, as Charleston wrote to Saxe-Gotha to berate local authorities for stopping the shipment to the Cherokees, Stuart, in Florida, appointed his brother, Henry, as a confidential agent to communicate Gage's instructions to various Indian agents throughout Florida, Georgia and South Carolina. Henry was instructed *"to proceed to the Upper Creek and finally to the Cherokee and in those nations, in cooperation with Taitt and Cameron and loyal traders, to seek to engage the Indians to act in His Majesty's service ... Stuart concluded ... with this warning: You will understand that an indiscriminate Attack upon the Provinces is not Meant, but to act in the Execution of any concerted Plan and to assist ... friends in distressing the Rebells and bringing them to a sense of their Duty."*[414]

Writing separately to Cameron and Taitt weeks later, Stuart repeated that he did not construe Gage's instructions *"as an order to attack frontier inhabitants."* Philip M. Hamer sums it up nicely in his article *John Stuart's Indian Policy during the Early Months of the American Revolution.* Stuart believed *"that the Indians should not be incited to a general attack upon the frontier settlements in which Rebels, Tories, women, and children would suffer indiscriminately, but that they should be prepared to be used as auxiliaries to regular troops of organized loyalists, and that this use of them should be made only when some concerted plan of campaign had been formulated."*[415]

There seems to be little difference between the Rebel and Loyalist approach to Indians in the south. Each initially encouraged them to remain neutral—to side with their respective patron only when hostilities began. But both sides remained suspicious of the other's motives, which is why Rebel leadership in Georgia and South Carolina, as Galphin had recommended, opted to prudently and selectively supply the Indians with arms. When this policy was disregarded by the men of Saxe-Gotha, the Council of Safety in Charleston became furious. Having vented its anger, the Council now ordered Saxe-Gotha: *"We desire you will do your endeavors to forward the Waggon with Safety & order the Waggoner to deliver the letter directed to Mr. Wilkinson ... to Mr. Pearis, as we suppose Mr. Wilkinson will be gone from Keowee to attend his duty at Salisbury—we have ordered an escort of Rangers to conduct the Waggon."*[416]

The Council wrote separate letters on this day to Wilkinson and Pearis, both at Keowee, to inform them that *"the ammunition ... intended for the Cherokees has been stopped and detained at Congaree ... authorized Mr. Pearis to transact the business"* while Wilkinson was attending the Salisbury *"meeting of the Indian commissioners ... on the 10th November."* The letter to Pearis also said that he would hear *"from the Provincial Congress in due time relative to recalling Mr. Cameron, but we desire that you will not abate your vigilance to counteract his schemes & projects."*[417] The reader will recall Cameron's intransigent reply of 16 October to Drayton's message of 26 September. Cameron's attitude did not sit well with the council. He was still very much suspected of nefarious activities, suspicions elicited from a recent Wilkinson letter regarding remarks made by Cameron to the Cherokees. Some Council members thought Wilkinson should have been more forceful in rebutting Cameron.

Criticism of Wilkinson may also have been generated by an earlier Pearis comment alluding to Wilkinson as a "rogue." Consequently, Henry Laurens, always a prudent pacifier, in his letter to Pearis, cautions him: *"We cannot forbear expressing our good opinion of Mr. Wilkinson & that our hopes upon further investigation you will find that you had mistaken his principles & his conduct—We have no partiality for any man but him who is a fast & steady friend to American Liberty—if Mr. Wilkinson shall here after be found to be or to have been faulty, he shall receive no countenance from us—but we cannot condemn any man unheard, we hope you will either prove clearly that he has acted contrary to the interest of America ... or that you will endeavor to coalesce with him for common benefit."*[418]

Laurens' reaction to Pearis was much like his reaction to the Rev.Tennent when the latter attempted to bad-mouth Galphin with unfounded accusations. Pearis was an opportunist and fence sitter who, a few weeks later, would become a turncoat, responsible for propagating the story that linked the arming of Cherokees to a deliberate Council policy for unleashing Indians upon Loyalists in the back country. Meanwhile, the time had arrived for the rangers, on leave since 29 September, to muster in Amelia on 24 October.

### Wednesday, 25 October

The Council now alerted Col. Thomson to the movement of arms, outlining its policy *"done after mature deliberation & after long consultation with our friends in Georgia as well as under the sanction & direction of the Representatives of the united colonies at Philadelphia."* In spite of this, *"the Committee at Congaree have thought proper to stop the waggon, under the pretence that the people in the frontier will not allow the ammunition to pass & ground their apprehensions upon a report made to them by Lieutenant Dutarque ... public business cannot be conducted if orders are to be thus questioned ... the Indians can procure Ammunition without our help—& therefore for every good and obvious reasons, we think it expedient to supply them ... we desire you will order an Officer's Guard immediately to escort & protect the Waggon & see that the powder & Ball are safely delivered to Mr. Richard Pearis."*[419]

The letter was sent to Thomson in Amelia, where his rangers were mobilizing for a march to Dorchester, 25 miles west of Charleston. It was here that other militia units [like that of Ezekiel Polk] were being asked to gather prior to the impending Second Provincial Congress. Before moving out from the Congarees, Thomson appointed a detail from Capt. Kershaw's company to remain behind and escort the ammunition train to Keowee. Before relinquishing its powers to the new Congress, the Council, still bristling with indignation over Cameron's alleged comments to the Cherokees, responded curtly to Wilkinson's letter of 20 October.

*Sunday, 29 October*

In its letter the Council berated its Indian agent for not rebutting Cameron, saying *"Mr. Pearis had some days before intimated to us what passed between Mr. Cameron & the Cherokees. We shall only observe to you, that when Mr. Cameron in his talk to the Indians said that but for the care of the Great King … they could not have had a foot of land left them by the white settlers,"* he should have been challenged. This remark was interpreted as implying that, but for British policies, greedy Carolina frontiersmen would long ago have stolen Indian land. Wilkinson was criticized for allowing such words to go unchallenged: *"Your silence was a Tacit Confirmation of a charge against us…. To render us odious in the sight of the Indians … we desire you will use your utmost endeavours … & all future opportunities to eradicate the belief of pernicious doctrines as Mr. Cameron has impressed upon the hearts of those People—He may pretend what Friendship he pleases for us but he could not have said more to undo us."* He could offer *"20 affidavits in proof of his pretended neutrality … we should not believe him …he has afforded us too much reason to say we are sure that whenever it shall be thought proper by his Employers to order the Cherokee to fall upon and murder our Frontier Inhabitants Man Woman & Children he will be found a ready and active instrument for promoting & Carrying into execution the Measure. We Referr you to a Particular Instruction by the Continental Congress towards such men."*[420]

While the Council was conceding its powers to a new Congress, which was about to commence, a momentous event was about to occur in the back country that would divert everyone's attention to the west.

*Tuesday, 31 October*

Having received its directive from the Council of Safety, the Saxe-Gotha Committee released the Cherokee ammunition train at *"about 9 o'clock in the morning"* on the 31st. Moses Cotter, wagon driver, left the Congarees heading for Keowee, a distance of approximately 126 miles. Keowee, a major

Cherokee center, was located some eight miles north of present day Clemson University. According to a contemporary account, Cotter was *"under escort of Col. Thompson's* [sic] *rangers consisting of Lieut. Col.* [sic] *Charleton and Mr. Uriah Goodwin, a cadet, 2 sergeants and 18 privates, and continued on their journey without the least molestation until noon this day* [3 November]" at which time the wagon, four days out of the Congarees, was attacked *"18 miles below Ninety Six."* [421]

# CHAPTER XVII

## *Congress Confronts a Hijacking*

THE POLITICAL ATMOSPHERE IN SOUTH CAROLINA HAD CHANGED considerably since the Rebels First Provincial Congress adjourned in late June. A provincial defense force had been raised to counter the King's men; a revolutionary government was functioning; the Royal Governor had been run out of town. Charleston's harbor was being fortified by Rebel forces as a precaution against possible British attack from the sea. However, there were no British troops in the colony—and only two gunboats in the harbor. Back country Loyalists had been neutralized by Drayton's Treaty of Ninety-Six. Except for a few isolated pockets of vocal belligerence from individual Loyalists, the back country seemed tranquil. The attitude of Indians toward British/American differences continued to remain a potential source of hostility, but attempts to win over the Indians had been initiated. Currently, as Rebel legislators gathered in Charleston on 1 November for the opening session of the Second Provincial Congress of South Carolina, they elected William Henry Drayton to serve as President in place of Henry Laurens—replacing a dove with a hawk.

### *Wednesday, 1 November*

No sooner had preliminaries been completed than it was learned *"that Capt. Robert Cunningham, charged with high crimes and misdemeanours against the liberties of America, had been taken into custody and brought to town by Capt. Benjamin Tutt."* This news created a sensation. It was *"Ordered, That Capt. Tutt be desired to attend the Congress at five o'clock this evening … Capt. Tutt attended according to order, and related the cause and manner of his having taken and brought Robert Cunningham to Charles Town. An affidavit of Capt. John Caldwell, taken before Richard Rapley, Esq., at Ninety Six, Oct. 23, 1775, which justified the measure, was produced and read … Ordered, that the thanks of this congress be returned to Captain Tutt for his service; and also to the several persons who accompanied him ... Resolved, That all expenses of bringing the said Cunningham to town, be defrayed by the public ... Ordered, That Capt. Charles Cotesworth Pinckney, and Mr. Thomas Heyward, Jun., be a Committee to collect the charges against Capt. Cunningham; and to draw up a state of his offences against the peace and liberties of America."* Furthermore it was *"Ordered, that Capt Robert Cunningham be forthwith brought before congress ... and being brought before the congress accordingly, and questioned by the President, he replied, that he could not deny, that he had made use of expressions somewhat like those mentioned in Capt Caldwell's affidavit, which had been read to him— that he believed Capt. Caldwell had not perjured himself as bound by the late treaty at ninety six, yet he since had constantly behaved himself as peaceably as any man,— and although he had opinions, he had not expressed them but when asked."*[422]

Freedom of expression was of no concern to congressmen in Cunningham's case, as it was now *"Ordered, That Mr. President do immediately issue his warrant, for committing the said Cunningham to safe custody, in the common gaol of Charles-Town ... and the following warrant was accordingly issued ... to the Sheriff of Charles-Town district, or his Deputy; or the keeper of the common gaol in Charles-Town ... you are hereby commanded and required to receive into your custody in the common gaol, and there safely keep until further order, the body of Robert Cunningham, herewith sent to you, charged with high crimes and misdemeanors against the Liberties of the colony."* Nevertheless, the sheriff was also *"Ordered ... to afford the said Robert Cunningham every reasonable and necessary accomodation, at the public charge; but that he do not suffer the said Cunningham, to converse or correspond with any person whatsoever, or to have the use of pen, ink or paper, unless by express leave from Congress, or authority derived from there."*[423]

In this manner was public enemy #1 incarcerated, undoubtedly as an example to other malcontents. In light of his letter of 20 October to brother James, one must wonder how outgoing President Henry Laurens really felt about such kangaroo court justice.

### Thursday, 2 November

In the normal course of business on 2 November, Congress *"Resolved, That the sum of eight hundred and twenty five pounds currency be paid to the said Capt. Tutt, to be distibuted as follws, viz. Three hundred pounds to himself ... one hundred and fifty pounds to Lieut. Robert Bryant,—and seventy five pounds each to the following privates, viz. James Coursey, Joseph Reed, Ezekiel*

*Williams, Richard Tutt, and Richard Doggett."* On this same day it was agreed that Cunningham *"might be permitted to write a letter."* The sheriff was *"commanded to admit Capt. Tutt and Mr. Gervais. You are also required to permit Mr. Gervais to furnish Mr. Robert Cunningham with such linen and cash as Mr. Gervais shall think proper."*[424]

The reaction from the back country in response to Cunningham's arrest was soon to provoke the most serious opposition to civil order yet encountered. Patrick Cunningham, younger brother of Robert, unable to prevent his capture, sought revenge. He was handed a fortuitous opportunity in the form of the delayed arms shipment to the Cherokee Indians which finally left the Congarees on 31 October. Capture of these arms would not only offer the satisfaction of revenge; it would also stand the Council's Indian policy on its head when Patrick Cunningham loudly declared that these arms were meant to encourage the Cherokees to attack Loyalist frontiersmen. Such words found eager ears among back country residents. Ironically, had this shipment been delivered in mid-October as intended, it would have reached its destination without incident. Now it became fair game for Loyalist raiders, not as a premeditated act, but one of chance—a fortuitous opportunity to slash back at Rebels for a dishonorable act on their part in capturing Robert Cunningham and charging him with treason. Patrick Cunningham and his band of followers made their attack upon the shipment on 3 November, just as the wagon, on its fourth day, was 58 miles distant from the Congarees.

*Friday, 3 November*

The hijack of this day is best described by Moses Cotter, driver of the arms wagon, in his sworn affidavit. After his wagon train was stopped and looted by Patrick Cunningham, Cotter took a horse from his wagon and rode to Ninety-Six, where he appeared the same evening before Justice of the Peace James Mayson. [Evidently Mayson had not yet left to rejoin the rangers or to partake in the Second Provincial Congress]. Cotter, *"Being duly sworn on the holy evangelist, of almighty God, makes oath and says ... about noon this day some men on horseback,"* led by Patrick Cunningham, who said, *"I order you to stop your wagon in his majesty's name, as I understand you have ammunition for the Indians to kill us, and I am come on purpose to take it in his majesty's name ..."* He then *" handed out every keg to his men who were prepared with bags to receive it ... the rangers were at some little distance behind the waggon, and were riding up pretty fast ... Cunningham's party said, there comes*

*the liberty caps, we will soon blow them all to hell; and such like scurrilous lan-
guage. Cunningham's men, as soon as Lieut. Charleton came up with his guard,
retreated behind trees on the road side, and called upon him to stop ... otherwise they would blow out his brains ... Lieut. Charleton, with his men, were
soon surrounded ... afterwards they tied Lieut. Charleton, Mr. Goodwin, and
William Witherford* [a private] *by their arms ... marched off with the ammunition, and the prisoners."* After taking Cotter's statement, Mayson explains
that *"they left the deponent, desiring him to return to the Congarees, but as soon
as they were out of sight he took a horse and came to Ninety six, to inform me of
what had happened ... he arrived about 8 o'clock, This unfortunate accident of
taking the ammunition, happened 18 miles below Ninety-six ... sworn before me,
this 3rd of Nov. 1775 ...James Mayson, J.P."*[425]

Mayson immediately sent a courier to alert Major Andrew Williamson
and his volunteer militia of the theft. The news was received by Williamson
around four the next morning, 4 November, at his home, Whitehall,
approximately ten miles west of Ninety-Six Courthouse. Col. Thomson, at
Dorchester, would be informed on 6 November by a rider from Lt. Charlton's
guard detail, after being set free. Members of Congress would also learn the
news on 6 November. On this same day Williamson would also dispatch a
message to Edward Wilkinson in the Cherokee town of Keowee.

During the interim, excitement over Robert Cunnigham's arrest had
subsided in Charleston, and Congress turned their attention to other matters.

*Saturday, 4 November*

With respect to back country affairs, the record shows that *"Captain
Polk having informed the Congress, that his company of militia Rangers, had,
according to orders, repaired to Dorchester, likewise applied for pay, and for
further orders ... Ordered, That Mr. President be desired to write to the officer
commanding at Dorchester, to take command of Capt. Polk's company ... and
that they do duty there until further order of Congress therein."*[426] Concern over
the back country lagged until the 6th.

*Monday, 6 November*

The morning session at Congress was devoted to housekeeping chores,
including an order to *"Lieut. Col. Thomson of the Rangers, to send for Isaac
Jordan, a private in his regiment, charged with horse-stealing and breaking
jail at Cheraws district."* It was during the afternoon session that legislators

were shocked by the *"information being laid before the Congress, that Patrick Cunningham had seized the public gun-powder sent by the late Council of Safety to be distributed among the Cherokee Indians; and that a person is now in Charles-Town, who saw the seizure aforesaid, Ordered, That one of the messengers do immediately endeavour to find out the said person, and cause him to appear before Congress."* This humiliating news would beat the Congress into a frenzy of activity over the next four days. For the moment, it was *"Ordered, That Mr. President, Col. Laurens, and Col. Parsons, be a Committee to enquire into and touching the conduct of Patrick Cunningham, in seizing the public gun-powder aforesaid; and to report to this Congress."*[427]

One can imagine the anxiety such news stimulated, and how much it must have chagrined Laurens and Drayton to have the delay in shipment compounded by its theft, especially as their credibility vis-à-vis the Cherokees, key to their strategy regarding Indian policy, was now compromised. Near the scene of the crime, Major Williamson began to mobilize his militia to pursue the hijackers, while quickly sending an express to Wilkinson in Keowee to alert him. Wilkinson was told: *"On Saturday morning last [4 November], about 4 o'clock, I received a letter from Major Mayson, which to my great surprise and astonishment, informed me, that the day before about 5 o'clock, Jacob Bowman and Patrick Cunningham, with about one hundred fifty armed men, from the north side of Saluda river, stopped a wagon loaded ammunition, about seventeen miles below ... which they took and carried off, making a guard of twenty rangers and officers prisoners; and as John Vann* [an Indian trader] *was here yesterday on his way to the nation, and on his arrival will be apt to inform the Indians of this robbery, and lest some young inconsiderate man of the Cherokees should think of revenging this on the people of that side of the Saluda, I have embodied part of this regiment, and this moment intend to march to Ninety-Six to join those that are there; and hope in a few days, to retake the ammunition, and bring those people to justice who committed this act ... I have thought it necessary to acquaint you of this by express, that you may be able to explain this matter properly to the warriors and head men, and I am confident that they will be able to prevent this affair being productive of any breach of comity between them and this Province, as I think the people who committed this act, were led to it, by two rash inconsiderate men ... And, as you wrote me in your last that you intended to be at Salisbury on the 10th day of the month, I have taken the liberty to direct this, in your absence, to Mr. Cameron, with my compliments, and hope he will do me the favor to explain it to the principal men ... your most obedient, Very humble servant, A. Wm'son."*[428]

No matter that the Council of Safety considered Cameron an enemy and dangerous provocateur. Here we have Williamson treating him as a friend and ally. Should Wilkinson be absent, Cameron's help is sought to maintain peace among the Indians. Evidently Williamson was unaware of the harsh words exchanged between Drayton and Cameron over the past month. Indeed, Williamson, Wilkinson and Cameron all appear to be good friends with a common cause—to maintain good relations with the Cherokees. Wilkinson was still at his post when the news reached him.

*Tuesday, 7 November*

Williamson's letter was *"received ... on the 6th instant."* Wilkinson replied on the 7th, offering insight into the way matters were unfolding. Williamson was informed that *"I sent off Pearis about six days ago to Ninety six in Order to know whether the ammunition promis'd to these People were coming up or not as several of the indians were waiting here for some days ... but being out of patience ... have returned home."* Upon receiving Williamson's letter, Wilkinson says *"this was in good time as the Warriors* [those who remained] *had a meeting here this day. I acquainted them of what you wrote me in regard to Bowman and Cunningham taking the Ammunition that was coming up for them ... they are very much displeased at the news and says that we have told them a great many Lies about giving them ammunition and that they will not believe any thing more We shall say about it, that they will now go & hunt for their Father Capt. Stuart & see if they cannot get a little from him, however they say we have Twice taken the Ammunition which was import for their Trade, first at Savannah & now near ninety six ... yet this shall not break their Friends with us, that they believe the Great man above* [King George] *is the occasion of it, by his making the White people mad."* Wilkinson concludes by saying he will now set off for Salisbury, *"Mr. Hugh Hambleton will take care & issue out the ammunition if it should come up & will transact every other Matter that may be necessary in my absence. Mr. Cameron desires his Comp'ts to you & Mrs. Williamson & Mrs. Winter."*[429]

Hambleton was designated in place of Pearis, who had not yet returned from Ninety-Six. In a second letter on the 7th, Wilkinson wrote to the Council of Safety. No copy has been found, but reference would later be made to it by William Henry Drayton when defending himself from Pearis' accusations. Allegedly Wilkinson said, *"I would never be concerned, or have anything to do to say to the Indians with Pearis."* His actions were suspect, he was *"a liar ... notorious among those who knew him ... honest men who knew him, avoided being connected with him."*[430]

This reading of the enigmatic Richard Pearis concurs with the opinion of Alexander Cameron. It may be a charge that followed Pearis from the days of the French and Indian War when he supplied Indian warriors to George Washington to fight against the French in western Virginia, Maryland and Pennsylvania. As an Indian trader on the Holston River in 1755, Pearis had partnered with Christopher Gist of the Ohio Company for a short time, before they had a falling out. As historian W.W. Abbot, editor of the papers of George Washington, observes: *"Richard Pearis, who seems to have misbehaved at every point in his long career on the frontier, left the service of Virginia after having held a captain's commission from Governor Dinwiddie for more than a year ... He remained in command of the 5th Maryland company for about one year, until Governor Sharpe removed him because of complaints. Shortly thereafter Gen. John Forbes gave Pearis command of Fort Cumberland. On 3 May 1759 Pearis secured a captain's commission in the Pennsylvania Regiment. After the war Pearis pursued a successful career among the Cherokees of South Carolina."*[431]

Given this background, it appears that Pearis' bad reputation followed him as he was wheeling and dealing in 1775. Currently, the 50-year-old Richard Pearis was deputy to Edward Wilkinson in the Cherokee Nation, so far as the Council of Safety was concerned. But, at the moment, he was absent when the ammunition hijacking took place. Pearis learned of the robbery while in Ninety-Six; he was still there on 7 November when Wilkinson departed and left Hambleton in charge in the Nation. On the same day, Congress was learning more about Cunningham's raid.

In Charleston we find that *"Mr. President laid before the Congress an information upon oath, taken this day before Thomas Bee, Esq., touching a quantity of ammunition being taken, by force of arms, by Patrick Cunningham, from a detachment of rangers."* The person who offered this information is not revealed. But, at the same time, it was *"Ordered, That Col. Thomson be summoned to attend: And being introduced into the congress, delivered an affidavit made on the 6th instant by John Joseph Witner before John Purves, Esq., relative to the taking the public ammunition, by Patrick Cunningham. And Col. Thomson declaring, that the ammunition taken, was sent by the late Council of Safety, to be distributed amongst the Cherokees; and that Lieut. Charlton commanded the detachment, from whom Patrick Cunningham took the ammunition stated in the information and affidavits."*[432]

Congress was gathering facts. It appears that there were two affidavits, one taken by Bee, the other by John Purves, a ranger Captain now with his company at Dorchester. Witner was a private with the escort that accompanied the ammunition wagon. He is the herald who brought news of the heist to Thomson in Dorchester. Congress now *"Ordered , that Mr. Arthur Middleton, the Rev. Mr. Tennent, Mr. Ferguson, Capt. Charles Cotesworth Pinckney and Mr. Salvador. Be a committee immediately to take into their consideration the above information and affidavit, and to report thereon ... ordered, that Lieutenant Charlton be immediately put under arrest, and brought to Charles-Town."* Drayton was now asked *"to write to Capt. Pearis, informing him, that the ammunition sent to be distributed among the Indians has been violently taken by Patrick Cunningham, in contempt of authority."*[433]

At this moment, Congress was not aware that Pearis had left the Cherokee Nation; nor did it know of the Cotter affidavit—how and when Mayson had submitted it is nowhere made clear. Nor was Congress aware that Williamson had been notified of the robbery and had taken steps to mobilize local militia. It was unaware of Wilkinson's negative attitude toward Pearis, and the fact that Wilkinson had been alerted to the robbery by Williamson. But the legislators, aroused by the affidavits taken by Bee and Purves, were definitely pre-occupied with forming their own posse to recover the stolen goods. They blamed Lt. Charlton for allowing the theft to take place; he was indeed taken prisoner—but soon set free as more pieces fell into place.

In its preparations to pursue Patrick Cunningham and his gang, Congress now *"Ordered, That the Committee at Dorchester be directed to supply the troops there with a proper quantity of powder and ball in the cartouche-boxes."* Later in the day, *"Arthur Middleton, from the Committee to whom was referred the consideration of the two affidavits relative to the seizure of the public ammunition ... reported thereon ... and the said report, being taken into immediate consideration, was amended, and agreed to as follows: Whereas information, on oath, hath been made and laid before this Congress, that on or about the 3rd day of this instant November, at or near a place called the Ridge in Ninety-six district, Patrick Cunningham, Henry O'Neal, Hugh Brown, David Reese, Nathaniel Howard, Henry Green, with sundry other persons, about sixty in number, did, by force of arms, rob a certain waggon in the service of the public, feloniously taking therefrom a quantity of lead, and sundry kegs of gun-powder, containing about one thousand weight, intended as presents for the Cherokee Indians; and that the above persons, having first disarmed a body of rangers, who escorted the said waggon, did violently carry off the said powder and lead, to the great loss and damage of the public, in violation of the public peace, and in open contempt of the public authority; thereby exposing the frontier inhabitants of the colony to the depredations and horrors of an Indian war. And whereas there is an absolute necessity of crushing such dangerous attempts to destroy the peace of the colony, by bringing such atrocious offenders to condign punishment."*[434]

In contrast to the information taken from wagon driver Cotter, the name of Jacob Bowman is omitted in the committee's report; the number of raiders is also reduced from 150 to 60.

*Wednesday, 8 November*

The seriousness with which Congress viewed Cunningham's raid can now be gauged by the tone of the letter drafted to Col. Richard Richardson, and the size of the army he was being asked to raise in pursuit of the thieves: *"There being a necessity of assembling six Companies of the regiment of Rangers, Capt. Polk's Company of volunteers, and draughts of the militia, to act in the interior parts of this colony; and you being the eldest field officer now ordered upon this service, of course the command of the detachments upon this service rests in you."* Richardson is asked to raise an army through *"the commanding officer in each of these regiments … and militia Volunteers …as you shall judge necessary."* The army so raised is *"to act under your command."*[435]

As the oldest and probably most highly venerated frontier soldier, Richard Richardson, age 71, was given temporary command over most of the colony's armed forces for this emergency in the back country. From the letter to Richardson, one also learns that six of nine companies from the Regiment of Rangers are currently based in Dorchester; Capt. Caldwell is still at Fort Charlotte and Major Mayson is still in the Ninety-Six area with the remnants of two other companies, ostensibly still recruiting. He and 37 rangers would later team up with Major Williamson to confront Loyalists at Ninety-Six. Although both Mayson and Williamson were elected delegates to the Second Provincial Congress, they obviously had not yet departed for Charleston when the robbery occurred; nor would they attend, given the circumstances. But, at the moment, neither man was yet aware of action being taken by the Congress.

Meanwhile, to appreciate the nature of congressional reaction, one must bear in mind that Rebel leaders in Charleston were furious, not only because the confiscated arms could be used against them, but because the revolutionary government could now be accused by Cherokees of reneging on a deal. They might indeed go on the warpath—as alluded to in Wilkinson's letter to Williamson. Moreover, the revolutionary government was in danger of losing face among the very back country settlers it wished to bring into the Association. If undecided frontiersmen concluded that Rebels were arming Indians as a form of intimidation against Loyalists to sign the Association, their resentment might be extreme. The Middleton report recognized this possibility. Indeed it wasn't long before anger and suspicion in the back country was inflamed, fueled by Patrick Cunningham's propaganda along these same lines.

At Congress on the 8th, not all legislators were anxious to launch precipitately into military action. The resolution to empower Richardson to raise an army narrowly passed by a vote of 51-49. Before adjourning on this day, Congress also *"Ordered, That Mr. President do transmit to Major Andrew Williamson, the thanks of this Congress, for conduct in causing the body of Robert Cunningham to be apprehended and sent to Charles-Town; and also for opposing the insurrection caused by Patrick Cunningham and his accomplices."*[436]

Just how the congress now knew that Williamson had mobilized his militia remains a mystery, unless the major sent a courier to inform them. If so, one wonders why Mayson's name was omitted from the gratitude of Congress. After all, it was Mayson who so alertly initiated action after taking Cotter's sworn statement.

It was also on the 8th that Congress learned that *"a brother to O'Neal and a brother to Bochman* [sic] *... were in town."* As O'Neal and Bowman were among the raiders, Congress wished to interrogate their brothers. Men were sent to apprehend them and *"Capt. Sumpter* [sic] *being returned, reported that he with Capt. Flood and Mr. Beard, had made diligent inquiry after O'Neal, Bochman, and Yates* [Thomas Yates] *... but could not meet with either of them,"* although evidence confirmed they had been in town and *"purchased some goods from a Mr. Rugeley."* Following this report, it was *"Ordered, That Col. Laurens and Capt. Cattell forthwith proceed to Mr. Rugeley's, and desire to examine his books."*[437] Rugeley knew nothing of their whereabouts. Such incidents merely serve to show how paranoid Congress had become over the hijacking, leaving no stone unturned in an effort to apprehend the culprits.

*Thursday, 9 November*

Adding to Rebel paranoia, rumors were circulating in Charleston suggesting that *"Thomas Brown passed yesterday through Dorchester ... Ordered, That Mr. President do immediately issue his warrant for apprehending the said Thomas Brown."* The warrant was sent to Col. Thomson for this purpose *"without delay, to use the most effectual means for apprehending and bringing to Charles-Town, the body of Thomas Brown, charged before this Congress with having violated the treaty of Ninety-six."*[438] The alarm proved false; Brown was long gone to Florida. A similar rumor about the return of Moses Kirkland also proved false. He, too, was in Florida awaiting passage to Boston.

Still fearful of Loyalists, Congress now sent letters to those who had signed the Treaty of Ninety-Six—Thomas Fletchall, John Ford, Thomas Green, Evan McLaurin and Benjamin Wofford. Signed by William Henry Drayton, the letters demanded: *"wherefore, in pursuance if the treaty … by order of congress, I now do hereby make requisition, that the said Patrick Cunningham, Henry O'Neal, Hugh Brown, David Reese, Nathaniel Howard, and Henry Green, together with their aiders and abettors, be by you, or one of you, surrendered and delivered up, to the authority of Congress."*[439] Congress was covering all contingencies.

On this same day, 9 November, still unaware of changing attitudes toward Richard Pearis, or his whereabouts, Congress sent a letter to him at Keowee, under Drayton's signature. It reviewed Pearis' promise to *"the good Warior and the Cherokee Indians, that a quantity of gun powder and lead should be sent to them"* and proceeded to explain how the wagon train had been hijacked. The letter notifies Pearis that *"Col. Richardson with the Rangers and militia"* have been detailed to capture the criminals. Pearis is asked *"to be so good as to cause these particulars to be generally published and made known to the Indians, that they may at once see that the Headmen of South Carolina are faithful to their engagements, and that they not suffer their lawful authority to be trampled with impunity … P.S. You will assure the Indians that, as soon as the powder and lead, or any part of it, is retaken, it will be forwarded without delay."* This letter from Drayton was to be relayed through Major Andrew Williamson to whom Drayton wrote a cover note, enclosing *"a copy of the instructions and orders to Col. Richardson, and you are to regulate your conduct thereupon. You are hereby ordered, with the militia under your command, to act against the insurgents with the utmost vigour, and that you will be attentive to the security of Fort Charlotte."*[440] No similar note to Major James Mayson, alerting him to the formation of a posse, has been found. If sent it probably would have come from Col. Thomson.

Pearis would never receive his message from Drayton. By the time it reached Williamson on 14 November, Pearis had changed sides—and Williamson probably knew it. As of the 9th, however, six days had elapsed since the robbery took place. A number of wheels had been set in motion by Congress to recover its stolen property, as well as its dignity. While waiting for its orders to take effect, Congress settled down to other duties. There remained the very serious business of defense from the two British gunboats, the HMS *Tamar* and HMS *Cherokee*, lying just outside Charleston Harbor; there was also the perennial fear of British troops being put ashore.

# CHAPTER XVIII

## *Prelude to Bloodletting*

OMMUNICATIONS BETWEEN DIFFERENT AREAS OF THE COLONY being what they were in 1775, it took time for the militia to get organized in order that Col. Richardson might assemble his posse.

*Friday, 10 November*

On the 10th, Polk was informed by Congress: *"you are hereby nominated and appointed Captain of a company of volunteer Rangers, in the service of the colony, subject to the orders of congress, and in their recess, to the council of Safety."* The appointment was retroactive to 3 November. The ordnance store-keeper at Dorchester was directed *"to deliver to Capt. Ezekiel Polk, thirteen pounds weight of gunpowder, lead in proportion, and three dozen flints, for use of his company of volunteer rangers."*[441] In Dorchester, on this same day, a letter of complaint from the officers of the Regiment of Rangers was forwarded to Congress, protesting the comparative discrimination in status and rank between the colony's regimental forces.

*Saturday, 11 November*

The complaint from ranger officers was read before Congress on the 11th, after which it was *"Ordered, That the same be referred to a Committee of the following gentlemen, viz, Col. Laurens, Col. Bull, Col. Gervais, Doctor Oliphant, and Capt. John Huger."* Elsewhere, intrigue and swiftly changing events were bringing matters to a head between Rebels and Loyalists in the back country.

On this day, an infamous affidavit was sworn to by Richard Pearis in *"South Carolina Ninety six District ... before me Evan McLaurin One of His Majesty's Justices of the Peace."* It was witnessed by Patrick Cunningham, James

Lindley, Daniel Jones, Jacob Bowman, and Henry O'Neall—Loyalists all. A later notation on the third page of this statement reads: *"Rich. Pearis affidavit 11 November 1775, Read in Council the 30th & considered as a false and malicious libel, calculated to disservice the people & to prejudice the Hon. Mr. Drayton Esquire—because of the active part which he has taken in favor of American Liberty."* Rebel leaders found malicious libel in the words: *"saith that he the deponent is assured that from what Drayton did say to the Indians—that he intended to Employ the Indians to fight against the white men for the committee."*[442]

Word of this accusation spread quickly throughout the back country; it would become a catalyst for enticing almost 2000 armed men to join the Loyalist side in their confrontation with Rebels at Ninety-Six in eight days time. Major Andrew Williamson would later report: *"I understood it was chiefly owing to an affidavit made by Capt. Richard Pearis, that so many men were embodied."* He enclosed a copy of the affidavit in his letter to Congress on 25 November.[443]

Williamson's opinion would be seconded by an unidentified Rebel officer who was present at the battle which would shortly take place at the Ninety-Six Courthouse. The officer's letter, dated 29 November, and later published in a Charleston newspaper, offers a delightful example of embellishment through rumor. In part, the writer states: *"it was certainly owing to Pearis' Oath and their Declarations, that they were in Possession of undoubted Proof, that the council of Safety intended letting the Indians on them; that the powder was sent for that very Purpose, and that the Associators were to be distinguished by a Piece of Bear's Skin and a Deer's Tail, or a piece of white paper wore in their hats, which was to be the signal by which the Indians were to know them from the king's faithful subjects, that so many Men embodied under Standards; this was certainly the most popular plan they could adopt to raise Men."*[444]

The "bear's skin and deer's tail" allegation is unsubstantiated—but rumors of this sort abounded. Back country inhabitants were easily frightened by possibilities of Indian attack, given their vulnerable position on the frontier. Anyone who would deliberately incite Indians to violence was damned as a vile creature. In this case, it was the Rebel side that was being accused of "hellish plots." The charge would greatly upset Rebel leaders in Charleston.

Although reasons for the Pearis deposition remain murky, its closing statements offer clues to Pearis' activities prior to the wagon train robbery. The affidavit states: *"at the Congrees Ralph Humphreys a Tavern Keeper & Secretary to one of the Committees—told him* [Pearis] *that the Ammunition from the Committee for the Indians had come some time ago—but that the*

*committee at the Congrees had Stoped it—sent advice to the council of Safety—
from where they soon had reply Reprimanding them severely for Stoping the
Ammunition—Ordering them forthwith to forward it for the Indians—on
which they sent it off by Moses Cotter a Waggon under the guard of Twenty
of committee Rangers Commanded by Lieut. Charleton and another officer—
Saith that upon receiving this advice he the Deponent did Immediately return
towards home— to Receive the Letters and the Ammunition which left three
days Before the Deponent was there ... saith— that on the Deponents way to the
Congarees he did hear that Capt. Robert Cunningham had been taken prisoner
by some of the committee party some days before ... sworn to this 11th day of
November 1775."*[445]

From this recitation one deduces that Pearis, aware of Cunningham's
capture, arrived at the Congarees [Saxe-Gotha] on 3 November. Here he was
told the wagon train had departed for Keowee on 31 October. He now left
for "home," unaware of the hijack until he reached Ninety-Six, probably on
the 5th. Here he remained to denounce Drayton and the revolutionary government on the 11th. Why? Historian John Drayton, son of William Henry
Drayton, writing in 1821, simply says that Pearis *"was urged by the violence of
his passions, and the support of his new associates, to make an affidavit in which
... he charged that late Council of Safety with a design of bringing down the
Cherokee Indians upon the settlements ... the populace thence naturally supposed,
he was acquainted with the intentions of the council ... And, this, with the
clamorous industry of the insurgent leaders, induced the uninformed populace, to
credit so absurd an affidavit ... Hence, they speedily swelled their numbers."* [446]

With Loyalist numbers swelling, armed confrontation against Rebels
was becoming a real possibility. At the same time Col. Richardson was organizing his forces to pursue the thieves.

*Sunday, 12 November*

On this day, *"Col. Laurens, from the committee to whom was referred
the complaint of the officers of the regiment of Rangers, regarding rank and precedence, delivered in their report ... being taken into immediate consideration,
the Congress came to the following resolution ... Resolved, That the regiment of
Rangers be considered as the third regiment in the service of the colony. That the
degrees of first and second Lieutenants be considered as giving rank regimentally
in the regiments respectively, and not otherwise. And that upon detachments and
courts-martial, officers of horse and foot of equal degree, shall take rank according to the date of commissions."* [447]

The number of ranger officers who joined in the original complaint, signed by Capt. John Purves, is not known. Nor is it known whether Col. Thomson approved of their grievances. But five months had elapsed since the two low country regiments, and the one back country regiment, had been created. During this time the rangers had been made to feel like a poor cousin by their low country counterparts—a situation that Congress was now attempting to rectify.

*Monday, 13 November*

Meanwhile, as military organization and mobilization to hunt down the Loyalist insurgents continued, rumors once again spread regarding Moses Kirkland's presence in town. Congress immediately issued a warrant for his arrest—false alarm. Congressional concerns now turned to the British gunships—the *Cherokee* and *Tamar*—anchored just outside Charleston Harbor. Yesterday, when Charlestonians had tried to block a channel entrance to the harbor, they were fired upon. This hostile reaction, although not unexpected, was pompously viewed by Congress as *"the actual commencement of hostilities by British arms in this colony against the inhabitants ... an event of the highest moment to the southern part of the United Colonies on this continent."*[448]

With this second crisis on its hands, Congress was propelled into a flood of activity, including *"erecting several new batteries for the more effectual defence of Charles Town."* The ship *Prosper* was armed for colony service and Congress now established *"a regiment of artillery ... formed a Committee of intelligence to correspond with, and communicate to, the inhabitants of the interior parts of this colony ... to seize, or cause to be seized and secured, and take the examinations of, all such persons, who being at large, may endanger the public safety, or prove injurious to the common cause of America."*[449]

In a belligerent mood, Congress would tolerate no dissension. If you were not for the Rebel cause, you were against it—and would have to suffer the consequences. Congress was gearing up for action on two fronts. Charleston, for the moment had priority. But the back country pot was coming to a boil. Meanwhile, a report from the meeting of Rebel Indian commissioners in Salisbury, forwarded to the Continental Congress in Philadelphia, provides further insight into the Indian question.

The report contains a *"Copy of Talk from the commission of Indian Affairs for the Southern Dept. to the Cherokee Indians."* Excerpts read: *"From talks with beloved men of Georgia and Mr. Galphin, you have already been told of the nature of the dispute between Great Britain and America, and it is like a dispute between a father and his children … you have no concern with it … keep an open path through your lands."*[450] Once again the Cherokees were being asked to maintain a state of neutrality.


*Tuesday, 14 November*

From Andrew Williamson's subsequent report of 25 November to William Henry Drayton, we learn that *"your letter by order of Congress dated the 9th inst., I received on the 14th."* This was 11 days after the hijack, 10 days after Williamson had been alerted, 8 days after his own letter to Wilkinson and 7 days since he had received Wilkinson's reply. Now, on the 14th, after receipt of this letter from Congress, Williamson gave orders for reinforcing Fort Charlotte, reporting on the 25th that he has furnished *"Captain Caldwell with iron for the carriages to mount the guns."* But it is the penultimate paragraph of Williamson's letter that offers additional insight into sensitivity over rank and privilege that was beginning to affect the egos of officers within the budding military organization of South Carolina. Major Williamson refers to an argument that arose when he received, on the 14th, Drayton's letter of the 9th. He replies to Drayton: *"I am sorry to acquaint your Honor that some difference arose between Major Mayson and me about the command of the militia … to prevent any bad consequences I agreed that if he would come to camp I would receive orders for the militia and volunteers, and give them myself until a gentleman should arrive who would command us both … but when I received [on the 14th] your letter with orders from the Congress, I thought myself no longer bound by that agreement, especialy when he told me he was ordered to attend the Congress."*[451]

The argument is simply another indication of how rank and status conscious officers were becoming regarding military protocol. Mayson, as a major in the "regular" army—Regiment of Rangers—outranked Williamson, a former Major in the King's militia, now commanding a Rebel voluntary militia. If Mayson should join him in the campaign against Loyalists, Williamson would grudgingly accept Mayson as his superior officer. However, upon receiving instructions from Congress, he interpreted them as giving him sole authority over his militia forces, even though a superior officer was present. The situation was left to ferment.

With respect to attending Congress, Mayson, as well as Williamson and Caldwell, were all elected representatives to the Second Provincial Congress. Due to the crisis, none would attend. Williamson's cryptic comment that Mayson had also been "ordered" to attend remains unexplained.

*Wednesday, 15 November*

A new Regiment of Artillery was commissioned by Congress. Major Robert Owens, taken from the First Regiment, was placed in command as a Lt. Colonel. His second in command was to be Major Barnard Elliott. In other actions taken, Congress imposed restrictions upon supplies of provisions to the governor and his ships in harbor. The Committee on the State of the Colony was expanded to add two more members from the back country—Capt. LeRoy Hammond from Ninety-Six District and Capt. Thomas Sumter from the District Eastward of the Wateree. Also, *"a motion was made, that the future meetings of the Provincial congress be held at Camden or some other more central and convenient place ... carried in the negative."*[452]

This was the first instance in which low country privilege was challenged regarding the geographical seat of government. One reason for the motion was the fact that attendance from back country delegates to Congress at Charleston was relatively low. A more central location for assembly would make participation more convenient. But it would be another 15 years before interior dwellers could force a change to move the capital from Charleston to Columbia. In 1775 Congress was still dominated by men from the low country. Representation from the back country, 83 out of 208, was disproportionate for a province in which 70-80% of the white population lived in the back country. The total population of South Carolina at this time was only 174,000, of which 104,000 were slaves. Of the 70,000 persons who comprised the white population, perhaps 15,000 resided in the low country. Yet, they were represented by 125 representatives in Congress.

Regrettably, journals of the Second Provincial Congress do not provide attendance figures but, judging from the appointments to committees, and from ad hoc comments, attendance in general was very low. In voting on resolutions, at no time were more than 100 votes recorded—less than 50% of the total number [208] of elected representatives. Logical deduction leads one to conclude that absenteeism among the delegates from the back country was proportionally higher than that of their counterparts from the low country.

*Thursday, 16 November*

On this day, approximately 13 days before Congress was scheduled to adjourn, selections to the next Council of Safety were made. These nominees contained only low country names. Of the 13 members, all were holdovers from the previous Council except for Henry Middleton, David Oliphant and Thomas Savage; they replaced Miles Brewton, John Huger and William Williamson.

*Friday, 17 November*

The back country would receive additional representation in the Committee on the State of the Colony when Capt. Patrick Calhoun from Ninety-Six and Capt. John Winn from the District Between the Broad and Catawba Rivers were called to serve by Congress.

*Saturday, 18 November*

This same committee [State of the Colony], on the 18th, reported on the *"regulation of the militia ...Mr. Caldwell* [not the commandant of Fort Charlotte], *Mr. Green and Mr. Newton from the back country attended, and were severally admitted, who gave very alarming accounts of the state of affairs in those parts."* Their accounts reflected tensions arising from the Pearis affidavit, of which legislators may not yet have been fully aware—a copy would be sent to them only on 25 November by Major Williamson. The accounts from these latecomers to Congress provided welcome intelligence but shocking news. Therefore, it was *"Ordered, That Mr. President be desired to prepare the draught of a Declaration, calculated to remove the prejudices entertained in some parts of the colony, against the measures of the late Council of Safety, in sending a small quantity of ammunition to the Cherokee Indians."*[453] Although understated, this issue was a smoking gun. Legislators, especially men such as Laurens and Drayton, knew it; the proposed "draft declaration" was aimed to get common sense policy back on track.

It was also on the 18th, as one learns from a later report dated 24 November, sent by Major James Mayson to Col. Thomson: *"about 4 o'clock in the afternoon, we* [Mayson and Williamson] *received intelligence that all the people assembled in arms over Saluda River, had marched over, and encamped about four and a half miles from our camps, in about two thousand ... We had at most, not more than five hundred men. At first consultation with Major Williamson, we agreed to march and meet the opposite party and give them battle; but upon consideration, we thought it most prudent to march all our men to Col. Savage's old field, near Ninety-Six ... we arrived there about daybreak* [on the 19th]."[454]

Another version of these same events is offered by Major Williamson, who reported to Drayton on the 25th that: *"he could obtain no certain intelligence from the opposite party until the seventeenth ... in the night ... when I learned their numbers amounted to at least fifteen hundred men ... On the eighteenth, in the evening, I received certain information that they were crossing the Saluda river on their march toward us, and then was joined by Maj. Mayson, with thirty-seven rangers. I immediately ordered the men under arms, and took the resolution of marching to meet them, and demanding their attentions, and if they were determined to come to action to be ready before them ... but after reflecting on the fatal consequences should we have been defeated, proposed in a Council of War, consisting of Major Mayson and all the Captains, to march from the camp near Ninety-six into the cleared ground of Col. Savage's plantation ... which was unanimously approved of, and early next morning we marched to Ninety-six with all our provision and baggage."*[455]

After describing the capture of Robert Cunningham, the hijacking of arms to the Cherokees and the mobilization of Richardson's posse, a newspaper report later recounted that *"Major James Mayson with about 46 men of the rangers and Major Andrew Williamson with about 460 of the militia, hearing that the insurgents were increasing daily in Numbers ... joined the force, and upon the 17th of last month, having received certain intelligence that the Enemy were within a few miles away hastily erected ... breastworks."*[456]

*Sunday, 19 November*

Quoting once more from Mayson's letter of the 24th, the Rebel forces arrived in the area of the court house, *"Col. Savage's old field ... about daybreak"* on the 19th. *"As our numbers were small ... began to fortify the same with the rails thereabouts ... and in about two hours a square of one hundred and eighty five yards was fortified in such a manner as to keep off the enemy."*[457]

These were the "breastworks" later mentioned in the newspaper account. In Williamson's words [letter of 25th], this was a *"kind of fortification of old fence rails joined to a barn and some out houses ... before we had quite completed they had surrounded us with a large body of men with drums and colors. I then sent out an officer to demand their intention, who, on his return reported that Major Robinson and Mr. Patrick Cunningham refused to have any conference but with the commanding officers. I then sent Major Mayson and Mr. Bowie, whom they and Mr. Evan McLaurin met between their men and the fort in sight of both, and after about fifteen minutes conference they returned, and reported that they insisted on our immediately delivering up our arms to them and which were the only terms they were determined to grant us, and at parting they told them to keep our people within the fort, which was the only place where they could be safe; and immediately they took two of our people just by the fort, before my face, whom I gave orders to retake, and a warm engagement ensued, which continued with very little intermission from three o'clock in the afternoon of Sunday, until Tuesday sunset."*[458]

One of the reasons why Rebel forces agreed to take a position at Savage's field on the morning of the 19th, according to Williamson, was that we were *"being in immediate expectation of being joined by Col. Thompson [sic] and the rangers, at last, and also some men from the lower part of this regiment and Augusta."*[459]

This expectation, not unreasonable, was based on the letter from Drayton received by Williamson on 14 November. He was aware that mobilization orders had been issued to Col. Richardson on 9 November and that Col. Thomson's rangers, in Dorchester, had been alerted. It was supposed that they would lose little time in marching into the interior. But two weeks would elapse before any such move would be made. Nor is there any record of ranger communication between Thomson and Mayson at the time. Williamson's expectations were based on wishful thinking.

In Charleston, on Sunday the 19th, as Rebels were confronting Loyalists at Ninety-Six, Congress was still in session, oblivious to violence in the back country. *"Mr. President delivered a draught of the Declaration which he had been directed to prepare, to quiet the minds of the misguided people in the Back Country ... being taken into immediate consideration."* While this declaration would be of no value, given the outbreak at Ninety-Six, it offers excellent insight into the formulation of policy and planning in 1775. Written by William Henry Drayton, the declaration states: *"It has ever been the policy of America in general, and of this colony in particular, to endeavour to cultivate a good correspondence with the neighbouring Indians; and especially so, since the commencement of the present unhappy disputes with the British administration. Experience has taught us, that occasional presents to the Indians has been the great means of acquiring their friendship ... the Continental Congress having divided the management of Indian affairs into three departments, have already allotted for the expences of this southern department the sum of ten thousand dollars, in order to preserve the friendship of the Indians on the back of our settlements ... it clearly and unfortunately appeared, that a general Indian War was inevitable, unless the Indians were furnished with some small supplies of ammunition, to enable them to procure deer skins for their support and maintenance ... Rather than draw on an Indian War, by an ill-timed frugality in withholding ammunition, our friends in Georgia resolved to supply the Creeks ... They also strongly pressed the late Council of Safety to supply the Cherokees.*

*About the end of September the Honourable William Henry Drayton ... met several of the Cherokee head-men at the Congarees. Nothing could in the least degree satisfy them but a promise of ammunition ... the Council the more readily agreed to this measure, because as they almost daily expected that the British arms would attack the colony in front on the sea coast, they thought they would be inexcusable, if they did not ... remove every cause to apprehend an attack at the same time from the Indians upon the Back Settlements ... But this measure, entered into by the council, upon principles of the soundest policy, of Christianity, breathing equal benevolence to the associators and non-associators in this Colony ... unfortunately has been, by some non-associators, made an instrument for the most diabolical purposes ... These wicked men, to the astonishment of common sense, have made many of their deluded followers believe, that this ammunition was sent to the Indians, with orders for them to fall upon the frontiers and to massacre the non-associators ... this is absurd in its very nature ... the Council of Safety is incapable of such inhumanity ...and that Mr. Drayton's conduct at Ninety Six, at the head of the army, fully shewed, that the blood of the non-associators was not the object of his policy. If men will but call reason to their aid, they must plainly see, that if the Indians were let loose upon the frontiers, they must indiscriminately massacre associators and non-associators, since there is no mark to distinguish either to the Indians ... the Congress in a body, and also individually, declare, in the most solemn manner, before almighty God, that they do not believe, any order was ever issued, or any idea was ever entertained, by the late Council of Safety ... to cause the Indians to commence hostilities upon the frontiers."* This declaration also takes pains to explain that the revolutionary government in Charleston, *"by various and a multitude of means is able to procure a constant, speedy and authentic information of the state of all parts of the colony ... being much better informed ... are the most competent judges of where ammunition ought to be sent; whether a small quantity to the Indians, with a view and probability of keeping them quiet, or a large quantity to the inhabitants necessarily to arm them against the Indians ... Common sense and common honesty dictate, that if there is a probability that by a present of a small quantity of ammunition the Indians can be kept in peace; that present ought not to be withheld at the hazard of inducing an Indian war."*[460]

As a passionate and logical appeal to reason, Drayton's policy outline is a belated attempt to salvage reputation as well as to promote unity in common cause. If back country political support is lost, the common cause of liberty could be jeopardized. The Rebels in Congress were well aware of this. But many of the Loyalists in the back country, suspicious of the motives of their low country brethren, are not yet convinced that they share a common cause.

On 19 November, at Ninety-Six, Rebels and Loyalists were poised for more than a battle for men's minds. Meanwhile, on this same day, the declaration on Indian policy was ordered *"distributed among the inhabitants of the back country."* But, to back up policy with arms, it was *"Ordered, that Mr. President be desired to instruct Col. Richardson, to apply to Col. Thomas Polk, of North Carolina, for the assistance of the six companies under his command, to be in the pay of this colony, if he shall judge such assistance necessary."*[461]

So, ten days after issuing initial orders to Col. Richardson, it appears that mobilization is far from complete. The colonel was still receiving instructions. But where is he—in Charleston, Dorchester, or still in Camden? Meanwhile, unknown to Richardson, Thomson or members of Congress, South Carolina's first armed confrontation of the Revolutionary War was about to escalate from words into bloodletting.

# CHAPTER XIX:

## *War and Peace at Ninety-Six*

V IOLENCE BROKE OUT AT NINETY-SIX ON THE AFTERNOON OF
Sunday, 19 November, and continued through to sunset on Tuesday,
21 November. A belated newspaper account of hostilities provides
a recapitulation of the battle through a Rebel's eyewitness report which,
says the editor, is an *"extract from a letter from an officer at Ninety Six."* The
letter writer is not identified, but his correspondence is dated 29 November:
*"On the second day after the engagement began they* [Loyalists] *set fire to the
fences and old grass in the Fields all around us, with an intent to burn up our
fort, which consisted of only old dry Fence Rails, and attack us from behind
but the ground was too wet, and saved us from the Trouble of extinguishing
the fire ... when they found that plan defeated, they set to work and made
some kind of rolling Battery, behind which they intended to come up and set
fire to Col. Savage's barn, and to burn us but this they afterwards dropt."* The
Rebels *"resolved in a council of War to make a Vigorous sally about midnight
and Captains Pickens, Hamilton, Robert Anderson, Singuefield, and Colton
from Georgia, with twenty picked Men each were appointed for this service, and
were to attack them in five different Quarters at the Same Time; When they
went out each Captain was to reconnoiter the Quarter he was to attack ...each
were to endeavor to make one sure fire and immediately retreat ... but a flag of
cessation of Hostilities was hung out ... We have since learned that their Reason
for offering of Arms was owing to some of our people who were absent on Furlow
when the Affair began, returning to their Duty with as many more as they
could raise, and engaging them on the Outside and learning from a Deserter
of us our intended sally."*[462] Reports later submitted by Majors Mayson and
Williamson are less embellished.

According to Major Williamson, in his report dated 25 November,
addressed to Drayton and received by Congress on the 29th, the battle continued *"until Tuesday sunset, when they* [Loyalists] *hung out a white flag from*

*the jail, and called to us that they wanted to speak to the commanding officers. I replied, if they wanted to send an officer or any message they should be safe. On which they sent a messenger carrying a lighted candle and a letter from Major Robinson directed to Col. Mayson, demanding of us one hour's time to return an answer; to which Major Mayson and myself jointly answered that we were determined never to resign our arms."* Two interesting points emerge: one being that Robinson appears to be the commanding officer on the Loyalist side, and the other being that he addressed his letter to Col. Mayson, addressing him in his old militia rank, rather than as a major in the rangers. The Rebel answer to Robinson was carried back by John Bowie, who then returned with Patrick Cunningham who, reports Williamson *"I met about fifty yards from the gate, where we conversed for some time, and then he came with us into the fort, where after some time, we agreed to have a conference on the morrow ay eight o'clock."*[463]

Mayson, far briefer in a report drafted on 24 November to his superior in the rangers, Col. Thomson, merely states: *"On Tuesday last, in the afternoon, the enemy held out a flag of truce and sent into our fort a messenger with a letter from Major Robinson to myself, which was the first beginning of a treaty."*[464] Negotiated and drawn up on the 22nd, a copy of the treaty was enclosed with Mayson's letter of the 24th to Thomson. He would receive it on the 27th at the Congarees.

In Charleston, Congress was still concerning itself with military preparations to defend the port city against shelling by British gunboats; it was completely unaware of developments in the back country.

## Monday, 20 November

Congress took several steps on this day. One was to allow *"Colonels of the several regiments of militia throughout the colony ... to enrol ... able male slaves, to be employed as pioneers and labourers, as public exigencies may require."* Another was *"to make provision for the support of all persons who may be maimed and disabled in the public service of the colony ... and also of the families of such as may be killed."* Concerning back country affairs, it was *"Ordered, That Col. Gervais, Capt. Hammond, and Mr. Rapley have leave to visit Capt. Robert Cunningham, in his confinement in Charles-Town Gaol."*[465] These men, all back country delegates to Congress, presumably would seek to enlist Cunningham's help in encouraging his brother to surrender on mutually acceptable terms.

*Tuesday, 21 November*

Still preoccupied with military matters, Congress *"Ordered, That the consideration of the report of the committee on the state of the colony, respecting the militia, be resumed."* Keen on tightening military organization throughout Carolina, legislators *"resolved, that the commissioned of the colony regular troops take precedence of officers of equal degree in the militia, without regard to prior dates of commission ... that precedency in the regular forces be according to the number and denomination of the regiments of infantry, and rangers, and the regiment of artillery, according to the custom of the British Army. That all corps of regulars take precedence of all corps of militia ... And that the regiments of militia shall take precedence in the following manner: Berkely County; Charles Town; Granville County; Colleton County; Craven County the lower part; Orangeburg; Craven County the upper part; Camden; Ninety Six north of the Fish-dam Ford between Enoree, Broad and Saludy Rivers; the New Acquisition South of the Fish-dam Ford, and between Broad and Saludy Rivers; North of Enoree, between Broad and Saludy Rivers."*[466]

Low country militia continued to take precedence over the back country. Procedures for drafting militia troops were tightened. Every company commander was required to *"assemble, muster, train and exercise his company once every fortnight, under a penalty of twenty-five pounds currency for every default ... every person liable to bear arms, shall appear completely armed, once every fortnight, on the day and at the place appointed by the Captain ... the privates under penalty not exceeding three pounds current money, the officers under penalty of twenty five pounds, for every default ...that there be no more volunteer troops of horse formed."* Congress needed infantry, not cavalry, to ward off any possible attack on Charleston. The port city was of highest priority at the moment. Therefore *"it was moved ... that an immediate draught of five hundred Militia from the country regiments be ordered to rendezvous ... convenient to and for the defence of Charles-Town."*[467]

The usual war of words ensued between hawk and dove over this resolution—the doves feeling such a proposal for mobilization was excessive. Brought to a vote, the doves won and an alternate resolution was adopted, requiring merely that *"Colonels of the militia throughout the colony ... to draught one third of their respective regiments ... and hold them in constant readiness to march at a minute's warning."* Curiously, given the belligerent mood toward Loyalists, Congress, on this same day, passed an act of leniency regarding Capt. Benjamin Wofford, a Loyalist signer of Drayton's 16 September treaty. Having behaved himself, it was *"Ordered, That Capt. Benjamin Wofford have leave to trade here, upon taking his oath to observe the strictest neutrality, agreeable to the late treaty of Ninety-six."*[468]

Wofford took the oath, was granted the promised trade privileges but later, upon leaving Charleston, was taken prisoner and jailed without trial when feelings against Loyalists were again running high, once the Rebels in Charleston became aware of the latest skirmish in the back country.

The first hints of trouble that reached Charleston ears occurred on Saturday, 25 November, when William Moore, a delegate from Ninety-Six, made a belated appearance at Congress. The record indicates that he *"gave some information of a skirmish, said to have happened last Monday between the enemies of this country, led by Patrick Cunningham, Jacob Bowman and others, and a band of militia, under the command of Major Williamson."*[469] As second hand intelligence based solely on hearsay, Moore's information aroused concern, but not panic. Indeed, although Moore had departed from Ninety-Six while the firefight was still taking place, he was not an eyewitness; he was simply relaying gossip. While Moore was enroute to Charleston, the combatants were preparing to negotiate a ceasefire and treaty.

*Wednesday, 22 November*

In his report to Drayton dated 25 November, which would arrive in Charleston on the 29th, Major Andrew Williamson gives his account of the ceasefire at Ninety-Six, commenting: *"Accordingly on Wednesday morning Maj. Mayson, Capt. Pickens, Mr. Bowie and myself met with Major Robinson, Messrs. Patrick Cunningham, Evan McLaurin and Richard Pearis, and agreed to a cessation of hostilities now inclosed you, which was lucky for us, as we had not above thirty pounds of powder, except what little the men had in their horns; but no scarcity appeared, as no person knew our stock but one gentleman and myself."* But, as Williamson noted, the Rebels still had *"thirty eight barrels of flour with five live beeves … and got good water the third day after digging upwards of forty feet, so that if we had a sufficiency of powder we could have withstood a siege for a considerable time."*[470]

Major Mayson's own words, regarding conditions, merely state: *"before three days expired, our men began to be outrageous for want of bread and water, and we had not above sixteen pounds of gunpowder left."*[471] The Rebels were ready to negotiate but, with respect to the treaty protocol, taking into account the festering tension between the two Rebel majors, one later learns from a Mayson account: *"rather than hurt the cause … I suffered his [Williamson's] name to be inserted in the Truce before mine, yet the means of our defense was planned by me; and the whole negotiation with the disaffected party was addressed to me."*[472]

Putting aside their differences, Mayson and Williamson, on the 22nd, hammered out a treaty entitled *"Agreement for a cessation of Arms, between Major Joseph Robinson, Commander of a body of His Majesty's Militia, now under arms, for himself and the troops under his command of the one part; and Major Andrew Williamson and Major James Mayson, commanders of the Fort at Ninety Six, for themselves and the troops therein, under the direction of the Provincial Congress:*

1st That hostilities shall immediately cease on both sides.

2nd That Major Williamson and Major Mayson, shall march their men out of the fort; and deliver up their swivels.

3rd That the fort shall be destroyed flat, without damaging the house therein; under the inspection of Captain Patrick Cunningham and John Bowie, Esquire: and, the well filled up.

4th That the differences between the people of this district, and others disagreeing with the present public measures, shall be submitted to his Excellency our Governor, and the Council of Safety; and for that purpose, that each party shall send dispatches to their Superiors—that the dispatches shall be sent unsealed—and the messengers of each party shall pass unmolested.

5th That Major Robinson shall withdraw his men over Saluda river, and there keep them embodied or disperse them, as he pleaseth: until his Excellency's orders be known.

6th That no person of either party, shall, in the mean time be molested by the other party; either in going home, or otherwise.

7th Should any reinforcements arrive for Major Williamson or Major Mayson, they also, shall be bound by this cessation.

8th That twenty days be allowed for the return of any messengers.

9th That all prisoners taken by either party, since the second day of this instant, shall be immediately set at liberty.

*In witness whereof, the parties to these articles have set their hands and seals, at Ninety-Six, this twenty-second day of November, one thousand seven hundred and seventy-five; and in the sixteenth year, of his Majesty's reign … before Pa. Cunningham; Rich'd Pearis; Andw. Pickens and John Bowie."*[473]

In comparison to the earlier Treaty of Ninety-Six, unilaterally imposed by Drayton on 16 September, this one has the earmarks of a joint Rebel/

Loyalist effort to save face on both sides—an attempt to preserve pride and dignity with a minimum of rhetoric. However, not all would view the cessation of hostilities favorably. Just as Loyalists Cunningham and Brown had denounced the treaty of 16 September, so Rebels Richardson and Thomson would denounce the treaty of 22 November. Although the treaties complemented one another, there was a glaring omission in the latest accord. Nothing was said of returning the hijacked arms or of bringing Cunningham and his gang to justice.

Major Mayson, following proper military protocol, sent a copy of the treaty to Col. Thomson, who would forward it to his superior, Col. Richardson. Major Williamson sent his copy and report directly to William Henry Drayton, President of the Congress, still in session. Robinson sent a copy by courier to Governor Campbell aboard his warship, the HMS *Cherokee*, berthed in Charleston Harbor. During the interim, Congress had other worries.

*Thursday, 23 November*

Discussion of military preparations continued, as legislators *"resolved ... to oblige all inhabitants to do duty in some company or other, so that no one, who is by law obliged to do duty in times of alarm, shall be excused."* An order was issued to the *"contractor for supplying the colony infantry with provisions, be desired also to supply the Rangers posted at Dorchester, until further orders."*[474]

This inference leads one to conclude that the rangers have not yet set out to join Richardson's expeditionary force which was authorized on 9 November. Indeed, Williamson and Mayson had long been expecting the rangers to show at Ninety-Six. Where was Richardson's army? Not until 27 November would it be confirmed that Richardson was at a "Camp near Congarees," where he had arrived the previous evening to join Col. Thomson. It was here that Mayson's letter of the 24th would reach both officers on the 27th.

*Friday, 24 November*

From his home at Island Ford on the Saluda, Major James Mayson reported on the confrontation at Ninety-Six, stating in his letter: *"We have only one man dead since this battle, and eleven wounded; some will be mortal by the doctor's opinion. The enemy say they had but one man dead, who is a Capt. Luper, and about the same number wounded as ours; by the best information they have buried at least twenty-seven men, and have as many wounded. I am certain that I saw three men fall at the first fire from our side. The swivels are to be delivered up this evening to us, although inserted in the articles of cessation as given by us up, as agreed to by the head men of the other party."*[475] Williamson's report would elaborate a bit more on this aspect.

*Saturday, 25 November*

Writing from his home, Whitehall, on the 25th, Williamson states: *"It will appear to your Honor by the articles that we gave up the swivels, but that was not intended either by them or us, for after the articles were agreed on and were ready for signing, their people to the number of between three and four hundred surrounded the house where we were and swore if the swivels were not given up they would abide by no articles, on which the gentlemen of the opposite party declared upon their honor that if we would suffer it to be so inserted in the agreement they would return them, which they have now done and I have sent them to Fort Charlotte."*[476]

A swivel gun of 1775 was a light, mobile cannon, mounted on a rotating stand which allowed for a 360 degree arc. It fired a three pound ball. The gentleman's agreement regarding the swivels, a face saving measure, speaks well for the negotiators of both sides in seeking an amicable reconciliation of differences. Otherwise, when commenting upon casualties, Williamson differs somewhat from Mayson. He says *"our loss was very small, owing chiefly to blinds of fence rails and straw with some beeves hides ... We had only thirteen men wounded, one of whom is since dead, most of the rest very slightly."* With his report, Williamson also enclosed a *"copy of a letter from Major Williamson to Edward Wilkinson, esq, ... camp near Long Cane, 6 November 1775 ... Mr. Wilkinson's answer, dated Nov. 7, 1775 ... return of the militia and volunteers in the fortified camp at Ninety Six, Nov. 19, 1775."*[477]

This return did not include Major Mayson's 37 rangers, but named 25 militia companies ranging in size from 4 to 54 men. Capt. James McCall from Georgia had 54 men; Capt. Andrew Pickens, 40; Capt. Benjamin Tutt, 34—all the others had fewer men in their companies. The total numbered 523 volunteer militia men who took part in the skirmish at Ninety-Six.[478]

In a second letter of the 25th, Williamson forwarded Drayton a copy of the Pearis affidavit of 11 November which, when received in December, would enrage the President of the Second Provincial Congress of South Carolina.

The dead Rebel to whom both Mayson and Williamson alluded was James Birmingham of the Long Canes region. He was wounded on the first day of battle and died on 22 November—his family was later awarded an annuity of one hundred pounds by the South Carolina General Assembly.

The battlefield upon which he was shot, sometimes described as a stockade, was said by Mayson to be "a square of one hundred eighty five yards." When excavated by archaeologists in 1972, investigators concluded that the fence rails *were set in palisade trench in the traditional stockade manner ... enclosing an area 85 x 150 feet.*"[479]

It was also on the 25th that William Moore, as previously stated, appeared in Charleston with rumors of a possible confrontation at Ninety-Six. His news caused alarm; Congress now ordered *"all public gun-powder ... in public hands"* to be gathered. Lt Col. Roberts was *"forthwith to go to Dorchester, and give directions for putting the Magazine Fort in such posture as he shall think will best enable it to repel any sudden attack."* The parish of St. George, Dorchester, was *"to be impowered to impress negroes, horses, wagons, carts, and every thing else, necessary for giving dispatch to the completing of the works of defence proper to be erected at that post."* Supplies for 1000 men for one month were to be gathered at Dorchester; it was also *"resolved, that this colony be now, and it is hereby declared to be, in a state of actual alarm ... as if the same had been proclaimed in the manner and form directed and appointed by the militia law."* A motion was made at this point to refer to committee *"to fix on a proper place of rendezvous, for the militia which may be thought necessary to be draughted."*[480]

Legislators were once more divided into hawks and doves. The question being put to a vote, the doves prevailed. The gathering of Loyalists at Ninety-Six was serious, but there was no need to panic. Therefore it was resolved merely to bolster Col. Richardson's expeditionary force with *"six hundred men from Col. Powell's regiment* [militia of the Cheraws] *and also six hundred men from Col. Rothmaler's* [militia of Craven County]" to be *"forthwith marched to rendezvous at Congarees."* An additional 150 men from Col. Bull's regiment [militia of Granville County] would go to Cherokee Ponds near Augusta to stand by. All were to *"act under the orders of Col. Richardson."* A company from the new Regiment of Artillery was also ordered to join Richardson.[481]

Congress was organizing a rather formidable force to meet any contingency that might arise in the back country. The leaders in Charleston were not yet aware of the treaty of 22 November.

*Sunday, 26 November*

All resolutions passed on the previous day were put into effect, and confirmation letters were sent out. Congress, about to adjourn in four days time, now put some finishing touches on the powers invested in the Council of

Safety, which would be the *de facto* government until Congress met for its second session in February 1776. The Council was given authority to act *"if any complaint be made against any officer of the militia … after having inquired into the truth of it, and heard the defence of the officer, if he hath any, may remove such officer, if they judge the complaint to be just, and forthwith appoint another in his stead."*[482]

This clause was adopted because numerous complaints had been received, not only from rangers, but from other regular regiments and the militia. With independence from England becoming an increasingly real possibility, men were becoming sensitive to status and recognition for their services under a budding revolutionary government. The need for discipline and a clear cut division of responsibility between the military and civilian branches of government also became imperative. Congress, therefore, ordained *"that no person holding a military commission in the regular forces of this colony, or in the continental army, shall be capable of possessing a seat, or of having a voice in the said Council of Safety."*[483]

The revolutionary government of South Carolina was beginning to gel, but it still had to reflect the desires of the Continental Congress sitting in Philadelphia. From there, the crisis of potential civil war in the back country barely registered; protection of Charleston had priority in its instructions to South Carolinians.

*Monday, 27 November*

Reviewing its instructions from Philadelphia, the Provincial Congress, on the 27th, observed: *"Inasmuch as it is the sense of the Continental Congress, that Charles-Town ought to be defended to the last extremity, against any attack … it is hereby recommended, that all such persons who are by law considered as residents in Charles-town, and liable to bear arms, and have departed, do forthwith return to Charles-Town; And that all persons, residents as aforesaid, and liable to bear arms, and who are in Charles-town, do not depart therefrom … all resolve respecting the militia of this colony, be forthwith printed and published, in hand bills, and also in the Gazettes."*[484]

With the Provincial Congress about to adjourn and the Council of Safety poised to resume authority, the Richardson expeditionary force finally entered the picture. On the 26th it reached the Congarees; on the 27th, Mayson's report on the skirmish at Ninety-Six caught up with both Richardson and Thomson. It may have prompted Richardson to send his first message back to Charleston, addressed to Drayton. From this letter we learn that Richardson *"has been very busy in getting the men's wagons, &c.; over the river, which I shall scarcely complete tomorrow."* He explains that *"The route I intended to have taken was very different from the one I at first anticipated; as when I heard of the fort at Ninety-Six being besieged, I altered my march, in order to make what I could to relieve them; but they had concluded the articles too soon, for a possibility of my reaching them."*[485]

These cryptic words are difficult to decipher. We only know that it was at the Congarees that Mayson's letter found Thomson on the 27th. Four hours after receiving it, Thomson shared it Richardson, after which Richardson wrote to Drayton. He wrestles with a guilty conscience, ruefully observing: *"Perhaps it may be said in Congress why did not Col. Thomson go and relieve them? I answer, he could not, was not able, nor had timely notice if he had been."* The meaning of this disingenuous explanation is puzzling at best. Richardson continues, lamely commenting, *"We have received no accounts from there but what I herewith enclose a copy* [Mayson's letter with the treaty], *together with a letter from Mr. McLaurin which was sent today to Col. Thomson."*[486]

Reviewing events, I suspect that Thomson received the Mayson and McLaurin letters at the same time, probably from the same courier. Following the treaty, the two sides at Ninety-Six had nothing to hide. Differences appeared to have been amicably dumped into the laps of the Governor and Council of Safety, respectively. But Richardson, it seems, refused to accept the terms at face value; he was still on the warpath and meant to hunt down all Loyalists regardless. This was already taking place. In this same letter to Drayton, which was completed piecemeal, Col. Richardson, in a post-script, reports that a returning patrol, led by Lt. Boykin of Capt. Kershaw's company, found Col. Thomas Polk *"22 miles from us … had three prisoners … Capt. Mayfield and two others."* Moreover, Col. Polk *"had received a letter that Major Robinson was pursuing him with a thousand men."* This dubious information had been passed on to Polk prior to the encounter at Ninety-Six, when Robinson may have indeed been on the road to Ninety-Six with a large force. But, following the cessation of hostilities, complying with article #5, Robinson was peacefully encamped across the Saluda awaiting results, or he may have dispersed his forces. Upon receiving news from Polk, Col. Richardson, ignoring the treaty, tells Drayton that he *"detached a party of rangers, volunteers and militia"* to chase after Robinson, suggesting that he may be on his way to Dorchester.[487] He wasn't; the Rebel forces were simply out of synchronization and in a muddled state at this point in time. Col. Thomas Polk, from North Carolina, was the brother of Ezekiel Polk who was currently in Dorchester. There is no confirmation that Ezekiel ever joined the Richardson expedition.

In assessing his situation on this evening of 27 November, still awaiting the arrival of troops, Richardson's letter comments, *"I cannot ascertain the number of my men, as I have not, from the bustle, been able to obtain regular returns, and which, I believe, at this time, amount to about one thousand, with daily additions, and soon expect as many more ... though we hear the opposers are very numerous and violent and desperate, yet we hope in a little time to give you a more full account of our army and our opposers, who are much elated and carry a high hand."*[488]

Again one wonders just how well informed Richardson was. Has he not read Mayson's letter? Had he not reviewed the treaty of 22 November? The Loyalists at Ninety-Six were indeed numerous in number but were no longer violent or desperate. They had disbanded, awaiting reaction to the treaty. Richardson seems to have chosen to disregard this; he was still uneasy. He wrote to Drayton, *"But though much, very much, depends upon this campaign, do not be under too great apprehension for the event. If God is for us, we have nothing to fear. I might tell a thousand hearsays, but nothing of moment to depend ... I am ready to receive any orders, and execute any commands that may redound to the peace and tranquility of my country."*[489]

Col. Richardson was a most righteous person, in the process of compiling a Christian coalition to crusade against evil. One story says that while on this campaign he carried a sermon by the Rev. Richard Furman. In 1775, Furman, ordained a teen-age preacher the year before, was barely 20 years old when he gave his *"Address on Liberty"* at the *"Baptist Church in the High Hills of Santee in November 1775."* According to one historian, the sermon was *"carried by Colonel Richard Richardson and his militia as a circular letter to the people of the back country in 1775 to explain the cause of unrest with Great Britain."*[490]

# CHAPTER XX

## *Retribution not Reconciliation*

C OL. RICHARDSON COMPLETED HIS LATE NIGHT LETTER STARTED ON the 27th in the early hours of 28 November. Meanwhile, on the 27th, Major Andrew Williamson, from his home, Whitehall, in the Long Canes area, was again writing to William Henry Drayton in Charleston, to report that he had just received a message from Patrick Cunningham. The Loyalists, writes Patrick, wished to appoint Robert Cunningham as their spokesman in Charleston.

### *Tuesday, 28 November*

William Goodwin was dispatched to carry Williamson's letter to Charleston, but he never made it. Enroute, outside of Ninety-Six, late on the 28th, Goodwin ran into a rider from Col. Richardson carrying a letter to Major James Mayson. This rider informed Goodwin that *"nothing could be done in Charlestown ... the matter was entirely left to Col. Richardson ... and that it was resolved in a Council of war of all officers that they should not abide by the cessation of Arms we had agreed to."* So wrote Major Williamson in a postscript addition to his letter of the 30th, which was then retransmitted to Laurens; Williamson now initiated direct communications with Richardson as well.[491]

The war council to which Richardson's courier referred was held on the morning of the 28th. Col. Thomson sheds some light on the meeting in his letter to Henry Laurens dated 28 November: *"You will see by the enclosed that our party and the opposite have had an engagement, and came to a cessation of arms on the 22nd and you will perceive how dilatory they were, in giving us information of it ... the moment I received it [Mayson's letter of the 24th] ... I acquainted Col. Richardson with the same, who was then about eight miles distant from us, and joined me four hours after. We immediately summoned our officers and held a consultation … whether according to our orders in the present situation, the cessation of arms stipulated have any weight upon our operations. Carried in the negative."* In brief, the expeditionary force chose to ignore the treaty; it decided "to take Cunningham, Robinson and Pearis, in custody, though they are the persons acceding to the cessation of arms at Ninety-Six."[492]

Richardson then sent for Mayson to appear in camp to tell his side of the encounter at Ninety-Six. He would arrive at the Congarees on the 29th, after Richardson and Thomson had dispatched their own letters to Charleston. The die was cast; Loyalists would be hunted down, captured and jailed, irrespective of the treaty of 22 November. Attitudes had hardened; a taste of this is provided by Col. Thomson in his same letter of the 28th, as he complains of being rebuffed by his own people in the Orangeburg area where he had been able to raise only 100 men for the expeditionary force. Thomson writes: *"When the Sergeants warned the draughted people about Orangeburg & the Congarees, they seemed very insolent, asked which camps they were to join, and, in fact, did as much as to declare themselves King's men … the same dissatisfaction seems to have reigned amongst a part of Col. Richardson's people. But I am persuaded, after all their murmurings, we shall have a sufficient number of men to vanquish all the disaffected people in South Carolina & I hope Col. Richardson will have orders so to do before we break up."* Such belligerence was supported by the troops; according to Thomson: *"We have had great uneasiness amongst them when the news arrived of the Cessation of Arms, & we had no other means of appeasing their disturbed minds but by signifying that the Cessation of Arms was not binding on us & so forth."*[493]

The expeditionary force was in a vindictive mood, fueled by rumors that were also reported by Thomson in his letter of the 28th: *"I have some reason to believe that the late mob* [Loyalists] *has privately murdered people in the Woods who have been Associates. I believe part of the disaffection among the People at Orangeburg proceeded part from Cowardice & part from the Speeches of disappointed Gent. In our parish … But I hope to have the liberty of putting Militia Law in force against the defaulters."*[494] Thomson was in a vigilante frame of mind; for the moment vengeance was in fashion both in Richardson's camp and in Charleston.

*Wednesday, 29 November*

It was *"Resolved, That the Congress shall be adjourned to the first day of February next."* At this time details of the affair at Ninety-Six had not reached Charleston; Rebel leaders were primarily concerned with an impending attack on the port city, reflecting the concern of the Continental Congress. Therefore, they reacted with urgency when it was learned *"that a certain person has been sent by General Gage, to raise recruits in this colony, for an army whose object it is to kill and destroy the innocent inhabitants of these colonies … It is therefore declared by authority of congress, that this colony will consider such an attempt, by any man, as the highest crime against the peace, liberty and safety of its inhabitants … all manner of persons are hereby requested to be watchful to detect and seize any and every such person … a handsome reward allowed for apprehending and securing him or them."* Low country militia Captain John Allston was *"Ordered to march the Volunteer Company of foot Rangers after the Indian Manner, under your Command, and scour the Sea-Coast from Sewee Bay to Haddrel's Point in Charles-Town Harbour, to repel the Landing of Men from British armed vessels, to prevent their Depredations."*[495]

Gage's spies and agitators, if they indeed existed, were never caught. But it was in this exaggerated mood of vigilance that Congress went into adjournment, and in this frame of mind that the Council of Safety would receive reports from the western front.

*Thursday, 30 November*

Col. Richardson, still at the Congarees, once again wrote to Drayton to report that Major James Mayson was now in camp and that he would be coming to Charleston to brief the Council: *"By Maj. Mayson setting out for Charlestown, I take the liberty of acknowledging the receipt of your favor of the 25th, by Lieut. Charleton … pray, if possible, send some ammunition."* But, as an afterthought, Richardson adds, *"I think we have little to fear from the oposers of our peace."* After talking to Mayson, the colonel was in a bit of a quandary. In this same letter, he admits: *"I am really at a loss how to proceed, as I do expect they will couch under their cessation, which we in Council of War have voted not to affect us."*[496]

Mayson set off for Charleston on the 30th; on the same day the Council of Safety would receive Major Williamson's letter of the 25th, to which it would reply three days later.

*Saturday, 2 December*

Although erroneously addressed to: *"Andrew Williamson, esq., Major in Col. Thomson's Regiment* [sic] *at Ninety-Six,"* the Council confirms: *"received your several dispatches directed to the President* [of the Congress] *which adjourned on the 29th."* Henry Laurens, once again in place as president of the Council, is the one who signed off on the letter to Williamson. He continues: *"Your country is greatly indebted ... for your attention to the safety of Fort Charlotte, but more especially for the Brave & very important defence ... at Ninety Six—had the Enemy broke through that post they would have been encouraged to penetrate the lower settlements & probably would have occasioned us ten fold embarrassmen—We highly applaud the whole of your conduct ... and with great pleasure on behalf of the good People of this Colony return you Thanks—we request you to signify in form the sense we have of their late services to Major Mayson & to all the Officers & Troops which were under your command."*[497]

The nicety of these words, since no mention is made of the squabble between Mayson and Williamson over command, implies that Williamson's version was accepted by the Council. However, given hyper-sensitivity over protocol, status and recognition among officers in Carolina's budding military establishment, Mayson was affronted. He would not be so easily brushed off when he learned of the Laurens letter.

As for the treaty itself, Laurens' letter to Williamson makes clear: *"At the expiration of the stipulated terms* [20 days] *our friends will be collected ... we shall then be prepared to demand submission to such articles as will secure the future Peace of this Colony against attacks of those misguided people."* Laurens did not reject the treaty out of hand, as had Richardson and Thomson. Then again, the Council *"has not heard properly either from Coll. Richardson or Coll. Thomson ... we cannot account for their slow progress."* Nonetheless, Laurens chastises Williamson: *"you cannot have meant ... to bind any Troops of this colony ... but such as might have been Marching directly to your Camp as a reinforcement, therefore if Colonel Richardson by virtue of Orders which he received from the congress should act offensively against the insurgent party even before the expiration of the twenty days, such Act cannot be construed an infraction ... of Article 7 ... although we do not mean to prompt him by any new orders ... we are not obliged to ... countermand those under which he took the field."*[498]

Splitting hairs with diplomatic double talk, the Council thus indicates that it, too, prefers unconditional surrender, rather than a truce. In this respect it would concur with Richardson and Thomson, once their reports were received. But the temper of Council members can be better gauged, at this time, by their reaction to the Pearis affidavit which was logged in on 30 November. In his same letter to Williamson, Laurens calls it *"groundless & malicious libel ... we are also of the opinion that the late attack was hastened by the instigation of that infamous Traitor who ... wantonly abandoned us & joined the Enemy ... your endeavours will not be wanting to lay hold of that grand*

*Offender, nor will we be deficient in proper rewards to Persons who will seize &*
*bring him to Charles Town … we need not urge the necessity for keeping this a*
*profound secret … we have every confidence in your Zeal & vigilance … which*
*assures us that not withstanding the present cessation of Arms, you will not stand*
*an idle spectator if attempts should be made to injure our Cause, contrary to the*
*letter or spirit of the Treaty either by our old or upstart Enemies, by any means or*
*by any pretence whatsoever—watchfulness & perseverance are necessary to guard*
*against the various machinations of a wicked Ministry who are resolved to attack*
*us in Front & Rear, who by secret Emissaries stir up enemies in our very bosom*
*& who leave no stone unturned no means unessayed to work our utter ruin."*[499]

This analysis of Loyalist intentions would concur with that of Richardson
in the field. Loyalists would be hunted down. By this same 2nd of December,
Richardson's forces had moved up into the fork between the Broad and
Saluda rivers. From McLaurin's store, Col. Richardson now reported to the
Council: *"we are just starting to March … as Yet unmolested by the Opposites*
*… have taken the persons herein named … Capts. John Mayfield, Benj. Wofford,*
*Wm. Hunt, Dan'l Stagner. Jacob Stack … I have been joined by Col.Thomas*
*with about 200, Col. Neel as many, Col. Lyles abt one hundred Together with*
*Col. Thomson's Regt. Rangers & Militia with my own, may make in the whole*
*about 2500 and I rec'd Last night Acct. of Col. Polk's being Near with 600."*[500]

Col. Richardson was in the process of amassing a formidable punitive
force. The inclusion of Benjamin Wofford among the prisoners provides
insight into prevailing jingoistic attitudes now widespread among the Rebels.
Just two weeks earlier this signer of the Drayton Treaty had been given
amnesty and free trade privileges. Now he was arrested and would soon be
clapped in jail. Excerpts from Wofford's own account, written six weeks after
being jailed, are illuminating. In a letter *"To the Honorable Council of Safety,"*
Wofford acknowledges that Cunningham's men approached him after the
arms hijack to raise a company to guard the stolen ammunition. Wofford
not only refused but went to Charleston to voice his objection to the robbery
and to declare his neutrality. He writes: *"I staid in town Ten days upon my*
*own expence while the Battle was over at Ninty six. The same time the Hon. Wm.*
*Henry Drayton, Esq gave me a permit from under his hand Granting me the*
*Privilege of free Trade. On my journey home I was taken a Prisoner & sent to Jail*
*Honorable Gentlemen I humbly implore your Honours to have me brought to a*
*trial … as I may be informed what accusations are against me … I have never*
*violated the Treaty of Peace … Very Humble Servant … Benjamin Wofford*
*… January 15th Day 1776 … Charles Town Jail."*[501] His request for a trial was
subsequently denied.

*Monday, 4 December*

On this day the Council received and read letters *"From Col. Richardson, dated Camp at Congarees, Nov. 27, 1775 … ditto, dated Nov. 30, 1775."* By this time it had also received Thomson's letter of the 28th and Williamson's interrupted one bearing the same date. The Council, abreast of developments in the back country, began to respond. Replies dated 4 December were drafted to all three correspondents—to be discussed in the Council on the 5th. At the Council session of the 4th, Article #4 of the recently concluded treaty at Ninety-Six came amusingly into play. Council journals reveal that *"Matthew Floyd, assuming to be a messenger from Major Robinson, with dispatches to the governor, which he pretended to have lost, applied for permission to wait on his Lordship, to relate to him the substance of the agreement for a cessation of arms, concluded on the 22nd ult. at Ninety Six … Ordered, That the said Floyd be permitted to wait upon Lord Wm. Campbell, attended by a proper person, in behalf of the council, who must be present at the interview & conversation between him and Lord William."*[502]

While it was well-known that the Loyalists would be sending a rider to Campbell carrying news of the treaty, as permitted under Article #4, it was not foreseen that he would turn up drunk. Although Floyd's appearance discombobulated Council members, he was allowed to see Campbell.

*Tuesday, 5 December*

In the Council's letter to Major Andrew Williamson, the Floyd incident was reviewed by Laurens: *"Major Robinson's messenger, or a person who pretends to be the messenger, and calls himself Floyd, has appeared before us & declared that being drunk, he had lost all his papers at Orangeburg. He was nevertheless extremely anxious to go on board the vessel in which Lord William keeps his court, in order to inform his lordship verbally all that he can recollect of the contents of the treaty and relative circumstances. As this man brought with him no credentials, we might without violation of treaty, not only refuse to grant his request, but also might have imprisoned him as a Spy, but unwilling to take advantage even of those who persevere in acting unjustly & cruely towards us … we have consented that he shall go to Lord William upon this express condition, that his whole conversation with his Lordship Shall be in the presence and hearing of a Witness whom we shall send for that purpose—this will be no more than equal to unsealed dispatches covenanted for in the 4th article."*[503]

This same letter to Williamson repeats, however, that Col. Richardson is not bound by the treaty: *"Col. Richardson received positive instructions from Congress under the 8th November to March an Army of Rangers & Militia into the Enemy's Country to 'Seize & apprehend the Bodies of those persons who Robbed the waggon near Ninety Six of Public Gun Powder & Lead, their Aiders & abettors, to use his best endeavours effectually to suppress the present insurrection & to deter all persons from attempting Insurrections for the future'* … *he was not prepared to reinforce your camp, therefore the 7th Article does not touch him."* Laurens further observes that Richardson has gathered *"upwards of 3000 men in the field … we have ordered auxiliary Troops from several quarters—& supplies of every kind Shall be given as occasions may require until the party with whom you have treated Shall lay down their Arms or Save themselves by flight & dispersion—We feel for their approaching distress but whatever calamities may befall them will appear to have been with equal folly & industry Sought by themselves."*[504]

In the letter to Col. William Thomson, the Floyd affair is again mentioned. And Laurens agrees: *"Your determination on the 7th Article of the late Treaty is certainly right, & accordingly I have confirmed the Orders"* to Richardson. Thomson is also reassured that he has *"power to fine all delinquent Militia Men according to Militia Law in time of Alarm."*[505]

In the Council's letter to Col. Richard Richardson, reviewed and dispatched on this day, Laurens refers to the Colonel's *"dispatches under the 27th and 30th November … Certainly your determination on the 7th article of the treaty is unanswerable … you were ordered to seize and apprehend persons who had committed an atrocious robbery, to suppress effectually an insurrection, & to deter all persons from attempting insurrections in the future. You were not ordered or destined as a reinforcement to Major Williamson's fortified camp, wherefore that Article cannot by the most strained construction be wrought to affect or touch your proceedings; it follows that your detention of Mayfield and other prisoners is justifiable."* So much for the neutrality of men such as Benjamin Wofford; Laurens forthrightly suggests: *"We refer you to your original instructions, recommending all possible expedition … Probably a proper declaration, inculcated among the lower classes of those misguided people under the influence of the enemies to liberty, may have the good effect of inducing many of them to come in to you, & to lay down ther arms; upon which condition, together with a solemn promise of the strictest neutrality, terms of mercy & protection may be granted."*[506]

This is the same tactic employed by William Henry Drayton on 30 August and 13 September when, in pursuit of Moses Kirkland, he issued a "circular" to intimidate the masses and discourage insurrection. The Council attached a brief addendum to Richardson for clarification: *"We think it neces-sary to explain, that we mean by 'laying down their arms,' that such men as may in consequence of a declaration come in to you, must surrender their arms, and put them in your custody ... in the meantime you may assure them of protection. The fears which some of them pretend to entertain, that Indians will be set upon them, are altogether groundless. Our great view by insisting upon a surrender of their arms, is to put it out of their power to disturb the public peace & safety. Their quiet and reasonable behavior will induce the Congress, or this Board, to reinstate & take them into favour, & to return their arms."*[507]

Clearly, the Rebel leaders in Charleston were greatly annoyed that fron-tiersmen did not trust them regarding a policy of arming Indians. By charging that Rebels were deliberately arming Cherokees, Loyalist leaders were able to mobilize support. It angered the Council of Safety to have its motives chal-lenged. This became quite evident from reaction to the Pearis affidavit, which prompted the Council to draft an "address" to the back country.

*Wednesday, 6 December*

The Council's first order of business on the 6th was: *"an address to the inhabitants of the frontier settlements ... which being read was approved."* Written by Drayton, it was impeccably argued in a barrister fashion specifi-cally designed to ridicule the opposition. Pearis' challenge to Drayton's honor and integrity stuck in Drayton's craw as he drafted a caustic 2000 word rebuttal. This is Drayton at his waspish best, from which only a few high-lights will be quoted as he *"endeavours to apply an antidote to a poison I should otherwise have disregarded ... Richard Pearis ... one of a considerable number of people who attended a public harangue I delivered at Mr. Woffords on the 21st August. I was then an utter stranger to Pearis, but knowing he had resided a considerable time among the Indians, and imagining he had some influence over them, I desired him to bring some of them to converse with me."*[508]

As a *quid pro quo* for escorting Indians to Amelia, Drayton makes it appear as though Pearis tried to blackmail him into a land purchase and into assistance for settling Pearis' debts in Charleston. *"On this subject we had some conversation ... but not in the manner stated by him, and I ended it by telling him his price was too high, but that I would defray the expense he mentioned & I would mediate with the sheriff not to distress him while absent on public business; he was content and we parted ... Upon my meeting Pearis & the Indians [at Congarees] ... Pearis again applied to me to satisfy his debt ... & to purchase part of his land; I declined both ... He then requested my interest with the Council of Safety, to procure him the Superintendent's place,"* to which Drayton agreed, but now explains, *"when I came to town, I found the Commissioners for Indian affairs had already been nominated."*[509]

Was Drayton stringing Pearis along? The Galphin and Wilkinson appointments had been made in July before Drayton and Tennent took up their propaganda mission to the back country. Surely he was aware of this. Equally suspicious is the manner in which Drayton slides over the accusation that he agreed to a partnership with Pearis to purchase Indian land—and to pay for it with the presents allotted to the Cherokees by the Council. Drayton beat around the bush regarding his complicity in any chicanery in a land deal with Pearis. He simply offers *"presumptive evidence,"* arguing circuitously *"it is notorious among those who know him, that he is a man of no principle,"* while offering Wilkinson's letter of 7 November to back up the charge. He concludes, *"In short I imagine Pearis is offended with me on four points: first, that I did not indulge him, by endeavouring to rid him of Mr. Wilkinson; secondly, that I did not purchase part of his land; thirdly, that I did not assume a debt … & fourthly, that I did not procure his being made commissioner of Indian affairs."*[510]

The main thrust of the Pearis affidavit, however, was not so much to question Drayton's integrity over a land deal; it was to accuse him of trying to employ Indians *"against the white men."* *"The folly of this calumny,"* says Drayton, is refuted by *"the declaration of the 19th of November last by authority of Congress."*[511]

This is an odd argument. The ammunition wagon was hijacked on 3 November, and Pearis' accusation was made on the 11th—the fat was already in the fire when the declaration of the 19th was offered to explain policy.

Nevertheless, Drayton's rhetoric on 6 December helped soothe the Council's guilt over this affair. It then proceeded on to other business.

Benjamin L. Marchant, who accompanied Matthew Floyd on his visit to Governor Campbell aboard the HMS *Cherokee* on 5 December, now reported that he presented Lord William with a copy of the cessation of arms accord and explained that he was accompanying Floyd in accordance with Article #4. After remaining on board throughout the afternoon of the 5th, holding sporadic, non-substantive conversations with the governor's aides—and with Floyd ill much of the time—Marchant says that he was told by Innes: *"my Lord desires you will return, and inform the persons who sent you, that as the other person is a messenger from a friend to government, he must detain him until he had determined on a proper answer."* Surprisingly, Marchant acceded to this subterfuge, which must have vexed members of the Council of Safety; they now had no way to monitor any conversation between Floyd and the governor. Therefore, it was ordered that Floyd be immediately apprehended when he returned ashore. As an additional measure, his horse was held in strict custody to prevent escape.

The record for 6 December also shows that Major James Mayson, who had earlier brought in Col. Richardson's letter of 30 November, was *"given leave to visit and converse with Robert Cunningham, Confined in Charles-Town jail,"*[512]

The nature of their talk is not in the record. But, while in Charleston, Mayson became aware of Major Williamson's letter of 25 November and of the Council's reply. He was offended. A proud and vain man, sensitive to perceived slights in questions of honor, duty and military protocol, Mayson impulsively drafted a rebuttal to Williamson's claim of "command" during the recent skirmish at Ninety-Six.

## Thursday, 7 December

In a letter to the Council, dated the 7th, Mayson sadly but forthrightly wrote: *"Gentlemen, it is with the greatest reluctance that I presume to trouble you with a matter, which principally relates to myself. But, as its example and tendency might perhaps hereafter be of some prejudice to the cause, in which we are all engaged, if no notice was taken of it; I find myself under a necessity, of not being entirely silent on the subject ... The few forces which were lately assembled at Ninety-Six, were drawn together by me, as well as by Major Williamson; and though I was Lieutenant-Colonel of the same regiment of militia in which Major Williamson held his commission, and also a Major in your Regular Troops, to my surprise Major Williamson disputed the command with me—but, rather than hurt the cause, I yielded some points to him; which, I am sensible as your soldier, I shall not be justifiable in, without the greatest indulgence from you. I however think it proper to mention, that although on account of the public good I suffered his name to be inserted in the Truce before mine, yet the means of our defense was planned by me; and the whole negotiation with the disaffected party, was addressed to me ... I thought the conduct of Major Williamson in this affair the more extraordinary, as he was a member of the very Congress, which settled these points of command; and which I find have been confirmed by the present congress, as well as by the Continental congress ... lest hereafter the same disputes may arise, I humbly submit it to this honorable board, whether Major Williamson should not be informed, that when we act together, and hold our present commissions, I am to have the command ... The thanks of my country, it will be my highest ambition to deserve, and I understand that Major Williamson is to return the thanks of Congress to the officers who were present at Ninety-Six; I shall with joy receive them … though delivered to me by an inferior officer …I cannot conclude without assuring you, that both Major Williamson and myself concealed our differences from all, except one or two of the officers."*[513]

His argument is unassailable; the records of the Provincial Congress bear him out. Officers in the regulars would most likely applaud Mayson's initiative to preserve discipline but, for the Council, it was preferable to avoid controversy—especially as this was a matter that involved the Council's judgment. In the time-honored, bureaucratic manner of saving face, the Council would offer a weasel-worded reply on 9 December.

## Friday, 8 December

Meanwhile, the Council session on the 8th indicates that: *"Matthew Floyd had last night been landed from the Cherokee … that he was immediately seized, and placed under the care of the militia guard; and that he had produced … a certificate of his detention on board the said ship two days and two nights, signed by John Ferguson, commander of the said ship, and dated on board, in Rebellion Road, 7th December 1775. … I detained the bearer hereof, Mr. Floyd … as the circumstance of his coming on board with the messenger of the Council of Safety, made it highly suspicious that he did not come with any message from His Majesty's faithful and loyal subjects in the back part of this Province."* The Council now *"Ordered, That the said Floyd be brought before the Council immediately … being brought … he confirmed the report that had been made by Mr. Marchant—then proceeded to relate what had passed between him and Lord William Campbell … he declared Lord William had directed him to 'tell the people in the back country to do every thing they can for the best, that he did not desire any effusion of blood; but whatever they should do would meet with his consent.'"* All this sounds harmless, but when Floyd was asked by the Council *"what he believed Lord William meant,"* Floyd answered, *"that if they [Loyalists] could obtain a good and beneficial peace, they should do so; if not, that they should make war."*[514]

Make war! The Council of Safety put the worst possible interpretation to these words. It was viewed as another "hellish plot" which only made the revolutionary government more determined to corral all non-associators who threatened their cause. William Campbell would later report on his conversation with Floyd, commenting: *"I learned that the friends of Government in the back country after besieging six hundred of the Rebels in a fort they had erected near 96 and obliging them to capitulate, for want of a leader of either*

*consequence or knowledge enough to direct their enterprise they agreed to a ces-*
*sation of Arms for twenty days and then dispersed.... It was much against my*
*judgement that any attempt should have been made till a force appeared here*
*to support them, but ... their zeal and the oppression they laboured under had*
*obliged them to arm."*[515]

Campbell clearly viewed the skirmish at Ninety-Six as a Loyalist victory,
although prematurely launched and botched by a lack of leadership. With
respect to the treaty, Campbell complains: *"the Rebels have broke every article*
*of it and are, I am told, determined to extirpate the whole Body of them out of*
*the Province bringing many principal people into Charlestown custody."* The
process, of course, was well underway when Campbell drafted his Despatch.
Interestingly, even before speaking with Floyd, the governor sought to
offer morale-boosting commissions to back country Loyalists, telling the
Foreign Office that: *"Captain Innes was ready to set out with them by way of St.*
*Augustine through the Creek and Cherokee Nations, when the news reached me*
*of their leaders being seized and the whole party dispersed."*[516]

Floyd was jailed on 8 December. It was *"Ordered, that Major Williamson*
*be wrote, and made acquainted with every circumstance relative to said Floyd*
*and ... that Floyd be permitted to write"* to Loyalist Major Robinson, but only
if his letters were *"submitted to inspection of Mr. President."*[517]

In the back country, anticipating Laurens' advice, Col. Richardson, on
8 December, was preparing a *"Declaration ... to insurgents under Cunningham."*
Like Drayton's declaration last August, it was designed to intimidate frontiersmen into submission. Richardson and the Council were on the same
wavelength. The Richardson declaration reviewed current Rebel administrative thinking: *"Whereas on the third day of November last past, Patrick*
*Cunningham, Henry O'Neal, David Russe, Nathaniel Howard, Henry Green,*
*& sundry other persons, did, on Ninety-six district raise a dangerous insurrection*
*& commotion, & did, near Mine Creek, in said District, feloniously take & carry*
*away a quantity of ammunition, the property of the public, & in contempt of*
*public authority, & did also, with further aid, & by force of arms, on the nine-*
*teenth, twentieth, & twenty first days of said month of November at Ninety-six*
*in the district aforesaid, attack, besiege, kill & wound a number of good people*
*of this Colony, & in manifest violation of peace & good order, & breach of*
*solemn treaty entered into on the eighteenth* [sic] *day of September Last, made*
*& concluded between the Honorable William Henry Drayton, on the one part,*
*& Col. Thomas Fletchall & others, on the other part, thereby becoming guilty of*
*the atrocious crimes of robbery, murder, & breach of treaty of peace. To satisfy*
*public justice in the just punishment of all which crimes & offences, as far as the*

*nature of the same will admit, I am now come into these parts, in the same &*
*behalf of the colonies to demand of the inhabitants, the delivery up of the bodies*
*of all the principal offenders herein, together with the said ammunition & full*
*restitution for the ravages committed, & also the arms & ammunition of all the*
*aiders & abettors of those robbers, murderers, & disturbers of the peace & good*
*order as aforesaid; &, in case of refusal or neglect, for the space of five days, I shall*
*be under a necessity of taking such steps as will be found disagreeable, but which*
*I shall certainly put into execution for the public good … Given under my hand*
*this eighth day of December 1775."*[518]

Copies were circulated in the back country. One had only to wait
and see whether this declaration would produce a mood of cooperation or
belligerency.

*Saturday, 9 December*

Richardson's letter of 2 December was read at the Council of Safety's
session on the 9th. It buoyed spirits; in this message Richardson confirmed
the arrival of Cols. Thomas, Neel and Lyles, adding that Polk's arrival was
imminent. The strength of Richardson's army was now approaching 3000.

On the 9th as well, a draft reply to Major Mayson's letter of remonstrance was *"laid before the council,"* reviewed and duly sanctioned. The
Council treaded gently to soothe bruised feelings, observing: *"we have duly
considered … your letter … & as we have received no complaint from Major
Williamson, & are satisfied that each of you had the real services of the colony
at heart … we wish to avoid a minute inquiry, which in our opinion would
produce no beneficial end."* The Council expected all concerned to forgive and
forget. Why beat a dead horse? The Council excused its approach with some
obsequious afterthoughts: *"The command of the militia was, by the Congress,
vested in Major Williamson, from considerations of the distance of Col. Savage …
as well as from an information that you were at the time extremely ill, unable to
take the field … it was therefor necessary to order that gentleman to call forth the
militia in his district, & to hold them in readiness to join the troops under Col.
Richardson …your junction, & what afterwards happened at the fortified camp
Ninety-six, were circumstances altogether adventitious & unexpected … Hence
we are convinced, that Major Williamson, when he took the command, acted in
conformity to the order of Congress, & you will perceive that those orders were
not intended to overlook your merit, nor to offer you an affront … We highly
applaud you, for having, after you had joined Major Williamson, yielded in any
point of mere punctilio, on acount of the public good … We are so sensible of your*

*services, that with pleasure we repeat to you the thanks to the officers and soldiers of the corps of rangers who were under your command."*[519]

The Council, to its credit, was trying its best to correct an oversight —and to avoid a court martial offense under the rules and regulations for military conduct adopted in a resolution by Congress on 26 November. The confrontation, after all, left no visible scars. However, in writing on this episode years later, John Drayton reflects his father's bias, self righteously proclaiming, the Council's *"confidence was greater in Major Williamson; and he was more influential in that part of the country."*[520]

On the same December 9th Mayson was ordered to *"repair immediately to Col. Richardson's camp … we are satisfied of your zeal and attachment in the cause, and particularly we confide that you will persevere in your endeav- ours to promote harmony within your sphere, and to discountenance every kind and degree of dissension, the bane of public service. We wish you health and success."*[521] With this pat on the head, Mayson returned to the back country, taking with him a message from the Council to Col. Richardson informing the supreme commander that his letter of the 2nd had been received and that the prisoners sent to Charleston, *"Capts. Mayfield, Wofford, Hunt, Stagner and Stack were safely lodged in charge of the guard at barracks. We have also in custody, Capt. Floyd, who assumed to be a public messenger from Major Robinson to Lord William Campbell; but as he brought no credentials to us, and that Lord William had declared in writing his suspicions of the said Floyd, the Council of Safety have judged it necessary to detain him until an explanation can be obtained."*[522]

The Council now turned its attention to Major Williamson; in a letter dated the 9th he was alerted to the Floyd encounter and asked *"to give the needful information to Major Robinson, and transmit us his answer. Major Robinson will perceive, as do us the justice to say, that we have acted with great consideration, and have not, in any respect, departed from the terms of the treaty of the 22nd of November."*[523]

The Council may not have *"departed from the terms of the treaty"* but they were implementing its conditions selectively—conceding to open com- munications on the one hand, while preparing to crush all opposition in a preemptive campaign on the other. The prisoners were already starting to trickle in; more captives from Richardson reached Charleston on the 9th, brought in *"by a party of rangers"* and left in the custody of Col. Moultrie at the barracks. On the same day, the council *"resolved, that Matthew Floyd, now in custody of the militia guard, and John Mayfield, Benj. Wofford, William Hunt, Dan'l Stagner, and Jacob Stack, in custody of the barrack guard, be removed from the places where they respectively are confined and committed to close custody in the common jail of Charlestown."*[524] Warrants for this purpose were immediately issued.

Finally, on the 9th, Indian Commissioner Galphin, recently returned from the meeting at Salisbury, now reported. In a letter dated the 9th, which the Council would receive on the 14th, Galphin encloses: *"Proceedings of the Commrs. At Salisbury."* In addition he comments on the need to replace Indian stocks of gunpowder to mollify their suspicions. Galphin reports that he is desperately trying to supply the shortfall, hoping *"it will be sufficient to kill meat for them but they cannot make hunts with it."* He is especially concerned because Wilkinson has informed him that *"there are about 40 Cherokees gone to Augustine to meet Mr. Stuart, to get ammunition and presents. I am afraid they will think but little of our presents, they will get so much from Mr. Stuart ... We must provide a good Quantity of Rum for without that the goods would be nothing."* Other than emphasizing the lubricating power of alcohol, Galphin, in closing, offers a fascinating bit of intelligence: *"there is a man Just come down from Cunningham's Settlement he says that they made a very strong fort & they are Fiddleing & dancing & tells every man that Joins them the King will give them 500 Acres of Land and pay beside ... he Says he heard ... they had 4 Hogsheads of Gunpowder Sent them ... & that they have a great many men."*[525]

Such rumors of Loyalist high jinks in the camp of a man who, barely two weeks earlier, had signed the treaty of 22 November at Ninety-Six, must have infuriated the members of the Council of Safety.

*Sunday, 10 December*

Except for some movements of the British ships in Charleston harbor, the 10th was a relatively quiet day. The Council issued a permit allowing *"John Cunningham to visit his brother, Patrick* [sic] *Cunningham, in jail, in the presence of John Lewis Gervais, and Richard Rapley."*[526]

Meanwhile, in the back country, Col. Richardson was making good progress.

# CHAPTER XXI

## The Final Roundup

T HE REVOLUTIONARY GOVERNMENT IN CHARLESTON HAD BY NOW come to terms with its own differences regarding Loyalists in the back country. In addition, there was no longer hope for reconciliation with Great Britain.

*Monday, 11 December*

Henry Laurens signed a follow-up letter to Col. Richardson, noting *"I wrote to you by Major Mayson, to which I refer ... we ordered payment to the party which brought down Capt. Mayfield and the other persons."* This letter also contained news from England which the Council *"just received ...to the 8th of September."* The news contained word of King George's proclamation of 23 August and British plans for mobilization. This led Laurens to comment: *"we are confirmed in our belief, that the administration are determined to persevere in hostile measures against America."*[527]

*Tuesday, 12 December*

The "Proclamation by the King for Suppressing Rebellion and Sedition," had reached Boston by 31 October, and the news spread quickly. The recently received "news from London" reconfirmed that reconciliation was impossible. The Council now *"Ordered, That the following circular letter, be sent to the commissioners of the high roads throughout the colony ... Gentlemen—The present circumstances of the colony, renders it highly necessary, that the roads and bridges throughout should be repaired, for the marching of troops & conducting cannon as occasion may require ... carry this service into execution."*[528]

By the 12th, Major Mayson had delivered the Council's letters of December 4th and 5th. On the 12th, Richardson was responding; he states:

*"in the evening of yesterday ...they came to hand by Express ... they convey the lenitive measure, which I have been happy at the distance of two hundred miles to adopt. The eighth instant I wrote & made public a kind of declaration, of which I herewith inclose a copy ... upon which they have come in, many of them, & delivered up their arms."* Having anticipated the Council's recommendation, Richardson's circular of 8 December appears to be having good effect. He is in a euphoric mood: *"Our army which is formidable strikes terror, and the opposite party have hitherto fled before us, keeping fifteen or twenty miles distant. We often are told they will give battle, but yet they have not attempted it ... should their behavior be otherwise we shall deal with them accordingly."* Best of all, the colonel writes: *"We have several prisoners, amongst whom are Col. Fletchall, who was hid in a cave, & taken by Col. Thomson & rangers ... papers have fallen into my hands which the Council will be glad to see, but which I cannot venture to send by this conveyance, but shall transmit by the officer of the guard, with the prisoners, which I intend to dispatch to-morrow."*[529]

The content of these captured papers is not revealed, but Col. Richardson is jubilant over the success of his mission. With Colonels Thomson, Thomas, Neel of South Carolina, and Colonels Polk and Martin of North Carolina on hand, with others expected, Richardson comments *"I conceive when we are all in conjunction we shall muster between four and five thousand men & hope we may be in liberty to afford you any aid you may have occasion for"* in Charleston. With glee, he states *"this minute ... Capts Plumer and Smith with thirty men surrender themselves ... All goes well ... by divine assistance, the Company may answer every good intention ... if the inclemency of the season does not impede us, as our troops are illy provided, but well fed."*[530]

The capture of Fletchall was quite a coup, in spite of the fact that he had been inactive since 16 September, and under the supposed protection of Drayton's treaty. The associators were taking no chances; former enemies, even though neutralized, were fair game, to be accused without due process for *"offending the proceedings of Congress or other authorities."*[531] The manhunt would continue for the Cunningham gang—the only potential opposition to Richardson's army.

*Thursday, 14 December*

George Galphin's letter of the 9th reached Charleston on the 14th and was read before members of the Council of Safety. Its enclosures included *"copy of resolves of said commissioners, at a meeting at Salisbury, 13th November 1775; Copy of a talk to the Cherokees, same date; Copy of a talk to the Creeks, same date; copy of a letter to the Continental Congress, same date."* The Council would answer Galphin on the 18th. For the moment, other matters had priority. British activities had picked up. Council of Safety records show that its members interviewed Capt. Alexander Wylly whose *"coasting schooner ... had been seized about five weeks ago ... Wylly come up to town last night ... been detained on board the Tamar, sloop of war, ever since the seizure of his vessel by order of Lord William Campbell."* Wylly had been held hostage so that he could be used as a coastal pilot, if required. But, as no British reinforcements were coming to Charleston, the captain was released. The Council brought him in for questioning. Wylly said *"that he saw a number of slaves belonging to the inhabitants of this town on board some of the ships of war, and on shore upon Sullivan's Island."*[532]

This information prompted the Council to order Col. Moultrie to procure additional boats to cruise the harbor channels *"to cut off all regular correspondence with the men of war and other ships in Rebellion-Road."* On this same day the Council *"read a letter from Captain Peyer Imhoff, of the Rangers, dated Dorchester, 14th December, 1775, inclosing a return."* Imhoff's company had escorted Richardson's first batch of prisoners to Charleston. It was now *"Ordered, That Capt.Peyer Imhoff be supplied with about one hundred yards of the cloth imported for the public, to clothe his company of rangers, and that he be desired to procure Doct. Chandler's accounts for attending sick rangers, properly certified, to be laid before the board."* It was also *"Ordered, That a commission be made out, for a second Lieut. in the regiment of rangers, in the room of Lieut. Monoghan, resigned; date this day, and that the same be delivered to Capt. Peyer Imhoff, he having promised not to have it filled up without the approbation of his field officers."*[533]

*Saturday, 16 December*

Flushed with success and exuding confidence, we find Col. Richard Richardson once again writing to the Council on the 16th from a camp some miles south of Duncan's Creek in Fair Forest, which was the most distant point of his campaign. It was while at Duncan's Creek, somewhere between modern day Spartanburg and Greenville, that the Rebel army captured Fletchall and Pearis. Col. Richardson then turned south and was now at Liberty Hill, a few miles south of the Enoree River, in contemporary Laurens County. From here Richardson proudly writes: *"I herewith send you the persons of Col. Thomas Fletchall, Capt. Richard Pearis, Capt. Jacob Fry, Capt. George Shuburg, John Mcwilliams, Philip Wells, James Davis, Capt. McDavid alias McDade, and Joseph Alexander. These being all adjudged by officers and people here to be offenders of such a nature … it would be dangerous to let them go … they are under guard of my son who … will appear before you."*[534]

The Colonel's son, Capt. Richard Richardson, Jr., from the Camden Regiment of Militia, would reach Charleston on Boxing Day, 26 December. In his letter of the 16th, the father continues: *"these unhappy people are in a great panic, still flying before us … it is told that young Pearis* [son of the captured Richard Pearis] *And others have gone to bring the Indians down … it could not be in a better time … should be glad the whole would come while we are here … though Cunningham, Robertson* [sic], *and others, are fled they may yet come in our way."*[535]

The campaign is progressing splendidly; Richardson is worried neither by an Indian attack nor by Loyalists such as Patrick Cunningham and Joseph Robinson. Rebel spirits would soon be bolstered even more by news from the north.


*Sunday, 17 December*

Though not yet known to Carolinians, Moses Kirkland had finally secured passage from St. Augustine to Boston. Enroute to meet General Gage, his vessel, the sloop *Betsey*, was captured by Capt. John Manley of the armed schooner *Lee* on 17 December off the Massachusetts coast. The *Betsey* was brought in to the port of Beverly *"where Moses Kirkland a passenger … was taken into custody. The intercepted correspondence was given to Gen. George Washington who forwarded it to John Hancock in Philadelphia."* Attested copies were later transmitted to the Council of Safety through South Carolina's delegates to the Continental Congress by a letter dated 2 January 1776, received in Charleston on 3 February.[536] Kirkland himself was jailed in Philadelphia.

Manley was one of six army officers with seafaring experience who were selected and detailed by George Washington to patrol the waters of Boston Harbor to prevent supplies from reaching King George's troops. At the same time that he captured the *Betsey*, Manley brought in another prize, the *Nancy*, loaded with 2000 muskets, 31 tons of musket shot, 3000 round shot, numerous barrels of powder and a 13-inch brass mortar which was promptly christened "Congress." For his efforts Manley was commissioned a commodore.

In Charleston on the 17th, Council members were still doling out gunpowder with care: *"Mr. President reported that the five hundred pounds of gunpowder, and one thousand pounds of lead ordered to Camden, for the use of the forces under Col. Richardson ... had yesterday been dispatched, properly packed in rum hogsheads, by Mr. Aaron Loocock.*"537 But, on the other hand, Galphin's request would be denied.

*Monday, 18 December*

Henry Laurens now replied to George Galphin's *"dispatch of the 9th instant ... we are glad to learn that you are returned Safely to silver Bluff ... It is not at present in our power ... to issue the quantity of Gun powder which you think will be wanted for Indian service ... we are ordered by the continental congress to defend Charles Town to the 'last extremity' ... you will agree with us that it would be extremely imprudent to part with 2000 pounds for indians at this critical juncture ... when our stock will bear it we Shall not be penurious ... must of necessity trust to Rum & good words for Soothing until we can Satisfy the further demands of our Red friends ... Pearis has proved himself to be an infamous Traitor ... chargeable with exciting the Insurrection by forging abominable Lies & Swearing to them in the most formal & Solemn manner."* Laurens doesn't comment on the rumor passed on by Galphin regarding revelry in the Cunningham camp, but simply states *"we have accounts that the party are distracted & broken to pieces ... Mr. Pearis & others must be taken, killed, or fly the Country."*538

The conservative Henry Laurens, having shed his tolerance for Loyalists, was becoming as bellicose as William Henry Drayton. His lust for revenge would be rewarded 24 hours later, when news of Pearis' capture was received.

*Tuesday, 19 December*

The Council journal for this day reveals that it *"read a letter from Col. Richardson, dated Camp Great Swamp, Duncan's Creek, 12th December 1775."* This was the message in which Richardson reported his successes, including the capture of Fletchall and Pearis. Laurens would draft a reply to Richardson, to be *"laid before the board"* on the 20th.

*Wednesday, 20 December*

Today, the Council acknowledged receipt of *"your letter of the 12th, which ... affords us great satisfaction. We congratulate you upon your success, and flatter ourselves with hopes, that you will persevere in the execution of your orders, until you are fully assured that the dangerous opposition which lately threatened the happiness of this colony, is effectually quelled, & so finish the campaign with equal benefit to your country & honour to yourself. We desire you will also present our gratulations and good wishes to the field officers and officers under your command, and more particularly our thanks to Col. Polk & Lieut. Col. Martin, for the assistance which they have given to you, and their further offers of services to come, if needful, to Charles Town ... at present we are able to stand our ground & the intelligence just received from Canada, inclines us to hope the enemy will find their hands full of employment far from our door, except that they may send a few ships to attempt destruction of this town, against which we are going ... to guard effectually ... Lord William Campbell has gone to great lengths in harbouring & protecting negroes on Sullivan's Island, from whence these villains made nightly sallies, & committed robberies & depredations on the sea-coast of Christ-Church. This alarming evil received such a check yesterday morning, as will serve to humble our negroes ...& perhaps to mortify his Lordship ... The company of Foot rangers ... under the command of Lieut. Withers, made a descent on that island, burnt the house in which the banditti were often lodged, brought off four negroes, killed three or four, & also took some white prisoners."*[539]

The Sullivan Island caper was reported by Lord William Campbell as follows: *"when the Scorpion ... sailed for Cape Fear ... the rebels were elated ... the very next morning* [18 December] *they landed a body of men on Sullivan's Island where they had never ventured before, burned the only house upon it, consumed the little all of three poor families who had taken refuge there, carried off the people."*[540]

The *Scorpion*, mentioned by Campbell, had previously been cruising North Carolina waters. Returning to Charleston for provisions, it brought Governor Martin for consultation with Governor Campbell. Lord William tried to retain the ship for service in Charleston harbor, but failed. The *Scorpion* returned to North Carolina for duty in the Cape Fear area.

There was a definite sea change in Laurens' letter of the 20th to Richardson. The back country crisis was coming to an end, dissident leaders had been caught, and arms are being turned in by settlers. Only a mopping-up operation was needed to apprehend culprits such as Patrick Cunningham; a huge army was no longer necessary. Therefore, on the 20th, the Council also directed letters to Col. George Gabriel Powell in the Parish of St. David and to Col. Job Rothmaler of Craven County, canceling orders for their militia to join Col. Richardson's expedition. Both militia commanders were informed: *"Intelligence which we have just received from Col. Richardson, induces us to believe, that he will be able to accomplish the business upon which he was ordered by the Congress, without further aid."*[541]

*Friday, 22 December*

Having moved from his last camp at Liberty Hill, we now find Col. Richardson's forces, on the 22nd, encamped near the forks of the Saluda and Reedy Rivers, a site at Raborn's Creek, Hollingsworth's Mill, from where the supreme commander was drafting another message to the Council. Six days have elapsed since his last letter, *"constant marching, and multiplicity of cares"* had prevented him from writing sooner. But, *"now, as we have got to the very extremity of the roads north-westward … I take the liberty to inform you, that on Saturday last, the 16th instant, we were joined by Col. Rutherford, of Rowan, and Col. Graham, of Tryon counties, in North Carolina, with about five hundred men … to give their aid in common cause."*[542] A total of four militia units from North Carolina were now joining up with the South Carolinians—led by Colonels Polk, Martin, Rutherford and Graham.

By the "very extremity of the roads north-westward" Richardson refers to a position near that juncture on the borders of the Cherokee Nation known as DeWitt's Corner, where the eastern and southern border of Indian lands meet, on the Reedy River. While marching to this spot from Liberty Hill, *"on Wednesday, the 20th inst … was joined by Maj. Andrew Williamson, Capt. Hammond, and a small party of Col. Bull's regiment amounting in the whole to about eight hundred, so that our army is now formidable, between four and five thousand—a number most desirable to view—though we have had no occasion for more than my own regiment to have done the business."* [543]

The colonel was in high spirits; he could afford to boast. Loyalist opponents, after the confrontation at Ninety-Six, had dispersed. The Rebels' massive forces were intimidating. In his dispatch of the 22nd Richardson observes: *"the number has had a good effect, strikes terror, and shows what can be done on occasion … we have been successful in disarming most of this unhappy people; they are coming in with fear and trembling, giving up their arms, with a sensible contrition for the errors they have been guilty of. The spirit of discord being much abated, the most of the Captains have come in, and a good part of the companies under them. I use every method in my power for the honor of the Colonies, and the salutary and peaceable establishment of tranquility in these distracted parts."* Nevertheless, *"there is still a camp which we cannot yet come up with, consisting of the principal aggressors, which were, by best information, camped on Cherokee land."*[544] He refers, of course, to Patrick Cunningham and his merry band who, two weeks earlier, as Indian agent George Galphin reported, were fiddling and dancing at camp in Indian Territory. In addition, Major Joseph Robinson has not been seen or heard from.

As for concern over a potential Indian attack, Col. Richardson reports: "*They* [Loyalists] *have had expectations of the Indians joining them, but by a letter from Mr. Wilkinson to Major Williamson, they will be disappointed in that ... the Indians are well satisfied, & they say the Saluda people are devils.*" Wilkinson made his assessment in a letter dated 17 December to Williamson, who now shared it with his commanding officer. Richardson continues, "*I detached yesterday about thirteen hundred horse and foot ... under the command of Cols. Thomson, Martin, Rutherford, Neel, Polk, Lyles, Major Williamson and others ... I don't expect them in until tomorrow, or perhaps some days hence.*" These parties were sent out to search for Cunningham, who still retained most of the gunpowder he had hijacked, although Richardson reported "*We have at times got small parts of the ammunition they got ... and have a slight information of some more.*"⁵⁴⁵

In the rest of his letter, Richardson provides an excellent summary of his situation. He writes: "*I shall, while I stay do every thing I can for the good of my country, but the winter is advanced, the men, from their precipitate collecting and marching, illy provided, no tents, shoes wore out, and badly clothed, make it very difficult to keep them here. If they should break off abruptly, it might have a very bad effect. I shall, therefore, crave your permission to discharge the North Carolinians, to make their way from hence through the upper parts by the indianline to their own colony ... and Cols Neel and Thomson through a middle direction to their different quarters.*" Whether or not Cunningham is caught, Richardson was ready to bring the campaign to a close due to inclement weather—snow was threatening. Troops need refurbishing; morale was a critical factor, so much so that Richardson laments: "*Had I but forces to garrison a fort, it might be proper to establish one, but the militia will not be prevailed upon to stay, but I hope ... the spirit of discord will so far subside, that they will hardly raise any more commotion.*" Once before, Richardson had to quell "*this same spirit, which prevailed greatly on the north of the Wateree river and Lynche's creek.*" Therefore, he now reasons, it might be best to cut short the campaign "*when I think it well with us, lest it should be worse ... if our present expedition should fail, we shall yet have these principals ... We have many prisoners, yet think we shall not trouble you with many of them, as they are not of the first class.*"⁵⁴⁶

The Colonel's analysis seems a sensible one, taking into account the limitations of vengeance. If the search party sent out yesterday doesn't turn up any more foes or arms, it may be prudent to call off the hunt. Indeed, a large force is no longer necessary. As Richardson points out, "*Maj. Williamson's Ninety six militia may be best concerted*" to keep pressure on Cunningham.

Before he finished his letter, however, contingency planning became unnecessary. In a postscript Richardson adds, "*This minute since, or while I was writing my name, a messnger from Col. Thomson … arrived with the agreeable account that they had surprised and taken the camp of Cunningham, &c, & taken the greatest part prisoners, with all their ammunition, guns, wagons, and utensils. P. Cunningham has escaped, and some principals, but the most are taken, &c. I hasten the messenger express … & desire you will send him back as quick as possible, with a state of affairs in Charles Town, and such orders as you may think proper.*"[547]

To Thomson, Mayson and their fellow rangers went the glory of previously capturing Col. Thomas Fletchall and now of destroying the Cunningham gang. At this moment Fletchall was still enroute to jail in Charleston, in the custody of Capt. Richard Richardson, Jr. The captain, with all his prisoners, had set out four days earlier carrying his father's letter dated the 16th. As of the 22nd, the Council was yet unaware of Fletchall's capture. It had only Richardson's letter of the 12th, which had been read on the 19th and answered on the 20th— response that Richardson had not yet received. Everyone was playing catch up. Regarding Charleston, Col. Richardson, as of the 22nd, knows only that British ships in Charleston Harbor have shelled Rebel boats trying to blockade a port channel; he is cognizant of the Council's fear that British troops might be landed; he knows of the increase in spy and sabotage activities by pro-British elements; and he is aware of the order from the Continental Congress to defend Charleston "to the last extremity." Thus, Richardson now stands ready to offer his services for Charleston's defense, if necessary. On the other hand, he fears that demobilization may be essential before current hardships provoke volunteer militias to mutiny. For its part, the Council of Safety, at this point, was unaware that the back country insurrection had been extinguished. Only when the expresses caught up with Richardson and the Council, would everyone be able to breathe a sigh of relief. Meanwhile the Council pursued its daily deliberations while running the revolutionary government.

## Saturday, 23 December

With the Christmas season upon them, Charlestonians turned to thoughts of holiday festivities. On this day the Council "*read a letter from Captain John Purves, of the Regiment of Rangers, dated 22nd of December, 1775 … Ordered, That Capt. Purves … upon duty at Dorchester, have leave of absence, not exceeding three weeks … pay bill for his company of Rangers, from 20th November to 20th December, at Dorchester,"* was sent to Purves and to *"Capt. Peyer Imhoff"* on the 23rd.[548] The companies of Purves and Imhoff had escorted the first groups of prisoners to Charleston. They were ready for Christmas leave. Another group of prisoners was on its way under Capt. Richardson. Meanwhile, the captain's father, Col. Richardson, at DeWitt's Corner in the back country, was preparing to send off the last contingent of prisoners, from Cunningham's gang.

An account of their capture would be included in a Richardson letter dated 2 January 1776, which provides insight into the last days of his expedition. Cunningham's camp had been found *"at a convenient place called the Brake of Canes on the Cherokee land … Our people surrounded their camp by daylight in the morning of the 22nd … after a long march of near twenty five miles … then attacked and took one hundred and thirty prisoners, with baggage, arms, ammunition … but Patrick Cunningham escaped on a horse bare backed without breeches … none of our men was killed or wounded, except the son of Col. T. Polk … was shot through the shoulder … some five or six of the other party, I am told, were killed."* The raiding parties returned to camp at Raborn's Creek the next day.[549]

On this same day, 23 December, like a scene from a Shakespearean play, *"the snow set in, and continued for thirty hours without intermission which, with the hardship and fatigue the men had suffered before, made them very uneasy, and seeing no more could be done they grew so uneasy it was out of my power to keep the troops together any longer … I, therefore, on christmas Day dismissed the North Carolina troops, viz: Rutherford, Col. Graham, Col. Martin & Col. Polk to all of whom, in behalf of my country, I returned my cordial & hearty thanks … the same day Col. Neel and Thomas, and Major Williamson were dismissed, with proper orders to pursue such measures in their different marches, as I was convinced would be necessary for the public service … the snow then lying at least fifteen inches deep … I marched out in the best manner we could downward."*[550]

# CHAPTER XXII

## *Coming Together in Charleston*

HAVING DISMISSED HIS NORTH CAROLINA FORCES, COL. Richardson and the remaining South Carolinian army marched "downwards" to the Congarees for eight harrowing days. It was from the Congarees that Richardson would send his last dispatch to the Council of Safety in Charleston.

### *Christmas to the New Year*

After breaking camp on Christmas Day, writes Richardson, *"eight days we never set on the earth or had a place to lie, till we had spaded or grabbed away the snow, from which circumstance, many were frost bitten … and on the third day a heavy cold rain fell, together with sleet; and melted the snow and filled every creek and river with a deluge of water."*[551]

While this remnant of Richardson's force was sloshing its way to the Congarees with their prisoners, on Christmas Day in Charleston the Council of Safety was facing its recurring problem of management and discipline at Dorchester which, since early November, had been designated as a central base camp *"for effectually guarding the cannon, gun powder, stores and public records, at that place."*

Dorchester slowly expanded into a garrison and supply depot for the South Carolina military. As the post grew, so did problems of administration. It was from Dorchester that Capt. Purves of the rangers, on 20 November, had submitted a letter to Congress complaining of "inconveniences" at Dorchester. Capt. William Cattell, a militia officer, personally grumbled to Congress on the same subject two days later. Commandants at Dorchester were constantly being reproached or replaced. On 9 December Col. Joseph Glover, Commander of the Colleton County Militia Regiment, had been told *"to order immediately a field officer from your regiment, to repair forthwith to Dorchester, and there to take command of the troops of rangers and militia at that post."*[552]

Glover appointed Major James LaRoche, who promptly resigned his commission rather than accept what he viewed as a thankless posting. The major's superior officer, Lt. Col. Samuel Elliott, took over on temporary duty, which dragged on. In due course, having received another letter *"from Lt. Col. Elliott at Dorchester, who signified a desire to be relieved from the command,"* the Council on 25 December wrote again to Col. Joseph Glover insisting that he personally *"should succeed Col. Elliott ... we are of the opinion, that, if you were on the spot, you would ... by your own application and direction, soon cause such barracks, guard room, and place for confinement of prisoners, to be fitted up, or built, as would remove all ground for complaint."*[553]

Col. Elliott was advised that he would be relieved by his superior, Col. Glover, but the Council reprimanded him for all the complaints and grievances *"which we had hoped would have been long since redressed, by the attention and discretion of the commander."* Paradoxically, the Council also compliments Elliott: *"it affords us great satisfaction to know that perfect harmony has subsisted between the rangers and the militia, and that a resolution to do duty, and decorum, has governed the whole."*[554]

All was not lost; nevertheless, the task of creating a disciplined revolutionary military force was proving to be an arduous task. The application of rules and regulations, while at the same time satisfying the personal egos of men in uniform, had been exasperating the Provincial Congress and Council of Safety for the past six months. While harmony between rangers and militia may have improved, latent jealousies remained. They would continue to plague discipline as the revolution wore on.

On this Christmas Day, however, news coming from the back country would, for the moment, overshadow the petty squabbles at Dorchester. In a letter to the Council, dated 25 December, dateline Eutaw, Capt. Richardson alerted the Council of his impending arrival with Loyalist prisoners captured by his father's forces. Eutaw was approximately 50 miles from Charleston, and 25 miles from Dorchester. The captain's letter was sent ahead by a courier who arrived in Charleston on the 26th. However, since Council members seem to have been celebrating Boxing Day, they did not meet until the 27th, when they *"read a letter from Richard Richardson, Jun., dated 25th Dec. 1775 ... To which Mr. President sent the following answer: Sir ... you may come forward as quick as you conveniently can—you will probably be in Charles Town tomorrow evening—when you come to the Quarter House ... inform me ... The council of Safety ... will give you notice before you come within the town, where the prisoners are to be lodged."*[555]

The Quarter House was *"a tavern situated six miles north of Charleston on the main road just before it branched to Dorchester or Goose Creek and the Congarees ... a favorite destination for Charlestonians on pleasure drives."*[556]

On the same morning, the Council read the letter dated 22 December from Col. Richardson, sent while still encamped at Raborn's Creek. From its contents, the Council became aware that that Cunningham's camp had been found, that the back country insurrection was over and that Col. Richardson was anxious to demobilize. That very afternoon another messenger arrived from Capt. Richardson who *"attended to acquaint the board, that ... he was arrived at the Quarter House with ten prisoners."* He sought instructions. The courier returned with the Council's *"desire for Capt. Richardson's immediate attendance with the intercepted papers."* In the early evening of the 27th, *"Capt. Richardson attended ... delivered to Mr. President a packet from Col. Richardson containing a letter from Col. Richardson, dated 17th Dec. 1775, Inclosing a list of the following prisoners, viz., Colonel Thomas Fletchall, Capt. Richard Pearis, Capt. Jacob Fry, Capt. George Subergh, Philip Wells, James Davis, David George, Capt McDavid alias McDade. Joseph Alexander, and John McWilliams; and also a number of letters found in the possession of Col. Fletchall ... warrant was issued to the sheriff of Charles town, or his deputy, or the keeper of the Common Jail in Charles Town ... to receive into your custody, in the common jail ... prisoners charged with high crimes and misdemeanors against the liberties of these colonies."*[557]

When the Council met on the 28th the first order of business was to read and review a letter directed to Col. Richardson, dated 27 December, referring to the Colonel's *"important dispatch of the 22nd, by the hand of Mr. Newton, the contents of which require that we should repeat our declaration of being greatly satisfied with your conduct and your success in a campaign, which will be a topic in American history, always reflecting honor upon your name."*[558]

President Laurens goes on to generously laud the efforts of others, desiring Richardson: *"to repeat our thanks also to all the officers and men of the colony regiments of rangers and militia, and the companies of volunteers, and then you may proceed to discharge the whole in the manner which you have proposed ... but we must not lose sight of Patrick Cunningham and Major Robinson ... offering proper rewards for apprehending those troublesome enemies."* Laurens closes in the hope that Richardson will be able to attend the second session of the Second Provincial Congress when it opens on 1 February *"where you* *will receive the highest reward to a faithful Servant of the public—the unfeigned thanks of his country."*⁵⁵⁹

On the 28th payment was also authorized to *"Capt. Richard Richardson, thirteen hundred pounds, to be applied in payment to officers and men in the detachment with prisoners from Col. Richardson's camp."* One of the officers who accompanied Richardson was Capt. John Coutourier with *"a volunteer group of horse."* He *"acquainted the board that he had information of Euan* [sic] *McLaurin's being harbored at Wassamassaw, offering his services to go in quest of him … to apprehend and take the said McLaurin."* He was so authorized, although the quest ultimately proved unnecessary.⁵⁶⁰

In a more personal vein, Laurens wrote separately to Col. Richardson, eloquently saying: *"permit me to add my particular congratulations as a member in common & my thanks for the Services which you have rendered your Country—Conquest without bloodshed bespeaks at once the bravery & humanity of the Conqueror … beg my Compliments to Col. Thomson & particularly to my good friend Col. Rutherpurd* [sic]—*when Shall I see him again & where? … I heartily wish you health & a Safe return to your habitation being with a great regard & esteem."*⁵⁶¹

The Council's letter to Richardson was delayed at this point due to an invasion scare. An express had been received from the Committee at Georgetown, regarding *"a fleet of ships having been seen sailing southerly on Christmas evening, said to be eighteen sail, five of which are very large."* This prompted a postscript, informing Richardson of the sighting and advising him that the Council was going *"to direct Col. Thomson to march his Regiment of Rangers immediately to Monck's Corner, and if you can prevail upon a body of volunteer foot, from 500 to 1000 men … also to march to the same place, we desire you to do so … we confine our application wholly to volunteers because we would not harrass the militia who have already been engaged in severe service."* Three days later, on the 31st, Thomson was directed *"to march that part of your regiment of Rangers now with you, with all expedition to Monck's Corner, and upon your approach to that place, to give notice to this board."*⁵⁶²

Preparation for the defense of Charleston had actually begun in earnest earlier in December, much of it carried out by William Henry Drayton. On 14 December he had *"made an offer of his service in the naval department of this colony."* On the 15th his offer was accepted. On the 16th Drayton was appointed *"captain and commander of the colony armed ship Prosper."* On the 17th he and fellow member of the Council of Safety, Dr. David Oliphant, became a coordinating authority for the defense of Charleston. Others, such as Col. William Moultrie, were directed *"to confer with the*

*Hon. William Henry Drayton and Doct. Oliphant"* regarding any military preparations. [563]

After the 16th of December, Drayton did not attend meetings of the Council of Safety, in deference to the ruling of Congress *"that no person holding a regular commission in the regular forces of this colony ... shall be capable of possessing a seat, or of having a voice in the said Council."* In his new role, Drayton recommended that priority be given to a request for 500 able-bodied seamen from the northern colonies of Massachusetts, Rhode Island and Connecticut. It was thought to pay these men from funds originally allocated to *"the commissioners of Indian Affairs in the Southern Department."* Capt. Robert Cochran, age 40, a native of Massachusetts, who had established a shipyard in Charleston around 1763, was sent north to recruit seamen. [564]

Although the British invasion proved false this time, the threat remained real. It helped knit low country and back country associators closer in solidarity.

Cooperation later proved essential at Sullivan's Island on 28 June 1776, when the Regiment of Rangers became a critical part of Col. William Moultrie's defense in order to repel a British landing.

During this period between Christmas and the New Year, Col. Richardson's army, marching through snow, sleet and rain toward the Congarees, as yet knew nothing of the frenzy in Charleston. Having now moved approximately 55 miles from his previous camp, Richardson was still riding his wave of success as, on 2 January, he reported to his peers. Richardson had not yet received the Council's letters of the 27th. Referring to his letter of 22 December with respect *"to the detachments I has sent out, & in a postscript, of my intelligence of success,"* the Colonel now elaborates: *"Yesterday we reached this place with our prisoners, whom we have used in the best manner we could—about ten Captains and a hundred and twenty of the most mischievous men ... some of whom will make good soldiers ... we took seven kegs of gun-powder, six of which I delivered to Maj. Williamson to be sent up to Mr. Wilkinson for the Cherokees ... many arms have been delivered up, & I caused the men to sign an instrument of writing, which they did willingly with fear & trembling, by which they forfeit their estates, real and personal, if they ever take up arms against, or disquiet the peace & tranquility of the good people of this colony again, & to assist them if they are ever called upon ...the arms taken by Maj. Williamson & those from that quarter I ordered to be stored at Fort Charlotte ... Those taken by the upper regiments are to be sent down, & many lodged in the hands of the committees to be sent to Mr. Chestnut's Store at the congarees, & about two hundred stand I have ordered to Camden."* [565]

Now encamped at the Congarees, Richardson tells the Council, in this letter of 2 January 1776, that he will send the prisoners *"in a boat from this place to Wilson's Ferry, under the command & guard of Capt. Thomas Sumter ... from thence Col. Thomson with the Rangers ... on this expedition I constituted Capt. Sumter Adjutant General, who had behaved very well & has been to me & the cause, of extra service."* In this manner we learn that Sumter is no longer under suspicion of having been too close to Moses Kirkland. Praise is also lavished upon *"Col. Thomson who, with Major Mayson & officers under them have been obliging in behavior & alert in service, & must recommend them to your particular notice ... Major Joseph Kershaw, who I constituted Major of the Brigades ... has been more than commonly serviceable, as he has been Major, Commissary-General, Treasurer, and every thing to help the service ...&, thus, sir, I have been oblged to end this campaign before I received orders, as the last express is not yet returned; & I am happy when I say & think it has answered every desire, wish or expectation ...The lenitive measures have had a good effect; the spirit & power is gone from them & I am sure, if not interrupted by designing men on our side, that country, which I had it in my power to lay waste, & which people expected, will be happy, & peace & tranquility take take place of ruin & discord."*[566]

On the subject of honor and duty, so much valued among Carolinians, Col. Richardson has one more point to make in his letter of the 2nd. He expected discipline from men under his command; therefore he indignantly criticizes the behavior of Major Andrew Williamson: *"I am informed Maj. Williamson has sent an immediate detail of occurrences from Raborn's Creek of the 23rd or 24th ult. to the council of Safety which I must ask pardon for not doing sooner, as I then was & till within two hours have been too much incumbered to do."* This precipitate, self-serving behavior to curry favor with the Council annoyed Richardson who, as Williamson's superior officer makes plain: *"I think if that gentleman wrote to the council of Safety while under my wing ... he might have let me know it."* Not without sarcasm, he adds, *"I hope he has not omitted his own merit, which I should always take care to give him ... as I am still broke in upon every time ... I shall refer you to Col. Thomson and Maj. Mayson for further particulars ... by Col. Thomson you will receive the prisoners we thought proper to detain, which upon examination find were the most leading and active, in taking the powder at Ninety Six ... they were long out before taken, & have been some time since in durance, from which circumstances they ... will make a despicable appearance."*[567]

So falls the curtain in 1775 on "so violent an opposition to our cause" that Pickens would recall in his letter of 1811—with more than one hundred malodorous Loyalists herded toward incarceration in Charleston—the men who had, according to Andrew Pickens, became "so exasperated" when "Mayson got the commission" instead of Cunningham "that they immediately took to the other side of the question." In retrospect, that offhand, simplistic comment, remains but one man's biased opinion of a far more complex struggle.

# *Epilogue*

## *Lord William Campbell*

Within one week after he had written his last dispatch on 1 January 1776, the self-exiled Royal Governor of South Carolina, Lord William Campbell, was picked up in Charleston Harbor by a new British Frigate, the HMS *Syren*, which had sailed in from the Cape Fear area. The Syren took Campbell and his Tory wife, Sarah, daughter of wealthy Charleston merchant, Ralph Izard, to Jamaica. A few months later Campbell joined up with General Henry Clinton, when British forces tried to invade Charleston in late June 1776, and he took part in the Battle of Sullivan's Island.

## *Moses Kirkland*

On *"11 January 1776 at the Gael of Philadelphia,"* Moses Kirkland wrote a pitiful and pathetic *apologia pro vita sua* *"To the Honourable Henry Learance* [sic], *Esqr and president of the Counsel of Safety at Charles Town in South Carolina,"* which Laurens received around 20 March.[568] Kirkland requests forgiveness and amnesty, having seen the error of his ways, and asks for Laurens' help to secure his release from jail. He wasn't released—but escaped in May 1776 and fled to Florida. There British authorities appointed Kirkland a *"Deputy Superintendent to the Seminoles."* He *"advised Sir Henry Clinton in 1778 to instigate a slave rebellion."* In 1780 he *"was commissioned a Major and resumed command of a Tory regiment in Ninety Six,"* rising to the rank of a Lt. Colonel. Kirkland later fell out with the British when he was denied promotion to Brigadier General. After the war he moved to Jamaica. In 1787 the 62-year-old Moses Kirkland was enroute to England when his ship was lost at sea.[569]

## Robert Cunningham

At the Charleston jail on 25 February 1776, Robert Cunningham was joined by Thomas Fletchall, Richard Pearis, Benjamin Wofford and 30 other Loyalist prisoners in signing a petition to Henry Laurens requesting amnesty and *"the Freedom to Enter into any Honorable Terms of Unity to preserve the peace in the Disturbed Province ... we shall on any Forfeit Promise to settle peace to your Satisfaction and the Unity of the Different Settlements on the Frontiers."*[570] The petition was read at the Second Provincial Congress of South Carolina during a sitting for its second session on 26 February. It was rejected. Two months later, in April, a general amnesty was passed and most Loyalist prisoners were released on their word of honor that they would not take up arms against the American cause. Those, such as Robert Cunningham, who refused to take the oath of neutrality, remained incarcerated. In July 1776 Robert Cunningham underwent a change of heart. Having been convinced that the British *"were so wicked as to instigate the Savages to War against us ... his conscience freed him from his old obligations & he most heartily desired to take the Oath of fidelity to the United Colonies & to have an opportunity of giving proofs of his sincerity."* So wrote Henry Laurens to his son John on 14 August 1776.[571] Cunningham was freed but his offer to fight on the Rebel side was rejected by Andrew Williamson, newly designated commander of a forthcoming campaign against the Cherokees. The rejection was due to lingering, wary opposition against former Loyalists among back country settlers. According to Williamson, some of these freed Loyalists had already violated their parole.[572] Instead, Cunningham defected to Florida where, like Thomas Brown, he was given a commission by Governor Tonyn, rising to the rank of a Loyalist Brigadier General. Robert was not permitted to return to South Carolina after the war; he made his home in Nassau, where he died at age 74 in 1813.

## Patrick Cunningham

On 27 February 1776 the Provincial Congress learned that *"Jonathan Downs, Esq ... was on his way to Charles Town with Patrick Cunningham, Hugh Brown and William Duggins, three of the late insurgents, as prisoners."*[573] They had been captured by the militia of Major Andrew Williamson and were now jailed along with the previously captured Loyalists. Upon release from the Charleston jail in the summer of 1776, Patrick Cunningham, like his brother, went to Florida. He was permitted to return to South Carolina in 1785 where, upon petition, his banishment was repealed. Patrick served two terms in the state legislature but was never fully accepted by his colleagues. He died in 1795 at age 54.

## Joseph Robinson

Joseph Robinson managed to elude capture by the forces of the Richardson expedition after signing the Treaty of Ninety-Six, but his home was supposedly plundered and burned by Col. Thomas' militia. Robinson took his family to East Florida where he was commissioned by Governor Tonyn as a Lt. Colonel of the South Carolina Royalist Regiment. In 1781/82 Robinson's regiment fought Rebels in various back country skirmishes following the fall of Charleston, but In December 1782 he and his family were among the Tories evacuated by the British from Charleston. He first went to Jamaica and later, in 1786, moved his family to Prince Edward Island in Canada, where he died in 1807 at age 59.

## Andrew Williamson

Andrew Williamson reached the rank of a Brigadier General as head of the Ninety-Six Militia but continued to equivocate with respect to his personal values. After the surrender of Charleston in 1780, Williamson became a "double agent" and was accused of treason by the Rebels. Taking British protection, he retired to his home in Long Canes. When the South Carolina General Assembly met in exile in January 1782, at Jacksonboro, it passed several confiscation acts. Among the 227 persons listed, whose property was to be confiscated, Williamson was condemned under the category of "obnoxious persons."[574] However, due to the intervention of General Nathaniel Greene, his lands were not confiscated, merely subjected to a twelve percent amercement. Andrew Williamson died at his plantation home, Whitehall, in 1786. He was 56 years old.

## The Regiment of Rangers

After delivering their prisoners, the Regiment of Rangers under Lt. Col. William Thomson and Major James Mayson remained in the Charleston area. The regiment would play a role in the Battle of Sullivan's Island on 28 June 1776, defending against a British landing force. On 24 July the Continental Congress passed a resolution, signed by John Hancock, part of which stated: *"Resolved that the Regiment of Rangers now in the pay of the State of South*

*Carolina be placed upon Continental establishment."*[575] Then, on 23 December 1776, the rangers were upgraded, receiving authority for three field officers, to place them on a par with the 1st and 2nd Regiments. They became the 3rd South Carolina Regiment of Washington's Continental Army. Thomson was promoted to full Colonel; Mayson to Lt. Colonel; and Samuel Wise to Major. The rangers took part in the defense of Savannah, where Samuel Wise was killed.

*William Thomson*

Due to ill heath, William Thomson resigned from the rangers in 1779 and returned home to command the Orangeburg Militia. He continued to lead an active political life in service of his community and served as a state senator in the 5th thru 11th general assemblies. In 1796 he traveled to Sweet Springs, Virginia, in hopes of regaining his health. He died there the same year at age.[69]

*James Mayson*

During the euphoria that followed the Rebel victory over the British at Sullivan's Island, James Mayson, age 43 and a widower for approximately one year, married, on 7 August 1776, the 16-year-old Henrietta Hart, daughter of an Episcopalian Minister. He would raise a second family of nine children. Son Luke, from his first wife, joined the rangers in 1776 as a lieutenant; he died in April 1780. Mayson himself had resigned from the rangers in January 1780 and returned to the legislature. Soon after the fall of Charleston, he accepted British parole from further military activity. When New York Loyalist Col. John Harris Cruger took over command of the Star Fort at Ninety-Six in June 1780, Mayson's plantation home, Glasgow, became Cruger's headquarters and residence, until the Loyalists retired from the fort in June 1781. Mayson continued to serve as a representative to the 3rd, 7th and 9th General Assemblies of South Carolina. He sided with Rawlins Lowndes in 1788 to oppose adoption of the Federal Constitution. From 1785 on, he also served as a judge in Newberry County. In 1799 James Mayson, age 66, died at his plantation home, where he lay buried until 1934 when his remains were exhumed and reinterred by a local DAR chapter at the entrance to the Ninety-Six Star Fort, now a National Historic Site.

## Richard Richardson

Richard Richardson attended the Second Provincial Congress in February 1776, where he received the accolades of his colleagues for a successful campaign against the back country Loyalists. As a delegate, Richardson served in this Congress, as well as in the next general assembly. He was appointed a Brigadier General in 1778. Like Mayson, he took parole from the British in 1780 after the fall of Charleston; he died later in the same year at age 76.

## Henry Laurens

The Second Provincial Congress, at the close of its session, designated itself as the First General Assembly of South Carolina. It adopted a Constitution on 26 March 1776, in order to establish a government; Henry Laurens became Vice President. In 1777 he was elected a delegate to the Continental Congress, over which he presided from November 1777 to December 1778. Laurens was then appointed to negotiate a loan from the Dutch Government in 1779, but was captured at sea and spent 15 months as prisoner in the Tower of London. Upon release he served as an American Peace Commissioner in Europe until 1784, returning to Charleston only in January 1785. From that point on Laurens eschewed public life, spending his time trying to rebuild his ravaged estate. Henry Laurens died in 1792 at age 70.

## William Henry Drayton

William Henry Drayton became Chief Justice of South Carolina when the new government was established according to the Constitution of 26 March 1776. He was elected to the Continental Congress in 1778, where he served until his death in Philadelphia in 1779 at the age of 37.

## William Tennent

Drayton's companion in the Bible and sword crusade through the back country, William Tennent, continued to serve in the next General Assembly. As a "firebrand preacher" Tennent remained a leading advocate of the disestablishment of the Church of England. He died in 1777 at age 37.

In retrospect, one might say that during the year 1775 the South Carolina ship of state had undergone a shakedown cruise with an untested crew composed of low country and back country freedom fighters—aristocrats and frontiersmen—learning to work together in common cause. These men weathered an insurrection, stabilized course and stood firm against a British counter attack the following year. The marriage of convenience entered into by low country elitists and back country planters in that crucible year of 1775 set the tone for a South Carolina that has endured to the present day.

# Reference Sources

**PRIMARY**

British Public Records Office, *America and the West Indies*, Vol. 229, Books 35 & 36. Micofilm 1188, Reel #11, Woodruff Library, Emory University, Atlanta.

Historical Manuscripts Commission; Fourteenth Report, Appendix, Part X; The Manuscripts of the Earl of Dartmouth; Vol. II; American Papers; Presented to both Houses of Parliament by Command of her Majesty; London; Printed for Her Majesty's Stationery Office, by Eyre and Spottiswoode; 1895.

*English Historical Documents: American Colonial Documents to 1776;* edited by Merrill Jensen, M.A.; Ph.D.; Professor of History at the University of Wisconsin; Oxford University Press, New York, 1964.

*American Archives: A Documentary History of the English Colonies from the King's Message to Parliament of March 4, 1774, to the Declaration of Independence by the United States*; fourth series; edited by Peter Force and M. St. Clair Clarke; published under an Act of Congress, passed on the second of March 1833; six volumes. Volume one published in Washington, December 1837.

*Documents of American History*; edited by Henry Steele Commager; sixth edition; Appleton-Century-Crofts, Inc.; New York, 1958.

*Letters to Delegates to Congress 1774-1789;* Paul H. Smith, Ed.; August 1774-August 1775; published 1976; and September-December 1775; Library of Congress, Washington, D.C., 1977

*Correspondence of the American Revolution being Letters of Eminent Men to George Washington from the time of his taking command of the Army to the end of his Presidency;* edited from the original manuscripts by Jared Sparks; Volume I; Books for Libraries Press, Freeport, New York.

*The Revolutionary Diplomatic Correspondence of the United States;* edited under the Direction of Congress by Francis Wharton; published in conformity with Act of Congress of August 13, 1888; Volume I; Washington, Government Printing Office, 1889.

*Historical Statistics of the United States: Colonial Times to 1970;* Part II; U.S. Dept. of Commerce; Bureau of the Census, 1970.

*Extracts from the Journals of the Provincial Congresses of South Carolina 1775-1776;* William Edwin Hemphill, Ed.; Wylma Anne Bates, Asst. Ed.; Columbia, South Carolina Archives Dept., 1960.

*Biographical Directory of the Commons House of Assembly of South Carolina 1692-1775;* Vol. II, Walter B. Edgar and N. Louise Bailey, Eds.; University of South Carolina Press, 1977.

*Biographical Directory of the House of Representatives of the State of South Carolina 1775-1791;* Vol. III; N. Louise Bailey and Elizabeth Ivey Cooper; Eds.; University of South Carolina Press; 1981.

*Collections of the South Carolina Historical Society;* Volume II; Charleston, 1858.

*Collections of the South Carolina Historical Society;* Volume III; Charleston, 1859.

*The Papers of Henry Laurens;* David R. Chestnutt, Ed.; Published for the South Carolina Historical Society by the University of South Carolina Press, Columbia; Volume Ten: Dec. 12, 1774-Jan. 4, 1776; published 1985; Volume Eleven: Jan. 5, 1776-Nov. 1, 1777; published 1988.

*Documentary History of the American Revolution 1764-1776;* Letters and Papers Relating to the Contest for Liberty, Chiefly in South Carolina, from Originals in the Possession of the Editor, and Other Sources; by R.W. Gibbes, M.D.; New York; D. Appleton & Co.; 1855.

*Journals and Letters of the Late Samuel Curwen, Judge of the Admiralty, A Loyalist-Refugee in England, during the American Revolution to which are added Illustrative Documents and Biographic Notices of many Prominent Loyalists and other Eminent Men;* Third Edition; by George Atkinson Ward, member of the New York Historical Society, and corresponding member of the Massachusetts Historical Society; New York: Leavitt, Trow & Co.; 194 Broadway; London: Wiley and Putnam, Paternoster Row, 1845.

*Kendall Collection;* Letters of Henry Laurens and other correspondence; Micofilm, books #30, #31, #32; pertaining to the years 1775-1776; The South Caroliniana Library; University of South Carolina, Columbia. Indexed at the library under the title *Simms Collection of Laurens Papers.*

*The Colonial Records of North Carolina;* Vol. X, 1775-1778; Published under the Supervision of the Trustees of the Libraries, by order of the General Assembly; Collected and Edited by William L. Saunders, Secretary of State; Raleigh; Joseph Daniels, Printer to the State, 1890.

*The Colonial Records of Georgia;* Vol. XVII; Journal of the Upper House of Assembly – January 17, 1763 to March 12, 1776 inclusive; Compiled and Published under Authority of The Legislature by Allen D. Candler; Atlanta, Georgia; The Franklin-Turner Company; Printers, Publishers, binders, 1908.

*The Revolutionary Records of Georgia;* Volume I, 1769-1782; by Allen D. Candler; Published by the Franklin-Turner Co; Atlanta, 1908.

*An Order book of the Third Regiment, South Carolina Line, Continental Establishment, December 23, 1776 – May 2, 1777;* Edited by A.S. Salley, Secretary of the Historical Commission of South Carolina; Printed for the Historical Commission of South Carolina by The State Company, Columbia, 1942.

*South Carolina and American General Gazette;* Number 893-900; June – December 1775; Charleston, S.C.

*South Carolina Gazette;* January 23 – February 6, 1775, Charleston, S.C.

## SECONDARY
### Books

Alden, John Richard; *John Stuart and the Southern Colonial Frontier: A Study of Indian Relations, War, Trade, and Land Problems in the Southern Wilderness, 1754-1775;* Ann Arbor, The University of Michigan Press; Humphrey, Oxford, Oxford University Press, 1944.

Barck, Oscar Theoore Jr.; Wakefield, Walter L.; Lefler, Hugh Talmage; *The United States: A Survey of National Development through 1865;* Volume I; The Ronald Press Company; New York, 1952.

Bass, Robert D; Ninety Six: *The Struggle for the South Carolina Back Country;* The Sandlapper Store, Inc., 1978.

Bell, William Watts; *The State That Forgot: South Carolina's Surrender to Democracy;* Columbia, 1972.

Boatner, Mark Mayo; *Encyclopedia of the American Revolution;* David McKay Company, Inc., New York.

Bridenbaugh, Carl; *Myths and Realities: Societies of the Colonial South;* Louisiana State University Press, Baton Rouge, 1952.

Brinsfield, John Wesley; *Religion and Politics in Colonial South Carolina;* Southern Historical Press, Inc., 1983.

Brown, Richard Maxwell; *The South Carolina Regulators;* The Belknap Press of Harvard University Press; Cambridge, 1963.

Carroll, B.R.; *Historical Collections of South Carolina—embracing many Rare* and Valuable Pamphlets and other Documents relating to the History of that State from its First Discovery to its Independence in the year 1776; in two volumes; New York; Harper & Brothers, 1836.

Coulter, E. Merton; with Stephenson, Wendell Holmes; Eds.; *History of the South;* Volume III, *The South in the Revolution,* by John Richard Alden; Louisiana State University Press, 1957.

Craven, Wesley Frank; *A History of the South: The Southern Colonies in the Seventeenth Century 1607-1689;* Volume I.

Crow, Jeffrey J. and Tise, Larry E., Eds., *The Southern Experience in the American Revolution;* The University of North Carolina Press; Chapel Hill; 1978. Article: *Rebelliousness: Personality Development and the American Revolution in the Southern Colonies,* by Robert M. Weir.

Davis, Nora Marshall; *Fort Charlotte on Savannah River and its Significance in the American Revolution;* reprinted by the McCormick County Historical Commission, McCormick County Historical Society, McCormick, South Carolina, 1976.

Drayton, John L; *Memoirs of the American Revolution: from its commencement in the year 1776 inclusive as relating to the State of South Carolina and occasionally referring to the States of North Carolina and Georgia;* two volumes, Charleston, 1821.

Fleming, Thomas; *1776 Year of Illusions;* W.W. Norton & Co., New York, 1975.

Gregg, Rt. Reverend Alexander; *History of the Old Cheraws—extending from about A.D. 1730 to 1810 with notices of families and sketches of individuals;* New York, Richardson and Company, 1867.

Howe, George; *History of the Presbyterian Church in South Carolina;* Vol. I; Prepared by order of the Synod of South Carolina; Columbia; Duffie and Chapman, 1870.

Ivers, Larry E; *Colonial Forts of South Carolina 1670-1775;* Tercentennial Booklet Number 3; University of South Carolina Press; Columbia, South Carolina, 1970.

Jones, Louis Pinckney; *The South Carolina Civil War of 1775;* The Sandlapper Store, Inc.

Klein, Rachel K.; *Unification of a Slave State: The Rise of the Planter Class in the South Carolina Backcountry; 1760-1808;* The University of North Carolina Press, Chapel Hill and London, 1990.

Lambert, Robert Stansbury; *South Carolina Loyalists in the American Revolution;* University of South Carolina Press, 1987.

McCrady, Edward; *The History of South Carolina under the Royal Government*

*1719-1776;* and *The History of South Carolina in the Revolution 1775-1780;* New York, The MacMillan Company, 1901.

Miller, John C; *Origins of the American Revolution;* Little, Brown and Company; Boston, 1943.

Moultrie, William; *Memoirs of the American Revolution;* two volumes; printed by David Longworth for the author; New York, 1802.

O'Neall, John Belton and Chapman, John A.; *The Annals of Newberry South Carolina,* 1892.

Salley, A.S.; *The History of Orangeburg County South Carolina—from its first settlement to the close of the Revolutionary War;* Orangeburg, S.C.; R. Lewis Berry, Printer, 1898.

Seller, Leila; *Charleston Business on the Eve of the American Revolution;* Chapel Hill, The University of North Carolina Press, 1934.

Skelton, Lynda Worley; *General Andrew Pickens, an Autobiography;* edited by Skelton; published by the Pendleton District Historical and Recreational Commission in cooperation with the Andrew Pickens Chapter, DAR, Clemson, South Carolina, January 1976.

South, Stanley; *Archaeological Excavation at the site of Williamson's Fort of 1775,* University of South Carolina Press, 1972.

Tocqueville, Alexis de; *Democracy in America;* edited by Richard D. Hefner; A Mentor Book, 1956.

Utley, Francis Lee and Hemperley, Marion R; Eds.; *Essays of: Place Names in Georgia;* article by John H. Goff, *The Buffalo in Georgia.*

Wallace, David Duncan, Ph.D., Litt. D., LL.D.; Professor of History and Economics in Wofford College; *The History of South Carolina;* Volume II; The American Historical Society; New York, 1934.

Watson, Margaret; *Greenwood County Sketches: Old Roads and Early Families;* The Attic Press Inc.; Greenwood, South Carolina, 1982.

Whitney, Edson L; *Government of the Colony of South Carolina;* Johns Hopkins University in Historical and Political Science, Herbert B. Adams, Ed., Baltimore; The Johns Hopkins Press, January-February, 1895.

Young, Alfred F; *The American Revolution: Explorations in the History of American Radicalism;* Northern Illinois University Press; DeKalb,1976; Article by Ronald Hoffman, *Disaffected in the Revolutionary South.*

## Periodicals

*The Mississippi Valley Historical Review;* Vol. XVII, 1930/31, *John Stuart's Indian Policy,* by Philip M. Hamer.

*The South Carolina Historical and Genealogical Magazine;* Vol. I, 1900,

#1,2,3,4; *Papers of the first Council of Safety of the Revolutionary Party in South Carolina, June-November 1775;* Ibid., Vol. II, 1901, #1,2,3,4; Ibid., Vol. III, 1902; Also *Notes From the American Jewish Historical Society;* Also *Col. Moses Thomson and some of his Descendants.* Vol. V, January 1904; *Historical Notes,* Vol. IX, 1908; *Miscellaneous Papers of the General Committee, Secret Committee and Provincial Congress 1775,* Vol. XVII, #1, January 1926; *Correspondence of Hon. Arthur Middleton.* Vol. XVIII, 1917; *Historical Notes,* Vol. 67, January 1966; *A Loyalist view of the Drayton-Tennent-Hart Mission to the Upcountry.* Vol. 68, #4, October 1967; *Loyalists and the American Revolution: Thomas Brown and the South Carolina Backcountry 1775-1776.* Vol. 69, #1, January 1968; Ibid. Vol. 76, *Prelude to the War: The First Battle of Ninety Six, November 19, 1775.*

# Source Notes

**INTRODUCTION [PAGES XV–XVII]**

1   *General Andrew Pickens an Autobiography, Lynda Worley Skelton (Mrs. B.R.), ed., p.10.*

2   *Documents of American History, edited by Henry Steele Commager, p. 84.*

3   *Ibid., p. 86.*

4   *Extracts from the Journals of the Provincial Congresses of South Carolina, 1775-1776, William Edwin Hemphill, ed., p. 39.*

5   *Ibid., p. 44-45.*

**CHAPTER I [PAGES 3-8]**

6   *1776 Year of Illusions, by Thomas Fleming, p. 29-30.*

7   *The History of South Carolina Under the Royal Government 1719-1776, by Edward McCrady, p.757.*

8   *Ibid.*

9   *British Public Record Office [BPRO], Vol. 229, America and the West Indies, Book 30, Emory University, Microfilm 1188, #11. Despatch #74, 3 August 1774, from Bull to the Earl of Dartmouth at Whitehall.*

10   *Historical Statistics of the United States: Colonial Times to 1970, Part II, U.S. Dept. of Commerce, Bureau of the Census, p. 1168.*

11   *McCrady, op. cit., Royal Government, p. 758-760.*

12   *Johns Hopkins University Studies in Historical and Political Science, Thirteenth series, I-II, Government in the Colony of South Carolina, by Edson L. Whitney, p. 118.*

13   *McCrady, op. cit., Royal Government, p. 761-762.*

14   *South Carolina Historical and Genealogical Magazine [SCHGM], Vol. II, No. 3, July 1901, p. 190.*

15   *The Papers of Henry Laurens, Vol. 10, David R. Chestnutt, ed., p. 22. Letter dated 4 January 1775 to Richard Oswald, his agent in London.*

16   *Ibid.*

17   Ibid., p. 23

18   *Memoirs of the American Revolution: from its commencement to the year 1776 inclusive as relating to the State of South Carolina and occasioinally referring to the States of North Carolina and Georgia, Vol. II, by John L. Drayton, p. 274.*

19   *South Carolina and American General Gazette, Vol. XVIII – from Friday January 6 to Friday January 13, 1775, p. 1.*

### CHAPTER II [PAGES 9–15]

20   *Laurens, op. cit., Vol. 10, p. 27-28.*

21   *Extracts 1775-1776, op. cit., p. 21.*

22   *Ibid., p. 24*

23   *Ibid., p. 29.*

24   *The History of South Carolina in the Revolution, 1775-1780, by Edward McCrady, p. 4.*

25   *McCrady, op. cit., Revolution, p. 29.*

26   *Memoirs of the American Revolution, Volume I, by William Moultrie, p. 57-58.*

27   *Laurens, op. cit., Vol. 10, p. 71.*

28   *McCrady, op. cit., Royal Government, p. 786-787.*

29   *Moultrie, op. cit., Vol. I, p. 59.*

30   *Letters of Delegates to Congress, August 1774-August 1775, by Paul H. Smith, ed., p. 570.*

31   *South Carolina Gazette and Country Journal, 9 May 1775.*

32   *Fleming, op. cit., p. 109.*

33   *The Mississippi Valley Historical Review [MVHR], Vol.XVII, 1930/1931, article entitled John Stuart's Indian Policy, by Philip Hamer, p. 353. NB: William Legge, the Earl of Dartmouth, became Secretary for the Colonies in 1772 and remained in this post until 10 November 1775 when he was replaced by George Sackville, Lord Germain. Dartmouth was sacked because he was considered too friendly toward the colonies. General Thomas Gage, whose letter started the controversy, was relieved of command as Chief of British Troops in America on 10 October 1775. He was replaced by General William Howe who remained in charge until 1778.*

34   *Ibid., p. 354.*

35   *Colonial Records of North Carolina, Vol. X, 1775-1776, William L. Saunders, ed., p. 1260.*

36   *The Encyclopedia Americana, 1956 edition, p. 613.*

37   SCHGM, op. cit., Vol. I, p. 63-64.

38   Laurens, op. cit., Vol. 10, p. 115-116.

39   Ibid., p. 119.

## Chapter III [pages 16–27]

40   McCrady, op. cit., Royal Government, p. 792.

41   Extracts 1775-1776, op. cit., p. 34.

42   Ibid., p. 35.

43   Ibid., p. 36.

44   Biographical Directory of the Commons House of Assembly 1692-1775, Vol. II, Walter B.Edgar and N. Louise Bailey, eds., p. 301-302.

45   Ibid., p. 37.

46   Ibid., p. 38.

47   Ibid., p. 39.

48   Ibid., p. 43.

49   Ibid.

50   Ibid., p. 45.

51   Ibid., p. 48.

52   Ibid., p. 49.

53   Journals of the Council of Safety for the Province of South Carolina 1775, Collections of the South Carolina Historical Society, Volume II, p. 23.

54   Biographical Directory, op. cit., Vol. II, p. 672.

55   Extracts 1775-1776, op. cit., p. 55.

56   Ibid., p. 56. Actually the 2nd congress would convene on 1 November.

57   Collections, op. cit., Vol. II, p. 23-24.

58   Historical Records Commission, Fourteenth Report, Appendix Part X, The Manuscripts of the Earl of Dartmouth, Vol. II, p. 207.

59   Ibid., p. 256.

60   Ibid.

61   BPRO, op. cit., Vol. 229, Book 35, Despatch #1 from Campbell to Dartmouth, dated 2 July 1775.

62   Hamer, op. cit., MVHR, VVII, p. 355.

63   Laurens, op. cit., Vol. 10, p. 186-187.

64   Ibid., p. 190-192.

65   Ibid., p. 194

## Chapter IV [pages 28–43]

66   Collections, op. cit., Vol. II, p. 26.

67   McCrady, op. cit., Revolution, p. 34.

68   *The History of Orangeburg County,* by A.S. Salley, p. 389.

69   *Collections, op. cit.,* Vol. II, p. 29.

70   *SCHGM, op. cit.,* Vol. I, p. 42.

71   *Collections, op. cit.,* Vol. II, p. 28.

72   *Hamer, op. cit., MVHR, Vol.XVII,* p. 237.

73   *Collections, op. cit.,* Vol. II, p. 28.

74   *Hamer, op. cit., MVHR,* Vol. XVII, p. 355-356.

75   *Salley, op. cit.,* p. 391.

76   *BPRO, op. cit.,* Vol. 229, Book 35; Microfilm 1188, #11.

77   *Ibid.*

78   *Ibid.*

79   *Collections, op. cit.,* Vol. II, p. 31.

80   *Documentary History of the Revolution 1764-1776,* by R.W. Gibbes, p. 123. Fletchall's reply was directed to Henry Laurens and dated 24 July 1775.

81   *BPRO, op. cit.,* Vol. 229, Book 35; Microfilm 1188, #11.

82   *Origins of the American Revolution,* by John C. Miller, p. 203.

83   *Ibid.,* p. 204.

84   *Documents of American history,* by Henry Steele Commager, ed., 6th edition, p. 92-95. While Commager implies that the Olive Branch Petition was signed on 6 July, B.F. Stevens, in his *Facsimiles of Manuscripts Relating to America,* shows that it was signed on 8 July. I have accepted the latter.

85   *SCHGM, op. cit.,* Vol. III, p.49.

86   *SCHGM, op. cit.,* Vol. I, p. 67.

87   *Collections, op. cit.,* Vol. II, p. 35.

88   *SCHGM, op. cit.,* Vol. I, p. 46. Letter from Mayson to Thomson dated 18 July 1775.

89   *Ibid.,* Vol. I, p. 48.

90   *Ibid.,* p. 45

91   *Fort Charlotte on the Savannah River and its Significance in the American Revolution,* by Nora Marshall Davis, p. 14.

92   *Collections, op. cit.,* Vol. II, p. 55-56.

93   *Collections, op. cit.,* Vol. II, p. 37-39; Salley, op. cit., p. 392-395.

94   *Ibid.*

## Chapter V [pages 44–55]

95   *Laurens, op. cit.,* Vol. 10, p. 244-246.

96   *Kendall Collection, Papers of Henry Laurens and Other*

*correspondence. Books #30, #31, #32 of this collection pertaining to the
years 1775-1776 are on microfilm at the South Caroliniana Library,
University of South Carolina, Columbia. Microfilm of #31, p. 001043-
001044 contains the original document.*

97  *SCHGM, op. cit., Vol. I, p. 39.*

98  *Collections, op. cit., Vol. II, p. 40.*

99  *SCHGM, op. cit., Vol. I, p. 45.*

100  *Ibid., p. 51.*

101  *Collections, op. cit., Vol. II, p. 55-56.*

102  *Collections, op. cit., Vol. II, p. 40-43. Laurens, op. cit., vol. 10, p.
214-218.*

103  *Ibid., p. 40-43; Ibid., p. 214-218*

104  *Salley, op. cit., p.401.*

105  *Collections, op. cit., Vol. II, p. 46. Laurens, op. cit., Vol. 10, p.
225-227.*

106  *Ibid.; Ibid.*

107  *The United States: A Survey of National Development Through `865,
by Oscar Theodore Black, Jr. p. 90*

108  *Religion and Politics in Colonial South Carolina, by John Wesley
Brinsfield, p. 59-60.*

109  *SCHGM, op. cit., Vol. I, p. 46.*

110  *McCrady, op. cit., Revolution, p. 38.*

111  *Edgefield County, S.C., Abstracts of Deed Books 1-12, Vol. I,
abstracted by Lee Corley Hendrix, p. 244.*

112  *SCHGM, op. cit., Vol. III, p. 50.*

113  *Salley, op. cit., p. 397-398.*

114  *SCHGM, op. cit., Vol. II, p. 173-193. Deduced from A General
Return of Col. William Thomson's Regiment of Rangers from the
tume of inlisting to this 20th Day of September 1775.*

115  *Collections, op. cit., Vol. II, p. 49.*

116  *Letters of Delegates to Congress 1774-1799, Augst 1774-August 1775,
Paul H. Smith, ed., p. 570.*

117  *SCHGM, op. cit., Vol. I, p. 46.*

118  *American Archives: A Documentary History of the English Colonies
in North America from the King's Message to Parliament, of March
7, 1774, to the Declaration of Independence by the United States, 4th
series, Peter Force and M. St. Claire Clark, eds., six volumes, Vol. I,
p. 1681.*

119  *SCHGM, Vol. I, p. 62-65.*

## Chapter VI [pages 56–66]

120 Salley, op. cit., p. 398.

121 Salley, op. cit., p. 398-399.

122 Collections, op. cit., Vol. II, p. 53.

123 BPRO, op. cit., Vol. 229, Book 35, Micofilm 1188, #11.

124 Ibid.

125 Ibid.

126 Collections, op. cit., Vol. II, p. 69-70.

127 Ibid.

128 Dartmouth Mss., op. cit., Vol. II, p. 355

129 Collectiions, op. cit., Vol. II, p. 67-68.

130 SCHGM, op. cit., Vol. I, p.129-130.

131 Salley, op. cit., p. 406.

132 SCHGM, op. cit., Vol. I, p. 70.

133 Ibid.

134 Salley, op. cit., p. 408.

135 History of the Presbyterian Church in South Carolina, by George Howe, Vol. I, p. 428

136 Salley, op. cit., p. 404.

137 Collections, op. cit., Vol. II, p. 33.

138 Ibid., p. 399-400.

139 Ibid., p. 409.

140 Ibid., p. 408-409.

141 Ibid., p. 410

142 Ibid., p. 406.

143 Collections, op. cit., Vol. II, p. 58.

144 Journal and Letter of the late Samuel Curwen, Judge of the Admiralty, etc., a loyalist refugee in England to which are added illustrative documemts and biographic notices of prominent loyalists and many other eminent men, by George Atkinson Ward, 3rd edition, p. 622-623.

145 Collections, op. cit., Vol. II, p. 59.

## Chapter VII [pages 67–75]

146 BPRO, op. cit., Vol. 229, Book 35, microfilm 1188, #11.

147 Gibbes, op. cit., p. 123-124.

148 Collections, op. cit., Vol. II, p. 63.

149 Ibid.

150  *Ibid., p. 64.*

151  *Ibid.*

152  *SCHGM, op. cit., Vol. I, p. 68-70*

153  *Ibid.*

154  *Salley, op. cit., p. 406.*

155  *Laurens, op. cit., Vol. 10, p. 246.*

156  *Laurens, op. cit., Vol. 10, p. 285. Gibbes, op. cit., 1764-1776, p. 133.*

157  *Salley, op. cit., p. 406-407.*

158  *Salley, op. cit., p. 408-410.*

159  *SCHGM, op. cit., p. 69.*

160  *Salley, op. cit., p. 415-416. This letter is incorrectly noted in Thomson's Order Book as being dated 20 July.*

161  *BPRO, op. cit., Vol. 229, Book 35, Microfim 1188, #11.*

162  *Laurens, op. cit., Vol. 10, p. 256-257.*

163  *Ibid.*

164  *Ibid.*

165  *Miller, op. cit., p. 423-424.*

166  *SCHGM, op. cit., Vol. 9, p. 69.*

## CHAPTER VIII [PAGES 76–87]

167  *Dartmouth MSS, op. cit., Vol. II, p. 355.*

168  *Ibid., p. 356.*

169  *Encyclopedia of American Quaker Genealogy, by William Wade Hinshaw, Vol. 1, p. 1015.*

170  *Gibbes, op. cit., p. 225.*

171  *Ibid.*

172  *Salley, op. cit., p. 410; Laurens, op. cit., Vol. 10, p. 266-267.*

173  *Ibid.*

174  *Ibid.*

175  *Ibid.*

176  *Gibbes, op. cit., p. 226.*

177  *Gibbes, op. cit., p. 128. Laurens, op. cit., Vol. 10, p. 278.*

178  *Gibbes, op. cit., p. 226.*

179  *Gibbes, op. cit., p. 133. Laurens, op. cit., Vol. 10, p. 285.*

180  *Gibbes, op. cit., p. 226.*

181  *Ibid., p.166*

182  *Gibbes, op. cit., p. 128; Laurens, op. cit., Vol. 10, p. 279.*

183  *Ibid., p. 130. Ibid., p. 279-283.*

184  Ibid., p.130-131; Ibid., p. 279-283.

185  Ibid., p. 133; Ibid., p. 284-285.

186  Ibid., p. 132-133; Ibid., p. 284.

187  Ibid., p.129; Ibid., p. 279-280

188  Salley, op. cit., p. 414. Kirkland/Polk letters not found.

189  Gibbes, op. cit., p. 127.

190  Gibbes, op. cit., , p.227.

191  Biographical Directory, op. cit., Vol. III, p. 320.

192  Ibid., p. 511.

193  Kendall Collection, op. cit., Microfilm #31.

## Chapter IX [pages 88–97]

194  Gibbes, op. cit., p. 227.

195  Gibbes, op. cit., p.135; Laurens, op. cit., Vol. 10, p. 287.

196  Ibid., p. 135; Ibid., p. 287.

197  Ibid.., p. 135; Ibid., p. 287

198  Salley, op. cit., p. 415; Laurens, op. cit., vol. 10, p. 289.

199  SCHGM, op. cit., Vol. I, p. 124-125.

200  Ibid., p. 124-125.

201  BPRO, op. cit., Vol. 229, Book 36, Microfilm 1188, #11.

202  Gibbes, op. cit., p. 227.

203  Ibid., p..227.

204  Salley, op. cit., p. 417-418. Laurens, op. cit., Vol. 10, p. 291-292.

205  Ibid.

206  Ibid.

207  Gibbes, op. cit., p. 141.

208  Salley, op. cit., p. 421.

209  Gibbes, op. cit., p. 136.

210  SCHGM, op. cit., Vol. I, p. 126.

211  Laurens, op. cit., Vol.10, p. 323.

212  SCHGM, op. cit., Vol. I, p. 126.

213  Gibbes, op. cit., p. 144.

214  Ibid., p. 228.

215  Ibid.

216  Gibbes, op. cit., p. 148-149.

217  Ibid., p. 137.

218  Ibid., p. 138.

219  Ibid., p. 141.

220  Ibid., The name reference is either to John Adams Summer, age 31, or

*his father Johannes Adams Summer, German planters residing near Crims Creek between the Broad and Saluda rivers.*

221 *Salley, op. cit., p. 418; Laurens, op. cit., Vol. 10, p. 301-302.*

## Chapter X [pages 98–115]

222 *Salley, op. cit., p. 419; Laurens, op. cit., Vol.10, p. 302-303.*

223 *Ibid., p. 419; Ibid., p. 302-303.*

224 *Laurens, op. cit., Vol. 10, p. 296-297.*

225 *Gibbes, op. cit., p. 228.*

226 *Ibid., p. 142.*

227 *Force, op. cit., Vol. I, p. 1413.*

228 *Gibbes, op. cit., p. 228.*

229 *Ibid., p.142.*

230 *Ibid.*

231 *Ibid., p.143.*

232 *Salley, op. cit., p. 423. Williamson's "10th instant" may be a mistake.*

233 *Ibid., p. 428-429.*

234 *Gibbes, op. cit., p. 150-151; Laurens, op. cit., Vol. 10, p. 345.*

235 *McCrady, op. cit., Revolution, p. 35-36.*

236 *Gibbes, op. cit., p. 154; Laurens, op. cit.,Vol. 10, p. 345.*

237 *Gibbes, op. cit., p. 145.*

238 *Gibbes, op. cit., p. 151; Laurens, op. cit., Vol.10, p. 346.*

239 *Gibbes, op. cit., p. 152; Laurens, op. cit., Vol.10, p. 347.*

240 *Ibid.; Ibid.*

241 *Gibbes, op. cit., p. 147.*

242 *BPRO, op. cit., Vol. 229, Book 35, Microfilm 1188, #11*

243 *Gibbes, op. cit., p. 146. Laurens, op. cit., Vol. 10, p. 339-340.*

244 *Gibbes, op. cit., p. 229.*

245 *Laurens, op. cit., Vol. 10, p. 325.*

246 *Ibid..*

247 *Gibbes, op. cit., p. 153; Laurens, op. cit., Vol. 10, p. 347-348.*

248 *Kendall Collection, op. cit., Microfilm Vol. 31.*

249 *Gibbes, op. cit., p. 153. Laurens, op. cit., Vol. 10, p. 348-349.*

250 *Ibid., p. 154-155; Ibid., p. 349.*

251 *Kendall collection, op. cit., Vol. 31.*

252 *A History of the South: The Southern Colonies in the Seventeenth Century 1607-1689, by Wesley Frank Craven, Vol. I, p. 340-341.*

253 *Myths and Realities: Societies in the Colonial South, by Carl Bridenbaugh, p. 114.*

254 Kendall Collection, op. cit., Vol. 31.

255 Ibid..

256 Gibbes, op. cit., p.150; Laurens, op. cit., Vol. 10, p. 344.

257 Gibbes, op. cit., p. 154.

258 Salley, op. cit., p. 420-421.

259 Ibid., p. 424.

## Chapter XI [pages 116–126]

260 Gibbes, op. cit., p. 155.

261 SCHGM, op. cit., Vol. I, p. 133-134.

262 Ibid., Vol. I, p. 134.

263 Ibid.

264 Ibid.

265 Ibid., p. 135.

266 Laurens, op. cit., Vol. 10, p. 329.

267 SCHGM, op. cit., Vol. I, p. 136.

268 Gibbes, op. cit., p. 155.

269 BPRO, op. cit., Vol. 229, Book 35, Microfilm 1188, #11.

270 Ibid.

271 Gibbes, op. cit., p. 156.

272 Ibid.

273 Salley, op. cit., p. 424.

274 Ibid., p. 425.

275 Ibid.

276 Gibbes, op. cit., p. 231.

277 Ibid.

278 Ibid.

279 SCHGM, op. cit., Vol. I, p. 188.

280 Gibbes, op. cit., p. 232.

281 Ibid., p. 232.

282 Gibbes, op. cit., p. 159-162.

283 The Revolutionary Records of Georgia, Vol. I, 1769-1782, by Allen D. Candler, p. 129.

284 Gibbes, op. cit., p. 159-161.

## Chapter XII [pages 127–139]

285 Gibbes, op. cit., p. 162-163; Laurens, op. cit., Vol. 10, p. 352.

286 Ibid.; Ibid.

287 Ibid.; Ibid.

288  Laurens, op. cit., Vol. 10, p. 290.

289  Gibbes, op. cit., p. 163-164

290  Laurens, op. cit., Vol. 10, p. 353.

291  Ibid., p. 354.

292  Memoirs of the American Revolution, by John L. Drayton, Vol. I, p. 396.

293  Ibid., p. 397.

294  BPRO, op. cit., Vol. 229, Microfilm 1188, #11.

295  SCHGM, op. cit., Vol. I, p. 193.

296  Gibbes, op. cit., p. 232.

297  Gibbes, op. cit., p. 165-166; Laurens, op. cit., Vol. 10, p. 359-360.

298  Gibbes, op. cit., p. 232.

299  Salley, op. cit., p. 435.

300  Ibid., p. 430.

301  Gibbes, op. cit., p. 166-167.

302  Gibbes, op. cit., p. 234.

303  Ibid., p. 166-168.

304  Ibid., p. 234.

305  Ibid.

306  Laurens, op. cit., Vol. 10, p. 364-365.

307  Ibid.

308  Ibid., p. 366.

309  Salley, op. cit., p. 431-432.

310  Ibid., p. 432.

311  Salley, op. cit., p.433; Laurens, op. cit., Vol. 10, p. 370-371.

312  Ibid., p. 434; Ibid., p. 371.

313  Salley, op. cit., p. 436.

314  SCHGM, Vol. I, p. 199-200.

## CHAPTER XIII [PAGES 142–155]

315  Gibbes, op. cit., p. 236.

316  Ibid., p. 239.

317  Salley, op. cit., p. 436-437.

318  Gibbes, op. cit., p. 237.

319  Ibid., p. 169.

320  Ibid., p. 231.

321  SCHGM, op. cit., Vol. II, p. 198.

322  Gibbes, op. cit., p. 170-171

323  Ibid., p. 170.

324  Gibbes, op. cit., p.173-174; Laurens, op. cit., Vol. 10. p. 376-377.

325  Ibid.; Ibid.

326  Ibid.; Ibid.

327  Ibid.;Ibid.

328  Ibid., p. 1745-175; Ibid., p. 378

329  Gibbes, op. cit., p. 174.

330  Ibid.

331  Ibid., p. 178.

332  Ibid.

333  Ibid., p. 179.

334  Documents of the American Revolution 1770-1781, edited by K.G. Davies, Vol. XI, p. 177; Laurens, op. cit., Vol. 10, fn p. 394.

335  SCHGM, op. cit., Vol. I, p. 205.

336  Laurens, op. cit., p. 386.

337  Moultrie, op. cit., Vol. I, p. 67-68.

338  Gibbes, op. cit., p. 181-182.

339  Ibid., p. 188.

340  Laurens, op. cit., Vol. 10, p. 387.

341  Gibbes, op. cit., p. 186-187.

342  Biographical Directory, op. cit., Vol. III, p. 632.

343  Gibbes, op. cit., p.187; Laurens, op. cit., Vol. 10, p. 390-391

344  Ibid.; Ibid.

345  Ibid.; Ibid.

346  Ibid.; Ibid.

## Chapter XIV [pages 157–168]

347  BPRO, op. cit., Vol. 229. Book 35, Microfilm 1188, #11. Brown's letter was enclosed with Campbell's Despatch #8 to Lord Dartmouth; SCHGM, op. cit., Vol. 67, p. 17-26

348  Ibid.; Ibid.

349  Ibid.; Ibid.

350  Ibid.; Ibid.

351  Ibid.; Ibid.

352  Ibid.; Ibid.

353  Ibid.; Ibid.

354  Ibid.; Ibid.

355  Ibid.; Ibid.

356  Laurens, op. cit., Vol. 10, p. 396-399.

357 *Ibid.*
358 *Ibid.*
359 *BPRO, op. cit., Vol. 229, Book 35, Microfilm 1188, #11.*
360 *Ibid.*
361 *Ibid.*
362 *Ibid.*
363 *Gibbes, op. cit., p. 191-192.*
364 *Gibbes, op. cit., p. 192. Laurens, op. cit., Vol. 10, p. 411-412.*
365 *Drayton, op. cit., Vol. I, p. 419.*
366 *Ibid.*
367 *Ibid.*
368 *Kendall Collection, op. cit., Microfilm Vol. 31.*
369 *Ibid.*
370 *Ibid.*
371 *Gibbes, op. cit., p. 194-195.*
372 *SCHGM, op. cit., Vol. II, p. 9-14.*
373 *Curwen, op. cit., p. 638-641*
374 *Laurens, op. cit., Vol. 10, p. 428.*

## Chapter XV [pages 169–182]

375 *Gibbes, op. cit., p. 196; Laurens, op. cit., Vol. 10, p. 431.*
376 *Salley, op. cit., p. 426; Laurens, op. cit., Vol. 10, p. 439.*
377 *Ibid.; Ibid.*
378 *Ibid., p. 427; Ibid., p. 440-441*
379 *History of the Old Cheraws, by Rev. Alexander Gregg, p. 247.*
380 *Ibid.*
381 *Laurens, op. cit., Vol. 10, p. 445-446.*
382 *SCHGM, op. cit., Vol. II, p. 99-100.*
383 *Ibid.*
384 *Laurens, op. cit., Vol. 10, p. 449.*
385 *Ibid.*
386 *Gibbes, op. cit., p. 200; Curwen, op. cit., p. 628.*
387 *Gibbes, op. cit., p. 200-201.*
388 *SCHGM, op. cit., Vol. II, p. 262-264.*
389 *Ibid., p. 264-265.*
390 *SCHGM, op. cit., Vol. V, p. 189-190.*
391 *Gibbes, op. cit., p. 202-203.*
392 *SCHGM, op. cit., Vol. III, p. 75.*

393 *Ibid., p. 76.*

394 *SCHGM, op. cit., Vol. III, p. 7; Laurens, op. cit., Vol. 10, p. 467-468.*

395 *Gibbes, op. cit., p. 207.*

396 *Ibid., p. 207-208.*

397 *SCHGM, op. cit., Vol. III, p. 84-85.*

398 *BPRO, op. cit., Vol. 229, Book 35, Microfilm 1188, #11*

399 *Ibid.*

400 *BPRO, op. cit., Vol. 229, Book 35, Micofilm 1188, #11.*

401 *Laurens, op. cit., Vol. 10, p. 477-478.*

402 *Drayton, op. cit., Vol.I, p. 318.*

403 *Laurens, op. cit., Vol. 10, p. 479.*

404 *Ibid.*

## CHAPTER XVI [PAGES 183–190]

405 *Laurens, op. cit., Vol. 10, p. 491.*

406 *Ibid.*

407 *Curwen, op. cit., p. 619.*

408 *Extracts 1775-1776, op. cit., p. 82.*

409 *Force, op. cit., Vol. III, p. 160.*

410 *McCrady, op. cit., Revolution, p. 86.*

411 *Laurens, op. cit., Vol. 10, p. 500-501*

412 *Ibid.*

413 *MVHR, op. cit., Vol. XVII, p. 360-361.*

414 *Ibid.*

415 *Ibid., p. 362.*

416 *Laurens, op. cit., Vol. 10, p. 501-503.*

417 *Ibid.*

418 *Ibid., p. 503.*

419 *SCHGM, op. cit., Vol. III, p. 81.*

420 *Laurens, op. cit., Vol. 10, p. 506.*

421 *Moultrie, op. cit., Vol. I, p. 97*

## CHAPTER XVII [PAGES 191–201]

422 *Extracts 1775-1776, op. cit., p. 82-83.*

423 *Ibid., p. 83-84.*

424 *Ibid., p. 86-87.*

425 *Salley, p. 305-307; Moultrie, op. cit., Vol. I, p. 97-98; Force, op. cit., Vol. III, p. 1338-1340.*

426  *Extracts 1775-1776, op. cit., p. 91.*

427  *Ibid., p. 95-99*

428  *Gibbes, op. cit., p. 209-210. Mayson's actual message to Williamson is not on record.*

429  *Kendall Collection, op. cit., Vol. 31.*

430  *Collections, op. cit., Vol. III, p. 54.*

431  *The Papers of George Washington, Colonial Series 4, W.W. Abbot, Editor, fn. 4, p. 196-197.*

432  *Extracts 1775-1776, op. cit., p. 100.*

433  *Ibid., p. 101.*

434  *Ibid., p. 101-102.*

435  *Ibid., p. 103.*

436  *Ibid., p. 104.*

437  *Ibid., p. 105.*

438  *Ibid., p. 106.*

439  *Ibid., p. 106-107.*

440  *Ibid., p. 107-108.*

## Chapter XVIII [pages 202–212]

441  *Extracts 1775-1776, op. cit., p. 114.*

442  *Kendall Collection, op. cit., Vol. 31.*

443  *Gibbes, op. cit., p. 217.*

444  *South Carolina American and General Gazette, Charleston, #900, from Friday 14 November to Friday 2 December 1775.*

445  *Kendall Collection, op. cit., Vol. 31.*

446  *Drayton, op. cit., Vol. II, p. 116-117.*

447  *Extracts 1775-1776, op. cit., p. 120.*

448  *Extracts 1775-1776, op. cit., p. 123.*

449  *Ibid., p. 126-128.*

450  *Kendall Collection, op. cit., Vol. 31.*

451  *Gibbes, op. cit., p. 216-218; Laurens, op. cit., Vol. 10, p. 514-517.*

452  *Extracts 1775-1776, op. cit., p. 128-131.*

453  *Ibid., p. 135.*

454  *Gibbes, op. cit., p. 215.*

455  *Gibbes, op. cit., p. 215-217.*

456  *South Carolina and American Gazette, #900, from 15 November to 2 December 1775.*

457  *Ibid., p. 216.*

458  *Ibid., p. 217*

459  *Ibid., p. 218.*

460  *Extracts 1775-1776, p. 137-139.*

461  *Ibid., p. 40.*

CHAPTER XIX [PAGES 213–223]

462  *South Carolina and American Gazette, #900, From Friday 14 November to Friday 8 December 1775, p. 2.*

463  *Gibbes, op. cit., p. 218; Laurens, op. cit., Vol. 10, p. 516.*

464  *Gibbes, op. cit., p. 221.*

465  *Extracts 1775-1776, op. cit., p. 141.*

466  *Ibid., p. 142.*

467  *Ibid., p. 143.*

468  *Ibid., p. 144-145.*

469  *Ibid., p. 151.*

470  *Gibbes, op. cit., p. 218; Laurens, op. cit., Vol. 10, p. 517.*

471  *Gibbes, op. cit., p. 216.*

472  *Drayton, op. cit., Vol. II, p. 151, Letter 7 December 1775 from Mayson to Council of Safety.*

473  *Ibid., p. 148-149.*

474  *Extracts 1775-1776, op. cit., p. 147.*

475  *Gibbes, op. cit., p. 216.*

476  *Gibbes, op. cit., p.218; Collections, op. cit., Vol. III, p. 36.*

477  *Ibid.; Ibid.*

478  *Gibbes, op. cit., p. 221.*

479  *Archaeological Excavation at the site of Williamson's fort of 1775, by Stanley South, p. 24-28.*

480  *Extracts 1775-1776, op. cit., p.151.*

481  *Ibid., p. 152.*

482  *Ibid., p. 155*

483  *Ibid.*

484  *Ibid., p. 160.*

485  *Gibbes, op. cit., p. 219.*

486  *Ibid.*

487  *Ibid.*

488  *Ibid.*

489  *Ibid.*

490  *Religion and Politics in Colonial South Carolina*, by John Wesley Bronsfield, p. 75.

## CHAPTER XX [PAGES 224–238]

491  *Kendall Collection, op. cit., Vol. 30.*

492  *Gibbes, op. cit., p. 222; Laurens, op. cit., Vol. 10, p. 522.*

493  *Ibid.; Ibid.*

494  *Ibid.; Ibid.*

495  *Extracts 1775-1776, op. cit., p. 161.*

496  *Gibbes, op. cit., p. 223-224.*

497  *Laurens, op. cit., Vol. 10, p. 525.*

498  *Ibid., p. 526*

499  *Ibid., p. 526-527.*

500  *Laurens, op. cit., Vol. 10, p. 529-530.*

501  *Kendall Collection, op. cit., Vol. 31.*

502  *Collections, op. cit., Vol. III, p. 46.*

503  *Laurens, op. cit., Vol. 10, p. 536.*

504  *Ibid.*

505  *Ibid., p. 537.*

506  *Ibid., p. 533-534.*

507  *Ibid., p. 534.*

508  *Collections, op. cit., Vol. III, p. 53*

509  *Ibid., p. 54.*

510  *Ibid.*

511  *Ibid.*

512  *Collections, op. cit. Vol III, p. 58.*

513  *Drayton, op. cit., p. 151.*

514  *Collections, op. cit., Vol. III, p. 66.*

515  *BPRO, op. cit., Vol. 229, Book 36. Despatch #10, 1 January 1776.*

516  *Ibid.*

517  *Collections, op. cit., Vol. III, p. 66.*

518  *Gibbes, op. cit., p. 224-225.*

519  *Collections, op. cit., Vol. III, p. 67-68; Laurens, op. cit., Vol. 10, p. 551.*

520  *Drayton, op. cit., Vol. II, p. 119.*

521  *Collections, op. cit., Vol. III, p. 68; Laurens, op. cit., Vol. 10, p. 551.*

522  *Gibbes, op. cit., p. 69; Laurens, op. cit., Vol. 10, p. 552.*

523  Ibid.; Ibid., p. 553

524  Collections, op. cit., Vol. III, p. 70.

525  Laurens, op. cit., Vol. 10, p. 557-558.

526  Collections, op. cit., Vol. III, p. 75. Actually, it was Robert, not Patrick, who was in jail.

## Chapter XXI [pages 239–248]

527  Ibid., p. 76

528  Ibid., p. 80.

529  Gibbes, op. cit., p. 239-240.

530  Ibid., p. 241.

531  Ibid., p. 185-186.

532  Collections, op. cit., Vol. III, p. 84.

533  Ibid., p. 85-86.

534  Gibbes, op. cit., p. 241.

535  Ibid.

536  Laurens, op. cit., Vol. 11, p. 92.

537  Collections, op. cit., Vol. III, p. 93.

538  Laurens, op. cit., Vol.10, p. 572-573.

539  Ibid., p. 574-576.

540  BPRO, op. cit., Vol. 229, Book 36, Despatch #10, 1 January 1776.

541  Collections, op. cit., Vol. III, p. 104.

542  Gibbes, op. cit., p. 242-243.

543  Ibid.

544  Ibid.

545  Ibid.

546  Ibid.

547  Ibid., p. 244-245.

548  Collections, op. cit., Vol. III, p. 110-111.

549  Gibbes, op. cit., p. 246.

550  Ibid.

## Chapter Twenty–Two [pages 249–255]

551  Ibid., p. 246-247.

552  Collections, op. cit., Vol. III, p. 111.

553  Ibid., p. 113-114.

554  Ibid., p. 114-115.

555  Laurens, op. cit., Vol. 10, p. 589.

556  SCHGM, op. cit., Vol. 19, p. 43-44.

557   *Collections, op. cit., Vol. III, p. 119-120.*
558   *Laurens, op. cit., Vol. 10, p. 590.*
559   *Ibid., p. 593.*
560   *Collections, op. cit., Vol. III, p. 113-114.*
561   *Laurens, op. cit., Vol. 10, p. 593.*
562   *Collections, op. cit., Vol. III, p. 129-131.*
563   *Ibid., p. 85-91.*
564   *Laurens, op. cit., Vol. 10, fn. p. 385.*
565   *Gibbes, op. cit., p. 246-247.*
566   *Ibid., p. 247-248.*
567   *Ibid., p. 248.*

## Epilogue [pages 257–262]

568   *Gibbes, op. cit., p. 254-255; Laurens, op. cit., Vol. 11, p. 21-23.*
569   *Biographical Directory, op. cit., Vol. II, p. 381.*
570   *Kendall Collection, op. cit., Vol. 31.*
571   *Laurens, op. cit.. Vol. 11, p. 231.*
572   *Ibid., fn., p. 231.*
573   *Extracts 1775-1776, op. cit., p. 211.*
574   *Royal Gazette, Charles Town, 20 March 1782.*
575   *Revolutionary Records of Georgia, Vol. I, p. 195.*

# Index

# Acknowledgments

The idea for a more balanced perspective on relations between the people of South Carolina on the eve of the American Revolution, 1775, originated from the works of South Carolina historian Edward McCrady, who observed that the colony's residents overwhelmingly lived in the back country. Yet most histories touching on this period in South Carolina history have been written from a low country point of view.

Over the past twenty years, during which time I have been collecting documentation for this narrative, I have received unstinting guidance from the research staff at the South Carolina Historical Society, the South Carolina Department of Archives & History, and the South Caroliniana Library at the University of South Carolina, as well as from Emory University in Atlanta. Their help has been invaluable in ferreting out all primary documentation relating to individuals involved in South Carolina's attempt, in 1775, to carry out a resolution passed by the First Continental Congress in October 1774.

For much of this work, the late Dr. David Fischer, a lifetime friend, college classmate and former professor at the University of South Carolina, offered me a home base in Columbia for forays into the area for research purposes. His selfless cooperation in offering guidance toward sources was of inestimable value, as was that of Dr. Donald Weatherbee, Professor Emeritus at USC.

I am especially grateful to the staff of the South Caroliniana Library for leading me to the correspondence of back country Loyalists such as Joseph Robinson.

And I would be remiss in not acknowledging the encouragement and advice received from historians Thomas Fleming and the late C. Vann Woodward during the earlier stages of this project.

Finally, I would like to thank David E. Kane of American History Imprints for his insightful editorial assistance and tireless efforts in preparing the manuscript, my first venture into this field, for publication.

Edmund A. Bator
Atlanta, Georgia

## About the Author

Edmund A. Bator is a retired Foreign Service Officer with 25 years of service in Finland, Italy, Yugoslavia, Kuwait and Washington, D.C. Born in New Bedford, Massachusetts, after service with the U.S. Navy, he graduated from Oglethorpe University (B.A.1953) and continued his education at Johns Hopkins University, School of Advanced International Studies (M.A.1956).

After retiring to Atlanta, Georgia, he became a guest lecturer on the Middle East at Oglethorpe University for five years while continuing to pursue serious research in early American history and genealogy.

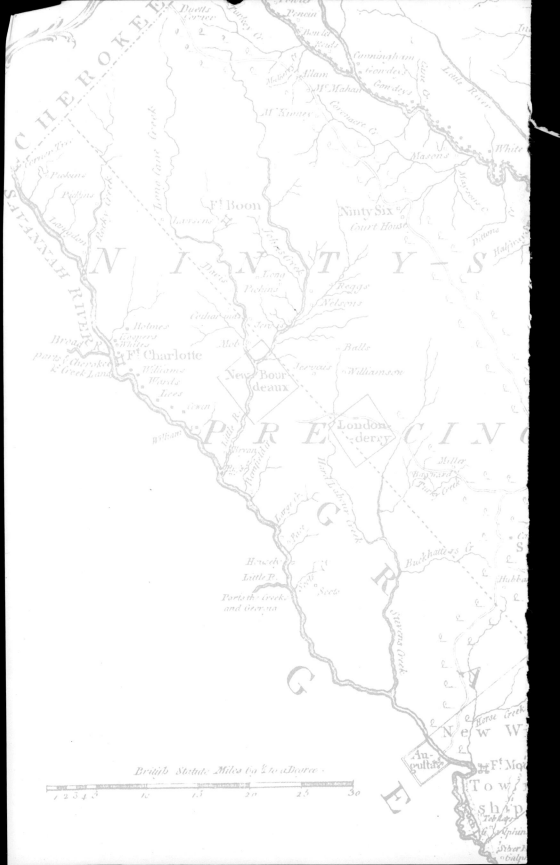